Australian & New Zealand Edition

Starting an Online Business

FOR DUMMIES®

Australian & New Zealand Edition

Starting an Online Business

FOR

DUMMIES®

**by Melissa Norfolk and
Greg Holden**

WILEY

Wiley Publishing Australia Pty Ltd

Starting an Online Business For Dummies®

Australian & New Zealand Edition published by

Wiley Publishing Australia Pty Ltd
42 McDougall Street
Milton Qld 4064
www.dummies.com

Copyright © 2009 Wiley Publishing Australia Pty Ltd

Original English language edition text and art copyright © 2008 Wiley Publishing, Inc. This edition published by arrangement with the original publisher, Wiley Publishing, Inc., Indianapolis, Indiana, USA.

The moral rights of the authors have been asserted.

National Library of Australia
Cataloguing-in-Publication data

Author:	Norfolk, Melissa.
Title:	Starting an Online Business For Dummies/ Melissa Norfolk, Greg Holden.
Edition:	Australian and New Zealand ed.
ISBN:	978 0 7314 0991 4 (pbk.)
Series:	For Dummies
Notes:	Includes index.
Subjects:	Business enterprises — Computer networks. Internet marketing. Electronic commerce. Web sites — Design.
Other Authors/ Contributors:	Holden, Greg.
Dewey Number:	658.8720681

Printed in Australia by Ligare Book Printer

10 9 8 7 6 5 4 3 2

About the Authors

Melissa Norfolk set up Internet marketing company, Norfolk Internet Group Pty Ltd, in 1998. The company provides keynote presentations and workshops on effective use of the Internet as well as Web design and email marketing advice. Now employing four staff, the business has grown rapidly over the past four years and celebrated ten years in business in 2008!

After completing her Bachelor of Computer Science, Melissa worked for Mobil Oil, Alcoa, GE Capital and Melbourne University before branching out to start her own Web design and consultancy business.

She is a professional speaker and Web designer specialising in building search-engine-friendly Web sites and marketing savvy email newsletters that connect businesses with more customers online.

A member of the NSAA, APESMA and BNI, Melissa speaks to business, school and community groups about effective use of the Internet, finding what you need online, Internet safety and online marketing.

Her monthly public workshops on Search Engine Optimisation, Email Marketing and Pay Per Click Advertising, educate both clients and members of the general public about how to best market their businesses on the Internet. Melissa regularly contributes to both online and offline publications including *Parenting Ideas*, *Flying Solo*, *Women's Network Australia* and *CEO Online*. Her audio CD 'How to Turn Your Website into a Lead Generating Profit Machine' also aims to help small- to medium-sized business owners maximise their use of the Internet as a business marketing tool.

Greg Holden started a small business called Stylus media, which is a group of editorial, design and computer professionals who produce both print and electronic publications. He has been self-employed for the past ten years. Greg is an avid user of eBay, both as a buyer and seller, and he recently started his own blog.

One of the ways Greg enjoys communicating is through explaining technical subjects in non-technical language. The first US edition of *Starting an Online Business For Dummies* was the ninth of his more than thirty computer books. He also authored *eBay PowerUser's Bible* for Wiley Publishing Inc. Over the years, Greg has been a contributing editor of *Computer Currents* magazine, where he writes a monthly column. He also contributes to *PC World* and the University of Illinois at Chicago alumni magazine.

Dedications

Melissa says ...

To my partner in life, Carlos, who supports me in everything I do.

I am a very ambitious person. At our wedding during his speech, Carlos joked that he often has to make an appointment to see me because I am always busy! After more than 14 years together, this is still not far from the truth because as an entrepreneurial business owner I always have a lot of projects on the go at the one time. He supports me 100 per cent and listens to my constant chatter, random thoughts and at times frustrated rants. Thanks so much Carlos.

Greg says ...

To my best friend Ann Lindner, who makes everything possible.

Authors' Acknowledgements

Melissa says ...

When I took on the challenge of writing this book I was nine months pregnant with my first child. I had wanted to write a book for quite some time and *Starting an Online Business For Dummies*, Australian & New Zealand Edition, seemed like the perfect opportunity. I thought I would have some spare time at home during my maternity leave — little did I know quite how challenging it would be with a new baby, a business to run and a house to keep!

I want to thank my husband Carlos for all his support and patience because I could not have finished the book without his support.

I wish to acknowledge the help of my acquisition editor Charlotte Duff, editor Robi van Nooten, technical reviewer Matthew Baulch and all the capable people at Wiley who contributed to this project.

And a special thank you to all the business owners who gave generously of their time to be profiled for the case studies: Glenda from Million Dollar Baby, Sandra from Kiwi Cake Supplies, Sue from Norfolk Corporate Support and Kathie from A Clayton's Secretary. As a business owner myself, I understand the multitude of pressures on your time and appreciate you sharing your online successes.

Greg says . . .

One of the things I like best about this book is that it's a teaching tool that gives me a chance to share my knowledge — small-business owner to small-business owner — about computers, the Internet and communicating your message to others in an interactive way. As any businessperson knows, most large-scale projects are a team effort.

While the online business landscape has changed since the first US publication of this book, some basic principles remain the same. One is the fact that the most successful entrepreneurs also tend to be the ones who were the most generous with their time and experience. They taught me that the more helpful you are, the more successful you'll be in return.

I want to thank all those who were profiled as case studies. Thanks go to: John Moen of Graphic Maps; Lucky Boyd of MyTexasMusic.com; Jeffrey E Edelheit; Lars Hundley of Clean Air Gardening; Mark Lauer of General Tool and Repair; Doug Laughter of The Silver Connection; John Raddatz of SoftBear Shareware; Sarah-Lou Morris of Alfresco; and Marques Vickers.

I would also like to acknowledge some of my own colleagues who helped prepare and review the text and graphics of this book and who have supported and encouraged me in other lessons in life. Thanks to Ann Lindner, whose teaching experience proved invaluable in suggesting ways to make the text more clear, and to my assistant Brendan Stephens.

Last but certainly not least, the future is in the hands of the generation of my two daughters, Zosia and Lucy, who allow me to learn from the curiosity and joy with which they approach life.

Publisher's Acknowledgements

We're proud of this book; please send us your comments through our online registration form located at www.dummies.com.

Some of the people who helped bring this book to market include the following:

Acquisitions, Editorial and Media Development

Project and Copy Editors: Robi van Nooten, On-Track Editorial Services; Catherine Spedding

Acquisitions Editors: Charlotte Duff, Kyle Looper

Technical Reviewer: Matthew Baulch

Editorial Managers: Gabrielle Packman, Leah Cameron

Production

Layout and Graphics: Wiley Composition Services, Wiley Art Studio

Cartoons: Glenn Lumsden

Proofreader: Pam Dunne

Indexer: Karen Gillen

The authors and publisher would like to thank the following copyright holders, organisations and individuals for their permission to reproduce copyright material in this book.

MyTexasMusic.com: page 27 © MyTexasMusic.com. Photos by Lucky Boyd, Jinelle Boyd • © Triple R Luxury Car Hire: page 28 • © WorldAtlas.com: page 32 • © Emma Wright: page 49 • © Lars Hundley: page 76 • Microsoft Corporation: pages 119, 123, 140, 153, 212, 216, 263, 300, 301 Screenshots reprinted by permission from Microsoft Corporation • Adobe: page 125 Adobe product screenshot reprinted with permission from Adobe Systems Incorporated. • © LP2CD Solutions, Ltd: page 128 • © Hewlett Packard: page 130 • © SBDcreative: page 133 • © Sensis Pty Ltd: page 141 • © Miami Hotel: page 143 • © 6J's Wine Merchants: page 144 • Citiwide Mortgage Services: page 144 © Citiwide, www.citiwide.com.au • © PayPal: page 190 • © TheNile.com.au: page 195 • © TNT Express: page 194 • © WebCentral: page 209 • Alfresco Limited: page 220 © Alfresco Limited, www.alfresco.uk.com • © Banner Maker Pro: page 275 • Google Inc.: pages 295, 296, 297, 323, 324, 325, 328 Reproduced with permission of Google Inc. • © Silk Road Trading Concern: page 344

Every effort has been made to trace the ownership of copyright material. Information that will enable the publisher to rectify any error or omission in subsequent editions will be welcome. In such cases, please contact the Permissions Section of John Wiley & Sons Australia who will arrange for the payment of the usual fee.

Publishing and Editorial for Technology Dummies

Richard Swadley, Vice President and Executive Group Publisher

Andy Cummings, Vice President and Publisher

Mary Bednarek, Executive Acquisitions Director

Marcy C. Cordner, Editorial Director

Publishing for Consumer Dummies

Diane Graves Steele, Vice President and Publisher

Joyce Pepple, Acquisitions Director

Composition Services

Gerry Fahey, Vice President of Production Services

Debbie Stailey, Director of Composition Services

Contents at a Glance

Table of Contents

Introduction

You've been thinking about starting your own business for a while now. You've heard about young entrepreneurs who've made billions online by creating popular Web sites. But you've been slow to jump on the bandwagon. You may have had a great idea but haven't known how to get started. Or perhaps you're still waiting for a great idea to hit you on the head! You're a busy person, after all. You have a full-time job, whether it's running your home or working outside your home. Maybe you've been through some life-changing event and are ready for a change in direction. Well, news is good: *Now* is the perfect time to turn your dream into reality by starting your own online business. More people than ever before are making money and improving their lifestyle by operating businesses online. Whether through selling on eBay, blogging or starting up your own unique Web site, the hours you work and your location are no longer limiting factors. Small-business owners can now work any time of the night or day in their spare bedroom, garage, local library or coffee shop.

If you like the idea of being in business for yourself but you don't have a particular product or service in mind, relax and keep yourself open to inspiration. Many diverse businesses have 'made it big' on the Internet from the ordinary to the weird and wonderful. Among those profiled in this book are a woman who sells her own insect repellent, a mapmaker, a retired woman who sells handmade cot sheets on eBay, a painter, a tool company selling power tools online, and several people who create Web pages for other businesses. With the help of this book, you can turn your own idea into reality and launch your business in cyberspace.

You Can Do It!

What's that? When we start talking about domain names, merchant accounts, or clickthrough advertising your first reaction is to think that we may as well be speaking in a foreign language! Don't worry: The Internet (and this book) levels the playing field so a novice has just as good a chance at succeeding as MBAs who love to throw around business terms at cocktail parties (Chapter 17 gives some great examples).

The Internet is a vital part of running a business these days. Whether you've been in business for 20 years or 20 minutes, the keys to success are the same:

- ✔ **Having a good idea:** If you have something to sell that people have an appetite for, and if your competition is slim, your chances of success are high.

- ✔ **Working hard:** When you're your own boss, you can make yourself work harder than any of your former bosses ever could. And, if you put in the effort and persist through the inevitable ups and downs, you're bound to be a winner.

- ✔ **Believing in yourself:** One of the most surprising and useful things we discovered from the online businesspeople we interviewed was that if you believe you're going to succeed, you probably can. Believe in yourself and proceed as though you're about to be successful. Together with your good ideas and hard work, your confidence can pay off.

If you're the cautious type who wants to test the waters before you launch your new business on the Internet, allow this book to lead you gently up the learning curve. After you're online, you can master techniques to improve your presence. This book includes helpful hints for doing market research and reworking your Web site until you get the success you want.

The Online Landscape

The Internet as we know it has been around for more than 15 years but even in the last couple of years we've seen some simple ideas that have had phenomenal success: The likes of YouTube, MySpace, Facebook, Flickr, Twitter and Blogger. Closer to home sites like SEEK, RSVP, realestate.com.au and Trade Me have taken over from traditional media for job seeking, dating, finding a new home, and buying and selling second-hand goods. Social networking and photo- and video-sharing are growing in popularity and becoming commonplace. Search engines (like Google, Yahoo!, ninemsn, MSN NZ), pay per click advertising and blogging are enabling entrepreneurs to start new businesses, advertise and gain a following online.

As the Web becomes more of a way of life and broadband Internet connections become widespread around the world, doing business online isn't a matter of speculation any more. Still, you may have reasonable concerns about the future of e-commerce for the very entrepreneurs this book seeks to help — individuals who are starting their first business on the

Web. Your fears quickly evaporate when you read this book's case studies of our friends and colleagues who do business online. They're either thriving or at least treading water, and they enthusiastically encourage others to jump right in.

'I feel the best time to start an online business is when you are positioned to begin. I do not feel that there is an advantage/disadvantage to waiting for a "better time" to start', says Mark Cramer, who runs a business called MePage.com as well as a Web site devoted to 'sport ballooning' enthusiasts. Mark's online business is proof that you can make money online doing just about anything as long as you have the right level of knowledge and enthusiasm.

About This Book

Online business isn't just for large corporations, or even just for small businesses that already have a physical shopfront in the real world and simply want to supplement their marketability with a Web site.

The Internet is a perfect venue for individuals who want to start their own business, who like using computers, and who believe that cyberspace is the place to do it. You don't need much money to get started. If you already have a computer as well as an Internet connection and can create your own Web pages (something this book helps you with), making the move to your own business Web site may cost only $2000 or less. After you're online, the overhead is pretty reasonable, too: You may pay only $10 to $75 per month to a Web hosting service to keep your site online.

With each month that goes by, the number of Internet users increases exponentially. And the growth is greatest outside Australia and New Zealand. To be precise, in late 2007 Internet World Stats released data indicating that more than 510 million Internet users are in Asia, compared with fewer than 20 million in Australia – New Zealand; more than 74 per cent of the Australian – New Zealand population had access to the Internet at home, compared to only 13.7 per cent of Asia. The OECD reported in September 2007 that 22.8 per cent of users who surf the Internet in Australia do so with a broadband connection. We have now reached that critical mass where most people are using the Internet regularly for everyday shopping and other financial activities. The Internet is already becoming a powerhouse for small businesses.

How to Use This Book

Looking for an overview of the whole process of going online and be inspired by one man's online business success story? Jump right in to Chapter 1. Want to find out how to accept credit card payments? Zip ahead to Chapter 7. Feel free to skip back and forth to chapters that interest you. This book is an easy-to-use reference tool that you're going to be comfortable with, no matter what your level of experience with computers and networking. You don't have to scour each chapter methodically from beginning to end to find what you want. The Net doesn't work that way and neither does this book!

If you're just starting out and need to do some essential business planning, see Chapter 2. If you want to prepare a shopping list of business equipment, see Chapter 3. Chapters 4–8 are all about the essential aspects of creating and operating a successful online business, from organising and marketing your Web site to providing effective online customer service and security. Chapters 9–12 explore a variety of marketplaces and services you can exploit, including eBay and Google Adwords. Later chapters get into legal issues and accounting. The fun thing about being online is that continually improving and redoing your presentation is easy. So start where it suits you and come back later for more.

What This Book Assumes about You

This book assumes that you've never been in business before but that you're interested in setting up your own commercial site on the Internet. We also assume that you're familiar with the Internet, have been surfing for a while, and may even have put out some information of your own in the form of a home page.

This book also assumes that you have or are ready to get the following:

✔ **A computer and a modem:** Don't worry, Chapter 3 explains exactly what hardware and software you need.

✔ **Instructions on how to think like a businessperson:** We spend a good amount of time in this book encouraging you to set goals, devise strategies to meet those goals, and do the sort of planning that successful businespeople need to do.

> ✔ **Just enough technical know-how:** You don't have to do it all yourself. Plenty of entrepreneurs decide to partner with someone or hire an expert to perform design and technical work. This book can help you understand your options and give you a basic vocabulary so that you can work productively with the consultants you hire.

What's Where in This Book

This book is divided into five parts. Each part contains chapters that discuss stages in the process of starting an online business.

Part I: Strategies, Tools and Planning for Your Online Business

In Part I, we describe what you need to do and how you need to think in order to start your new online business. The first chapter follows the story about how a business started by a graphic-artist-turned-mapmaker has grown into an Internet success story. Subsequent chapters also present case studies profiling other entrepreneurs and describing how they each started their online businesses. Chapter 2 looks at mapping out your online business, different models and identifying your target customers. Within these pages is where we also describe the software that you need to create Web pages and perform essential business tasks, along with any computer upgrades that help your business run more smoothly. You also discover how to choose a Web host and find exciting new ways to make money online.

Part II: Establishing Your Online Business

Even if you only sell on eBay or only make money by placing affiliate ads, at some point you need to create a Web site — a series of interconnected Web pages that everyone in cyberspace can view with a Web browser. A Web site is a home base where people can find you and what you have to offer. This part explains how to create a compelling and irresistible Web site, one that attracts paying customers around the world and keeps them coming back to make more purchases. This part also includes options for attracting and keeping customers, making your site secure, and updating and improving your online business.

Part III: Running and Promoting Your Online Business

Some of the most exciting options for starting a business online are ways to generate sales revenue that don't involve setting up your own Web site from scratch. One of the most reliable is the online auction model. By signing up with sites like eBay, you get the chance to make some extra income and clear the unused items out of your wardrobe and storage areas. You also discover the ins and outs of starting a business on eBay or Trade Me — marketplaces that have changed lives and are quickly changing the landscape of online business. By starting out with such sites, you figure out how to do some merchandising and provide customer service. You can then look for regular wholesale suppliers and build your business into a full-time operation. Chapters 10 and 11 look at strategies to promote your online business including email newsletters, banner advertising and search engine optimisation. Chapter 12 introduces some of the many Google tools you can take advantage of.

Part IV: The Necessary Evils: Law and Accounting

This part delves into some less-than-sexy but essential activities for any online business. Find out about general security methods designed to make commerce more secure on the Internet. We also discuss copyrights, trademarks and other legal concerns for anyone wanting to start a company in the increasingly competitive atmosphere of the Internet. Finally, you get an overview of basic accounting practices for online businesses and suggestions of accounting tools that you can use to keep track of your e-commerce activities.

Part V: The Part of Tens

Filled with tips, cautions, suggestions and examples, The Part of Tens presents many titbits of information that you can use to motivate, plan and create your own business presence on the Internet, including ten hot new ways to make money on the Web.

Conventions Used in This Book

In this book, we format important bits of information in special ways to make sure that you notice them right away:

- ✔ **In This Chapter lists:** Chapters start with a list of the topics that we cover in that chapter. This list represents a table of contents in miniature.

- ✔ **Numbered lists:** When you see a numbered list, follow the steps in the specific order to accomplish a given task.

- ✔ **Bulleted lists:** Bulleted lists (like this one) indicate things that you can do in any order or list related bits of information.

- ✔ **Web addresses:** When we describe activities or sites of interest on the World Wide Web, we include the address, or Uniform Resource Locator (URL), in a special typeface like this: www.johnwiley.com.au. Because the newer versions of popular Web browsers don't require you to enter the entire URL, this book uses the shortened addresses. For example, if you want to connect to the Wiley Publishing Dummies site, you can get there by simply entering the following in your browser's Go To or Address box: www.dummies.com.

  Don't be surprised if your browser can't find an Internet address you type or if a Web page that's depicted in this book no longer looks the same. Although the sites were current when the book was written, Web addresses (and sites themselves) can be pretty fickle. Try looking for a missing site by using an Internet search engine. Or try shortening the address by deleting everything after the .com (or .org or .edu).

- ✔ **Currency:** When we give you an idea of costs — for example, how much software costs — all figures are in Australian dollars unless otherwise stated.

Icons Used in This Book

Starting an Online Business For Dummies, Australian & New Zealand Edition, also uses special graphical elements — *icons* — to get your attention. Here's what they look like and what they mean:

 This icon points out some technical details that may be of interest to you. A thorough understanding, however, isn't a prerequisite to grasping the underlying concept. Non-techies are welcome to skip items marked by this icon altogether.

 This icon calls your attention to interviews we conducted with online entrepreneurs who provided tips and instructions for running an online business.

 This icon flags practical advice about particular software programs or about issues of importance to businesses. Look to these tips for help with finding resources quickly, making sales or improving the quality of your online business site. This icon also alerts you to software programs and other resources that we consider to be especially good, particularly for the novice user.

 This icon points out potential pitfalls that can develop into more major problems if you're not careful.

 This icon alerts you to facts and figures that are important to keep in mind when you run your online business.

We're in It Together

Improving communication is the whole point of this book. Our goal is to help you express yourself in the exciting medium of the Internet and to remind you that you're not alone. Melissa's a businessperson herself, after all. So we hope that you let her know what you think about this book by contacting her with any questions or comments. Visit Melissa's own Web page at www.melissanorfolk.com or send an email to her at melissa@ melissanorfolk.com.

Part I
Strategies, Tools and Planning for Your Online Business

Glenn Lumsden

'My first goal is to provide quality goods online at a reasonable price. After that, it's the complete global domination of the Internet and its inhabitants.'

In this part ...

What's all the fuss about starting an online business? This part answers that question with a brief overview of the whole process. Happily, it doesn't need to involve a lot of fuss.

The following chapters help you set your online business goals, and show you how to move from the planning to the reality.

This part looks at the business equipment or technology tools that the online business owner needs, including hardware and how to choose the right software for your Web site as well as how to find a Web host.

Let the step-by-step instructions and real-life case studies in this part guide you through the process of starting a successful business online.

Chapter 1

Opening Your Own Online Business in Ten Easy Steps

In This Chapter

▶ Finding a unique niche for your business

▶ Identifying a need and targeting your customers

▶ Coming up with a business plan

▶ Collecting together your business tools

▶ Finding technical experts

▶ Turning your Web site into an indispensable resource

▶ Setting up a sales system

▶ Providing personal customer service

▶ Getting the word out

▶ Evaluating your success and revising your site

Starting an online business is no longer a novelty. It's a fact of life for individuals and established companies alike. In the early days of e-commerce and selling online, consumers were wary about the technology and the security; but, now, online shopping is an accepted and popular way to shop! New software and services are continually developed to make creating Web pages and transacting online business easier than ever. But the basic steps you need to follow to start a successful online business haven't really changed. And those steps are well within the reach of individuals like you and me who have no prior business experience. All you need is a good idea, a bit of start-up money, some computer equipment and a little help from your friends.

One of our goals in this book is (you guessed it) to be a couple of those friends who provide you with the right advice and support to get your business online and make it a success. In this chapter, we give you a step-by-step overview of the entire process of starting an online business.

Step 1: Identify a Need

E-commerce and the Web have been around for over 15 years now. But new products and ways to sell them are identified all the time. Think of the things that didn't exist when the first Web sites were created: blogs, search engines, ads, podcasts, RSS feeds, MP3s, wireless modems, DVDs, and eBay. (Some of these terms may be unfamiliar. To help you get into all the bells and whistles associated with the Web, check out *The Internet For Dummies*, 4th Australian Edition by Paul Wallbank, John R Levine, Margaret Levine Young and Carol Baroudi, Wiley Publishing Australia Pty Ltd.)

In fact, when Melissa was working on this chapter, she came across the *BRW* Top 100 Australian Web 2.0 Applications published in June 2008. This list includes many weird and wonderful ideas like RedBubble (www. redbubble.com) which allows artists to upload their art, network and receive feedback from other artists and sell their work online in many formats including wall art, greeting cards and T-shirts. Another on the list is PickupPal (www.pickuppal.com) described on its site as 'a global eco-friendly transportation revolution that connects drivers, passengers, and packages with the places they need to go'.

Your first job is to identify your *market* (the people who are going to be buying your stuff or using your services) and determine how you can best meet its needs. After all, you can't expect Web surfers to patronise your online business unless you identify services or items that they really need.

Getting to know the marketplace

The Internet is a worldwide, interconnected network of computers to which people can connect either from work or home, and through which people can communicate via email, receive information from the Web, and buy and sell items by using credit cards or other means.

Many people decide to start an online business with little more than a casual knowledge of the Internet. But when you decide to get serious about going online with a commercial endeavour, you must first get to know the environment in which you plan to be working.

A hotbed of commerce

Statistically, the Internet continues to be a hotbed of commerce — and it just keeps becoming more accepted among consumers in general. Listen to what the experts are saying:

✔ **Nielsen** (www.nielsen.com) reports more than 85 per cent of the world's online population has used the Internet to make a purchase — increasing the market for online shopping by 40 per cent in the past two years (November 2007). Globally, the most popular and purchased items over the Internet are books (41 per cent), clothing/accessories/shoes (36 per cent), videos/DVDs/games (24 per cent), airline tickets (24 per cent) and electronic equipment (23 per cent). Credit cards are by far the most common method of payment — 60 per cent of global online consumers use their credit card. Of those paying with a credit card, more than half (53 per cent) use Visa.

✔ **Hitwise** (www.hitwise.com.au) reports that the largest percentage of online sales occurs from mid-October to late-December each year. In 2007, Trade Me and eBay Australia were the leading sites in New Zealand and Australia, respectively, in the Shopping & Classifieds category. Pure-plays dominate the department stores industry in Australia and New Zealand, with Amazon taking the top position in both markets in October 2007. DealsDirect was the leading local brand in the Australian market, while the Web site of bricks-and-mortar store Farmers ranked at fifth position in New Zealand. Search engines remain a key source of traffic to Shopping & Classifieds Web sites in the Australian and New Zealand markets, accounting for 29.35 per cent and 29.47 per cent, respectively of upstream visits in October 2007.

One of your first steps is finding out what it means to do business online and determining the best ways for you to fit into the exploding field of e-commerce. For example, you need to realise that the Internet is a personal place; customers are active, not passive, in the way they absorb information; and the Net was established within a culture of people sharing information freely and helping one another. For another, you need to know that although the marketplace continues to grow into the second decade of 2000, most of the new growth is expected to come from experienced online shoppers rather than people who are making their first purchases online. That scenario means you need to address the needs of experienced shoppers who are becoming more demanding of Web-based merchants.

Some of the best places to find out about the culture of the Internet are blogs, newsgroups, chat rooms and bulletin boards where individuals gather and exchange messages online. Visiting discussion forums devoted to topics that interest you can be especially helpful, and you're likely to end up participating. Also visit commerce Web sites (such as eBay, Trade Me, Amazon, DealsDirect, or other online marketplaces) and take note of ideas and approaches that you may want to use.

'Cee-ing' what's out there

The more information you have about the 'four Cs' of the online world, the more likely you are to succeed in doing business online:

- ✔ **Competitors:** Familiarise yourself with other online businesses that already do what you want to do. Don't let their presence intimidate you. After all, you're going to find a different and better way to do what they already do.

- ✔ **Content:** Web sites often look the same. What distinguishes them is their content. Useful information attracts repeat visitors, which leads to increased sales.

- ✔ **Culture:** Explore the special language and style people use when they communicate.

- ✔ **Customers:** Investigate the various kinds of customers who shop online and who may visit your site.

When you take a look around the Internet, notice the kinds of goods and services that tend to sell in the increasingly crowded, occasionally disorganised and sometimes-complex online world. The things that sell best in cyberspace include four Cs:

- ✔ **Cheap:** Online items tend to be sold at a discount — at least, that's what shoppers expect.

- ✔ **Compelling:** Consumers go online to quickly read news stories that are available by subscription, such as newspapers and magazines, content that is exciting and eye-catching or that exist online only, such as homemade video on YouTube (www.youtube.com) or Web logs (*blogs*).

✔ **Convenient:** Shoppers look for items that are easier to buy online than at a 'real' store, such as a rare book that you can order in minutes from Amazon (www.amazon.com) or an electronic greeting card that you can send online in seconds from Hallmark (www.hallmark.com).

✔ **Customised:** Anything hard-to-find, personalised or unique sells well online.

Visit one of the tried-and-true indexes to the Internet, such as Yahoo! (www.yahoo.com) or the pre-eminent search service Google (www.google.com). Enter a word or phrase in the Web site's home page search box that describes the kinds of goods or services you want to provide online. Find out how many existing businesses already do what you want to do. Better yet, determine what they *don't* do and set a goal of meeting that specialised need yourself.

Working out how to do it better

After you take a look at what's already out there, the next step is to find ways to make your business stand out from the crowd. Direct your energies towards making your site unique in some way and providing things that others don't offer. The things that set your online business apart from the rest can be as tangible as half-price sales, competitions, seasonal sales or freebies. They can also involve making your business site higher in quality than the others. Maybe you can just provide better or more personalised customer service than anyone else.

What if you can't find other online businesses doing what you want to do? Lucky you! In e-commerce, being first often means getting a head start and being more successful than latecomers, even if they have more resources than you do. (Just ask the owners of the online bookstore Amazon.com.) Don't be afraid to try something new and outlandish. It just might work!

CASE STUDY

Mapmaker locates his online niche

John Moen didn't know a thing about computer graphics when he first started his online business, Graphic Maps, in 1995. He didn't know how to write *HyperText Markup Language* (HTML), the set of instructions used to create Web pages. (Not too many people in 1995 did.) But he did know a lot about maps. And he heard that setting up shop on the Web was 'the thing to do'. He scraped together US$300 in start-up costs, found out how to create some simple Web pages without any photos (only maps and other graphics), and went online.

At first, business was slow. 'I remember saying to my wife, "You know what? We had ten page views yesterday."' The Graphic Maps site (www.graphicmaps.com) was averaging about 30 page views a day when Moen decided to do something that many beginners may find counterproductive, even silly: He started giving away his work for free. He created some free art (called *clip art*) and made it available for people to copy. And he didn't stop there: He began giving away his knowledge of geography. He answered questions submitted to him by school children and teachers.

Soon, his site was getting 1,000 visits a day. Today, he reports: 'We are so busy, we literally can't keep up with the demand for custom maps. Almost 95 per cent of our business leads come from the Web, and that includes many international companies and Web sites. Web page traffic has grown to more than 3 million hits a month, and banner advertising now pays very well.'

John now has a half dozen or so employees, receives many custom orders for more than US$10,000, and has done business with numerous Fortune 500 companies. To promote his site, John gives away free maps to non-profit organisations, operates a daily geography contest with a US$100 prize to the first person with the correct answer, and answers email promptly. 'I feel strongly that the secret on the Web is to provide a solution for a problem, and for the most part, do it free,' he suggests. 'If the service is high quality, and people get what they want ... they will tell their friends, and all will beat a path to your URL, and then, and only then, will you be able to sell your products to the world, in a way you never imagined was possible.'

Moen created a second site called WorldAtlas.com (www.worldatlas.com) that is devoted to geography. That site generates revenue from pop-up and banner ads that other companies place there because so many people visit. 'It is not unusual to have 20 million impressions on that site and hundreds of thousands of questions a month from teachers and students who need an answer to a geography question,' says Moen.

When asked how he can spare the time to answer questions for free when he has so much paying business available, he responds: 'How can you not? I normally work 12-hour and sometimes 16- or 18-hour days. If some little kid, some student, comes home from school, and says, "Grandpa, I need to find out what's the tallest mountain in North America", and he does a search on Google that directs him to go to WorldAtlas.com, we will try to answer that question.'

His advice for beginning entrepreneurs: 'Find your niche and do it well. Don't try to compete with larger companies. For instance, I can't compete with Microsoft or Rand McNally, but I don't try to. Our map site, GraphicMaps.com, is one of the few custom map sites on the Web. There is no software yet available that will do automatic mapping for a client. If you need a map for a wedding or for your office, we can make you one. I fill some needs that they don't fill, and I learned long ago how to drive business to my site by offering something for free. The fact is that if you have good ideas and you search for clients, you can still do well on the Web.'

Step 2: Determine What You Have to Offer

Business is all about identifying customers' needs and figuring out exactly what goods or services you can provide to meet those needs. The same approach applies both online and off. (Often, you perform this step before or at the same time that you scope out what the business needs are and figure out how you can position yourself to meet those needs, as we explain in the earlier section 'Step 1: Identify a Need'.)

To determine what you have to offer, make a list of all the items you have to put up for sale or all the services that you plan to provide to your customers. Next, decide not only what goods or services you can provide online, but also where you're going to obtain them. Are you going to create sale items yourself? Are you going to purchase them from another supplier? Jot down your ideas on paper and keep them close at hand while you develop your business plan.

The Internet is a personal, highly interactive medium. Be as specific as possible with what you plan to do online. Don't try to do everything; the medium favours businesses that do one thing well. The more specific your business, the more personal the level of service you can provide to your customers.

Step 3: Come Up with an Online Business Plan

The process of setting goals and objectives and then designing strategies for achieving them is essential when starting a new business. What you end up with is a *business plan*. A good business plan applies not only to the start-up phase but also to day-to-day operations and as a business grows.

While reading, keep a piece of paper handy so you can jot down your ideas, which then becomes part of your business plan.

To set specific goals for your new business, ask yourself these questions:

- ✔ Why do you want to start a business?
- ✔ Why do you want to start it online?
- ✔ What would *you* want to buy online?
- ✔ What would make you buy it?

These questions may seem simple. But many businesspeople never take the time to answer them. And only *you* can answer these questions for yourself. Make sure you have a clear idea of where you're going so that you can commit to making your venture successful over the long haul. (See Chapter 2 for more on setting goals and envisioning your business.)

To carry your plan into your daily operations, observe these suggestions:

- ✔ Write a brief description of your company and what you hope to accomplish with it.
- ✔ Draw up a marketing strategy. (See Chapter 10 for tips.)
- ✔ What is your budget and how will you keep track of your finances? (See Chapter 14 for specifics.)

Consider using specialised software to help you prepare your business plan. Programs such as MasterPlan by MAUS (www.maus.com.au) lead you through the process by asking you a series of questions to identify what you want to do. The Professional edition of the program retails for $299. If you prefer not spending money on software, you can try the free guides to business planning on www.business.gov.au in Australia or www.business.govt.nz in New Zealand. Alternatively, you can source a free business plan template from a site such as office.microsoft.com/en-au/templates/.

If you run your business from a home office, you're eligible for tax deductions. Exactly how much you can deduct depends on how much space you use. You can depreciate your computers and other business equipment, too. On the other hand, your municipality, local council or region may require you to obtain a licence if you operate a business in a residential area; check with your local authorities. You can find out more about tax and legal issues, in Chapters 13 and 14 of this book.

Step 4: Choose Your Tools of the Trade

One of the great advantages of opening a store on the Internet rather than on Main Street is money — or rather, the lack of it. Instead of renting a space and setting up furniture and fixtures, you can buy a domain name, sign up with a hosting service, create some Web pages, and get started with an investment of only a couple of thousand dollars or perhaps even less.

In addition to your virtual storefront, you also have to find a real place to do your business. You don't necessarily have to rent a warehouse or other large space. Many online entrepreneurs use a home office or perhaps a corner in a room where computers, books and other business-related equipment reside.

Picking your Web address

Choosing your domain name(s) is a lot like choosing a name for your company; and your choice is a critical part of your success. Here's how:

1. **Decide on the extension (see Table 1-1) that suits you.**

    The dotcom (.com) domain name space is by far the most popular — 'com' stands for commercial and is representative of a business or company that trades globally. Others such as '.com.au' and '.co.nz' extensions are for a company in Australia or New Zealand respectively.

2. **Aim to keep the domain name short, catchy and representative of what you do.**

    Have a guess what these businesses do:

    - www.quinnys.com.au
    - www.ad-hoc.co.nz
    - www.daydreamers.com.au
    - www.everythingbutflowers.com.au

    You probably had a good guess but you haven't got a clue, right? How about these ones:

    - www.landscapephotography.com.au
    - www.homeprojects.co.nz
    - www.petdeli.com.au
    - www.childsplayfitness.com.au

Much clearer. You can literally spell it out or come up with a clever name that still describes what the business does, like the last one Childsplay Fitness.

3. **Consider registering more than one domain name.**

If you're worried about others starting up a similar business or registering your business name, you may want to think about grabbing the .biz, .net or .info versions of your name — or both the .com and country-specific versions of your business name such as .com.au or .co.nz.

Also, if you have a clever business name, you may want to register both your business name and the generic word or phrase that describes what you do. For example, in this fictitious example a photographer specialising in children's photography goes out and registers the name www.bundleofsmiles.com.au because that is his chosen business name and he loves it. But he finds that childrensphotographer.com.au is also available so he registers both domain names and arranges for both to point to the same Web site.

Table 1-1	Domain Name Extensions
Top Level Domain Names (TLDs)	*Domain Name Meaning/Uses*
Generic TLDs (such as .com, .net and .org)	**.com** represents the word 'commercial' and is the most widely used extension in the world.
	.net represents the word 'network' and is most commonly used by Internet service providers, Web hosts and Web design companies.
	.org represents the word 'organisation' and is primarily used by non-profit organisations.
Country-specific TLDs (such as .com.au and .co.nz)	Each country has a two letter country-code such as .au (Australia), .ca (Canada), .cn (China), .fr (France), .jp (Japan) and .nz (New Zealand).
Alternative TLDs (such as .biz, .name and .info)	**.biz** is used for small-business Web sites.
	.info is for credible resource Web sites and signifies an informational Web site.
	.name is the only domain extension specifically designed for personal use. It is commonly used for easy-to-remember email addresses and personal Web sites that display photos or personal information about an individual.

Domain names are cheap as chips so, if it helps you to protect your brand name or secure a generic word that describes what you do, reserving two or three or even a half a dozen domain names makes good business sense.

Finding a host for your Web site

Although doing business online means you don't have to rent space in a shopping centre or open a real, physical store, you do have to set up a virtual space for your online business. You do so by creating a Web site and finding a company to host it. In cyberspace, your landlord is a Web hosting service. A *Web host* is a company that, for a fee, makes your site available 24 hours a day by maintaining it on a special computer — a Web *server*.

A Web host can be as large and well known as Telstra Bigpond, which gives all its customers a place to create and publish their own Web pages. Some Web sites, such as Yahoo! GeoCities (`geocities.yahoo.com`) or Tripod (`www.tripod.lycos.com`), act as free hosting services and provide easy-to-use Web site creation tools as well. Web hosts such as Netregistry (`www.netregistry.com.au`) and Webwidgets (`www.webwidgets.co.nz`) provide hosting plans including an easy-to-use, site-builder tool starting at around $25 to $29 a month.

In addition, the company that gives you access to the Internet — your Internet service provider (ISP) — may also publish your Web pages. Make sure your host has a fast connection to the Internet and can handle the large numbers of simultaneous visits, or *hits*, that your Web site is sure to get eventually. You can find a detailed description of Web hosting options in Chapter 4.

Assembling the equipment you need

Think of all the equipment you *don't* need when you set up shop online: You don't need shelving, a cash register, a car park, electricity, fire protection systems, a burglar alarm ... the list goes on and on. You may need some of those for your home, but you don't need to purchase them especially for your online business.

For doing business online, your most important piece of equipment is your computer. Other hardware — such as scanners, modems and monitors — are essential, too. Make sure your computer equipment is up to speed because you're going to spend a lot of time online: answering email, checking orders, revising your Web site, and marketing your product. Expect to spend anywhere between $1,000 and $6,000 for equipment, if you don't have any to begin with.

TIP

Remember that online shoppers are expecting a higher level of customer service. You don't want substandard equipment to slow down responses and performance. Shop wisely and get the best setup you can afford up front so that you don't have to purchase upgrades later on. (For more suggestions on buying business hardware and software, see Chapter 3.)

Keeping track of your inventory

Try not to overlook inventory and setting up systems for processing orders when you're just starting out. As Lucky Boyd, an entrepreneur who started MyTexasMusic and other Web sites, pointed out to Greg, make sure you have a 'big vision' early in the process of creating your site. In his case, it meant having a site that could handle lots of visitors and make purchasing easy for them. In other cases, it may mean having sufficient inventory to meet demand.

Having too many items for sale is preferable to not having enough. 'We operated on a low budget in the beginning, and we didn't have the inventory that people wanted', one entrepreneur commented. 'People who are online get impatient if they have to wait for things too long. Make sure you have the goods you advertise. Plan to be successful.' Co-founder Jinele Boyd adds that they treat every order with urgency and make an effort

to ship the same day the order arrives — or no longer than 36 hours. 'We also hand-write a note inside every box', she says. 'We get emails and calls all the time from people telling us how amazed they were that a "real person" handled their order and took the time to hand-address the boxes.'

Many an online business keeps track of its inventory (and thus fulfils orders quickly) by using a database connected to its Web site. When someone orders a product from the Web site, that order is recorded automatically in the database, which then produces an order for replacement stock.

In this kind of arrangement, the database serves as a so-called *back end* or *back office* to the Web-based storefront. This sophisticated arrangement may not be suitable for beginners. However, if orders and inventory get to be too much for you to handle, consider hiring a Web developer to set up such a system for you.

Choosing business software

For the most part, the programs you need in order to operate an online business are the same as the software you use to surf the Internet. You do, however, need to have a wider variety of tools than you would use for simple information gathering.

Because you're going to be in the business of information *providing* now, as well as information gathering, you need programs such as the following:

- **A Web page editor:** These programs, which you may also hear called *Web page creation tools* or *Web page authoring tools*, make it easy for you to format text, add images and design Web pages without having to master HTML.

- **Graphics software:** If you decide to create your business Web site yourself rather than find someone to do it for you, you need a program that can help you draw or edit images to include on your site.

- **Storefront software:** You can purchase software that leads you through the process of creating a fully-fledged online business and getting your pages on the Web.

- **RSS feed software:** RSS (Real Simple Syndication) is a way of formatting Web content in the form of an eXtensible Markup Language (XML) file so it can be read quickly and easily by people who subscribe to it. You can find instructions on how to create an RSS feed and a list of feed creation tools at www.rss-specifications.com/create-rss-feed.htm.

- **Accounting programs:** You can write your expenses and income on a sheet of paper. But a far more efficient way is to use software that acts as a spreadsheet, helps you with billing and even calculates GST.

Some businesspeople prefer blog software rather than a full-blown Web editor to create a Web site's content.

Step 5: Find Help

Conducting online business does involve relatively new technologies, but they aren't impossible to figure out. In fact, the technology is becoming more accessible all the time. Many people who start online businesses find out how to create Web pages and promote their companies by reading books, attending classes, or networking with friends and colleagues. Of course, just because you *can* do it all doesn't mean that you have to. Often, you're better off hiring help, either to advise you in areas where you aren't as strong or simply to help you tackle the growing workload — and help your business grow at the same time. Hence the saying 'Do what you do best and outsource the rest'.

Hiring technical experts

Spending some money up front to hire professionals who can point you in the right direction can help you maintain an effective Web presence for years to come. Many businesspeople who usually work alone hire knowledgeable individuals to do design or programming work that they would find impossible to tackle otherwise.

Don't be reluctant to hire professional help to get your business online. The Web is full of development firms that perform several related functions: providing customers with Web access, helping to create Web sites and hosting sites on their servers. The expense for such services may be considerable at first. The programming involved in setting up databases, creating purchasing systems, and programming Web pages can run over $10,000 for particularly extensive Web sites, but they can pay off in the long term. Choose a designer carefully and check out sites he or she has done before. Tell the designer your plan for the organisation and content and spell out clearly what you want each page to do. Another area where you may want to find help is in networking and computer maintenance. Know how to do troubleshooting and find out how to keep your computers running. Find out if you have a computer expert in your neighbourhood who is available on short notice.

Gathering your team members

Many entrepreneurial businesses are family affairs. A successful eBay business, Maxwell Street Market (www.maxwellstreetmarket.com), is run by a husband-and-wife team as well as family members and neighbours: The husband does the buying; the wife prepares sales descriptions; the others help with packing and shipping. John Moen found some retired teachers to help answer the geography questions that come into his WorldAtlas.com site. The convenience of the Internet means that these geography experts can log on to the site's email inbox from their respective homes and answer questions quickly.

Early on, when you have plenty of time to do planning, you're probably not going to feel a pressing need to hire others to help you. Many people wait to seek help when they have a deadline to meet or are under financial pressure. Waiting to seek help is okay — as long as you realise that you *are going to* need help, sooner or later.

Of course, you don't have to hire family and friends, but you must find people who are reliable and can make a long-term commitment to your project. Keep these things in mind:

- ✔ Pick someone who already exhibits experience with computers and the Internet.
- ✔ Always review a résumé, get at least three references and ask for samples of the candidate's work.
- ✔ Pick someone who responds promptly and courteously and who provides the talents you need.
- ✔ If your only contact is by phone and email, references are even more important.

If you do find a business partner, make sure the person's abilities balance your own. If you're great at sales and public relations, for example, find a writer or Web page designer to partner with.

Step 6: Construct a Web Site

Although you can make a living buying and selling full time on eBay, a Web site is still likely to be the focus of your online business. Fortunately, Web sites are becoming easier to create. You don't have to know a line of HTML in order to create an effective Web page. Chapter 5 walks you through the specific tasks involved in organising and designing Web pages. Chapter 5 also gives you tips on making your Web pages content-rich and interactive.

Make your site content-rich

The textual component of a Web site is what attracts visitors and keeps them coming back on a regular basis. The more useful information and compelling content you provide, the more visits your site is going to receive. This means the words, headings or images that induce visitors to interact with your site in some way. You can make your content compelling in a number of ways:

- ✔ Provide a call to action, such as Click Here! or Buy Now!
- ✔ Explain how the reader benefits by clicking a link and exploring your site. ('Visit our News and Specials page to find out how to win 500 frequent flyer points.')
- ✔ Briefly and concisely summarise your business and its mission.
- ✔ Scan or use a digital camera to capture images of your sale items (or of the services you provide), as Chapter 5 describes, and post them on a Web page called Products.

Don't forget the personal touch when connecting with your customers' needs. People who shop online don't get to meet their merchants in person, so anything you can tell your visitors about yourself helps to personalise the process and put your visitors at ease. For example, one of Lucky Boyd's primary goals for his MyTexasMusic.com site is to encourage people to become members so they're more likely to visit on a regular basis. His photos of music fans (see Figure 1-1) personalise the site and remind visitors they're members of a community of music lovers. Let your cyber visitors know they're dealing with real people, not remote machines and computer programs.

Figure 1-1:
Personalise
your
business
to connect
with
customers
online.

Peeking in on other businesses' Web sites — to pick up ideas and see how they handle similar issues — is a natural practice. In cyberspace, you can visit plenty of businesses that are comparable to yours from the comfort of your home office, and the trip takes only minutes.

Establishing a visual identity

When you start your first business on the Web, you have to do a certain amount of convincing. You need to convince customers that you're competent and professional. One factor that helps build trust is a graphic identity. A site with an identity looks a certain way. For example, take a look at Figure 1-2. This Web page is from the Triple R Luxury Car Hire Web site (www.tripler.com.au). You can see how the page has a black background, a distinctive logo, a photo in the header and similar fonts used throughout. Notice, too, that the Triple R Web site pages all have these same elements. Using such elements consistently from page to page creates an identity that gives your business credibility and helps viewers find what they're looking for.

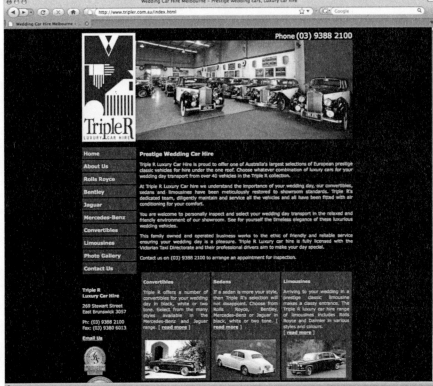

Figure 1-2:
Through
careful
planning
and design,
the Triple R
Luxury Car
Hire site
maintains a
consistent
look and
feel (or
graphic
identity) on
each page.

Step 7: Set Up a System for Processing Sales

Many businesses go online and then are surprised by their own success. They don't have systems in place for finalising sales, shipping out purchased goods in a timely manner and tracking finances as well as inventory.

An excellent way to plan for success is to set up ways to track your business finances and to create a secure purchasing environment for your online customers. That way, you can build on your success rather than be surprised by it.

Providing a means for secure transactions

Getting paid is the key to survival as well as success. When your business exists only online, the payment process isn't always straightforward. Make your Web site a safe place for customers to pay you. Provide different payment options and build a level of trust any way you can.

Some Web surfers are still squeamish about submitting credit card numbers online. And beginning businesspeople are understandably intimidated by the requirements of processing credit card transactions. In the early stages, you can simply create a form that customers have to print out and mail to you along with a cheque. (The Graphic Maps site is successful without having an online credit card system; clients phone in their orders.)

When you can accept credit cards, make your customers feel at ease by explaining what measures you're taking to ensure their information is secure. Such measures include signing up for an account with a Web host that provides a *secure server*, a computer that uses software to encrypt data and uses digital documents, or *certificates*, to ensure its identity. (See Chapters 6 and 7 for more on Internet security and secure shopping systems.)

Becoming a credit card merchant

Electronic commerce, or *e-commerce*, brings to mind visions of online forms and credit card data being transmitted over the Internet. Do you have to provide such service in order to run a successful online business? Not necessarily. Being a credit card merchant makes life easier for your customers, to be sure, but it also adds complications and extra costs to your operation.

The traditional way to become a credit card merchant is to apply to a bank. Small and home-based businesses can have difficulty getting their applications approved. Alternatively, you can sign up with a company that provides electronic shopping-cart services and credit card payments online to small businesses. See Chapter 7 for suggestions. These days, you can also accept credit card payments through the popular electronic payment service PayPal. Your customers have to have an account with PayPal and have their purchase price debited from their credit card accounts, but the service is popular enough that a substantial number of your online shoppers are probably members already.

If you do get the go-ahead from a bank to become a credit card merchant, you have to pay a fee per transaction processed (typically, 2 to 3 per cent of each transaction). You sometimes have to pay a monthly service charge of $10–$25 as well. Besides that, you may need special software or hardware to accept credit card payments — provided by your chosen bank.

To maximise your sales by reaching users who either don't have credit cards or don't want to use them on the Internet, provide low-tech alternatives (such as toll-free phone numbers and fax numbers) so that people can provide you with information using more familiar technologies.

After much searching, Lucky Boyd signed with a company called GoEmerchant (www.goemerchant.com), which provides him with the payment systems that many online shoppers recognise when they want to make a purchase. First, GoEmerchant has a *shopping cart* — a set of pages that acts as an electronic holding area for items before they are purchased. Next, it has a secure way for people to make electronic purchases by providing online forms where people can safely enter credit card and other personal information. The note stating that the payment area is protected by Secure Sockets Layer (SSL) encryption tells people that even if a criminal intercepts their credit card data, he can't read it.

Keeping your books in order

In the simplest sense, 'keeping your books' means recording all financial activities that pertain to your business, including any expenses you incur, all the income you receive, as well as your equipment and tax deductions. The financial side of running a business also entails creating reports, such as profit-and-loss statements, that banks require if you apply for a loan. Such reports not only help meet financial institutions' needs, but also provide you with essential information about how your business is doing at any time.

You can record all this information the old-fashioned way, by writing it down in ledgers and journals, or you can use accounting software. (See Chapter 14 for some suggestions of easy-to-use accounting packages that are great for financial novices.) Because you're making a commitment to using computers on a regular basis by starting an online business, choosing to use computers to keep your books, too, is only natural. Accounting software can help you keep track of expenses and provide information that may save you some headaches at tax time.

After you save your financial data onto your hard drive, make backups so that you don't lose information you need to do business. See Chapter 6 for ways to back up and protect your files.

Step 8: Provide Personal Service

The Internet, which runs on wires, cables and computer chips, may not seem like a place for the personal touch. But technology didn't actually create the Internet and all of its content; *people* did that. In fact, the Internet is a great place to provide your clients and customers with outstanding, personal customer service.

In many cases, customer service on the Internet is a matter of making yourself available and responding quickly to all inquiries. You check your email regularly; you make sure you respond within a day; you cheerfully solve problems and hand out refunds if needed. By helping your customers, you help yourself, too. You build loyalty as well as credibility among your clientele. For many small businesses, the key to competing effectively with larger competitors is to provide superior customer service. See Chapter 8 for more ideas on how you can do this.

Sharing your expertise

Your knowledge and experience are among your most valuable commodities. So you may be surprised when we suggest you give them away for free. Why? It's a 'try before you buy' concept. Helping people for free builds your credibility and makes them more likely to pay for your services down the track.

When your business is online, you can easily communicate what you know about your field and make your knowledge readily available. One way is to set up a Web page that presents the basics about your company and your field of interest in the form of Frequently Asked Questions (FAQs). Another technique is to become a virtual publisher/editor and create your own newsletter in which you write about what's new with your company and about topics related to your work. See Chapter 8 for more on communicating your expertise through FAQs, newsletters and advanced email techniques.

Greg's brother was sceptical when he recommended that his brother include a page full of technical information explaining exactly what equipment he uses and describing the steps involved in audio restoration. He didn't think anyone would be interested; he also didn't want to give away his 'trade secrets'. *Au contraire, mon frère!* People who surf the Internet gobble up all the technical details they can find. The more you wow them with the names and model numbers of your expensive equipment, not to mention the work you go through to restore their old records, the more they're likely to trust you. And trust gets people to place an order with you.

Making your site appealing

Many *ontrepreneurs* (online entrepreneurs) succeed by making their Web site not only a place for sales and promotion but also an indispensable resource, full of useful hyperlinks and other information, that customers want to visit again and again. For example, the Graphic Maps Web site, profiled earlier in this chapter, acts as a resource for anyone who has a question about geography. To promote the site, John Moen gives away free maps for non-profit organisations, operates a daily geography contest with a US$100 prize to the first person with the correct answer (as shown in Figure 1-3), and answers email promptly. 'I feel strongly that the secret on the Web is to provide a solution to a problem and, for the most part, to do it for free', he suggests.

The MyTexasMusic site (`www.mytexasmusic.com`) uses the concept of membership to strengthen connections with customers. The main purpose of the site is to make money by selling the works of Texas musicians as well as tickets to concerts. But in order to make money, you can give people a reason to visit your site on a regular basis. When people are *members*, for example, rather than *shoppers*, they feel connected and privileged.

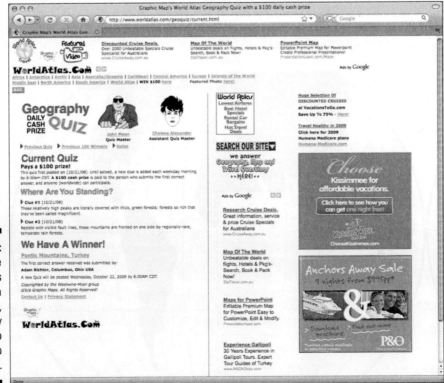

Figure 1-3:
This site uses free art, a mailing list, and daily prizes to drum up business.

The site encourages music lovers and musicians to become members: Members then provide information about who they are and where they live, and they create their own username and password so they can access special content and perform special functions on the site, such as selling their own CDs or posting song clips online. For an online business, knowing the names and addresses of people who visit and who don't necessarily make purchases is a goldmine of information. The business can use the contact information to send members special offers and news releases; the more frequently contact is maintained, the more likely that those casual shoppers eventually turn into paying customers.

The concept of membership also builds a feeling of community among customers. By turning the e-commerce site into a meeting place for members who love Texas musicians, those members make new friends and have a reason to visit the site on a regular basis. Community building is one way in which commerce on the Web differs from traditional bricks-and-mortar selling, and it's something you should consider, too.

Another way to encourage customers to congregate at your site on a regular basis is to create a discussion area. Chapter 8 shows you how to provide a discussion page right on your own Web site.

Communicating effectively to build relationships

Email is, in our humble opinion, the single most important marketing tool you can use to boost your online business. Becoming an expert email user increases your contacts and provides you with new sources of support, too.

The two best and easiest email strategies are

- Checking your email as often as possible
- Responding to email inquiries immediately

Additionally, you can email inquiries about co-marketing opportunities to other Web sites similar to your own. Ask other online business owners if they're willing to provide links to your site in exchange for you providing links to theirs. And always include a signature file with your message that includes the name of your business and a link to your business site. See Chapter 8 for more information on using email effectively to build and maintain relations with your online customers.

Spamming is bad for business

Use email primarily for one-to-one communication. The Internet excels at bringing individuals together. Mailing lists and newsletters can use email effectively for marketing, too. However, don't send out mass quantities of unsolicited commercial email. That practice turns off almost all consumers and can get you in trouble with the law.

Spam artists have been convicted, and the sentences are getting more severe. In October 2006, a Perth company and its director were fined $5.5 million for bombarding Internet users with millions of unsolicited email messages. In May 2008, a judge ordered two spammers to pay MySpace $247 million when they sent more than 725,000 emails to users of the social networking site pretending to be friends.

Step 9: Alert the Media and Everyone Else

In order to be successful, small businesses need to get the word out to the people who are likely to purchase what they have to offer. If this group turns out to be only a narrow market, so much the better; the Internet is great for connecting to niche markets that share a common interest. (See Chapter 10 for more on locating your most likely customers on the Internet and figuring out how best to communicate with them.)

The Internet provides many unique and effective ways for small businesses to advertise, including search services, email, newsgroups, electronic mailing lists, and more. It's encouraging to note, though, that you don't always have to depend on high-tech solutions to get publicity. 'We still do not spend money on print advertising and have more business than we can handle from word-of-mouth', says Jinele Boyd of MyTexasMusic.com.

Listing your site with Internet search services

How, exactly, do you get listed on the search engines such as Yahoo! and ninemsn? Frankly, it's getting more difficult. Many of the big search services charge for listings (Yahoo!'s fees for commercial listings in its directory are particularly steep — US$299 annually). But some allow you to contribute a listing for free, though be aware that you don't get a guarantee you're going to see your site included in their databases.

You can increase the chances that search services list your site

✔ By including special keywords and site descriptions in the titles, body text and HTML commands for your Web pages. You place some of these keywords after a special HTML command (the <meta> tag), making them invisible to the casual viewer of your site.

✔ By creating multiple Web sites for different purposes. One purpose is to reach different markets. Another is to improve rankings on search engines, such as Google. By linking one site to several other sites, the site is considered more popular, and its ranking rises.

Chapter 11 looks at how to optimise your Web site for the search engines.

Reaching the entire Internet

Your Web site may be the cornerstone of your business, but if nobody knows about it being out there, it can't help you generate sales. Perhaps the most familiar form of online advertising is *banner ads* — those little electronic billboards that seem to show up on every popular Web page you visit.

But banner advertising can be expensive and may not be the best way for a small business to advertise online. In fact, the most effective marketing for some businesses isn't traditional banner advertising or newspaper/magazine placements. Rather, the e-marketers who run those businesses target electronic bulletin boards and mailing lists where people already discuss the products being sold. You can post notices on the bulletin boards where your potential customers congregate, notifying them that your services are now available. (Make sure the board in question permits such solicitation before you do so, or you're going to chase away the very customers you want.)

This sort of direct, one-to-one marketing may seem tedious, but it's often the best way to develop a business on the Internet. Reach out to your potential customers and strike up an individual, personal relationship with each one.

Chapter 10 contains everything you need to know about advertising with mailing lists, newsgroups and even traditional banner ads.

Step 10: Review, Revise and Improve

For any long-term endeavour, you need to establish standards by which you can judge its success or failure. You must decide for yourself what you consider success to be. After a period of time, take stock of where your business is and then take steps to do even better.

Taking stock

Your business's one-year anniversary is a good time to take stock. Your site may be online, but if it isn't getting many page views, you should consider improvements or rebuilding the site — for example, by increasing the number of promotions or giveaways to encourage increased traffic.

HTML is a markup language: It identifies parts of a Web page that need to be formatted as headings, text, images and so on. It can be used to include scripts, such as those written in the JavaScript language. But by creating your pages from scratch with Hypertext Preprocessor (PHP) programming language, you can make your site more dynamic and easier to update. You can rotate random images, process forms and compile statistics that track your visitors by using PHP scripts, for instance. You can design Web pages in a modular way so they can be redesigned and revised more quickly than with HTML, too.

When all is said and done, your business may do so well that you can reinvest in it by buying new equipment or increasing your services. You may even be in a position to give something back to not-for-profit organisations and those in need. Mother and daughter team, Carol and Natalie, of Baby Delight (www.babydelight.com.au) give $1 from every nappy sale to the Princess Margaret Hospital Foundation in Perth. Perhaps having enough money left over means you can reward yourself, too — as if being able to tell everyone 'I own my own online business' isn't reward enough!

Money is only one form of success. Plenty of entrepreneurs are online for reasons other than making money. That said, it *is* important from time to time to evaluate how well you're doing financially. Accounting software, such as the programs described in Chapter 14, makes it easy to check your revenues on a daily or weekly basis. The key is to establish the goals you want to reach and develop measurements so that you know when and if you reach those goals.

Updating your data

Getting your business online now and updating your site regularly is better than waiting to unveil the perfect Web site all at one time. In fact, seeing your site improve and grow is one of the best things about going online. Over time, you can create competitions, strike up cooperative relationships with other businesses, and add more background information about your products and services.

Consider *4 Ingredients*, created by two Queensland mums Rachael Bermingham and Kim McCosker. Their idea was to create a cookbook where all the recipes use no more than four ingredients. They compiled 340 recipes and pitched the idea to publishers who rejected the project. So, not to be deterred, they self-published the book, found a distributor and set up a simple Web site (www.4ingredients.com.au) to allow for online sales. The book was released in March 2007, hit the bestseller list in both Australia and New Zealand, and sold more than 420,000 copies (making more than $1 million). The Web site has evolved with the business and now lists stockists and free recipes, while asking visitors to submit their personal favourite four-ingredient recipes. Rachael and Kim have since released a second book and produced their own TV show for cable television.

Businesses on the Web need to evaluate and revise their practices on a regular basis. By studying reports of where visitors come from before they reach your site, and what pages they visit on the site, you can attract new customers. Online business is a process of trial and error. Some promotions work better than others. The point is that the process needs to be ongoing and a long-term commitment. Taking a chance and profiting from your mistakes is better than not trying in the first place.

Chapter 2

Planning Your New E-Business

· ·

In This Chapter

▶ Drawing up a plan for your own successful online business

▶ Understanding your options: sales, services, auctions!

▶ Understanding your potential customers: who's coming to visit?

· ·

Starting your own online business is like renovating an old house —
something Greg is constantly doing. Both projects involve a series of
recognisable phases:

- ✔ **The idea phase:** You tell people about your great idea. They hear the
  enthusiasm in your voice, nod their heads, and say something like,
  'Good luck'. They've seen you in this condition before and know how
  it usually turns out.

- ✔ **The decision phase:** Undaunted, you begin honing your plan. You read
  books (like this one), ask questions, and shop around until you find
  just the right tools and materials to get you started. Of course, when
  the time comes to get your hands dirty and start work, you may start
  to panic, asking yourself whether you're really up for the task.

- ✔ **The assembly phase:** Still determined to proceed, you forge ahead. You
  plug in your tools and go to work. Drills spin, sparks fly and metal moves.

- ✔ **The test-drive phase:** One fine day, out of the dust and fumes, your
  masterpiece emerges. You invite everyone over to enjoy the fruits of
  your labour. All of those who were sceptical before are now full of
  admiration. You get enjoyment from your project for years to come.

If renovating a house doesn't work for you, think about restoring a vintage
car, planning a wedding or trekking the Kokoda Trail. The point is that
starting an online business is a project like any other — one that you can
understand and accomplish in stages. Right now, you're at the first stage of
launching your new business. Your creativity is working overtime. You may
have some rough sketches that only a mother could love.

This chapter helps you get from idea to reality. Your first step is to imagine how you want your business to look and feel. Then you can begin to develop a plan and implement strategies for achieving your dream. In Melissa's ten-plus years spent advising clients about developing Web sites, the single biggest reason for failure is a lack of a proper *business plan* (setting goals and objectives and then designing strategies to achieve them). And second to that reason is not devoting the time and resources needed to get the business idea off the ground. You now have a big advantage over those who started new businesses a few years ago: You have plenty of models to show you what works and what doesn't.

Take the time to write a business plan and map out your ideas. This disciplined approach starts you off on the right track. Preparing a business plan helps you to focus on what you hope to achieve, how you plan to get there and what your budget is. Having a business plan handy also helps you to give a brief to any contractors you want to hire and to pitch to bankers or investors if the opportunity arises.

Don't rush into signing a contract to design or host your online business until you know what you want and you have written a brief. We've encountered experienced businesspeople who prepaid for a year's worth of Web hosting with nothing else yet in place. Be sure that you know your options and have a business strategy, no matter how simple, before you sign anything. If you need software or a business plan template to help you write your plan, refer to Chapter 1.

Mapping Out Your Online Business

How do you get to square one? Mapping out your goals in the form of a written business plan (refer to the previous section) is the key to crystallising your ideas and getting started.

Start by imagining the kind of business that is your ultimate goal. Now is the time to indulge in some brainstorming and to answer the all-important questions:

- ✔ Why do you want to start an online business? (Consider your main purpose or goal.)
- ✔ Who is going to use your Web site? (Define your ideal target customer.)
- ✔ How do people find out about your business?
- ✔ What are they going to do when they get there? (Make a purchase, download a trial, pick up the phone?)

✔ When are they likely to come back? How often does your Web site need to be updated?

✔ What is your budget to develop, market and keep your business online?

Table 2-1 illustrates some possible goals and suggests how to achieve them.

Table 2-1	Online Business Models	
Goal	*Type of Web Site*	*What to Do*
Make millions	Sales	Sell items, gain paying advertisers
Gain credibility and attention	Marketing	Put your résumé and samples of your work online
Promote yourself	Personal	Promote yourself so that people hire you or want to use your goods or services
Turn an interest into a source of income	Hobby/special interest	Invite like-minded people to share your passion, participate in your site, and generate traffic so that you can gain advertisers

Looking around

You don't have to completely reinvent the wheel. The Internet can be the best source of information on how to build your online business. Sometimes, spending just half an hour surfing the Net can stimulate your own mental network. Find sites with qualities you want to emulate. This book suggests good business sites you can visit that illustrate good models to follow.

Don't feel obligated to keep moving in the same direction all the time, either. One of the many advantages of starting an online business is the ability to change direction with relative ease. For example, you may start out with an eBay store to sell your wares; then, as you grow, you may need to develop your own Web site with a fully-featured, online store.

Because you're not unlike your target audience, your likes and dislikes have value. Each time you surf for ideas, make a list as you go of what you find appealing, and jot down notes on logos, designs, text and site features. That way, your list becomes a treasure trove of data to draw upon when you begin to refine what you want to do.

Putting your business plan on paper

Your head is probably spinning with ideas for your new business. But the important first step to running any successful business is being able to put your ideas and goals on paper in the form of a business plan. This written plan then becomes your road map or action plan and can help you when applying for finance or briefing any consultants you may hire to help you reach your goals.

To help you prepare a business plan, follow these key points:

✔ **Executive summary:** Normally a short version, or summary of everything within the plan. This includes what the business does, your goals and objectives, how you plan to get there and what financial goals you hope to achieve.

✔ **Business profile:** A description of your business, what products and services you offer,

what makes up the business in terms of people and assets, and where you're going to operate.

✔ **Marketing:** Identifies your target market in terms of geography, income and demographic; as well as your plan for how to reach or market to your prospective customers.

✔ **Objectives and plans:** Lays out your business goals for the next one to five years and how you plan to achieve them.

✔ **Finances:** Includes a start-up budget as well as sales and profit forecasts — the costs to set up and run your business and how much you hope to sell.

For more help with writing your business plan, check out *Business Plans For Dummies*, by Paul Tiffany, Steven Peterson and Veechi Curtis (Wiley Publishing Australia Pty Ltd).

Making your mark

The Web and other parts of the online world have undergone a population explosion that still shows no signs of slowing. According to Internet Systems Consortium's Domain Survey (www.isc.org), in January 2008, 541.7 million computers that hosted Web sites were connected to the Internet, compared with 433.1 million in 2007 and 395 million in 2006. Of those computers, 17.6 per cent host Web addresses that end with the commercial (.com) designation, 2 per cent end with (.au) and 0.3 per cent end with (.nz).

As an ontrepreneur (online entrepreneur), your goal is to stand out from the crowd — or to 'position yourself in the marketplace', as business consultants like to say. Consider the following tried-and-true suggestions if you want your Web site to be a go-to place:

✔ **Pursue something you know well:** Experience adds value to the information that you provide. In the online world, expertise sells.

- ✔ **Make a statement:** On your Web site, include a *mission statement* that clearly identifies what you do, the customers you hope to reach, and how you're different from your competitors.

- ✔ **Give something away for free:** Giveaways and promotions are surefire ways to gain attention and develop a loyal customer base. In fact, entire Web sites are devoted to providing free stuff online, like ShopFree (www.shopfree.com.au) or Blinky (www.blinky.co.nz). You don't have to give away an actual product; it can be words of wisdom based on your training and experience. One good idea Melissa came across lately was a jam manufacturer that gave away free recipes on its Web site for cooking with its products.

- ✔ **Find your niche:** Web space is a great place to pursue niche marketing. In fact, sometimes, the quirkier the item, the better it sells. Some of the most successful sellers Melissa knows deal in things like antique tyres, water tanks, martial arts uniforms, personalised wine labels, and the like. Don't be afraid to target a narrow audience and direct all your sales efforts to a small group of devoted followers.

- ✔ **Do something you love:** The more you love your business, the more time and effort you're bound to put into it and, therefore, the more likely it is to be successful. Such businesses take advantage of the Internet's worldwide reach, which makes it easy for people with the same interests to gather at the same virtual location.

Scan through the list of *BRW* magazine's (www.brw.com.au) Fast 100 and Young Rich 100, and you find many examples of businesses that follow all the aforementioned strategies:

- ✔ RedBalloon Days (www.redballoondays.com.au) has a niche selling experiences as gifts such as hot air ballooning, sky diving and jet boat riding. Google 'Naomi Simson' and read how this entrepreneur started her online business — pure inspiration.

- ✔ DealsDirect (www.dealsdirect.com.au) began in 1999 on eBay and is now one of Australia's biggest online department stores selling everything from towels, rugs and tools, to computer monitors, furniture, toys and more.

- ✔ eCareer (www.ecareer.com.au) is an IT recruitment company with a great reliance on its Web site because most job hunters now use the Internet to find their next job rather than traditional media such as newspapers.

- ✔ realestate.com.au (www.realestate.com.au) came within two weeks of closing its doors in its early days (2001). The company now dominates the online real estate market, is the number one site in Australia and has a global presence with sites in more than eight other countries including New Zealand, Italy, France, Germany and Hong Kong.

Evaluating commercial Web sites

How is your business the same as others? How is it different from others? Your customers are going to ask these questions, so you may as well start out by asking them also. Commercial Web sites — those whose Internet addresses end with `.com`, `.com.au`, `.co.nz` or `.biz` — are the fastest-growing segment of the Net. This is the area you're entering, too. The trick is to be comfortable with the size and level of complexity of a business that's right for you. In general, your options are

- ✔ **A big commercial Web site:** The Web means big business, and plenty of big companies create Web sites with the primary goal of supplementing a product or business that's already well known and well established. Just a few examples are the Holden Web site (`www.holden.com.au`), the Fisher & Paykel Web site (`www.fisherpaykel.co.nz`) and the Huggies Web site (`www.huggies.com.au`). True, corporations with thousands of dollars to throw into Web design created these commercial Web sites, but you can still look at them to get ideas for your own site.

- ✔ **A mid-sized site:** Many a small business of ten to twelve employees makes good use of the Web to provide customer service, disseminate information, and post a sales catalogue. You may find some features that mid-size companies use, such as a Frequently Asked Questions (FAQ) page or a sales catalogue, useful to you. Look at the Finest Wedding Cars site (`www.finestweddingcars.com.au`) for good ideas.

- ✔ **A site that's just right:** You don't need prior business experience to guarantee success on the Web. A business can also start out as a single person, couple or family. In fact, the rest of this book is devoted to helping you produce a very fine, homegrown entrepreneurial business. This chapter gets you off to a good start by examining the different kinds of businesses you can launch online and some business goals you can set for yourself.

Choosing Models of Online Businesses to Test Drive

If you're easily overstimulated, you may feel like you need blinders when you comb the Internet for ideas to give your online business a definite shape and form. Use the following brief descriptions of online businesses to create categories of interest and then zero in on the ones that are likely to be most useful to you.

Selling consumer products

According to the Nielsen Global Online Survey on Internet shopping habits (November 2007) — more than 85 per cent of the world's online population has used the Internet to make a purchase — increasing the market for online shopping by 40 per cent in the past two years.

Some 87 per cent of Australian and 92 per cent of New Zealand Internet users have made a purchase over the Internet. In 2006, e-commerce sales in Australia and New Zealand exceeded $45 billion. The online marketplace is a great venue if you have products to sell. The most popular items purchased over the Internet are books, clothing, shoes, accessories, videos, DVDs, airline tickets and electronic equipment. The Web has always attracted those looking for unique items or something customised just for them. Consider taking your wares online if one or more of the following applies to you:

✔ Your products are high in quality.

✔ You create your own products; for example, you hand-paint dishes, make truffles or sell gift baskets of wine.

✔ You specialise in some aspects of your product that larger businesses can't achieve. Perhaps you sell regional foods such as Tasmanian seafood or wine from New Zealand.

Sites such as Put it on a T-shirt (www.putitonatshirt.com) allow customers to customise their own unique message on a T-shirt. Other sites don't sell consumer goods directly, but they support consumer goods. For instance, the Boost Juice Web site (www.boostjuice.com.au) focuses on its unique juice and smoothie menu, and the health and nutrition of its ingredients, as well as its healthy fun culture and high standards.

So come on in; the water's fine. The key is to find your niche, as many small-but-successful businesses have done. Use your Web space to declare your love for your products (and, by implication, why your customers can't but love them, too).

Marketing your professional services

Either through a Web site or through listings in indexes and directories, offering your professional services online can expand your client base dramatically. A Web presence also gives existing clients a new way to contact you: through email. Here are just a few examples of professionals who are offering their services online:

- ✔ **Barristers and solicitors:** Harjeet Golian is based in Auckland and specialises in immigration law. Through his Web site (www.golian.co.nz), he can reach individuals from around the world who want to come to New Zealand.

- ✔ **Consultants:** Experts who keep their knowledge up to date and are willing to give advice to those with similar interests and needs are always in demand. Consultants in a specialised area often find a great demand for their services on the Internet. For example: Feng Shui (www.fengshuiliving.com.au), Property (www.petermarsh.co.nz) and Generation Y (www.petersheahan.com.au).

- ✔ **Dentist:** Dr Yvonne King, who has a practice based in Caulfield, Victoria, has a Web site (www.cldc.com.au) that explains what she does that sets her apart from other dentists: she specialises in cosmetic and laser dentistry and helping people achieve a 'perfect smile'.

- ✔ **Virtual assistant:** Anita Kilkenny has a simple Web site (www.akavirtualpa.com.au) to market her services — she provides outsourced administrative and secretarial services over the Internet.

We're busy people who don't always have the time to pore over the fine print. Short and snappy nuggets of information can draw customers to your site and make them feel as though they're getting 'something for free'. One way you can put forth this professional expertise is by starting your own online newsletter. You get to be editor, writer and mailing-list manager. Plus, you get to talk as much as you want, network with loads of people who are interested enough in what you have to say to subscribe to your publication, and put your name and your business before lots of people. Michael Grose puts out a regular newsletter called *Happy Kids* that supplements his online business site (www.parentingideas.com.au).

Becoming a resource and sharing knowledge

The original purpose of the Internet was to share knowledge via computers, and information is the commodity that has fuelled cyberspace's rapid growth. As the Internet and commercial online networks continue to expand, information remains key.

Finding valuable information and gathering a particular kind of resource for one location online can be a business in itself. People love to get knowledge they trust from the comfort of their own homes. For example, Aussie shoppers are keen to access independent reviews on products before buying important big ticket items such as a pram, digital camera or washing machine. (See the Choice Web site, www.choice.com.au, run by the Australian Consumers' Association, for example.)

Other online businesses provide gathering points or indexes to more specific areas. Here are just a few examples:

- **Portals:** A portal aims to provide a single access point to the Internet for its visitors by providing a search engine, news, weather, TV guides, email and more, all in one place. The biggest Web site of this kind in Australia is ninemsn (www.ninemsn.com.au). The site is a joint venture between Microsoft and media giant PBL. Being linked with Channel 9 and Hotmail in Australia, it is one of the most visited Australian Web sites. MSN NZ (www.msn.co.nz) is just as popular in New Zealand, is also run by Microsoft, and is one of the top five most-visited sites in New Zealand.

- **Directories:** Directories or indexes for a particular industry or market segment often make their income from paid listings and advertisers. They aim to build a steady stream of traffic and become the most popular and well-ranked site in their area. For example, Natural Therapy Pages (www.naturaltherapypages.com.au) dominates in health and wellness and Realestate.co.nz (www.realestate.co.nz) dominates in the property market. Travelbug (www.travelbug.co.nz) is popular in the holiday accommodation market, as is Stayz (www.stayz.com.au), which earnt its inventors a fair profit when it was sold to Fairfax Media in 2005.

- **Links pages:** The site Lottos (www.lottos.com.au) gathers links to current competitions and give-aways along with short descriptions of each one. The site generates income through advertising and premium membership registrations. Made up of a collection of blogs, Share My NZ (www.sharemynz.co.nz) allows Kiwis to share links with each other. This Web site makes money by charging annual fees to businesses listed on the site.

Resource sites, such as these, can transform information into money in a number of ways. In some cases, individuals pay to become members; sometimes, businesses pay to be listed on a site; other times, a site attracts so many visitors on a regular basis that other companies pay to post advertising on the site. Big successes — such as realestate.com.au — carry a healthy share of ads and strike lucrative partnerships with big companies, as well.

Making opportunities with technology

What could be more natural than using the Web to sell what you need to get and stay online? The online world itself, by the very fact that it exists, has spawned all kinds of business opportunities for tech entrepreneurs:

- **Computers:** Suppliers like TechBuy (www.techbuy.com.au) and Computer Store (www.computerstore.co.nz) have had success by going online and offering equipment for less than conventional retail stores. Being on the Internet means that they save on overheads, staff wages, and other costs, and they can pass those savings on to their customers.

- **Hardware and electronics:** The popularity of all the peripheral gadgets like MP3 players, USB keys, iPods and mobile phones have seen sites such as Mr.Gadget (www.mrgadget.com.au), GadgetPeople (www.gadgetpeople.co.nz) and Digital Cameras Online (www.digitalcameras.com.au) take off. As well, some sites review and report on the latest gadgets such as Good Gear Guide (www.goodgearguide.com.au) and Gizmodo (www.gizmodo.com.au).

- **Internet service providers:** These businesses provide access to the Internet through either a dial-up or broadband connection. Many ISPs, such as Telstra Bigpond or OptusNet in Australia and iHug or Slingshot in New Zealand, are big concerns. But smaller companies are succeeding as well — for example, Netspace (www.netspace.net.au), which is based in Melbourne, Australia, and services more than 60,000 customers, and Broadband Choice (www.broadbandchoice.com.au), which is an independent online community where surfers can compare and read reviews on different ISPs.

- **Software:** Matt Wright is well known on the Web for providing free computer scripts that add important functionality to Web sites, such as processing information that visitors submit via online forms. Matt's Script Archive site (www.scriptarchive.com) now includes an online survey system for sale and an invitation to businesses to take out advertisements on his site.

Being a starving artist without the starving

Being creative no longer means you have to live out of your flower-covered van, driving from art fairs to craft shows. If you're simply looking for exposure and feedback on your creations, you can put samples of your work online. Consider the following suggestions for virtual creative venues (and revenues):

✔ **Online galleries and directories:** Thanks to online galleries, artists whose sales were previously limited to one region can get enquiries from all over the world. Art2Muse (`www.art2muse.com.au`) promotes and sells the art of more than 55 established artists. Online art portal artsConnect (`www.artsconnect.com.au`) profiles artists from all walks of life including painters, sculptors, musicians and filmmakers.

✔ **Promote your artwork:** New Zealand painter Emma Wright uses her Web site (`www.emmawright.co.nz`) to display her artwork and raise her profile (see Figure 2-1). Australian artist Richard Claremont makes money online by painting commissioned portraits for people from photographs (`www.paintedmemories.com.au`).

✔ **Publish your writing:** *Blogs* (Weblogs, or online diaries) are all the rage these days. The most successful, like the one run by New Zealand–based Richard MacManus (`www.readwriteweb.com`), are generating ad revenue. To find out how to create one, check out Blogger (`www.blogger.com`) or BlogTown (`www.blogtown.co.nz`).

✔ **Sell your music:** Songwriter-performer Jacqueline Amidy promotes and sells her music through her Web site (`www.jacquelineamidy.com`).

Figure 2-1:
A New Zealand artist created this Web site to gain recognition and sell her artwork.

You can, of course, also sell all that junk cluttering your spare room or garage, as well as junk from other family members, on eBay; see Chapter 9 for more information on this exciting business opportunity.

Identifying Your Target Customers

After you map out the type of online business you're looking to develop, thinking about who is likely to use your Web site is crucial. In the planning stages you need to consider things like the age, sex, education, location and interests of your target audience so you can build a site attractive to this demographic.

Look at who's coming to visit

The key to your online success is determined by how well you're able to identify and attract your target customers. After all, a site with no visitors is a 'cyber-ghost town'! While Internet surfers may come in all shapes and sizes, if you try to narrow down and be as specific as you can when identifying who your ideal customers are likely to be, you're going to be in a better position to reach the right people from the start.

Use the following list to help you to focus on defining your target market:

- **Age group:** Is your site aimed at a specific age demographic such as new mothers, teenagers, baby boomers or retired professionals? This factor can affect decisions such as what colours and the type of language you choose for setting up your Web site (see Chapter 5), as well as what type of attractors or give-aways you decide on. In general, the younger your audience the shorter their attention span so, if you're targeting young kids, you need to take this factor into account.

- **Location:** Is your site for a specific local area? Or, do you need to consider whether your target customers are likely to live in a city or rural area or even overseas. This factor may affect things like how accessible the Internet is to your customers and, also, the cost of delivering to these areas.

- **Internet connection:** Is your target market travelling salespeople, farmers in a rural area or staff of big corporates that are behind a firewall? This factor then can affect how they access and use your site. For example, you would need to consider things like *load times* (the amount of time your site takes to appear after someone types in your Web address) and how much multimedia you use such as animation and video.

✔ **Profession, education and income:** Are you specifically targeting a profession or industry such as tradespeople, teachers, lawyers or stay-at-home parents? The job, education, salary and background of your visitors can affect how they use your site, how they make decisions and how much they're prepared to spend.

✔ **Interests/hobbies:** Are you starting a niche Web site for collectors, scrapbookers, sporting fans or similar? If so, the hobbies and interests of your target market are an important factor.

Building credibility

Building credibility and trust is very important for any business and especially so for an online business. If people are to consider making a buying decision without physically seeing you, your shop or your product, you can boost their confidence to do business with you (and not the other bloke down Cyber Street) by giving them the information they want to know — a bit about you and how long you've been around. Here's how:

✔ **Background and mission:** Your site should include a bit of background about you and your business. Include how long you've been around, where your business is physically located and the standards you set for your business.

✔ **Awards and testimonials:** If you're recognised with any awards or media attention, wave your flag — include details of these on your site. Collecting and displaying comments from satisfied customers also helps to build confidence in what your business has to offer.

✔ **Contact details:** Don't hide your contact details; instead, give people a choice of how they can contact you. Include your phone, fax, email, physical and postal addresses, and make them clearly visible from all pages on your Web site. (Chapter 8 provides more tips on how to provide good customer service online.)

✔ **Site policies:** Make details such as your secure payment options, terms and conditions, delivery method, returns and privacy policies clearly visible so prospective customers can access these before making a buying decision. (Find out more about building trust with online shoppers in Chapter 6 and about setting these policies and keeping it legal in Chapter 13.)

Use audio or video testimonials instead of written comments. Making use of multimedia clips such as sound or video can add credibility to your customer comments due to the fact that your site visitors can hear or see the person's genuine enthusiasm.

Spreading the word online

As soon as your Web site is launched, your main objective, besides keeping customers happy, is getting noticed or making sure people know your site exists.

On the Internet, announcing your business's cyber existence means getting your site listed or mentioned on as many other Web sites as possible. In the planning stages, you can research relevant places to list your site or exchange links. Here's how:

- ✔ **Look at search engines and directories:** Submit your site to the search engines and get your site listed in all the relevant directories such as the Yellow Pages and business or industry directories. (Chapters 11 and 12 show you how to use search engines and Google to your advantage.)

- ✔ **Get published online:** Mention your site on online community or forum sites, write your own blog or submit articles to online magazine or resource sites such as HomebizBuzz (`www.homebizbuzz.co.nz`). (For more tips on these free publicity strategies, see Chapter 10.)

- ✔ **Exchange links:** Find complementary sites to exchange links with businesses that are not in competition with you. For example, if you're a doctor, you may exchange links with a radiologist, pathology lab or podiatrist. If you're in a local shopping strip, you may choose to exchange links with other neighbouring businesses.

- ✔ **Consider auctions and classifieds:** Depending on your product type, you can consider listing items with online classified or auction Web sites to get the word out and increase sales — for example, eBay PowerSeller Nathan Huppatz sells musical instruments via his eBay store called Marquez Music (`stores.ebay.com.au/Marquez-Music`). (Find out more about how to run a business through online auctions from Chapter 9.)

- ✔ **Advertise:** Choosing to pay to advertise on another site or in a third-party email newsletter (that is, someone else's email newsletter) can help you build your database especially in the early stages. (Chapter 10 gives you lots of great advice about advertising and publicity.)

Chapter 3

Equipping Your New E-Business

- -

In This Chapter

▶ Obtaining or upgrading your computer hardware

▶ Connecting to the Internet: choosing the right plan

▶ Assembling a business software suite

▶ Exploring RSS and other new technologies to boost your business

- -

*B*efore opening the 'cyber-doors' to your new venture, you must also consider properly equipping your online business — just like you would have to equip a traditional, bricks-and-mortar business. One of the many exciting aspects of launching a business online, however, is the absence of much *overhead* (that is, operating expenses). Many non-Internet businesses choose to take out loans, pay rent, remodel their shopfronts, and purchase fixtures and fittings. In contrast, the primary overhead for an online business is computer hardware and software. Being able to afford top-of-the-line equipment is a nice bonus, but the latest bells and whistles aren't absolutely necessary in order to get a business site online and maintain it effectively. However, in order to streamline the technical aspects of connecting to the online world and creating a business Web site, some investment is always necessary.

Technology is changing at such a rapid rate that even the techno-savvy geeks of this world find it hard to keep up with all the changes — let alone you, the busy small-business operator just starting out in the maze of online business. So many different options and tools are available to choose from, plus with all the jargon and acronyms from RAM to VoIP and kilobytes to terabytes, you may feel a bit overwhelmed at first. But have no fear!

This chapter gives a no-nonsense, easy-to-understand run down of many of the technology tools you're going to come to rely on to run your business effectively online. After all, any tools that help automate or speed up aspects of your business can save you time and money in the long run.

Easyware (Not Hardware) for Your Business

Becoming an information provider on the Internet places an additional burden on your computer and peripheral equipment. When you're 'in it for the money', you may very well start to go online every day, and perhaps hours at a time, especially if you buy and sell on eBay. The better your computer setup, the more email messages you can download, the more catalogue items you can store, and so on. In this section, we introduce you to many upgrades you may need to make to your existing hardware configuration.

Some general principles apply when assembling equipment (discussed in this section) and programs (discussed in a subsequent section, 'Software Solutions for Online Business') for an online endeavour:

- ✔ **Look on the Internet for what you need.** You can find just about everything you want to get you started. Web sites such as staticICE (www.staticice.com.au) and PriceSpy (www.pricespy.co.nz) make searching for and comparing prices on computer hardware and software easy for you.

- ✔ **Be sure to pry before you buy!** Don't pull out that credit card until you get the facts on what warranty and technical support your hardware or software vendor provides. Make sure that your vendor provides phone support 24 hours a day, 7 days a week. Also ask how long the typical turnaround time is in case your equipment needs to be repaired.

If you purchase lots of new hardware and software, remember to update your insurance by sending your insurer a list of your new equipment. Also consider purchasing insurance specifically for your computer-related items from a company such as Protecsure (www.protecsure.com.au).

The right computer for your online business

You very well may already have an existing computer setup that you believe is adequate to get your business online and to start the ball rolling. After all, personal computers are becoming more powerful and at the same time generally less expensive; your personal computer may be more than adequate for your business. Or you may be starting from scratch and looking to purchase a new computer. In either case, knowing what all the technical terms and specifications mean is going to help your decision making. Here are some general terms you need to understand:

- **Auxiliary storage:** Physical data-storage space on a hard drive, tape, CD-RW or other device, usually expressed in megabytes (MB) or gigabytes (GB).

- **Double data rate SDRAM (DDR SDRAM):** A type of SDRAM that can dramatically improve the clock rate of a CPU.

- **Gigahertz (GHz) and megahertz (MHz):** The unit of measure that indicates how quickly a computer's processor can perform functions. The central processing unit (CPU) of a computer is where the computing work gets done. In general, the higher the processor's internal clock rate, the faster the computer.

- **Hardware:** The collective term given to the physical parts that make up a computer.

- **Network interface card (NIC):** You need this hardware add-on if you have a cable or DSL modem or if you expect to connect your computer to others on a network, thus allowing you to share files, printers and/or Internet access. Having a NIC usually provides you with Ethernet data transfer to the other computers. (*Ethernet* is a network technology that permits you to send and receive data at very fast speeds.)

- **Random access memory (RAM):** The memory that your computer uses to temporarily store information needed to operate programs. RAM is usually expressed in millions of bytes, or megabytes (MB). The more RAM you have, the more programs you can run simultaneously. Data is stored in this temporary memory only while your computer is connected to the power, which is why if your power supply experiences a power surge, or your computer freezes and you haven't saved your work, you lose what you're working on.

- **Synchronous dynamic RAM (SDRAM):** Many ultrafast computers use some form of SDRAM synchronised with a particular clock rate of a CPU so that a processor can perform more instructions in a given time — that is, do more at once and faster.

- **Virtual memory:** A type of memory on your hard drive that your computer can 'borrow' to serve as extra RAM.

- **Wireless network card:** The laptop or desktop computer you purchase may have a wireless network card installed so you can connect to your wireless modem if you have one. If your home or office has a wireless network and you need to connect, you need to purchase a card as an add-on. You can find one at your local computer store for around $30 to $150.

Processor speed

Computer processors are getting faster all the time. Don't be overly impressed by a computer's clock speed (measured in megahertz or even gigahertz). By the time you get your computer home, another, faster, chip has already hit the streets. Just make sure you have enough RAM (memory) to run the types of applications shown in Table 3-1. (**Note:** These amounts of RAM are only estimates, based on the Windows versions of these products that were available at the time of writing.)

Table 3-1	Memory Requirements	
Type of Application	*Example*	*Amount of RAM Recommended*
Web browser	Internet Explorer	128 or 256MB
Web page editor	Dreamweaver	512MB
Word processor	Microsoft Word	256MB (as part of Office 2007)
Graphics program	Paint Shop Pro	512MB
Accounting software	MYOB or Quicken	64MB or 128MB
Animation/Presentation	Adobe Flash Professional	512MB

The RAM recommended for the sample applications in Table 3-1 adds up to more than 2GB. If you plan to work, be sure to get at least 2GB of RAM — more if you can swing it. Memory is cheap nowadays, so get all the RAM you can afford.

Hard drive storage

RAM is only one type of memory your computer uses; the other kind, the memory in the hard drive, stores information such as text files, audio files, programs and the many essential files that your computer's operating system needs. Most new computers on the market come with hard drives that store many gigabytes of data. Any hard drive with a few gigabytes of storage space should be adequate for your business needs if you don't do a lot of graphics work. But most new computers come with hard drives that are 80GB or larger in size.

CD-RW/DVD±RW drive

Although a DVD and/or CD recordable drive may not be the most important part of your computer for business use, it can perform essential installation, storage and data communications functions, such as installing software and saving, backing up and sharing data. A growing number of machines are now being made available with a *digital versatile disc* (DVD) drive. You can fit 4.7GB or more of data on a DVD±RW, compared with the 700MB or so that a conventional CD-RW can handle.

As soon as your Web site is finished being built, make a backup copy by burning it to CD or DVD. You can also make a backup copy of important files (such as your end-of-financial year bookwork) by burning these files to CD for your records and for your accountant.

Be sure to protect your equipment against electrical problems that can result in loss of data or substantial repair bills. At the very least, make sure that your home office has grounded power outlets and a *surge protector*. A common variety is a four- or five-outlet power board that has a protection device built in. Also consider the option of an uninterruptible power supply (UPS), which keeps devices from shutting off immediately in the event of blackouts.

Monitor

In terms of your online business, the quality or thinness of your monitor doesn't affect the quality of your Web site directly. Even if you have a poor-quality monitor, you can create a Web site that looks great to those who visit you. The problem is that you're not going to know how good your site really looks to customers who have high-quality monitors.

Flat-panel LCD (liquid crystal display) monitors are commonplace now, replacing traditional CRT (cathode-ray tube) monitors, and they're becoming more affordable, too. The quality of a monitor depends on several factors:

✔ **Resolution:** The resolution of a computer monitor refers to the number of pixels (or dots) it can display horizontally and vertically. A resolution of 800 × 600 means the monitor can display 800 pixels across the screen and 600 pixels down the screen. Higher resolutions, such as 1024 × 768 or 1280 × 1024, make images look sharper but require more RAM in your computer. Anything less than 800 × 600 is unusable these days.

✔ **Size:** Monitor size is measured diagonally, as with TVs. Sizes, such as 17 inches, 19 inches and up to 30 inches are available. (The most popular size is 22-inch, which is now available for less than $250.)

✔ **Refresh rate:** This is the number of times per second a video card redraws an image on-screen (at least 60 Hz [hertz] is preferable).

Keep in mind that lots of Web pages seem to have been designed with 17-inch or 21-inch monitors in mind. The problem isn't just that some users (especially those with laptops) have 15-inch monitors, but you can never control how wide the viewer's browser window is. The problem is illustrated in a page from the Web Style Guide, one of the classic references of Web site design (www.webstyleguide.com/page/dimensions.html).

Computer monitors display graphic information that consists of little units — *pixels*. Each pixel appears on-screen as a small dot — so small that it's hard to perceive with the naked eye unless you magnify an image to look at details close up. Together, the patterns of pixels create different intensities of light in an image as well as ranges of colour. A pixel can contain one or more bytes of binary information. The more pixels per inch (ppi), the higher a monitor's potential resolution. The higher the resolution, the closer the image appears to a continuous-tone image such as a photo. When you see a monitor's resolution described as 1280 × 1024, for example, that figure refers to the number of pixels the monitor can display. *Dot pitch* refers to the distance between any two of the three pixels (one red, one green and one blue) a monitor uses to display colour. The lower the dot pitch, the better the image resolution you obtain. A dot pitch of 0.25 millimetres is a good measurement for a 22-inch monitor.

Fax equipment

A fax machine is an essential part of many home offices. If you don't have the funds available for a stand-alone machine, you can install software that helps your computer send and receive faxes. You have three options:

✔ You can install a fax modem, a hardware device that usually works with fax software. The fax modem can be an internal or external device.

✔ You can use your regular modem but install software that enables your computer to exchange faxes with another computer or fax machine.

✔ You can sign up for a service that receives your faxes and sends them to your computer as an email message. Check out mBox (www.mbox.com.au) or Kiwifax (www.kiwifax.com).

If you plan to fax and access the Internet from your home office, get a second phone line or a direct connection, such as DSL or cable modem. The last thing a potential customer wants to hear is an engaged signal.

VoIP

Traditionally, a telephone or mobile phone is used to call someone across the country or overseas for talking long distance. But what's wrong with using a computer for talking to people by carrying on voice conversations? For an increasing number of individuals around the world the answer is: 'Nothing at all.'

VoIP, or Voice over Internet Protocol, is the transmission of a phone call over a computer network rather than over a telephone line — that is, making cheap calls over your broadband Internet connection. Basically, using VoIP allows you to make calls using software on your computer, or hardware connecting your phone to the Internet, to make calls over the Internet (to the phone numbers you would usually call) at an extremely reduced cost or, in some cases, for free.

When you talk on a landline, you connect with someone else over the cable owned and maintained by the phone company. But the DSL (Digital Subscriber Line) connections that bring relatively high-speed Internet into most homes can carry both voice and data signals: In fact, they both share the same line. If you can use the same cable to talk over the phone, you can certainly talk over your computer, too.

To connect your phone to the Internet, you can get a modem with a VoIP device built in that allows you to plug a standard phone into your modem. Alternatively, if your modem doesn't have this option, you can buy a separate VoIP device that plugs into your phone at one end and your modem at the other end. These devices are approximately $100 and can be purchased through your Internet Service Provider (ISP) or your local computer hardware store.

VoIP can help your business's bottom line. Melissa's own ISP, iiNet (www.iinet.net.au), offers a residential VoIP service for around $30 a month, and combined broadband Internet plus VoIP for $50 a month. Compare those amounts to what you're paying now for your landline and your Internet access, and you can save quite a bit (for Melissa, the difference is around $50 a month), thus saving your startup business lots of money as well.

To use a software solution (instead of a hardware solution) that allows you to make phone calls on your computer, look into the most popular software in the field, Skype (www.skype.com). For more on Skype, check out the section 'Software Solutions for Online Business', later in this chapter.

VoIP presents some potential downsides: An important consideration is the fact that if your Internet connection goes down for some reason, your phones stop working; and, if your connection is slow due to weather or heavy usage by others in your area, your voice signal may suffer.

Image capture devices

When you're ready to move beyond the basic hardware and on to useful gadgets, think about obtaining a tool for capturing photographic images. (By *capturing*, I mean *digitising* an image or, in other words, saving it in computerised, digital format.) Photos are often essential elements of business Web pages: They attract a customer's attention, they illustrate items for sale in a catalogue, and they can provide before-and-after samples of your work. If you're an artist or designer, having photographic representations of your work is vital.

Including a clear, sharp image on your Web site greatly increases your chances of selling your product or service. You have two choices for digitising: A digital camera or scanner. To decide which, read on.

Digital cameras

Not so long ago, digital cameras cost thousands of dollars. These days, you can find a good digital camera made by a reputable manufacturer, such as Nikon, Fuji, Canon, Olympus or Kodak, for around $150 to $300. You have to make an investment up front, but this particular tool can pay off for you in the long run. With the addition of a colour printer, you can even print your own photos, which can save you a pile in photo processing or printing costs.

Don't hesitate to fork over the extra cash to get a camera that gives you good resolution. Cutting corners doesn't pay when you end up with images that look fuzzy, but you can find many low-cost devices with good features. For example, the Canon PowerShot A580, which retails for around $200, has a resolution of more than 8 megapixels — fine enough to print on a colour printer and enlarge to a size such as 8 × 10 inches — and a zoom feature. *Megapixels* are calculated by multiplying the number of pixels in an image — for instance, when actually multiplied, $1984 \times 1488 = 2{,}952{,}192$ pixels or

2.9 megapixels. The higher the resolution, the fewer photos your camera can store at any one time because each image file requires more memory.

Having super-high resolution images isn't critical for Web images, because they display on computer monitors (which have limited resolution). Before being displayed by Web browsers, you have to compress your images by using the GIF or JPEG formats. (See Chapter 5 for more scintillating technical details on GIF and JPEG.) Also, smaller and simpler images (as opposed to large, high-resolution graphics) ordinarily appear more quickly on the viewer's screen. If you make your customers wait too long to see an image, they're likely to go to someone else's online store.

When shopping for a digital camera, look for the following features:

- ✓ The ability to download images to your computer via a FireWire or USB connection
- ✓ Bundled image-processing software
- ✓ The ability to download image files directly to a memory card that you can easily transport to a computer's memory card reader
- ✓ A macro function that enables you to capture clear close-up images
- ✓ An included LCD screen that allows you to see your images immediately

Digital photography is a fascinating and technical process, and you can read more about it in other books, such as *Digital Photography All-in-One Desk Reference For Dummies*, 3rd Edition, by David Busch or *Digital Photography For Dummies*, 6th Edition, by Julie Adair King and Serge Timacheff (both by Wiley).

Scanners

Scanning is the process of turning the colours and shapes contained in a photographic print or slide into digital information (that is, bytes of data) that a computer can understand. You place the image in a position where the scanner's camera can pass over it, and the scanner turns the image into a computer document that consists of tiny bits of information — *pixels*. The type that we find easiest to use is a flatbed scanner. You place the photo or other image on a flat glass bed, just like what you find on a photocopier. An optical device moves under the glass and scans the photo.

The best news about scanners is they've been around for a while, which, in the world of computing, means prices are going down at the same time that quality is on the rise. You can pick up a basic model to do everything you need for between $100 and $200.

A type of scanner that has lots of benefits for small or home-based businesses is a *multifunction device*. You can find these units, along with conventional printers and scanners, at computer outlets. A multifunction device sends and receives faxes, scans images, acts as a laser printer and makes copies — plus it includes a telephone and answering machine. Now, if it could just make a good cappuccino …

For more details about scanners, check out *Scanners For Dummies*, 2nd Edition, by Mark L. Chambers (Wiley).

Getting Online: Connection Options

After you purchase the computer hardware for your business needs, telephone bills are likely to be the biggest monthly expense associated with your online business. At least, they are for us: We pay for local service, long-distance service, mobile phone service, plus DSL (Digital Subscriber Line) service over our phone lines. It pays to choose your *telco* (telephone company) connection wisely.

A second phone line

Having a second line is pretty much a given if you plan to do business online regularly. A mobile phone works fine for business purposes if you don't want to pay your telephone company's line rental fees for the extra landline. Having a separate phone line dedicated to your business also makes your operation look more legitimate.

Ask your telco about a *nominated number discount* so you can call one number a lot for the same rate: 10 minutes for 20 cents, for example.

Another alternative is to take up a *bundled plan* with your phone company (such as Telstra or Optus) that can include fixed line, mobile, Internet and/ or pay TV services. These plans often include a percentage discount or free calls each month for taking up multiple services with the one provider.

Cable modem

Cable modem connections offer a really attractive way to get a high-speed connection to cyberspace:

- ✔ In Australia, just two main providers offer cable Internet access — Telstra Bigpond (www.bigpond.com) and Optus (www.optus.com.au).
- ✔ In New Zealand, cable modem connections are limited but are available through TelstraClear (www.telstraclear.co.nz) in Wellington and parts of Christchurch, and through Compass Communications (www.compass.net.nz) in the Auckland/Hamilton region.

Cable Internet access plans start at around $29.95 to $59.95 depending on the plan you choose. As well, you can be up for additional costs for a modem and installation depending on whether or not you sign up on contract (which can mean you agree to stay with the one supplier for a set period, usually two years).

The advantages of having a cable modem connection are many: This system provides a direct connection, frees up a phone line, and is super fast. Cable modems have the capacity to deliver 4 or 5MB of data per second. But some providers don't tell you what kind of connection you're getting: You might pay for the speed of the connection instead.

One of the downsides of cable Internet access is that all subscribers within a local area share a single cable connection to the Internet. This means the speed of your connection is affected by the number of people using the cable — the more people who join the service, the slower your access becomes. Plus, you have to purchase or lease the cable modem itself, pay an installation fee, and purchase an Ethernet card (if your computer doesn't already have one installed). But a cable modem is going to be far faster than a dial-up connection.

You can find out which cable modem and DSL providers cover your area and compare plans by using the tools provided by Broadband Choice (www.broadbandchoice.com.au) or Internet Choice (www.internetchoice.co.nz).

DSL

If your telephone company offers its customers Digital Subscriber Line (DSL) connections, you can get a connection that isn't quite as fast as cable but that is still 100 times faster than a 56 Kbps dial-up modem. And you can use your existing conventional phone lines rather than installing a new line to your house. You get this option because DSLs 'borrow' the part of your phone line that your voice doesn't use, the part that transmits signals of 3,000 Hz (hertz) or higher. DSLs can *upload* (send) data to another location on the Internet at 1.088 Mbps (megabits per second) and *download* (receive) data at more than twice that rate: 2.560 Mbps.

DSL comes in different varieties. Asymmetrical Digital Subscriber Line (ADSL) transmits information at different speeds, depending on whether you're sending or receiving data. Symmetrical Digital Subscriber Line (SDSL) transmits information at the same speed in both directions. As DSL gets more popular, it becomes more widely available and the pricing drops. While Melissa is writing:

- ✔ In Australia, ADSL plans start from $29.95 through ISPs such as Telstra, TPG and iiNet.
- ✔ In New Zealand, ADSL plans start from around NZ$24.95 through ISPs such as Slingshot, Telecom and TelstraClear.

These days, you can often find a local phone provider that offers discounted plans for bundling your phone line and Internet access together.

ADSL2+ extends the capability of basic ADSL by doubling the speeds that can be achieved. The data rates for downloads can be as high as 24 Mbps and for uploads as high as 1 Mbps depending on the distance from the exchange to the customer's home. So if you have a 'need for speed' then ADSL2+ plans start from around $39.95.

NakedDSL has been made available in both Australia and New Zealand in the last 12 months. NakedDSL (or stand-alone DSL) allows you to have DSL Internet access without the need to have a traditional landline connected, saving you on line rental costs. Instead, NakedDSL plans are bundled with VoIP (voice over Internet Protocol) to allow subscribers to make their phone calls over their Internet connection instead of via the traditional analogue telephone line.

Software Solutions for Online Business

One of the great things about starting an Internet business is that you get to use Internet software. As you probably know, the programs you use online are inexpensive (sometimes free), easy to use and install, and continually being updated.

Although you probably already have a basic selection of software to help you find information and communicate with others in cyberspace, the following sections describe some programs you may not have as yet that may come in handy when you create your online business.

Anyone who uses firewall or antivirus software will tell you how essential these pieces of software are, for home or business use. Find out more about such software in Chapter 6 or in Greg's book *Norton Internet Security For Dummies* (Wiley). See Chapter 14 for suggestions of accounting software — other important software you need.

Web browser

A *Web browser* is software that enables a user to search for and display the images, colours, links and other content contained on the Web. The most popular such programs are Microsoft Internet Explorer, Firefox, Safari and Opera.

Your Web browser is your primary tool for conducting business online, just as it is for everyday personal use. When it comes to running a virtual store or consulting business, though, you have to run your software through a few more paces than usual. You need your browser to

- ✔ Preview the Web pages you create

- ✔ Display animations, movie clips and other goodies you plan to add online

- ✔ Support some level of Internet security, such as Secure Sockets Layer (SSL), if you plan to conduct secure transactions on your site

In addition to having an up-to-date browser with the latest features, installing more than one kind of browser on your computer is a good idea. For example, if you use Microsoft Internet Explorer because it came with your operating system, be sure to download the latest copy of Firefox, as well. That way, you can test your site to make sure it looks good to all your visitors.

Web page editor

HyperText Markup Language (HTML) is a set of instructions used to format text, images and other Web page elements so that Web browsers can correctly display them. But you don't have to master HTML to create your own Web pages. Plenty of programs — *Web page editors* — are available to help you format text, add images, make hyperlinks and do all the fun assembly steps necessary to make your Web site a winner.

Sometimes, programs that you use for one purpose can also help you create Web documents: Software you use to create blogs can help you format other types of Web content. Microsoft Word enables you to save text documents as HTML Web pages, and Microsoft Office 98 and later (for the Mac) or Office 2000 or later (for Windows) enables you to export files in Web page format automatically.

Triple the benefits with W3C

Putting your Web site together is made easy with a Web page editor. But you need to make sure that the Web page editor you choose produces valid HTML code that meets the world standards as set by the W3C (World Wide Web Consortium). Some programs produce too much code, use invalid code or put HTML tags in the wrong order, which causes Web pages to not display properly in all browsers and makes it harder for search engines to read the code behind your site when indexing your site. The W3C (www.w3.org) develops Web standards and provides free validation tools (validator.w3.org) to help Web site owners and developers build Web sites that meet the world standards.

Taking email a step higher

You're probably very familiar with sending and receiving email messages. But when you start an online business, make sure your email software has some advanced features:

- ✓ **Attaching:** Attaching a file to an email message is a quick and convenient way to transmit information from one person to another.

- ✓ **Autoresponders:** Some programs automatically respond to email requests with a form letter or document of your choice.

- ✓ **Detecting junk email:** Some programs automatically detect and filter spam email. You can also mark email that arrives in your inbox as 'safe' or 'junk' so that future emails of this type do not get through.

- ✓ **Mailing lists:** With a well-organised address book (a feature that comes with some email programs), you can collect the email addresses of visitors or subscribers and send them a regular update of your business activities or, better yet, an email newsletter.

- ✓ **Quoting:** Almost all email programs allow you to quote from a message to which you're replying, so you can respond easily to a series of questions.

- ✓ **Rules or Filters:** Some programs automatically sort email messages by detecting either who the message is from or by the subject or words contained within the email and files messages to a folder of your choice. The more the volume of email you receive increases, the more you're going to appreciate a way to quickly sort orders and new enquiries from junk, regular newsletters or bills, so that you can respond to customers quickly and deal with the admin and spam later.

- ✓ **Signature files:** Make sure your email software automatically includes a simple electronic signature at the end. Use this space to list your company name, your title and your Web site URL.

Both Outlook Express, the email component of Microsoft Internet Explorer, and Mozilla Thunderbird, which is the email companion to Firefox, include most or all these features. Because these functions are essential aspects of providing good customer service, we discuss them in more detail in Chapter 8.

Discussion group software

When your business site is up and running, consider taking it a step further by creating your own discussion area right on your Web site. This sort of discussion area isn't a newsgroup as such; it doesn't exist in Usenet, and you don't need newsgroup software to read and post messages. Instead, you're providing your visitors with a Web-based discussion area where they can compare notes and share their passion for the products you sell or the area of service you provide.

Programs, such as Microsoft FrontPage and phpBB, enable you to set up a discussion area on your Web site. See Chapter 8 for more information.

FTP software

FTP (File Transfer Protocol) is one of those acronyms you see time and time again when you move around the Internet. You may even have an FTP program that your ISP gave you when you obtained your Internet account. But chances are you don't use it that often.

In case you haven't used FTP yet, start dusting it off. When you create your own Web pages, a simple, no-nonsense FTP program is the easiest way to transfer them from your computer at home to your Web host. If you need to correct and update your Web pages quickly (a regular need), you're going to benefit by having your FTP software ready and set up with your Web site address, username and password so that you can transfer files right away.

If you use software such as Dreamweaver or Contribute to update your Web site, FTP is built in, which means you don't need a separate piece of software. Alternatively, you can look into the popular shareware application CoreFTP or similar.

Image editors

You need a graphics-editing program either to create original artwork for your Web pages or to crop and adjust your scanned images and digital photographs. In the case of adjusting or cropping photographic image files, the software you need almost always comes bundled with the scanner or digital camera, so you don't need to buy separate software for that.

In the case of graphic images, the first question to ask is, 'Am I really qualified to draw and make my own graphics?' Three popular programs are Adobe Photoshop Elements 7 (www.adobe.com), LView Pro by Leonardo Haddad Loureiro (www.lview.com) and Paint Shop Photo Pro by Corel (www.corel.com). You can download all these programs from the Web to use on a trial basis. After the trial period is over, you need to pay a small fee to the developer in order to register and keep the program. Photoshop Elements 7 costs $135; LView Pro costs US $40; Paint Shop Pro Photo costs $159.

The ability to download and use free (and almost free) software from shareware archives and many other sites is one of the nicest things about the Internet. Keep the system working by remembering to pay the shareware fees to the nice people who make their software available to individuals like you and me.

Instant messaging

You may think that MSN Messenger, Yahoo! Messenger and ICQ are just for social 'chatting' online, but instant messaging has its business applications, too. Here are a few suggestions:

- ✔ If individuals you work with all the time are hard to reach, you can use a messaging program to tell you whether those people are logged on to their computers. You can contact them the moment they sit down to work (provided they don't mind your greeting them so quickly, of course).
- ✔ You can cut down on long-distance phone charges by exchanging instant messages with far-away colleagues.
- ✔ With a microphone, sound card and speakers, you can carry on voice conversations through your messaging software.

MSN Messenger enables users to do file transfers without having to use FTP software or attaching files to email messages.

Internet phone software

Skype (pronounced *skipe*; rhymes with *snipe*) is the best-known of a group of software programs that provide you with Internet phone service. Skype allows you to talk to other computer users over the Internet, provided you have a microphone connected to your computer and a headset if your built-in speakers aren't loud enough. Skype gives you a cost-effective alternative to long-distance or international phone calls. Skype really works best if both parties have a high-speed Internet connection. The program is free; find out more at www.skype.com.

Skype is hardly the only VoIP (Voice over Internet Protocol) service around. We mention Skype because it gives you immediate, personal access to your customers, especially those on eBay. For instance, if you sell on eBay and someone has a question about one of your auctions, he can talk to you if you both have Skype.

Backup software

Losing copies of your personal documents is one thing, but losing files related to your business can hit you hard in the hip pocket. That reason alone makes it even more important to make backups of your online business computer files. USB devices such as thumb drives or portable hard drives come in varying sizes and often come with software that allows you to automatically make backups of your files. If you don't own one of these programs, we recommend you get really familiar with the backup program included with Windows XP or look into Backup Exec by Symantec (www.symantec.com).

Understanding What's New — the Latest Web 2.0 Tools

The move towards a collaborative Internet is driving the trend towards more interactive Web sites. The Internet (as we have come to know it) has been around for 10-plus years now and typically people have used a search engine to browse, find and read static information sites.

In what is being coined the 'Web 2.0 era', the Internet is now about *interactivity*. No longer do Internet users want to just look at and read a page — they want to interact, leave comments, upload music or photos, etc ... and be involved in the Internet community.

This is now possible with very little technical knowledge.

Web 2.0 is simply the set of technologies that enable collaboration and sharing between Internet users. They can be Web pages, Web-based communities or hosted services such as social-networking sites, blogs and podcasts. This section introduces you to some of these tools.

RSS

Half the battle with an online business is simply making yourself available to the people who choose to find out more about you. Greg is a fan of the radio program 'Le Show', for instance (www.harryshearer.com/news/le_show/). At the end of every broadcast, the host, Harry Shearer, lists the different formats in which the program is distributed: via public radio, the Internet, satellite radio and shortwave radio. Why stick with one format when putting in just a little more effort can multiply your audience dramatically?

RSS: Not really simple, but still effective

RSS stands for *Really Simple Syndication*. Frankly, the name is misleading. If your head tends to reel when you think about JavaScript, PHP, XML, DHTML and the many alphabet-soup types of Web page languages, RSS just adds a new level of complication. RSS is a new language that leads to a method for distributing words and images on the Web. The system works like this:

1. **You get some content in the form of an RSS file. You have two options to obtain the content: You convert some of your own to RSS or you obtain someone else's RSS file.**

2. **You post the file on your Web server.**

3. **You validate the XML to make sure news aggregators can read it correctly.**

4. **You publicise your RSS feed in the directories that specialise in RSS listings.**

5. **Users around the Web use programs called news aggregators or feed readers to subscribe to your feed. The feed reader checks automatically to see if the RSS file has new content since the last time it checked. If it does, the reader downloads the feed so the end-user can read it.**

6. **You keep your file fresh by updating it regularly so news aggregators continue to retrieve it for your audience.**

After you wrap your mind around that scenario, you have to absorb another fact: RSS isn't a single format. Rather, RSS is a whole family of RSS format standards: They carry version numbers like 0.91, 1.0 and 2.0. Some publishers favour one variety, some another. You don't need to pick the latest and greatest standard; just pick the one you're comfortable with. News aggregators come in lots of options, including FeedDemon, NewsGator and many others.

Should you climb the RSS learning curve and become a news feed publisher? If you produce content that you intend to update on a regular basis, the answer is yes. RSS is the wave of the future and will only grow more popular. And most of the software you use to create feeds or aggregate them is absolutely free, so your only expense is the usual sweat equity — something you get used to expending very quickly when you become an online entrepreneur.

To some extent, making your online business available is a matter of putting your sales catalogue and your Web site contents in a form that people can read. Lots of people put out an RSS (Really Simple Syndication) feed of their Web site along with the conventional pages created in HyperText Markup Language (HTML), eXtensible Markup Language (XML), Hypertext Preprocessor (PHP) or another markup language.

HTML, XML and *PHP* are languages used to format or process information that appears on Web pages. *RSS* is a technology used to format content as an XML file so an RSS reader can display it. You don't need to know any of these techy-sounding languages in order to use them; you only have to use the right applications that do the formatting/programming 'in the background' for you.

Setting up site feeds

Like many ways of publishing content online, you don't have to be a programmer to make use of RSS. You do, however, have to meet one important requirement: You need to make a commitment to actually update your content on a regular basis. The whole point behind RSS is that it gives consumers of information a way to automatically view new comments put out by bloggers or other publishers without having to open the Web sites of those publishers on a regular basis. If you don't update your content, all those RSS feeders aren't going to retrieve it.

After you commit to being a periodic publisher, and after you have a text file you want to convert, you can go on to the next step: converting it to RSS format. You have several options:

- ✔ **Built-in software:** If you use a blogging tool, like WordPress (wordpress.org) or Blogger (www.blogger.com), you can use the built-in syndication software. Blogger supports Atom, a different type of syndication format; see the next section.

- ✔ **Stand-alone program:** You can use a stand-alone, Web-based syndication program such as RSS Channel Editor (www.webreference.com/cgi-bin/perl/rssedit.pl). Figure 3-1 shows the form for RSS Channel Editor that you fill out, and then it quickly builds your file. You simply make a link to the file you want to convert, and the program 'fetches' it for you. Use RSS Channel Editor only if you plan to create RSS feeds on a regular basis and if you don't want to install and maintain a stand-alone application on your system.

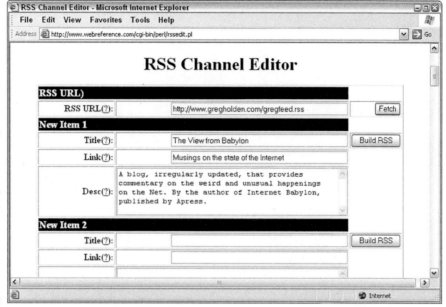

Figure 3-1:
You can reach a new audience of tech-savvy information consumers by creating an RSS feed.

No matter what option you choose, you end up with a file that you upload to your server space on your Web site. You then need to make a link to the file on one of your Web pages and publicise the link so people find out about it. After you get the system worked out, you can more easily update as well as re-post your files and reach a wider audience than you ever could otherwise.

Validate your RSS file to make sure it's in a form that news aggregators can read. An RSS file is comprised of XML commands, which need to be free of errors. Use an application like Userland RSS Validator (`rss.scripting.com`) to make sure your file's correctly formatted.

Atom

Atom is a syndication tool that doesn't use RSS. Instead, it's an alternative to RSS. If you use the popular blogging tool Blogger, you automatically create a feed of your blog in Atom format. Blogger claims that Atom is superior to RSS because it feeds content not only to news aggregators but to Web sites and even handheld devices.

FeedBurner and other RSS syndicators

FeedBurner (`www.feedburner.com`) calls itself a 'feed management provider'. It not only turns (or *burns*, to use the correct term) your blog into an RSS file but helps promote it as well. When you create a feed, you post an XML or RSS logo on your blog that advises others they can subscribe.

After you 'burn' your feed with FeedBurner or another tool, you publicise it by using a directory of such feeds. Look into Syndic8 (`www.syndic8.com`), which is free to use.

Blogging

In the late 1990s, Web pages were where they were at as far as e-commerce was concerned. In the late 2000s, the *blog* is the tool of choice for many online entrepreneurs. On the surface, a blog doesn't seem like something that can actually make you money. A blog is a sort of online diary: a running commentary that you add to as often as possible — every few days, every day or, perhaps, even several times a day.

Blogs do make money, however. When you have a dependable number of viewers, you can generate revenue from your blog by these methods:

- ✔ **Placing ads:** You can use a service like Google's AdSense (`adsense.google.com`).
- ✔ **Asking for donations:** You make use of the PayPal Tip Jar (see Chapter 13).
- ✔ **Placing affiliate ads:** You sign up for well-known programs that steer potential buyers to Amazon.com or eBay.
- ✔ **Building interest in your Web site:** By talking about yourself, your knowledge or your services, you encourage customers to commit to them.

Creating a blog to support your business is a powerful method to reach potential customers and strengthen connections with current ones. The word-of-mouth marketing that results from successful blog publishing is effective while being cost-efficient: Advertising costs are minuscule compared to a traditional marketing effort.

What's the first step in creating a blog? We usually advocate thinking before clicking: Give at least a few minutes' thought to the kind of blog you want to create. An article titled 'How Blogs Can Deliver Business Results' in *Entrepreneur* magazine describes several different types of blogs created by Denali Flavors to promote its Moose Tracks line of ice-cream flavours. Each one took a different approach to promoting the same product:

- ✔ **Entertainment:** A blog, *Moosetopia*, is written by the Moose Tracks Moose, the product mascot.

✔ **Useful advice:** A blog, Free Money Finance, provides something that everyone needs — advice on how to handle their money. The connection to the product is a 'sponsored by' Moose Tracks ice-cream logo near the top of the blog.

✔ **Public relations:** Another blog, Team Moose Tracks, concerns efforts of the company's cycling team to raise money for an orphanage in Latvia. It reflects positively on the company and the brand.

✔ **Behind the scenes:** A fourth blog, Denali Flavors, takes a look at what goes on in the company.

The 'How Blogs Can Deliver Business Results' article also reports that site visits went up 25.7 per cent after the blogs went online; the company spent less than US$700 on all four blogs, too. You can take any or all these approaches in your own blog, depending on the product you're trying to sell and your available resources. If you're selling a 'fun' product, you may decide to take the entertainment approach; if you work for a big company, you may take the behind-the-scenes approach.

After you have a general idea of the approach you want to take, the first step is to choose your blog host. You don't necessarily have to pay to do this; most of the best-known blog hosts offer hosting for free. They include:

✔ **Blogger (**`www.blogger.com`**):** Blogger doesn't have as many features as other blog utilities, but the site is free.

✔ **BlogHarbor (**`www.blogharbor.com`**):** Hosting packages start at US$8.95 a month; you get security and templates for designing blogs.

✔ **TypePad (**`www.typepad.com`**):** TypePad has lots of features, but it costs US$14.95 a month or US$149.50 a year.

Take some time to look at other business blogs and examine how they use type and colour. Often, for a purely personal blog, you don't need to be concerned about clever or aesthetic design. But for a blog that has a business purpose, you need to present a professional front.

Next, determine who is going to do the blogging. You may not want to do it all yourself. If you can gather two or three contributors, you increase the chances that you can post entries on a daily basis, which is important for blogs. And if someone goes out of town, you're set with backup contributors being on tap.

When you configure your blog, no matter which host you choose, the main features tend to be more or less the same. Figure 3-2 shows Gardening Gift Buyer's Guide, one of the many blogs created by expert marketer

Lars Hundley, who we profile in the sidebar 'Blogs plant seeds, gardening business blooms' later in this chapter. The blog includes some Google AdSense ads to drum up extra revenue; a link for visitors to post comments; categories that organise past blog posts; a chronological archive of posts; and links to other relevant sites, including Hundley's main Clean Air Gardening Web site (www.cleanairgardening.com).

For detailed instructions on how to create a business blog, turn to *Buzz Marketing with Blogs For Dummies* by Susannah Gardner and published by Wiley.

Perhaps the most difficult aspect of blogging isn't actually creating the blog, but maintaining it. Developing a schedule whereby you publish regular blog posts is important. Also important is being able to measure how many visits your blog and your business Web site get so you can measure results — be sure to do a benchmark test beforehand so you can judge results afterward. Adjust your site as needed to attract more visitors but remember to stay 'on topic' so you don't drive away the audience you already have.

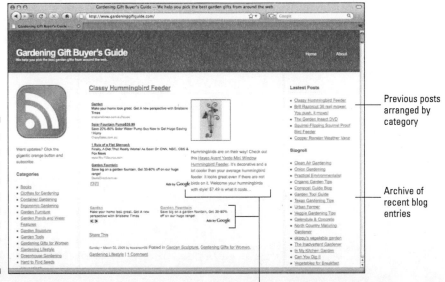

Figure 3-2: Make sure your blog organises past entries and gives visitors a way to comment.

Previous posts arranged by category

Archive of recent blog entries

Google AdSense ads

Blogs plant seeds, gardening business blooms

Lars Hundley is an expert with blogs, photo sharing and social networking sites to market his products. His Dallas Texas–based business, Clean Air Gardening (www.cleanairgardening.com), posted sales of US$1.5 million in 2006.

Products, such as tools for collecting leaves in the autumn, occasionally receive the attention of traditional media. In October 2006, for example, Clean Air Gardening was mentioned in *The New York Times* as well as on *Good Morning America*.

Lars uses a variety of blogs and online video sites to promote his Clean Air Gardening online business:

- **Practical Environmentalist** (www.practicalenvironmentalist.com): This blog isn't branded for Clean Air Gardening or directly linked to the company, but it is intended to attract the same kind of environmentally aware person that is its typical customer. This blog is more of a free service than a hard-selling kind of blog.

- **Gardening Gift Buyer's Guide** (www.gardeninggiftguide.com): This blog is a sort of Gizmodo or Engadget for gardening products. It promotes both products from Clean Air Gardening and interesting gardening products from other competing sites.

- **Compost guide** (compostguide.com/info/): This blog promotes several different companies. It's designed to generate a lot of composting-related educational information, as well as keyword-rich pages and product promotion pages that give Clean Air Gardening a growing body of search engine-friendly composting content over time.

- **Flash-based video on Clean Air Gardening:** Flash-based video helps sell products. Hundley films the videos with his Canon PowerShot S1 digital camera that also shoots video. Then he edits them with his Mac Mini and converts them to Flash so that people can watch them with their Web browser directly on the page. One example is at www.cleanairgardening.com/patdesaustum.html.

- **Videos on YouTube.com:** Hundley uploads videos so that he doesn't have to pay for the bandwidth. Then he embeds the YouTube video on his product page. That also allows people to find the products on the YouTube site and then click through to Clean Air Gardening.

- **Product and testimonial photos at Flickr:** He puts all his customer testimonial photos on Flickr and links to them from his testimonials page on his Web site. People can access these photos directly on Flickr (www.flickr.com/photos/cleanairgardening), and they can then use a link to return to the Clean Air Gardening page.

Social networking

In the days when the telegraph and telephone were the most high-tech communications technologies, people walked around town from merchant to merchant to do their shopping. Chances are they knew the merchant, and he or she knew them by name as well.

Social networking sites are the modern-day equivalent of the town square. When you go to a social networking site, you again strike up a personal relationship with a merchant; after you do, you're that much more likely to buy something from that person. They give potential customers another place where they can find you and get to know you. According to Hitwise's (www.hitwise.com.au) Asia Pacific Social Networking Report of January 2008, the top 5 sites in Australia and New Zealand are

- ✔ MySpace (www.myspace.com)
- ✔ Facebook (www.facebook.com)
- ✔ Bebo (www.bebo.com)
- ✔ Orkut (www.orkut.com)
- ✔ Windows Live Spaces (spaces.live.com)

If you want to reach a younger generation of consumers, places like Facebook (www.facebook.com) are among the best ways to find them. If you sell services that depend on personal contact with a customer, such as a group of musicians that plays for weddings or a wedding planner, people sometimes hire you as much for your personality and personal approach as for your actual work. In these kinds of fields, social networking sites are even more important.

Another networking site, LinkedIn (www.linkedin.com) allows you to build a network of business contacts that can get in touch with one another and hopefully build a community.

Flickr and YouTube

If you're lucky, your products sell themselves. But for some products, photos are a necessity. If you have a big piece of furniture, like a couch or a rare antique or a work of art, a description that consists solely of words just doesn't cut it. Photos give you a real selling point. Where can you post them online? You can put photos on your own Web site, of course. But the cool and trendy place for them to appear is at the popular photo sharing site Flickr (www.flickr.com).

Flickr is free and easy to use. There is no better business use for the site than the Clean Air Gardening customer photos, as shown in Figure 3-3. Lars Hundley (who we profile in the sidebar earlier in this chapter) invites his customers to submit photos of the products they purchase, such as push reel lawn mowers and weathervanes.

Similarly if you're a fashion designer, photographer, hairdresser or builder, for example, you can post photos on Flickr to represent your work. Flickr is organised by groups. For example, John of Xenedis Photography (www.xenedis.net) is a member of the Australian Portraits group (www.flickr.com/groups/australian_portraits), and he generates an income online through the sale of his photography.

YouTube (www.youtube.com) is the free video sharing Web site. YouTube has had huge online business success selling to Google for US$1.65 billion in late-2006. The reason for its success has been the decreasing cost of bandwidth making it possible to watch reasonable quality videos over the Internet and also social networking sites like MySpace allowing the videos to be distributed and shared.

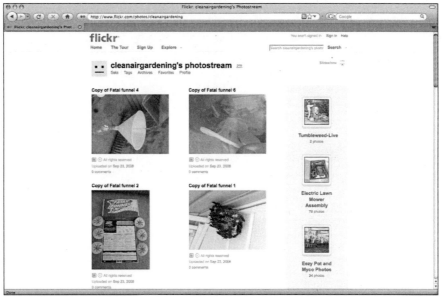

Figure 3-3: Use photo-sharing sites to publish photos of your products in action.

YouTube is a great marketing tool for business (when used properly) due to its viral nature. You can upload a video demonstration, infomercial or comedy sketch and then post it on your blog, embed it on your Web site and include it on your MySpace page. YouTube has millions of visitors watching videos on its site every single day so, if your video is good enough to capture even a small percentage of these eyeballs, your online business is going to do well. Popular formats include:

- ✔ **Commercial/comedy sketch:** Rather than just a straight out commercial, the current rage is to post a funny commercial, comedy sketch or so-called banned commercial (because, of course, more people click on something that says it has been banned!) such as this video titled Banned Toyota Commercial (www.youtube.com/watch?v=LCk9yvEpvtc) or this fun promo by small Australian beer maker Barons Brewing (www.youtube.com/baronsbrewing).

- ✔ **Demonstration:** A tutorial, how-to or demonstration is a great use of video whether it be for a product like Bokashi Bins for composting (au.youtube.com/billjackjane) or cooking with celebrity chef Benjamin Christie (www.youtube.com/chefsaustralia).

- ✔ **Own video channel:** Anyone can start a channel on YouTube. Current channels cover every topic imaginable from how to play the guitar, to documentaries on the environment to Internet addicts who post videos on themselves and issues they feel strongly about. The University of New South Wales has its own channel for both promotion and education (au.youtube.com/unsw), and regular YouTuber Pauly has his own channel TrueBlueAustralian (www.youtube.com/TrueBlueAustralian).

- ✔ **Virtual tour:** Often used by the tourism, hospitality or real estate industries. You can post a video that gives a tour of a property for sale or a city or country you're promoting. For example, Pure Zealand (www.youtube.com/purenewzealand) promotes New Zealand as a holiday destination. Real Estate New Zealand (www.youtube.com/realestatenewzealand) has over 550 videos of properties available in New Zealand.

When you sign up for a YouTube account you can choose the type of account you would like from the special account types: Musician, Reporter, Director, Comedian and Guru. One way to generate sales through YouTube is if you're a musician or a comedian you have the option to place a link on your profile page to purchase your CD.

YouTube earns income from ads placed on the Web site. Videos are rated in terms of how many times they're being watched as well as having a viewer rating from 1–5 stars. Channels are rated by how many subscribers they have. As soon as you have over 100 subscribers, you can apply to become a YouTube partner, which allows you to share in the ad revenue earned by your videos.

Podcasting and vodcasting

A *podcast* is an audio file or series of audio files that can be shared with others.

You can subscribe to a podcast in much the same way as you subscribe to an email newsletter. The 'author' or 'broadcaster' records an audio file on a given topic and places it on a server where it can be accessed by 'subscribers'.

Podcasts that you subscribe to are then automatically downloaded to your computer or MP3 player when new content is made available. This procedure happens using an RSS feed. An RSS feed contains a content summary from an associated Web site and makes it possible for subscribers to keep up to date automatically with changes or new content on their favourite Web sites.

Publishing a podcast can be a great way to raise your profile, get your name out there and keep your current and prospective clients up to date with the latest news from your business or industry. A podcast is a bit more personal than an email newsletter because instead of just reading, people can listen to the sound of your voice and make a more personal connection.

Some examples of podcasts include:

- ✔ ANZ Podcasts (www.anzpodcasts.com.au)
- ✔ Choice Online (www.choice.com.au/feeds/podcast/102314.xml)
- ✔ Radio New Zealand (www.radionz.co.nz/podcasts)
- ✔ Small Business Mentor Club (www.dsbn.com.au/smallbusiness mentorclub/Podcasts.asp)

A *vodcast* (or video podcast) is the delivery of on-demand video content. Vodcasts can be viewed on your computer using standard software such as Windows Media Player and Apple QuickTime. You can also save the video to your portable video player device such as the Apple iPod or the Sony PlayStation Portable (PSP). Due to the amount of data that needs to be transmitted for vodcasting you need to use a broadband Internet connection.

Some examples of vodcasts include:

- ✔ Wine education with Hospitality Crew (www.hospitality-crew.com/ content/shiraz-vodcast)
- ✔ Learn English with English Bites (http://australiannetwork.com/ learnenglish/vodcast/)
- ✔ Showcase of student work at Ringwood North Primary School (www.ischool.net.au/)

If you're providing useful information, a regular podcast (or vodcast) can help to keep your business top of mind. But the key is 'regular' so, if you don't have the time or resources to record regular topics, podcasting may not be for you.

Chapter 4

Selecting the Right Web Host and Design Tools

In This Chapter

▶ Choosing software to create and edit your Web pages

▶ Selecting a hosting service for your Web site

▶ Finding a Web page shortcut with a template

*Y*ou *can* sell items online without having a Web site. But do you really want to? Doing real online business without some sort of online 'home base' is time consuming and inefficient. The vast majority of online commercial concerns use their Web sites as the primary way to attract customers, convey their message and make sales. A growing number of ambitious, budding entrepreneurs use online auction sites, such as eBay (www.ebay.com.au), to make money, but the auctioneers who depend on eBay for regular income often have their own Web pages as well, where they can gather all the profit without having to pay fees to the auction marketplace.

The success of a commercial Web site depends in large measure on two important factors: Where it's hosted and how it's designed. These factors affect how easily you can create and update your Web pages, what special features (such as multimedia or interactive forms) you can have on your site, and even how your site looks. Some hosting services provide Web page creation tools that are easy to use but that limit the level of sophistication you can apply to the page's design. Other services leave the creation and design up to you. In this chapter, we provide an overview of your Web hosting options as well as different design approaches that you can implement.

Plenty of Web hosting services and CDs claim that they can have your Web site up and running online 'in a matter of minutes' using a 'seamless' process. The actual construction may indeed be quick and smooth — as long as you do all your preparation work beforehand. This preparation work includes identifying your goals for going online, deciding what market you want to reach, deciding what products you want to sell, writing descriptions and capturing images of those products, and so on. Before you start assembling your site, be sure that you do all the groundwork that we discuss in Chapter 1, such as identifying your audience and setting up your hardware.

Getting the Most from Your Web Host

An Internet connection and a Web browser are all you need if you're primarily interested in surfing through cyberspace, consuming information and shopping for online goodies. But when you're starting an online business, you're no longer just a consumer; you're becoming a provider of information and consumable goods. Along with a way to connect to the Internet, you need to find a hosting service that will make your online business available to your prospective customers.

A *Web hosting service* is the online world's equivalent of a landlord. Just as the owner of a building gives you office space or room for a storefront where you can hang your hat, a hosting service provides you with space online where you can set up shop.

You can operate an online business without a Web site if you sell regularly on eBay. But even on eBay you can create an About Me page or an eBay store; eBay itself is your host in both cases. (You pay a monthly fee to eBay in order to host your store. See Chapter 9 for more information.)

A Web host provides space on special computers — *Web servers* — that are connected to the Internet all the time. Web servers are equipped with software that makes your Web pages visible to people who connect to them by using a Web browser. The process of using a Web hosting service for your online business works roughly like this:

1. **Decide where you want your site to appear on the Internet.**

   Do you want it to be part of a virtual shopping mall that includes many other businesses? Or do you want a stand-alone site that has its own Web address and doesn't appear to be affiliated with any other organisation?

2. **Sign up with a Web host.**

   Sometimes you pay a fee. In some cases, no fee is required. In all cases, you're assigned space on a server. Your Web site gets an address, or *URL*, that people can enter in their browsers to view your pages.

3. **Create your Web pages.**

   Usually, you use a Web page editor (refer to Chapter 3) to do this step.

4. **Transfer your Web page files (HTML documents, images and so on) from your computer to the host's Web server.**

   You generally need special File Transfer Protocol (FTP) software to do the transferring. But many Web hosts can help you through the process by providing their own user-friendly software. (The most popular Web editors, such as Dreamweaver, allow you to do this, too.)

5. **Access your own site with your Web browser and check the contents to make sure that all the images appear and that any hypertext links you created go to the intended destinations.**

   At this point, you're open for business — visitors can view your Web pages by entering your Web address in their Web browser's Go To or Address box.

6. **Market and promote your site to attract potential clients or customers.**

Carefully choose a Web host because the host affects which software you use to create your Web pages and get them online. The Web host also affects the way your site looks, and it may determine the complexity of your Web address. (See the sidebar 'What's in a name?' for details.)

If you have a direct connection to the Internet, such as DSL, and you're competent with computers (or know someone who is), you can host your own site. However, turning your own computer into a Web server is more complicated than signing up with a hosting service. (Your ISP may not allow you to set up your own server anyway; check your user agreement first.) You need to install server software and set up a domain name for your computer. You also have to purchase a static IP address for your machine. (An *IP address* is a number that identifies every computer connected to the Internet, and that consists of four sets of numerals separated by dots, such as 206.207.99.1. A *static IP address* is one that doesn't change from session to session.) If you're just starting a simple home-based or part-time business, hosting your own Web site may be more trouble than you care to handle, but you should be aware of having that option.

Before you sign up with a host, check out customer service options. Specifically, find out when the service staff is available by telephone. Also ask if telephone support costs extra.

✔ In Australia, Netregistry (www.netregistry.com.au), Jumba (www.jumba.com.au) and Ilisys (www.ilisys.com.au) offer a pretty typical selection of hosting options and are well regarded for their pricing, uptime and customer service.

✔ In New Zealand, check out Web Drive (www.webdrive.co.nz) and Net24 (www.net24.co.nz).

Instead of getting locked into a long-term contract with a Web host, go month to month or sign a one-year contract. Even if you're initially happy with your host, you want a chance to back out if the company takes a turn for the worse or your needs change.

Domain name registration

Some ISPs or Web hosts also function as domain name registrars by enabling anyone to purchase the rights to use a domain name for one or more years. That way you can have the name associated with your site instead of having to point the name at the server that holds your site.

By *pointing* your domain name at your server, you purchase the rights to a domain name from a registrar. You then need to associate the name with your Web site so that when people connect to your site, they won't have to enter a long URL such as users.bigpond.net.au/username. Instead, they enter www.mybusiness.com. To do this, you tell the registrar that your domain name should be assigned to the IP address of your server. Your ISP or Web host tells you the IP address to give to the registrar.

New domains have been made available that can provide you with an alternative in case your ideal name on the dot-com-dot-au (.com.au) or dot-co-dot-nz (.co.nz) domain is unavailable. Even if you do get your ideal domain name, you may want to buy the same name with .com, .net, .biz, .info or .tv at the end so that someone else doesn't grab it.

Database connectivity

If you plan on selling only a few items at a time, your e-commerce site can be a *static* site, which means that every time a customer makes a sale, you take the time to manually adjust inventory. A static site also requires you to update descriptions and revise shipping charges or other details by hand, one Web page at a time. In contrast, a *dynamic* e-commerce site presents catalogue sales items on the fly (dynamically) by connecting to a database whenever a customer requests a Web page.

If you need to create a dynamic Web site, another factor in choosing a Web host is whether it supports the Web page and database software that you want to use. For Doug Laughter of The Silver Connection, LLC (which is profiled in a sidebar in this chapter), the choice of host was essential. He wanted to develop his site himself by using technologies he was familiar with and regarded highly, such as Microsoft Active Server Pages (ASP) technology. If you use a database program, such as MySQL, you may want to sign up with a Web host that allows you to run SQL Server on one of its servers.

Decide on which technology you're going to use to build your Web site before choosing your Web hosting package. This way, you know whether you require any special features such as the ability to use programming languages ASP or PHP or the need for an SQL database. If you seek the help of a Web developer, he or she can offer advice on the best Web hosting package based on the type of site you're building and the technology needed.

Finding a Web Server to Call Home

So you're not sure exactly what kind of Web site is right for you, and you want to see all the options? Just open your favourite Web browser and enjoy this tour of the many different options:

- ✔ **Online Web-host-and-design-kit combos:** WebAlive and eKnowHow among others.

- ✔ **Out-of-the-box shopping cart products:** ezimerchant and X-Cart, to name two.

- ✔ **Your own store on an online auction site:** eBay, Trade Me and OO all allow their users to create their own Profile pages and their own stores.

- ✔ **Your current Internet service provider (ISP):** Many ISPs are only too happy to host your e-commerce site — for an extra monthly fee in addition to your access fee.

- ✔ **Companies devoted to hosting Web sites full time:** These are businesses whose primary function is hosting e-commerce Web sites and providing their clients with associated software, such as Web page building tools, shopping carts, catalogue builders and the like.

The first three options combine Web hosting with Web page creation kits. Whether you buy these services or get to use them on the Web for free, you simply follow the manufacturer's instructions. Most of these hosting services enable you to create your Web pages by filling in forms; you never have to see a line of HTML code if you don't want to. Depending on which service you choose, you have varying degrees of control over how your site ultimately looks.

The last two options (ISPs and full-time Web hosts) don't include the building of your Web site so you either have to do it yourself or hire a Web developer to help you. You sign up with the host, you choose the software, and you create your own site. However, the distinction between this category and the others is blurry. As competition between Web hosts grows keener, more and more companies are providing ready-made solutions that streamline the process of Web site creation for their customers. For you, the end user, this competition is a good thing: You have plenty of control over how your site comes into being and how it grows over time.

If you simply need a basic Web site and don't want a lot of choices, go with one of the kits. Your site may look like everyone else's and seem a little generic, but setup is easy, and you can concentrate on marketing and running your business. You just have less control over what your Web site looks like and how it ranks in the search engines.

However, if you're the independent type who wants to control your site and have lots of room to grow, consider a do-it-yourself project. The sky's the limit as far as the degree of creativity you can exercise and the amount of sweat equity you can put in (as long as you don't make your site so large and complex that shoppers have a hard time finding anything, of course).

What to expect from a Web host

Along with providing lots of space for your HTML, images and other files (typically, you get anywhere from 50Mb to 2GB of space), Web hosting services offer a variety of related services, including some or all of the following:

- **Automatic data backups:** Some hosting services automatically back up your Web site data to protect you against data loss — an especially useful feature because disaster recovery is important. The automatic nature of the backups frees you from the worry and trouble of doing it manually.

- **Domain names:** Virtually all the hosting options that we mention in this chapter give customers the option of obtaining a short domain name, such as www.mycompany.com. But some Web hosts simplify the process by providing domain name registration in their flat monthly rates.

✔ **Email addresses:** You can likely get several email addresses for your own or your family members' personal use. Besides that, many Web hosts give you special email addresses called *auto-responders*. These are email addresses, such as `info@yourcompany.com`, that you can set up to automatically return a text message or a file to anyone looking for information.

✔ **Multimedia/CGI scripts:** One big thing that sets Web hosting services apart from other hosts is the ability to serve complex and memory-intensive content, such as RealAudio sound files or RealVideo video clips. They also let you process Web page forms that you include on your site by executing computer programs called *CGI scripts*. These programs receive the data that someone sends you (such as a customer service request or an order form) and present the data in readable form, such as a text file, email message or an entry in a database. See Chapter 6 for more about how to set up and use forms and other interactive Web site features.

✔ **Shopping cart software:** If part of your reason for going online is to sell specific items, look for a Web host that can streamline the process for you. Most organisations provide you with Web page forms that you can fill out to create sale items and offer them in an online shopping cart, for example.

✔ **Shopping and electronic commerce features:** If you plan to give your customers the ability to order and purchase your goods or services online by using their credit cards, be sure to look for a Web host that provides you with secure commerce options. A *secure server* is a computer that can encrypt sensitive data (such as credit card numbers) that the customer sends to your site. For a more detailed discussion of secure electronic commerce, see Chapter 6.

✔ **Site statistics:** Virtually all Web hosting services provide you with site statistics that give you an idea (perhaps not a precisely accurate count, but a good estimate) of how many visitors drop by. Even better is access to software reports that analyse and graphically report where your visitors are from, how they find you, which pages on your site are the most frequently viewed and so on.

✔ **Web page software:** Some hosting services include Web page authoring/editing software, such as Microsoft FrontPage. Some Web hosting services even offer Web page forms that you can fill out online in order to create your own online shopping catalogue. All you have to provide is a scanned image of the item you want to sell, along with a price and a description. You submit the information to the Web host that then adds the item to an online catalogue that becomes part of your site.

Having so many hosting options available is the proverbial blessing and curse. With so many possibilities and because the competition is so fierce, prices can be kept down. On the other hand, deciding which host is best for you can be difficult. In addition to asking about the preceding list of features, here are a few more questions to ask prospective Web hosts about their services to help narrow the field:

- **Do you limit file transfers?** Many services charge a monthly rate for a specific amount of electronic data transferred to and from your site. Each time a visitor views a page, that user is actually downloading a few kilobytes of data in order to view it. If your Web pages contain, say, 1MB of text and images and you get 1,000 visitors each month, your site accounts for 1GB of data transfer per month. If your host allocates you less than 1GB per month, you're probably going to be charged extra for the amount you go over the limit.

- **What kind of connection do you have?** Your site's Web page content appears more quickly in Web browser windows if your server has a super-fast T1 or T3 connection. Ask your ISP what kind of connection *it* has to the Internet. If you have a DSL line, speeds differ depending on the ISP: You may get a fast 1.5 Mbps connection or a more common 684 Kbps connection. Make sure you're getting the fastest connection you can afford.

- **What support is available?** Some hosting companies don't provide phone support and force you to email or submit an online ticket for help. This can be very frustrating especially if your email is the problem because obviously you can't send support an email to tell them your email isn't working! Check you can get a human being on the phone and that your potential host's support line is open extended hours and not just 9.00 am to 5.00 pm.

Besides these probing and necessary questions, the other obvious questions that you would ask of any contractor apply to Web hosting services as well. These include: 'How long have you been in business?' and 'Can you suggest customers who can give me a reference?'

The fact that we mention a particular Web hosting service in this chapter or elsewhere in this book doesn't mean that we are endorsing or recommending that particular organisation. Shop around carefully and find the one that's best for you. Check out the hosts with the best rates and most reliable service. Visit some other sites that they host and email the owners of those sites for their opinion of their hosting service.

What's in a name?

Most hosts assign you a URL that leads to your directory (or folder) on the Web server. For example, the typical personal account with an ISP includes space on a Web server where you can store your Web pages, and the address looks like this:

    http://homepage.speakeasy.
    net/~gholden

This URL is a common form that many Web hosts use. It means that my Web pages reside in a directory called ~gholden on a computer named homepage. The computer, in turn, resides in my provider's domain on the Internet: speakeasy.net.

However, for an extra fee, some Web hosts allow you to choose a shorter domain name, provided that the one you want to use isn't already taken by another site. For example, if I were to pay extra for a fully-fledged business site, my provider would allow me to have a catchier, more memorable address, like this:

    www.gregholden.com

Competition is tough among hosting services, which means prices are going down. But it also means that hosting services may seem to promise the earth in order to get your business. Be sure to read the fine print and talk to the host before you sign a contract and always get statements about technical support and backups in writing.

What's it gonna cost?

Because of the ongoing competition in the industry, prices for Web hosting services vary widely. If you look in the classified sections in the back of magazines that cover the Web or the whole Internet, you see ads for hosting services costing from $9.95 to $24.95 a month. Chances are these prices are for a basic level of service: Web space, email addresses, domain name and software. This package of features may be all you need.

The second level of service provides CGI script processing, the ability to serve audio and video files on your site, regular backups and extensive site statistics, as well as consultants who can help you design and configure your site. This more sophisticated range of features typically runs from $20 a month up to $100 or more a month. At Netregistry, for instance, you can conduct secure electronic commerce on your site as part of hosting packages that begin at $29.95 per month.

Hosting options: Parking for free

Free Web hosting is still possible for small businesses. If you're on a tight budget and looking for space on a Web server for free, turn first to your ISP, which probably gives you server space to set up a Web site. You can also check out one of a handful of sites that provide customers with hosting space for no money down and no monthly payments, either. Sometimes conditions apply and you may be required either to buy your domain name through your ISP or to display advertising on your site. But if you don't mind, here are some good deals you can enjoy:

- ✔ **Bravenet** (www.bravenet.com): In exchange for ads, which you're required to display if you set up a Web site on one of its servers, this site gives you add-ons (such as guest books and hit counters) and an online Web page building tool for creating your site — not to mention 50MB of server space.

- ✔ **Dot Easy Australia** (www.doteasy.com.au) **and Netfirms** (www.netfirms.com): These sites provide free hosting if you purchase your domain name through them.

- ✔ **Free Host** (www.freehost.net.au): This site promotes free hosting for Aussies with 'no catch'!

You can find other free Web hosting services on Yahoo! or Google by searching for the key phrase 'free Web hosting'.

Be sure the hosting service you choose allows you to set up for-profit business sites for free because some providers only provide free hosting for personal use or for not-for-profit organisations — such as Vicnet in Australia and Avatar in New Zealand.

Using software to build your Web site

Virtually all the free Web hosting services mentioned in the preceding section have caught on to the concept of making things easy and affordable for would-be *ontrepreneurs* (online entrepreneurs). These sites act as both a Web host and a Web page creation tool. You connect to the site, sign up for service, and fill out a series of forms. Submitting the completed forms activates a script on the host site that automatically generates your Web pages based on the data you entered.

Some Web site creation packages are available at the following sites:

- **Web hosts providing free site building tools:** Netregistry (`netregistry.com.au`) and TPP Internet (`www.tppinternet.com.au`) include Web site builder software with hosting packages starting from $29 a month. SmartyHost (`www.smartyhost.com.au`) has a budget package priced at $40 a year. Freeparking (`www.freeparking.co.nz`) includes SiteBuilder with hosting packages starting at NZ$199.95 per year. Web Widgets (`www.webwidgets.co.nz`) has packages starting at NZ$25 per month.

- **Online site building applications:** WebAlive (`www.webalive.com.au`) includes hosting and Web site builder packages starting at $49.50 a month (minimum 12-month contract). The basic plan doesn't include e-commerce. To sell products on your Web site the WebCommerce plan starts at $75.90 a month. eknowhow (`eknowhow.com.au`) packages start at $77 a month with an upfront setup cost of $495. Includes a Web site with unlimited pages, shopping cart and email marketing functionality all built in to the one tool.

- **Online market place:** CafePress (`www.cafepress.com`) allows you to easily create and sell T-shirts, music CDs, photos or artwork online for free. The hard part is deciding what you want to sell, how best to describe your sales items, and how to promote your site.

The saying 'you get what you pay for' well and truly applies with Web hosting and automatic Web creation tools. Be aware that free or very cheap services may not provide reliable servers and, consequently, may cause disruptions to your Web site; meaning, your site may be offline for periods of time. Getting good support by phone is often difficult, too. Automatic Web creation tools limit the control you have over what your Web pages look like, where they're placed and how much information or how many pages you can add and maintain.

Investigating electronic storefront software

All the other options that this chapter provides for publishing your business site are ones that you access and utilise online. Yet another option for creating a business site and publishing it online is to purchase an application that carries you through the entire process of creating an electronic storefront. The advantage is control: You own and operate the software and are in charge of the entire process (at least until the files get to the remote Web servers). The speed with which you develop a site depends on how quickly you master the process, not on the speed of your Internet connection.

Like hosting services, such as Netregistry Instant Store, WebAlive and StoreBuilder, electronic storefront software is designed to facilitate the process of creating Web pages and to shield you from having to master HTML. Most storefront software provides you with predesigned Web pages, *templates*, which you customise for your particular business. Some types of storefront options provide you with shopping cart systems that enable customers to select items and tally the cost at the checkout. They may also provide for some sort of electronic payment option, such as credit card purchases. Usually, you purchase the software and either download it online or obtain a CD, install the package like any other application, and follow a series of steps that detail the primary aspects of a business:

- ✔ **The storefront:** The Web pages that you create become the storefront. Some packages, such as ezimerchant, include predesigned templates or themes that you can use and customise with your own content.

- ✔ **The inventory:** You can stock your virtual storefront shelves by presenting your wares in the form of an online catalogue or product list.

- ✔ **The delivery truck:** Some storefront packages streamline the process of transferring your files from your computer to the server. Instead of using FTP software, you publish information simply by clicking a button in your Web editor or Web browser.

- ✔ **The checkout counter:** Most electronic storefront packages give you the option to accept orders by phone, fax or online with a credit card.

Besides providing you with all the software that you need to create Web pages and get them online, electronic storefronts instruct you on how to market your site and present your goods and services in a positive way. In addition, some programs provide you with a backend database for your business, where you can record customer information, orders and fulfilment.

The problem with many electronic storefront packages is that they're very expensive — some cost $5,000 to $10,000 or more. They're not intended for individuals starting their own small businesses, but rather for large corporations that want to branch out to the Web. However, a few packages (two of which we describe in the following sections) provide cheaper solutions, and cost of between $200 and $500 for the storefront software licence.

ezimerchant

ezimerchant Professional, by On Technology (www.ezimerchant.com), is software that you purchase and install on your computer. You download the program from its own Web site for $449 plus $29.95 per month for access to their Global Transaction Server. The software makes it easy for you to manage and upload your product catalogue, create your Web site from one of the 200 templates provided, and to set up a shopping cart. ezimerchant's Web site says you can have your online store live on the Internet in under 1 hour.

The costs mentioned above cover just the shopping cart software and not Web hosting. Web sites built with ezimerchant don't have any specific hosting requirements so you can choose to host with any Web hosting provider.

Examples of Web sites built with ezimerchant are

✔ Anixi Jewelry (www.jewelry-by-anixi.com)

✔ The Art Shop (www.theartstore.co.nz)

✔ The Pool Shop (www.poolshop.com.au).

X-Cart

X-Cart, by Qualiteam (www.x-cart.com), is a customisable shopping cart system with a wide range of e-commerce features. You can choose a design template, modify the look and feel and configure your online store, all with no programming knowledge.

X-Cart isn't software that you purchase and install on your desktop computer; instead, this Web-based software runs on a server at your Web hosting provider. You need to find a hosting service that runs X-Cart, such as Netregistry (netregistry.com.au) or Just X-Cart (justxcart.com.au). After you pick a company, you need to arrange for an account. Pricing varies depending on the host and the version of the software that you want. X-Cart comes in two varieties: X-Cart Gold and X-Cart Pro. The software licence itself costs between US$229 and US$599, and hosting for X-Cart costs between US$59 and US$99 a month.

Examples of Web sites built with X-Cart are

✔ Downunder Pilot Shop (downunderpilotshop.co.nz)

✔ Just for Bubs (justforbubs.com.au)

✔ Rapid Flowers (www.rapidflowers.com.au).

osCommerce

osCommerce is an *open source* online shop e-commerce solution available for free. An *open source* program is a program for which the source code is available to the general public to use and/or modify from its original design free of charge. osCommerce includes out-of-the-box online shopping cart functionality that allows store owners to set up, run and maintain online stores.

Because osCommerce is free, installing, setting up and maintaining the software is more difficult than the other options mentioned earlier in this section. So, you need to find a host that supports osCommerce shopping carts and then you need some knowledge of the PHP programming language. Alternatively, you can hire a Web developer with these skills. Find out more at oscommerce.com.

Examples of Web sites built with osCommerce are

- ✔ Jungle Mama (www.junglemama.co.nz)
- ✔ Party Balloon Online (partyballoononline.com.au)
- ✔ 6J's Wine Merchants (6js.com.au)

CASE STUDY

Finding a host that makes your business dynamic

Whether Telstra Bigpond or another ISP, which Web host you choose can have a big impact on how easy getting online and running your business successfully is. Just ask Doug Laughter. He and his wife Kristy own The Silver Connection, LLC, which sells sterling silver jewellery imported from around the world. They began their endeavour when Kristy brought back some silver jewellery from Mexico. The Silver Connection went online in April 1998 at www.silverconnection.com and is hosted by CrystalTech Web Hosting, Inc. (www.crystaltech.com).

Q. Why did you choose CrystalTech as your Web host?

A. Although many reliable companies today offer complete Web site hosting solutions, I settled on CrystalTech for a few reasons. It has a Windows-based environment that supports virtually every technology needed for your Web site development and needs. CrystalTech also offers a wide variety of hosting plans that are suitable for small personal Web sites to large business commercial sites at reasonable prices with options of shared hosting, dedicated hosting and SharePoint hosting.

Q. What makes CrystalTech such a good Web host?

A. CrystalTech offers a robust Control Center that allows complete administrative control for the Web site and business. Clients are able to manage every aspect of their sites, which includes administrative tools, such as automatic database connections, complete customer information overview, custom site and file permissions, domain setting, mail and much more. Some very nice resources also offer merchant applications and helpful information with legal forms to assist the client with Web site legalities.

Q. What kinds of customer service features do you use that other business owners should look for?

A. One feature that CrystalTech is very good with is keeping clients informed with informational items that include monthly newsletters and timely notifications of maintenance or system enhancement issues. CrystalTech also has a very knowledgeable and helpful technical support department, an in-depth knowledge base and various community forums to interact with other clients.

Q. What kinds of questions should small-business owners and managers ask when they're shopping for a hosting service? What kinds of features should they be looking for initially?

A. I would first suggest considering how you want to develop your Web site. Today's business site needs to be dynamic in nature, so the business needs to research and determine what Web server application it is going to use. A Web server application consists of the following:

- ✔ **Server Side Technology:** Active Server Pages (ASP, ASP.NET), ColdFusion, Java Server Pages, PHP, XML
- ✔ **Database Solution:** Microsoft SQL Server, MS Access, MySQL, Oracle
- ✔ **Server Application:** IIS, Apache, iPlanet, Netscape Enterprise
- ✔ **Operating Platform:** Windows, UNIX

So the decision about how the e-commerce Web site will be developed and in what technology is a very key decision to make from the onset. After this is decided, choose a Web host that supports your environment of choice.

Q. After the development platform is determined, what features should you look for?

A. Look for basic essentials that are wholesale elements to develop, maintain and enhance the Web presence. These items are common with most hosting plans but always need attention paid to them. This cursory list would include Web disk space, bandwidth limitations, FTP and mail accounts, site statistics, backup plans, merchant applications with payment gateways, and other customary plan offers. Finally, make sure the hosting service offers an application that can analyse traffic, such as WebTrends.

Take time to shop around and compare. Select a Web hosting company that you're comfortable with to avoid having to move shop too soon if something doesn't work out. After you select a hosting company, get down to the business of developing your presence on the Web instead of spending time wondering about moving your Web site identity.

Choosing a Web Page Editor

A woodworker has his or her favourite hammer and saw. A cook has an array of utensils, pots and pans. Likewise, a Web site creator has software programs that facilitate the presentation of words, colours, images and multimedia in Web browsers.

A little HTML is a good thing — but just a little. Knowing HTML comes in handy when you need to add elements that Web page editors don't handle. Some programs, for example, don't provide you with easy buttons or menu options for adding <meta> tags, which enable you to add keywords or descriptions to a site so that search engines can find them and describe your site correctly.

If you really want to get into HTML or to find out more about creating Web pages, read *HTML, XHTML & CSS For Dummies*, 6th Edition, by Ed Tittel and Jeff Nobel, or *Creating Web Pages For Dummies*, 8th Edition, by Bud E. Smith and Arthur Bebak (both by Wiley Publishing, Inc.).

It pays to spend time choosing a Web page editor that has the right qualities. What qualities should you look for in a Web page tool and how do you know which tool is right for you? To help narrow the field, this class of software is divided into different levels of sophistication. Pick the type of program that best fits your technical skill.

For the novice: Use your existing programs

A growing number of word-processing, graphics and business programs are adding HTML to their list of capabilities. You may already have one of these programs at your disposal. By using a program with which you're already comfortable, you can avoid having to install a Web page editor.

Here are some programs that enable you to generate one type of content and then give you the option of outputting that content in HTML, which means that your words or figures can appear on a Web page:

✔ **Adobe InDesign/Quark Xpress:** The most recent versions of these two popular page layout programs let you save the contents of a document as HTML — only the words and images are transferred to the Web, however; any special typefaces become generic Web standard headings.

✔ **Microsoft Office XP/2003/2007:** Publisher, Excel and PowerPoint all give users the option of exporting content to Web pages.

✔ **Microsoft Word:** The most recent versions of the venerable word-processing standby work pretty much seamlessly with Web page content — although most professional Web designers would say it generates messy code — and it does get the job done for beginners. You can open Web pages from within Word and save Word files in Web page format.

✔ **WordPerfect and Presentations:** These two component programs within Corel's suite of tools allow you to save files as an HTML page or a PDF file that you can present on the Web. If you choose to present one slide per Web page, the program adds clickable arrows to each slide in your presentation so that viewers can skip from one slide to another.

Although these solutions are convenient, they probably don't completely eliminate the need to use a Web page editor. Odds are you're still likely to need to make corrections and do special formatting after you convert your text to HTML.

Adobe Contribute is a great beginner tool for updating an existing Web site. It allows you to quickly and easily publish content to your Web site without any technical expertise. So it would be a good option if you convert your Web site into HTML with one of the tools mentioned in the previous section, but then need a tool to maintain the HTML Web pages you have created without having to learn any code. It is an affordable option too at around $230 a licence.

For intermediate needs: User-friendly Web editors

If you're an experienced Web surfer and eager to try out a simple Web editor, try a program that allows you to focus on your site's HTML and textual content, provides you with plenty of functionality, and is still easy to use. Here are some user-friendly programs that are inexpensive (or, better yet, free), yet allow you to create a functional Web site.

The following programs don't include some of the bells and whistles you need to create complex, interactive forms, page layouts or access a database of information from one of your Web pages. These goodies are served up by Web page editors that have a higher level of functionality, which we describe in the upcoming section for advanced commerce sites.

BBEdit

If you work on a Macintosh and you're primarily concerned with textual content, BBEdit is one of the best choices you can make for a Web page tool. It lives up to its motto: 'It doesn't suck.' BBEdit is tailored to use the Mac's highly visual interface, and version 8.5 runs on the Mac OS 10.3.9 or later. You can use Macintosh drag and drop to add an image file to a Web page in progress by dragging the image's icon into the main BBEdit window, for example. Find out more about BBEdit at the Bare Bones Software, Inc. Web site (barebones.com/products/bbedit/).

Other good choices of Web editors for the Macintosh are Taco HTML Edit by Taco Software (www.tacosw.com) or PageSpinner by Optima System (www.optima-system.com).

Macromedia HomeSite

HomeSite is an affordable tool for Web site designers who feel at ease working with HTML code. However, HomeSite isn't just a HTML code editor. HomeSite provides a visual interface so that you can work with graphics and preview your page layout. HomeSite also provides you with step-by-step utilities — *wizards* — to quickly create pages, tables, frames and JavaScript elements. HomeSite is available as a stand-alone program that works with Windows 98 or later; find out more about it at www.macromedia.com/software/homesite.

Microsoft FrontPage Express

Microsoft doesn't support FrontPage Express anymore, but if you still use Windows 98 and you're on a tight budget, give it a try. The software comes bundled with Windows 98, and you don't have to do a thing to install it. Just choose Start⇨Programs⇨Internet Explorer⇨FrontPage Express to open FrontPage Express.

CoffeeCup HTML Editor

CoffeeCup HTML Editor, by CoffeeCup Software (www.coffeecup.com), is a popular Windows Web site editor that contains a lot of features for a small price (US$49). You can begin typing and formatting text by using the CoffeeCup HTML Editor menu options. You can add an image by clicking the Insert Image toolbar button, or use the Forms toolbar to create the text boxes and radio buttons that make up an interactive Web page form. You can even add JavaScript effects and choose from a selection of clip art images that come with the software.

CoffeeCup HTML Editor doesn't let you explore database connectivity, add Web components, or other bonuses that come with a program like FrontPage or Dreamweaver. But it does have everything you need to create a basic Web page.

Amaya

Though Amaya may not be included in a list of reviews of Web page software, the program is ideal for an entrepreneur on a budget. Why? Allow me to spell it out for you: F-R-E-E.

The other great thing about Amaya is the software adheres to strict standards compliance. Amaya is the Web page editing tool developed by the W3C (www.w3.org). All you have to do is check it out and download from the W3C Amaya page (www.w3.org/Amaya/).

Editors to flip your whizzy-wig

Web browsers are multilingual; they understand exotic-sounding languages, such as FTP, HTTP and GIF, among others. But English is one language browsers don't speak. Browsers don't understand instructions, such as 'Put that image there' or 'Make that text italic'. HyperText Markup Language, or HTML, is a kind of translator between human languages and Web languages.

If the thought of HTML strikes fear into your heart, relax. Thanks to modern Web page creation tools, you don't have to master HTML in order to create Web pages. Although knowing a little HTML does come in handy at times, you can depend on these special user-friendly tools to do almost all your English-to-HTML translations for you.

The secret of these Web page creation tools is their WYSIWYG (pronounced whizzy-wig)

display. WYSIWYG stands for 'What You See Is What You Get.' A WYSIWYG editor lets you see on-screen how your page will look when on the Web, rather than force you to type (or even see) HTML commands like this:

```
<H1>This is a Level 1
Heading</H1>

<IMG SRC = 'lucy.gif'> <BR>

<P>This is an image of
Lucy.</P>
```

A WYSIWYG editor, such as CoffeeCup HTML Editor for Windows (www.coffeecup.com), shows you how the page appears even as you assemble it. Besides that, it lets you format text and add images by means of familiar software shortcuts such as menus and buttons.

For advanced commerce sites: Programs that do it all

If you plan to do a great deal of business online or even to add the title of Web designer to your list of talents (as some of the entrepreneurs profiled in this book have done), it makes sense to spend some money up front and use a Web page tool that can do everything you want — today and for years to come.

The advanced programs that are described here go beyond the simple designation of Web page editors. They not only let you edit Web pages but also help you add interactivity to your site, link dynamically updated databases to your site, and keep track of how your site is organised and updated. Some programs (notably, FrontPage) can even transfer your Web documents to your Web host with a single menu option. This way, you get to concentrate on the fun part of running an online business — meeting people, taking orders, processing payments, and the like.

Dreamweaver

What's that you say? You can never hear enough bells and whistles? The cutting edge is where you love to walk? Then Dreamweaver, a Web authoring tool by Adobe, is for you. Dreamweaver is a feature-rich, professional piece of software.

Dreamweaver's strengths aren't so much in the basic features, such as making selected text bold, italic or a different size; rather, Dreamweaver excels in producing Dynamic HTML (which makes Web pages more interactive through scripts) and HTML style sheets. Dreamweaver has ample FTP settings, and it gives you the option of seeing the HTML codes you're working with in one window and the formatting of your Web page within a second, WYSIWYG window. The latest version is a complex and powerful piece of software. It lets you create Active Server pages, connect to a ColdFusion database, and contains lots of templates and wizards. Dreamweaver is available for both Windows and Macintosh computers; find out more at the Adobe Web site (www.adobe.com/products/ dreamweaver/).

Microsoft FrontPage

FrontPage (www.microsoft.com/frontpage) is a powerful Web authoring tool that has some unique e-commerce capabilities. For one thing, it provides you with a way to organise a Web site visually. The main FrontPage window is divided into two sections. On the left, you see the Web page on which you're currently working. On the right, you see a tree-like map of all the pages on your site, arranged visually to show which pages are connected to each other by hyperlinks. The problem with FrontPage is that Microsoft no longer supports it (discontinued late 2006).

Microsoft Expression Web

Released in 2007, Microsoft's replacement product for FrontPage is Expression Web. Expression Web is a user-friendly yet powerful editor that has strong support for Cascading Style Sheets (CSS), a technology that allows you to format multiple Web pages consistently by using standard commands that all Web browsers can interpret. The program also lets you develop Web sites with ASP.NET and XML markup. Expression Web includes Dynamic Web Templates — sets of Web pages that have master areas that appear on each Web page: make a change to the master area, and the change is carried out through the whole site. It is definitely not for beginners and is aimed at experienced Web designers and programmers. Find out more at www.microsoft.com/expression/.

Part II
Establishing Your Online Business

Glenn Lumsden

'What do you think works best on my Web site? The tiny red text on the green background or the strobing yellow on the tartan?'

In this part ...

Just as business owners in the real world have to rent or buy a facility and fit it out to conduct their businesses, you have to develop an online storefront to conduct your online business. In this part, I explain how to put a virtual roof over your store and light a cyber-fire to welcome your customers. In other words, this part focuses on the nuts and bolts of your Web site itself.

The World Wide Web is the most exciting and popular place to open an online store. But merely creating a set of Web pages isn't enough to succeed online. Your site needs to be compelling — even irresistible. Chapter 5 shows you how to organise your site and fill it with useful content that attracts customers in the first place and encourages them to stay and browse. Chapter 6 looks at security issues for you and your customers, and Chapter 7 explains how to handle many different kinds of electronic purchases. And, to keep improving your site so that it runs more efficiently (with a cyber-smile, in fact), Chapter 8 encourages you to look at all areas of customer service.

Chapter 5

Organising Your Business Site Structure and Layout

In This Chapter

▶ Organising an easy-to-navigate business site

▶ Comprehending content

▶ Optimising type and images to build a graphic identity

▶ Creating content that holds your customer's attention and promotes trust

▶ Inviting interaction through forms, email and more

▶ Discovering the language of layout

*T*he same basic business principles work on the Web just as well as they do in the bricks-and-mortar world: Attracting customers is important, but real success comes from establishing relationships with customers who come to trust you and rely on you for providing excellent products and services.

Achieving these goals on the Web requires some special strategies, however. Loading your site with animations and flashy promotions won't work. Web surfers want results fast. They're increasingly mobile and increasingly accustomed to sophisticated content. The trick is to have no trick: Keep your site simple, well organised and content-rich.

This chapter examines some of the best ways for standing out from the crowd and attracting customers even as cyberspace becomes increasingly crowded and competitive. The chapter title might make it sound like organising a site and making it attractive are two mutually exclusive activities, but they go together: Creating an organised site is sure to attract first-time and returning customers. In this chapter, you explore ways to achieve these goals, including making your site easy to navigate; creating compelling content; optimising your images so they appear quickly; and building interactivity into your site so customers want to return to you on a regular basis.

Feng Shui Your Web Site

Feng shui is the art of arranging objects in an environment to achieve (among other things) success in your career, wealth and happiness. If that's true, try practising some feng shui with your online business environment — that is, your Web site. How you organise your Web site heavily influences how successful the site ultimately is likely to be. What elements you include and how you arrange them impacts how welcoming and how easy to navigate and purchase from the site is.

Although you may be tempted to jump right into the creation of a cool Web site, take a moment to plan. Whether you're setting off on a road trip across the country or building a new addition for your house, you'll progress more smoothly by drawing a map of where you want to go. Dig into your miscellaneous drawer until you find pencil and paper, then make a list of the elements you want to have on your site.

Look over the items on your list and break them into three or four main categories. These main categories branch off your *home page*, which functions as the grand entrance or shopfront for your online business site. You can then draw a map of your site in the form of an organisational chart that shows the hierarchy of pages, as shown in Figure 5-1.

Figure 5-1: A home page is the point from which your site branches into more specific levels of information.

The main areas on your site are likely to include:

- ✔ **About Us:** The purpose of this page (or area) is for detailed information about your online business. You can write about your experience with and your love for what you buy and sell, or anything else that personalises your site and builds trust. This may be introducing yourself and your team, or the history of how you came up with the idea for your business in the first place. A standard, and some might say 'boring', name for this page is About Us, but you can jazz it up or change it to suit your own business. Other possible names for this page may be About Me, Our Business, Background, Profile, Who We Are or Introducing [Business Name].

- ✔ **Our Products or Services:** If you have just one main product or service a better approach is to name this page in line with what you're offering — such as Legal Services, Lawn Mowing or Personalised Stationery — rather than using the generic terms 'Products' or 'Services'. This method is more helpful to visitors browsing because it spells out what you offer and is also helpful for later when you're trying to get your site listed in search engines. If you're offering a whole range of products or services, you can break up this area accordingly and, again, name the pages or categories of your catalogue with helpful descriptive titles (see Figure 5-2).

- ✔ **Free Resources:** Internet surfers are always on the lookout for freebies and giveaways. If you have something to give away, signposting this area and making it easy to find can help your visitor. Other possible names for this page may be Free Stuff, Free Articles or Free Ebook.

- ✔ **Contact Us:** This page may include your phone number, fax number, address and perhaps a fill-in email inquiry form that makes contacting and asking a question easy for potential customers. If you do have a physical location, a map is always handy on this page too.

The preceding example results in a very simple Web site. But, starting out simple and expanding or adding as you need to, works well, too.

If you're developing an online store to sell products, your resulting Web site map may look like Figure 5-2.

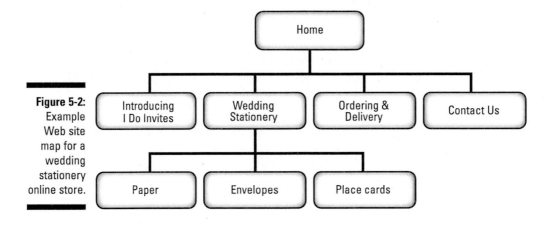

Figure 5-2:
Example
Web site
map for a
wedding
stationery
online store.

If you're developing an online store to promote your services, your resulting Web site map may look like Figure 5-3.

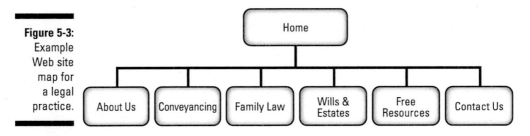

Figure 5-3:
Example
Web site
map for
a legal
practice.

Some Web design programs, like Microsoft's Expression Web, give you the ability to create your own visual site map. You can create new pages and see how they link to one another in Hyperlinks view.

Devising a structure for your Web site is only one way to organise it — the outer or top-down organisational method, you might say. Organisation also comes from the inside — from the content you create. The words, images and interactive features that help your site get organised are discussed in the following sections.

The All-Important Home Page

The home page of your Web site is a visitor's introduction to your business. You have 10–12 seconds to capture the attention of the average adult Internet surfer and even less for younger surfers. Remember to include the following items on your home page so that your visitors can immediately get a feel for what you do:

✔ The name of the store or business

✔ Your logo, if you have one

✔ Easy navigation or site menu — that is, links to the main areas of your site or, if your site isn't overly extensive, to every page

✔ A brief summary or profile of the business and the products and services you provide

✔ Keywords by which you want to be found (more about this item in Chapter 11)

✔ A clear 'call to action' to guide and encourage visitors to take the next step or the action you want them to take; for example, picking up the phone, downloading a file or buying a product

✔ Clear contact details, such as your email address, phone/fax numbers and your business or postal address so that people know how to reach you in the Land Beyond Cyberspace

Content is KING

What sells on the Web? Look no further than the search engine you probably use on a regular basis: Google. Google proves that information sells online. Making information easy to find and organising much of the Web's content in one place has helped make this one of the most successful businesses of recent years. When it comes to a business Web site, you need to present the *right* content in the *right* way to make prospective clients and customers want to explore your site the first time and then come back for more later on.

What is the 'right' content? The 'right' content:

✔ Helps people absorb information fast

✔ Makes it easy for visitors to find out who you are and what you have to offer

- Is friendly and informal in tone, concise in length and clear in its organisation

- Helps develop the all-important one-to-one relationship with customers and clients by inviting dialogue and interaction, both with you and with others who share the same interests

The place to begin is by identifying your target audience. Envision the customers you want to attract and make your site appear to speak directly to them, person to person. Ask around and try to determine what people want from your Web site. Speak informally and directly to them, by using 'you' rather than 'we' or 'us'. Ensure your site has plenty of action points — links to click, forms to fill out, or product descriptions to read. And follow the general principles outlined in the sections that follow.

Consider doing what professional marketing consultants do and write detailed descriptions of the individuals you're trying to reach. Make your customer profiles complete with fictitious names, ages, job descriptions, type of car they drive and so on. The more detailed you get, the better you can tailor your content to those people.

Making them fall in love at first site

First impressions are critical on the Web, where shoppers have the ability to jump from site to site with a click of their mouse. A few extra seconds of downtime waiting for complex images or mini-computer programs — *Java applets* — to download can cause your prospective buyer to lose patience and you to lose a sale.

How do you make visitors to your welcome page feel like they're being greeted with open arms? Here are some suggestions:

- **Remember, less is more:** Don't overload any one page with more than three or four images. Keep all images 20K or less in size.

- **Find a fast host:** Some Web servers have super-fast connections to the Internet and

others use slower lines. Test your site; if your pages take 10 or 20 seconds or more to appear, ask your host company why and find out whether it can move you to a faster machine.

- **Offer a bargain:** Nothing attracts attention as much as a competition, a giveaway, or a special sales promotion. If you have anything that you can give away, either through a competition or a discount, do it.

- **Provide instant gratification:** Make sure that your most important information appears at or near the top of your page. Visitors to the Web don't like having to scroll through several screens of material to get to the information they want.

Keep it simple

Studies of how information on a Web page is absorbed indicate that people don't really read the contents from top to bottom (or left to right) in a linear way. In fact, most Web surfers don't *read* in the traditional sense at all. Instead, they browse so quickly you'd think they have an itchy mouse finger. They 'flip through pages' by clicking link after link. More and more Internet users go online with palm devices, pocket PCs and Web-enabled mobile phones. Because your prospective customers don't necessarily have tons of computing power or hours of time to explore your site, the best rule is to *keep it simple*.

People who are looking for things on the Web are often in a state of hurried distraction. Think about a TV watcher browsing during a commercial or a parent stealing a few moments on the computer while the baby naps. Imagine this person surfing with one hand on a mouse, the other dipping chips into salsa. This person isn't in the mood to listen while you unfold your fondest hopes and dreams for success, starting with how you played checkout operator as a toddler. Attract them immediately by answering these questions:

- ✔ Who are you, anyway?
- ✔ All right, so what is your main message or mission?
- ✔ Well then, what do you have here for me?
- ✔ Why should I choose your site to investigate rather than all the others that seem to be about the same?

When it comes to Web pages, it pays to put the most important components first: Who you are, what you do, how you stand out from any competing sites and contact information.

Keep in mind that people who come to a Web site give that site less than a minute's attention (in fact, often less than 20 seconds).

If you have a long list of items to sell, you probably can't fit everything you have to offer on the first page of your site. Even if you could, you wouldn't want to: You're best to prioritise the contents of your site so that the 'breaking stories' or the best contents appear at the top and the rest of your catalogue's content is arranged in order of importance.

Think long and hard before you use features that may scare people away instead of wowing them, such as a splash page that contains only a logo or short greeting, then reloads automatically and takes the visitor to the main body of a site. Don't load your home page with Flash animations or Java applets that take precious seconds to load.

Striking the right tone with your text

Business writing on the Web differs from the dry, linear report writing used in the corporate world. So this is your chance to express the real you: Talk about your fashion sense or your collection of salt and pepper shakers. Add a personal touch but remember not to waffle! — keep it short, sweet and to the point. Your business also has a personality and the more striking you make its description on your Web page, the better. Use the tone of your text to define what makes your business unique and what distinguishes it from your competition.

Satisfied customers are another source of endorsements. Approach your customers and ask if they're willing to provide a quote about how you helped them. If you don't yet have satisfied customers, ask one or two people to try your products or services for free and then, if they're happy with your wares, ask permission to use their comments on your site. Your goal is to get a pithy, positive quote that you can put on your home page or scatter throughout your site (perhaps one on each page). Melissa suggests nobody is going to read a long scrolling page of testimonials, so you're best not to dedicate a separate page to quotes from your clients. After all, you're not likely to put a negative customer comment on your site so visitors short on time don't see a lot of value in scrolling through a long page of nice things people say about you.

Making your site easy to navigate

Imagine Web surfers arriving at your Web site with only a fraction of their attention engaged. Making the links easy to read and in an obvious location makes your site easier to navigate. And, having a row of clickable buttons at the top of your home page, each of which points the visitor to an important area of your site, is always a good idea. Such navigational pointers give visitors an idea of what your site contains in a single glance, and immediately encourage viewers to click into a primary subsection of your site and explore further. By placing an interactive table of contents up front, you direct surfers to the material they're looking for.

The links to the most important areas of a site can go at or near the top of the page on either the left or right side. The Dummies.com home page, as shown in Figure 5-4, has a navigation menu along the top that directs visitors to the *Dummies* titles by topic.

Figure 5-4:
Putting at
least five
or six links
near the
top of your
home page
is a good
idea.

Navigation can help with marketing: If you want to be ranked highly by search engines (and who doesn't), you have another good reason to place your site's main topics near the top of the page in a series of links. Some search services index the first 50 or so words on a Web page and follow any links. Therefore, if you can get lots of important keywords included in that index, your site is more likely to be ranked highly in a list of links returned by the service in response to a search. See Chapter 11 for more on embedding keywords.

Presenting the reader with links up front doesn't just help your search engine rankings, it also indicates that your site is content-rich and worthy of exploration.

CASE STUDY

Building an online presence takes time

Kathie M. Thomas, the *Virtual Assistant Queen*, knows all about running an online business and attracting clients over the Internet. She started her business A Clayton's Secretary (`www.asecretary.com.au`) in 1994 to be home full-time for her five daughters. Today, Kathie runs a global business via the Internet from her home office in Melbourne, Australia and her blogging efforts (`vadirectory.net/blog`) has placed her in the Top 100 Australian Blogs list.

She is a keen advocate for blogging and social networking and believes regularly participating in online communities is a great way to promote your business, learn from others and, above all, strike up relationships online through sharing what you've learnt. Altogether she regularly writes for more than 14 different blogs and is a member of a large and increasing number of social networks and discussion forums including Facebook, LinkedIn and Yahoo! Groups, just to name a few. She knows that on the Web, writing quality content and getting personal allows you to strike up relationships and build interest as well as trust.

Her passion is helping women return home to work, using skills they developed in the workforce, so they can be home full-time for their families. It was because of these community efforts that she was nominated for Australian of the Year in 2008.

Q. Can you briefly describe your business?

A. I began a home-based secretarial service in 1994, which changed considerably after the Internet entered the equation. Today, my small, sole-person, home-based secretarial service has morphed into a 200+ team of virtual assistants operating from their homes in 15 countries. We sell administrative, secretarial and Web-based services to clients worldwide. I began working from home to be present for my five daughters. Today, I provide a service that assists others to work from home and be present for their families, just as I have been. Ninety-eight per cent of my memberships are women/mothers. I didn't start out my business with the idea of going global — that development just happened along the way.

Q. What got you started online?

A. I was told by a Telecom technician in September 1995 that I could build a national business — at that stage I didn't really understand what she was trying to tell me and it took me three months before I really looked at what she suggested.

Q. What would you describe as the primary goal of your online business?

A. I have two audiences — the clients who need support and the virtual assistants who need help running their businesses. My goal is to gain exposure for my virtual assistants and to continue gaining clients for my team.

Q. How many hours a week do you work on your business sites?

A. Hard to give a figure. I do what's needed and more because I love it. I spend five hours a week at least on my own sites but probably more. Always tweaking, updating or adding. And then there's all the forum participation — hours unknown. I just do it.

Q. How do you promote your site?

A. Through printed materials, *Yellow Pages*, online directories, Google Adwords, blogs and forums. Also, through speaking engagements and books I've written. A lot has been through building personal relationships and getting to know people via virtual assistant forums online, client forums through LinkedIn.com and other places, Facebook, Blogging forums and so on. I spend a lot of time online networking and connecting with people. I often get asked how did something happen, or they comment on how lucky I've been. The reality is that I've worked for that luck — constantly. I have people who want to know how to get noticed or get the interest I've developed but when I outline my forum participation and networking they dismiss those things as not needed — I totally disagree. A lot of what happens online is because people constantly see my name and see me getting involved and helping others, giving free advice and just joining in.

Q. Has your online business been profitable financially?

A. Yes, but also emotionally — I get a great deal of emotional satisfaction.

Q. Who creates your business's Web pages?

A. I do — I'm constantly learning, reading, watching, absorbing, adapting.

Q. What advice would you give to someone starting an online business?

A. Do the research. Today there's absolutely no excuse for not being armed with the facts and not being able to find someone who can guide or mentor you. Thousands of online discussion forums are available via Yahoo! Groups, LinkedIn and many other sources today. Just do a search online for your key topic or theme and you're sure to find others who are connecting and discussing what it is you do. Join them and learn from them, absorb the information they give and be willing to give back as well. What you freely learn, be prepared to share with others. I firmly believe 'what goes around comes around'.

Pointing the way with headings

One hard-to-miss Web page element that's designed to grab the attention of your readers' eyes is a heading. Every Web page needs to contain headings that direct the reader's attention to the most important contents. This book provides a good example. The chapter title (we hope) piques your interest first. Then the section headings and subheadings direct you to more details on the topics you want to read about.

Most Web page editing tools designate top-level headings with the style Heading 1. Beneath this, you place one or more Heading 2 headings. Beneath each of those, you may have Heading 3 and, beneath those, Heading 4. (Headings 5 and 6 are too small to be useful on screen.) The arrangement may look like this (the headings are indented for clarity; you don't have to indent them on your page):

```
Miss Cookie's Delectable Cooking School (Heading 1)
  Kitchen Equipment You Can't Live Without (Heading 2)
  The Story of a Calorie Counter Gone Wrong (Heading 2)
  Programs of Culinary Study (Heading 2)
    Registration (Heading 3)
    Course Schedule (Heading 3)
      New Course on Whipped Cream Just Added! (Heading 4)
```

You can energise virtually any heading by telling your audience something specific about your business. Instead of 'Ida's Antiques Shop', for example, say something like 'Ida's Antiques Shop: The Perfect Destination for the Collector and the Crafter'. Instead of simply writing a heading like 'Stan Thompson, Pet Grooming', say something specific, such as 'Stan Thompson: We Groom Your Pet at Our Place or Yours'.

Becoming an expert list maker

Lists are simple and effective ways to break up text and make your Web content easier to digest. They're easy to create and easy for your customer to view and absorb. For example, suppose that you sell gifts and you want to offer certain lines at a discount during various seasons — such as Easter or Valentine's Day. Rather than bury the items you're offering within an easily overlooked paragraph, why not divide your list into subgroups so that visitors find what they want without being distracted? For example, gifts for new arrivals, birthdays, anniversaries, graduations, Christmas or Easter.

Lists are easy to implement. If you're using Microsoft Expression Web, open your Web page and follow these steps:

1. **Type a heading for your list and then select the entire heading.**

   For example, you might type and then select the words **This Month's Specials**.

2. **Choose a heading style from the Style drop-down list.**

   Your text is formatted as a heading.

3. **Click anywhere in Expression Web's Design View (the main editing window) to deselect the heading you just formatted.**

4. **Press Enter to move to a new line.**

5. **Type the first item of your list, press Enter, and then type the second item on the next line.**

6. **Repeat Step 5 until you enter all the items of your list.**

7. **Select all the items of your list (but not the heading).**

8. **Choose Format➪Bullets and Numbering.**

   The List Properties dialogue box appears.

9. **Choose one of the four bullet styles and click OK.**

   A bullet appears next to each list item and the items appear closer together on-screen so that they look more like a list. That's all there is to it! Figure 5-5 shows the result.

Most Web editors let you vary the appearance of the bullet. For example, you can make the bullet a hollow circle rather than a solid black dot, or you can choose a rectangle rather than a circle.

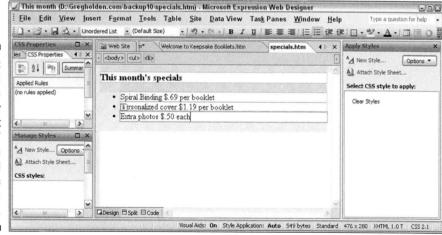

Figure 5-5:
A bulleted list is an easy way to direct customers' attention to special promotions or sale items.

Your Web page title: The ultimate heading

When you're dreaming up clever headings for your Web pages, don't overlook the 'heading' that appears in the narrow title bar at the very top of your visitor's Web browser window: The *title* of your Web page.

The two HTML tags `<title>` and `</title>` contain the text that appears within the browser title bar. But you don't have to mess with these nasty HTML codes: All Web page creation programs give you an easy way to enter or edit a title for a Web page. Make the title as catchy and specific as possible, but make sure that the title is no longer than 10 to 15 words. An effective title refers to your goods or services while grabbing the viewer's attention. If your business is Waterwise Rain Tanks, for example, you may make your title 'Complete Water Storage Specialists — Rainwater Tanks, Pressure Pumps, Level Indicators — Waterwise Rain Tanks' (15 words, which includes the dashes).

Leading your readers on with links

We mean for you to interpret the preceding heading literally, not figuratively. In other words, we're not suggesting that you make promises on which you can't deliver. Rather, we mean that you should do anything you can to lead your visitors to your site and then get them to stay long enough to explore individual pages. You can accomplish this goal with hyperlinked words and phrases throughout your content that leads to another page on your site.

For example:

- Within a paragraph:

    ```
    Here at Gifts Ideas for You, we provide a selection of
    gifts for all occasions including New Baby, Father's Day,
    Mother's Day, Christmas and Birthday.
    ```

    By clicking on any of the underlined or hyperlinked words visitors can jump straight to the area they're interested in.

- On a feature box or highlighted product:

    ```
    Father's Day is coming          New Baby
    We have a range of great        Visiting a new addition
    gifts for Dad                   in hospital? We have
    Find out more                   the perfect gift.
                                    Find out more
    ```

✔ On a bulleted list:

```
We offer:
```
• Farewell Gift Ideas

• Presents for Teenagers

• Retirement Gifts

• Golf Gifts

• Wine Gifts

• Gifts For Dad

<u>and many more ...</u>

You see words or phrases like 'More', 'Read more' and 'Find out more' all the time on Web pages that present a lot of content. If you're like Melissa, you're always interested in finding out what more they could possibly have to offer.

These days, your visitors are more likely to be Internet savvy about using links, so rather than presenting your link like this '<u>For more about our services, click here</u>' presenting, it like so — '<u>Find out more about our services</u>' — is probably sufficient.

Whenever possible, tell your visitors what they can expect to encounter as a benefit when they click a link. Give them a tease — and then a big pay-off for responding.

Enhancing your text with well-placed images

You can add two kinds of images to a Web page: an *inline image*, which appears in the body of your page along with your text, or an *external image*, which is a separate file that visitors access by clicking a link. The link may take the form of highlighted text or a small version of the image — a *thumbnail*.

The basic HTML tag that inserts an image in your document takes the following form:

```
<img src="URL">
```

This tag tells your browser to display an image (`<img>`) here. 'URL' gives the location of the image file that serves as the source (`src`) for this image. Whenever possible, also include `width` and `height` attributes (as follows) because they help speed up graphics display for many browsers:

```
<img height=51 width=48 SRC="target.gif">
```

Most Web page editors add the `width` and `height` attributes automatically when you insert an image. Typically, here's what happens:

1. **Click the location in the Web page where you want the image to appear.**

2. **Click an Image toolbar button or choose Insert⇨Image to display an image selection dialogue box.**

3. **Enter the name of the image you want to add and click OK.**

   The image is added to your Web page.

A well-placed image, points the way to text that you want people to read immediately. Think about where your own eyes go when you first connect to a Web page. Most likely, you first look at any images on the page; then you look at the headings; finally, you settle on text to read. If you can place an image next to a heading, you virtually ensure that viewers read the heading.

Making your site searchable

A search box is one of the best kinds of content you can put on your Web site's opening page. A *search box* is a simple text-entry field that lets a visitor enter a word or phrase. By clicking a button labelled Go or Search, the search term or terms are sent to the site, where a script checks an index of the site's contents for any files that contain the terms. The script then lists documents that contain the search terms in the visitor's browser window.

Search boxes are commonly found on commercial Web sites. You usually see them at the top of the home page, right near the links to the major sections of the site. The Dummies.com Technology page, as shown in Figure 5-6, includes a search box in the upper right corner of the page.

Search boxes allow visitors instantly to scan the site's entire contents for a word or phrase. They put visitors in control right away and get them to interact with your site. They're popular for some very good reasons.

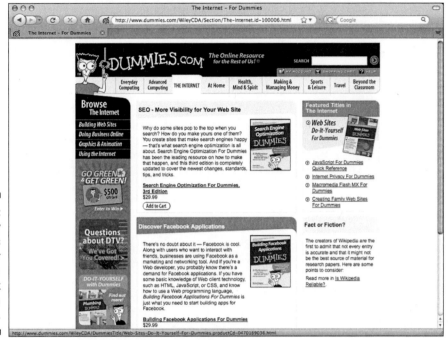

Figure 5-6:
Many
surfers
prefer
using a
search box
to clicking
links.

Yes, we recommend some sort of search utility for e-commerce sites. However, adding a search box to your site doesn't make much sense if you have only five to ten pages of content. And if your site has a sales catalogue driven by a database, your customers can use the database search tool instead.

The problem is that search boxes usually require someone with knowledge of computer programming to create or implement a program called a CGI script to do the searching. Someone also has to compile an index of the documents on the Web site so that the script can search the documents. An application such as ColdFusion works well, but this program isn't for beginners.

But you can get around having to write CGI scripts to add search capabilities to your site. Choose one of these options:

✔ **Allow your Web host to do the work:** Some hosting services do the indexing and creation of the search utility as part of their services.

✔ **Pay for a search service:** If you don't want to display ads on your search results pages, pay a monthly fee to have a company index your pages and let users conduct searches. For example, FreeFind (`www.freefind.com`) has some economy packages, a free version that forces you to view ads, and a professional version that costs US$5 per month for a site of 250 pages or less and US$9 per month for a site of 500 pages or less.

✔ **Use a free site search service:** The server that does the indexing of your Web pages and holds the index doesn't need to be the server that hosts your site. A number of services make your site searchable for free. In exchange, you display advertisements or logos in the search results you return to your visitors. For example, Google Site Search is a popular one (www.google.com/sitesearch/).

You say you're up to making your site searchable, and you shudder at the prospect of either writing your own computer script or finding and editing someone else's script to index your site's contents and actually do the searching? Then head over to Atomz (www.atomz.com) and check out the hosted application Site Search. Other organisations that offer similar services include FreeFind (www.freefind.com), PicoSearch (www.picosearch.com), and Webinator (www.thunderstone.com/texis/site/pages/webinator.html).

If a Web developer is helping to build your site, ask the developer to include a search feature in its quotation.

Nip and Tuck: Establishing a Visual Identity

The prospect of designing a Web site may be intimidating if you haven't tried it before. But just remember that it really boils down to a simple principle: *effective visual communication that conveys a particular message.* The first step in creating graphics is not to open a painting program and start drawing, but rather to plan your page's message. Next, determine the audience you want to reach with that message and think about how your graphics can best communicate what you want to say. Some ways to do this are

✔ **Gather ideas from Web sites that use graphics well.** Award-winning sites and sites created by designers who are using graphics in new or unusual ways can help you. To find some award winners, check out The Webby Awards (www.webbyawards.com) and NetGuide Web Awards (www.netguide.com.au/v2/webawards/ and www.netguide.co.nz).

✔ **Know your audience.** Create graphics that meet visitors' needs and expectations. If you're selling fashions to teenagers, go for loud colours and out-there graphics. If you're selling financial planning to senior citizens, choose a distinguished and sophisticated typeface.

✔ **Use graphics consistently from page to page.** You can create an identity and convey a consistent message.

TIP

How do you become acquainted with your customers when you're unlikely to actually meet them face to face? Find newsgroups and mailing lists in which potential visitors to your site are discussing subjects related to what you plan to publish on the Web. Read the posted messages to get a sense of the concerns and vocabulary of your intended audience.

Make a map of your Web site

Maps are especially important when navigating the information superhighway. When it comes to your e-commerce Web site, a site map can help you make your site easier to navigate. A *site map* is a graphical representation of your Web site — a diagram that graphically depicts all the pages in the site and how they connect to one another. Some Web page editing programs, such as Adobe Dreamweaver, have a site map function built into them. When you create pages and link them to one another, a site map is created. The following figure shows the site map on the left side of the window and a list of files on the right.

Keep in mind that you don't have to invest in a fancy (and expensive) software program in order to create a site map. You can also create

one the old-fashioned way, with a pencil and paper. Or you can draw boxes and arrows with a computer graphics program you're familiar with. The point is that your site map can be a useful design tool for organising the documents within your site.

If your sales are sluggish, make sure that your customers can actually find what they're looking for. Take a typical product in your sales catalogue and then visit your own site to see how many clicks someone would need to make in order to find it. Then see how many clicks that person would need to complete its purchase. Eliminating any unnecessary navigational layers (such as category opening pages) makes your site easier to use.

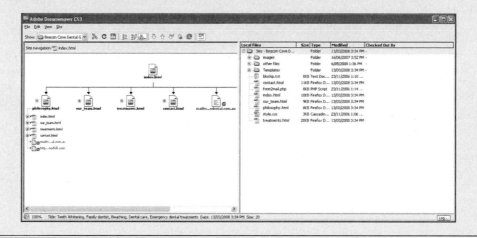

Choosing colours that appeal

The *background* is the solid colour or pattern that is behind the contents of a Web page. Most Web browsers display the background of a page as white unless you specify something different. If you choose the wrong background colour (one that makes your text hard to read and your images look like they've been smeared with mud), viewers are likely to get the impression that the page is poorly designed or that the author of the page hasn't put a great deal of thought into the project.

Most Web page creation programs offer a simple way to specify a colour or an image file to serve as the background of a Web page. For example, in Adobe Dreamweaver, you use the Modify menu and select Page Properties to set your Web page background colour or image.

Colour your Web site effectively

You can use background and other colours to elicit a particular mood or emotion and also to convey your organisation's identity on the Web. The right choice of colour can create impressions ranging from elegant to funky.

The basic colours chosen by the Nestlé Web site (www.nestle.com.au) and the Fisher & Paykel Web site (www.fisherpaykel.co.nz) convey to customers that they're staid and reliable companies. In contrast, the designers of the Yoplait site (www.yoplait.com.au) combine bright colours and glow effects to convey a fun, fresh and healthy image to mums and kids.

Consider the demographics of your target audience when selecting colours for your Web pages. Do some research on what emotions or impressions are conveyed by different colours and which colours best match the mission or identity of your business. Refer to resources, such as the online article by InKK Design (office.microsoft.com/en-us/frontpage/HA010429371033.aspx), which examines in some detail the subject of how colour choices make Web surfers react differently.

Even if you have the taste of a professional designer, you need to be aware of what happens to colour on the Web. The best colour choices for Web backgrounds are ones that don't shift dramatically from browser to browser or platform to platform. The best palette for use on the Web is a set of 216 colours that is common to all browsers. These are called *Web-safe colours* because they appear pretty much the same from browser to browser and on different monitors. The palette itself appears on the Wikipedia Web site (en.wikipedia.org/wiki/Web_colors).

Keep in mind that the colours you use must have contrast so that they don't blend into one another. For example, you don't want to put purple type on a brown or blue background, or yellow type on a white background. Remember to use light type against a dark background and dark type against a light background. That way, all the contents of your pages show up.

Tiling images in the background

You can use an image rather than a solid colour to serve as the background of a page. You specify an image in the HTML code of your Web page (or in your Web page editor), and browsers automatically *tile* the image, reproducing it over and over to fill the current width and height of the browser window.

This isn't the time to be totally wild and crazy. Background images work only when they're subtle and don't interfere with the page contents. Choose an image that doesn't have any obvious lines that create a distracting pattern when tiled. The effect you're trying to create should literally resemble wallpaper. Visit the Maine Solar House home page (www.solarhouse.com) for a rare example of a tiled background image that is faint enough to not interfere with foreground images and that adds something to the page's design.

Using Web typefaces like a pro

If you create a Web page and don't specify that the text be displayed in a particular font, the browser that displays the page uses its default font, which is usually Times or Helvetica (although individual users can customise their browsers by picking a different default font).

However, you don't have to limit yourself to the same old typeface. As a Web page designer, you can exercise a degree of control over the appearance of your Web page by specifying that the body type and headings be displayed in a particular non-standard font. A few of the choices available to you have names such as Verdana, Arial and Courier and so on. But just because you fall in love with a particular typeface doesn't mean your audience is going to admire it in all its beauty. The problem is that you don't have ultimate control over whether a given browser can display the specified typeface because you don't know for sure whether the individual user's system has access to your preferred typefaces. If the particular font you specified is not available, the browser falls back on its default font (which, again, is probably Times or Helvetica).

That's why you're better off picking a generic typeface that is built into virtually every computer's operating system. This convention ensures that your Web pages look more or less the same no matter what Web browser or what type of computer displays them.

Where, exactly, do you specify type fonts, colours and sizes for the text? Again, special HTML tags tell Web browsers what fonts to display, but you don't need to mess with these tags yourself if you're using a Web page creation tool. The specific steps you take depend on what Web design tool you're using. In Dreamweaver, you have the option of specifying a group of preferred typefaces rather than a single font in the Properties inspector (see Figure 5-7). If the viewer doesn't have one font in the group, another font displays. Check the Help files with your own program to find out exactly how to format text and what typeface options you have.

Not all typefaces are equal in the eye of the user. Sans-serif fonts such as Arial and Verdana are considered to be more readable on screen (such as for Web pages and PowerPoint presentations). Serif typefaces, such as Times Roman, are considered to be more readable for printed materials.

If you want to ensure that a heading or block of type appears in a specific typeface (especially a non-standard one that isn't displayed as body text by Web browsers), scan it or create the heading in an image-editing program and insert it into the page as a graphic image. But make sure it doesn't clash with the generic typefaces that appear on the rest of your page.

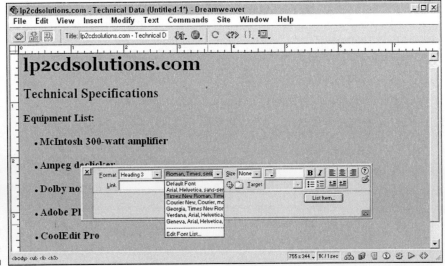

Figure 5-7: Most Web page design tools allow you to specify a preferred font or fonts for your Web page in a dialogue box like this.

Clip art is free and fun

Not everyone has the time or resources to scan photos or create their own original graphics. But that doesn't mean you can't add graphic interest to your Web page. Many Web page designers use clip-art bullets, diamonds, or other small images next to list items or major Web page headings to which they want to call special attention. Clip art can also provide a background pattern for a Web page or highlight sales headings, such as Free!, New! or Special!

In keeping with the spirit of exchange that has been a part of the Internet since its inception, some talented and generous artists have created icons, buttons and other illustrations in electronic form and offer them free for downloading.

Here are some suggestions for sources of clip art on the Web:

- Barry's Clipart Server (www.barrysclipart.com)
- Bravenet (resources.bravenet.com/clipart/)
- CoolArchive (www.coolarchive.com)
- Microsoft Office Online (office.microsoft.com/en-us/clipart/default.aspx)

If you use Microsoft Office, you have access to plenty of clip art images that come with the software. In Word, choose Insert⇨Picture⇨Clip Art to open the Insert Clip Art dialogue box. If these built-in images aren't sufficient, you can connect to the Microsoft Clip Gallery Live Web site by clicking the Clips Online toolbar button in the Insert Clip Art dialogue box. Web page editors — such as Microsoft FrontPage and CoffeeCup HTML Editor — come with their own clip-art libraries, too.

Be sure to read the copyright fine print *before* you copy graphics. All artists own the copyright to their work. Determining how they want to give someone else the right to copy their work is up to them. Sometimes the authors require you to pay a small fee if you want to copy their work, or they may restrict use of their work to non-profit organisations.

A picture is worth a thousand words

Some customers know exactly what they want before they arrive on your site and don't need any help from you. But most customers love to shop around or could use some encouragement to move from one item or catalogue page to another. This is where images can play an important role.

Even if you use only some basic clip art, such as placing stars or arrows next to sale items, your customer is likely to thank you by buying more. A much better approach, though, is to scan or take digital images of your sale items and provide compact, clear images of them on your site. Here's a quick step-by-step guide to get you started:

1. **Choose the right image to scan.**

   The original quality of an image is just as important as how you scan or retouch it. Images that are murky or fuzzy in print are even worse when viewed on a computer screen.

2. **Preview the image.**

   Most digital cameras let you preview images so that you can decide whether to keep or delete individual pictures before downloading to your computer. If you're working with a scanner, scanning programs let you make a quick *preview scan* of an image so that you can get an idea of what it looks like before you do the actual scan. When you press the Preview (or New Scan) button, the optical device in the scanner captures the image. A preview image appears on-screen, surrounded by a *marquee box* (a rectangle made up of dashes), as shown in Figure 5-8.

Figure 5-8: The marquee box lets you crop a preview image to make it smaller and reduce the file size.

3. **Crop the image.**

Cropping means that you resize the box around the image in order to select the portion of the image that you want to keep and leave out the parts of the image that aren't essential. Cropping an image is a good idea because it highlights the most important contents and reduces the file size. Reducing the file size of an image should always be one of your most important goals — the smaller the image, the quicker it appears in someone's browser window.

Almost all scanning and graphics programs offer separate options for cropping an image and reducing the image size. By cropping the image, you eliminate parts of the image you don't want and this *does* reduce the image size. But it doesn't reduce the size of the objects within the image. Resizing the overall image size is a separate step, which enables you to change the dimensions of the entire image without eliminating any contents.

4. **Select an input mode.**

Tell the scanner or graphics program how you want it to save the visual data — as colour, line art (used for black-and-white drawings), or greyscale (used for black-and-white photos).

5. **Set the resolution.**

Digital images are made up of little bits (dots) of computerised information called *pixels*. The more pixels per inch, the higher the level of detail. When you scan an image, you can tell the scanner to make the dots smaller (creating a smoother image) or larger (resulting in a more jagged image). This adjustment is called *setting the resolution* of the image. (When you take a digital photo, the resolution of the image depends on your camera's settings.)

When you're scanning for the Web, your images appear primarily on computer screens. Because many computer monitors can display resolutions only up to 72 dpi — a relatively rough resolution — this is an adequate resolution for a Web image. Using this coarse resolution has the advantage of keeping the image's file size small. Remember, the smaller the file size, the more quickly an image appears when your customers load your page in their Web browsers. (Alternatively, many designers scan at a fine resolution such as 300 dpi and reduce the file size in a graphics program.)

6. **Adjust contrast and brightness.**

Virtually all scanning programs and graphics editing programs provide brightness and contrast controls that you can adjust with your mouse to improve the image. If you're happy with the image as is, leave the brightness and contrast set where they are. (You can also leave the image as is and adjust brightness and contrast later in a separate graphics program, such as Paint Shop Pro Photo X2, which you can try out by downloading it from the Corel Web site, www.corel.com.)

7. **Reduce the image size.**

The old phrase 'good things come in small packages' is never more true than when you're improving your digital image. If you're scanning an image that is 8" × 10" and you're sure that it needs to be about 4" × 6" when it appears on your Web page, scan it at 50 per cent of the original size. This step reduces the file size right away and makes the file easier to transport — whether from your camera to your computer or your computer to your hosting service. Even more important, it appears more quickly in someone's Web browser.

8. **Scan away!**

Your scanner makes a beautiful whirring sound as it turns those colours into pixels. Because you're scanning only at 72 dpi, the process shouldn't take too long.

9. **Save the file.**

Now you can save your image to disk. Most programs let you do this by choosing File➪Save. In the dialogue box that appears, enter a name for your file and select a file format. (Because you're working with images to be published on the Web, remember to save either in GIF or JPEG format.)

Be sure to add the correct filename extension. Web browsers recognise only image files with extensions such as .gif, .jpg or .jpeg. If you name your image product and save it in GIF format, call it product.gif. If you save it in JPEG format and you're using a PC, call it product.jpg. On a Macintosh, call it product.jpeg.

For more details on scanning images, check out *Scanners For Dummies*, 2nd Edition, by Mark L. Chambers (Wiley Publishing, Inc.).

Creating a logo

An effective logo establishes your online business's graphic identity in no uncertain terms. A logo can be as simple as a rendering of the company name that imparts an official typeface or colour. Whatever text it includes, a *logo* is a small, self-contained graphic object that conveys the group's identity and purpose. Figure 5-9 shows some examples of logos.

Figure 5-9:
A good logo effectively combines colour, type and graphics to convey an organisation's identity or mission.

A logo doesn't have to be a fabulously complex drawing with drop-shadows and gradations of colour. A simple, type-only logo can be as good as gold. Pick a typeface you want, choose your graphic's outline version and fill the letters with colour.

GIF versus JPEG

Web site technology and HTML may have changed dramatically over the past several years, but for the most part, there are only two types of images as far as Web pages are concerned: GIF and JPEG. Both formats use methods that compress computer image files so that the visual information contained within them can be transmitted easily over computer networks. (PNG, a third format designed a few years ago as a successor to GIF, has never gained wide acceptance, and still isn't as widely used as GIF.)

GIF (pronounced either *jiff* or *giff*) stands for Graphics Interchange Format. GIF is best suited to text, line art or images with well-defined edges. Special types of GIF allow images with transparent backgrounds to be *interlaced* (broken into layers that appear gradually over slow connections) and animated. JPEG (pronounced *jay-peg*) stands for Joint Photographic Experts Group, the name of the group that originated the format. JPEG is preferred for large photos and continuous tones of greyscale or colour that need greater compression.

Interacting with Customers to Build Relationships

Quick, inexpensive and *personal:* These are three of the most important advantages that the Web has over traditional printed catalogues. The first two are obvious pluses. You don't have to wait for your online catalogue to be printed and distributed. On the Web, your contents are published and available to your customers right away and can be changed quickly and easily. Putting a catalogue on the Web eliminates (or, if publishing a catalogue on the Web allows you to reduce your print run, dramatically reduces) the cost of printing, which can result in big savings for you.

But the fact that online catalogues can be more personal than the printed variety is perhaps the biggest advantage of all. The personal touch comes from the Web's potential for *interactivity.* Getting your customers to click links makes them actively involved with your catalogue.

Getting positive email feedback

Playing hide and seek is fun when you're amusing your baby niece, but such an approach isn't a good way to build a solid base of customers. In fact, providing a way for your customers to interact with you so that they can reach you quickly may be the most important part of your Web site.

Add a simple *mailto* link like this:

Questions? Comments? Send email to: info@mycompany.com

A mailto link gets its name from the HTML command that programmers use to create it. When visitors click the email address, their email program opens a new email message window with your email address already entered. That way, they have only to enter a subject line, type the message and click send to send you their thoughts.

Most Web page creation programs make it easy to create a mailto link. For example, if you use Dreamweaver, follow these steps:

 1. **Launch and open the Web page to which you want to add your email link.**

2. **Position your mouse arrow and click the spot on the page where you want the address to appear.**

   The convention is to put your email address at or near the bottom of a Web page. A vertical blinking cursor appears at the location where you want to insert the address.

3. **Choose Insert➪Email Link.**

   The Insert Email Link dialogue box appears.

4. **In the Text box, type the text that you want to appear on your Web page.**

   You don't have to type your email address; you can also type **Webmaster**, **Customer Service** or your own name.

5. **In the email box, type your email address.**

6. **Click OK.**

   The Insert Email Link dialogue box closes and you return to the Dreamweaver Document window, where your email link appears in blue and is underlined to signify that it is now a clickable link.

Other editors work similarly but don't give you a menu command called Email Link. For example, in World Wide Web Weaver, a shareware program for the Macintosh OS, you choose Tags➪Mail. A dialogue box called Mail Editor appears. Enter your email address and the text you want to appear as the highlighted link and then click OK to add the mailto link to your page.

The drawback to publishing your email address directly on your Web page is that you're certain to get unsolicited email messages (commonly called *spam*) sent to that address. Hiding your email address behind generic link text (such as Webmaster) may help reduce your chances of attracting spam. But unfortunately spammers are clever and employing new tactics all the time. Doing business on the Web means publishing an email address on your Web site in some way is imperative, so keep your spam and antivirus software up to date to help minimise the amount of time-consuming junk that gets through to your mailbox. See Chapter 6 for more on security and antivirus protection.

Web page forms that aren't off-putting

You don't have to do much Web surfing before you become intimately acquainted with how Web page forms work, at least from the standpoint of someone who has to fill them out in order to sign up for Web hosting or to download software.

When it comes to creating your own Web site, however, you become conscious of how useful forms are as a means of gathering essential marketing information about your customers. They give your visitors a place to sound off, ask questions and generally get involved with your online business.

Be clear and use commonsense when creating your order form. Here are some general guidelines on how to organise your form and what you need to include:

- ✔ **Make it easy on the customer:** Keep forms short — minimise the amount of information that has to be filled out. Whenever possible, add pull-down menus with pre-entered options to your *form fields* (text boxes that visitors use to enter information). That way, users don't have to wonder about things such as whether you want them to spell out a state or use the abbreviation.

- ✔ **Validate the information:** You can use a programming language — for example, JavaScript — to ensure that users enter information correctly, that all fields are completely filled out and so on. You may have to hire someone to add the appropriate code to the order form, but the expense is worth it to save you from having to call customers to verify or correct information that they missed or submitted incorrectly.

- ✔ **Provide a help number:** Give people a phone number to call if they have questions or want to check on an order.

- ✔ **Return an acknowledgment:** Let customers know that you received their order and are shipping the merchandise immediately, or you're going to contact them if more information is needed.

As usual, good Web page authoring and editing programs make it a snap to create the text boxes, check boxes, buttons and other parts of a form that the user fills out. The other part of a form, the computer script that receives the data and processes it so that you can read and use the information, is not as simple. See Chapter 8 for details.

Not so long ago, you had to write or edit a scary CGI script in order to set up forms processing on your Web site. These days an alternative is available that makes the process of creating a working Web page form accessible to non-programmers like the rest of us. Web businesses, such as Response-o-matic (www.response-o-matic.com) and FormMail.To (www.formmail.to), lead you through the process of setting up a form and providing you with the CGI script that receives the data and forwards it to you.

Blogs that promote discussion

Most blogs give readers the chance to comment on individual comments the author has made. On Greg's blog, for instance, which was created with Blogger, he makes comments and readers can immediately respond. This is a standard feature to give readers the opportunity to comment on what you've written.

On blogs that attract a wide following, like David Nason (`blogs. theaustralian.news.com.au/davidnason/`) or Duncan Riley (`www.duncanriley.com`), comments by the respective authors generate long discussions by a community of devoted readers. Karen Cheng (`www.karencheng.com.au`) is a mum in Perth with two young kids and her blog is about her interests, family and everyday life. The blog is regularly in the top 20 most popular blogs in Australia. Find out more about blogs in Chapter 3.

Providing a guestbook

If you don't have a blog, a guestbook on your Web site can add a whole other dimension to your business by making your customers feel that they're part of a thriving community. When you provide a guestbook on one of your business's Web pages, your clients and other visitors can check out who else has been there and what others think about the site and then add their own comments as well.

If you set out to create your own Web page guestbook from scratch, you'd have to create a form, write a script (fairly complicated code that tells a computer what to do), test the code and so on. Thankfully, an easier way to add a guestbook is available: You simply register with a special Web business that provides free guestbooks to users. One such organisation, Lycos, offers a guestbook service through its Html Gear site (another organisation is Bravenet).

If you register with Html Gear's service, you can have your own guestbook right away with no fuss. (Actually, Html Gear's guestbook program resides on one of its Web servers; you just add the text-entry portion to your own page.) Here's how to do it:

1. **Connect to the Internet, start up your Web browser and go to** `htmlgear.lycos.com/specs/guest.html`.

2. **Scroll down the page and click the Get This Gear! link.**

   You go to the Network Membership page.

3. **Click the Sign Up button and follow the instructions on subsequent pages to register for the guestbook and other software on the Html Gear site.**

   The program asks you to provide your own personal information, choose a name and password for your guestbook, enter the URL of the Web page on which you want the guestbook to appear and provide keywords that describe your page.

   After you register, a page titled Gear Manager appears.

4. **Click Add Gear and then Get Gear next to Guest Gear.**

   After a few seconds, the Create Guest Gear page appears. This page contains a form that you need to fill out in order to create the guestbook *text-entry fields* (the text boxes and other items that visitors use to submit information to you) for your Web page.

5. **Fill out the Create Guest Gear form.**

   This form lets you name your guestbook and customise how you want visitors to interact with you. For instance, you can configure the guestbook to send you an email notification whenever someone posts a message.

6. **When you're done filling out the form, click Save & Create.**

   The Get Code page appears. A box contains the code you need to copy and add to the HTML for your Web page.

7. **Select the code.**

   Position your mouse arrow at the beginning of the code (just before the first line, which looks like this: `<!-- \/ GuestGEAR Code by http://htmlgear.com \/ ->`), press and hold down your mouse button and scroll across the code to the last line, which reads: `<!-- /\ End GuestGEAR Code /\ -->`.

   The code is highlighted to show that it has been selected.

8. **Choose Edit⇨Copy to copy the selected code to your computer's Clipboard.**

9. **Launch your Web editor, if it isn't running already, and open the Web page you want to edit in your Web editor window.**

   If you're working in a program (such as Dreamweaver) that shows the HTML for a Web page while you edit it, you can move on to Step 10. If, on the other hand, your editor hides the HTML from you, you have to use your editor's menu options to view the HTML source for your page. The exact menu command varies from program to program. Usually, though, the option is contained on the View menu. In FrontPage, for example, you click the HTML tab at the bottom of the window. The HTML for the Web page you want to edit then appears.

10. **Click the spot on the page where you want to paste the HTML code for the guestbook.**

    How do you know where this spot is? Well, you have to add the code in the BODY section of a Web page. This is the part of the page that is contained between two HTML tags, <BODY> and </BODY>. You can't go wrong with pasting the code just before the </BODY> tag — or just before your return email address or any other material you want to keep at the bottom of the page. The following example indicates the proper placement for the guestbook code:

    ```
    <HTML>
    <HEAD>
    <TITLE>Sign My Guestbook</TITLE>
    </HEAD>
    <BODY>
    The body of your Web page goes here; this is the part
    that appears on the Web.
    Paste your guestbook code here!
    </BODY>
    </HTML>
    ```

11. **Choose Edit⇨Paste.**

    The guestbook code is added to your page.

12. **Close your Web editor's HTML window.**

    Exactly how you do this varies depending on the program. If you have a separate HTML window open, click the close box (X) in the upper-right corner of the HTML window, if you're working in a Windows environment. (If you're working on a Mac, close the window by clicking the close box in the upper-left corner of the window that displays the HTML.)

    The HTML code disappears and you return to your Web editor's main window.

13. **Choose File⇨Save to save your changes.**

14. Preview your work in your Web browser window.

The steps involved in previewing also vary from editor to editor. Some editors have a Preview toolbar button that you click to view your page in a Web browser. Otherwise, launch your Web browser to preview your page as follows:

If you use Internet Explorer, choose File➪Open, click the name of the file you just saved in the Open dialogue box, then click Open to open the page.

The page opens in your Web browser, with a new Guestbook button added to it, as shown in Figure 5-10.

Now when visitors to your Web page click the Sign My Guestbook link, they go to a page that has a form they can fill out. Clicking the View My Guestbook link enables visitors to view the messages that other visitors have entered into your guestbook.

The problem with adding a link to a service that resides on another Web site is that it makes your Web pages load more slowly. First, your visitor's browser loads the text on your page. Then it loads the images from top to bottom. Besides this, it has to make a link to the Html Gear site in order to load the guestbook. If you decide to add a guestbook, images, or other elements that reside on another Web site, be sure to test your page and make sure that you're satisfied with how long the contents take to appear. Also make sure to use the 'Moderation' feature that enables you to screen postings to your guestbook. That way, you can delete obscene, unfair or libellous postings before they go online.

Figure 5-10:
Add a
guestbook
link to your
Web page.

Live chat

After visitors start coming to your site, the next step is to retain those visitors. A good way to do this is by building a sense of community by including a live chat option or a discussion area on your site.

Live chat allows you to offer immediate help to Web site visitors if they need it. Even if visitors don't use the live chat, having this option helps to build trust and credibility because they can see you're online and available to them. Usually you would have a live chat icon or button that visitors can click on, or a chat window like an instant messaging application where visitors can just start typing and you can both see a log of comments exchanged between each other.

A number of free Web-based live chat applications are available for you to download and add to your site. Check out Google Talk (www.google.com/talk), Meebo Me (www.meebome.com) and Digsby (www.digsby.com).

A discussion area takes the form of back-and-forth messages on topics of mutual interest. Each person can read previously posted messages and either respond or start a new topic of discussion. For an example of a discussion area that's tied to an online business, visit the TradingPost (forums.tradingpost.com.au) discussion areas, one of which is shown in Figure 5-11. TradingPost is a highly regarded classifieds site for buying and selling second-hand goods. The discussion boards give readers a place to bring up questions and issues they're having. This option encourages visitors to interact and visit the site more often, creating TradingPost's own online community.

The topics discussed don't have to be about your own particular niche in your business field. In fact, the discussions are likely to be more lively if your visitors can discuss concerns about your area of business in general — whether flower arranging, boat sales, tax preparation, clock repair, computers or whatever.

How do you start a discussion area? The basic first step is to install a special computer script on the computer that hosts your Web site. (Again, discussing this prospect with your Web hosting service beforehand is essential — check out Chapter 4 for information on what to expect from a Web host.) When visitors come to your site, their Web browsers access the script, enabling them to enter comments and read other messages.

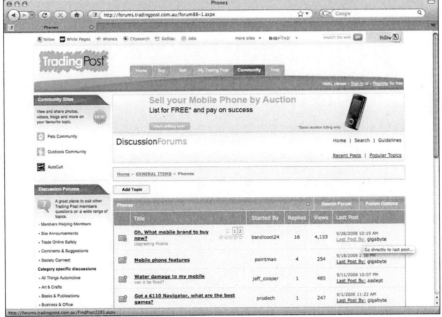

Figure 5-11:
A discussion area stimulates interest and interaction among like-minded customers.

Here are some specific ways to prepare a discussion area for your site:

- Copy a bulletin-board or discussion-group script from either of these sites:
    - phpBB.com (www.phpbb.com)
    - eXtropia.com (www.extropia.com/applications.html)
- Start your own forum on a service such as Google Groups or Yahoo!7 Groups:
    - groups.google.com.au
    - au.groups.yahoo.com

Setting Up Extreme Web Pages: Advanced Layouts

People who have some experience creating Web sites typically use cascading style sheets (CSS) these days. On the other hand, you may be an adventurous type who wants to start an online business but you haven't created a Web site before. You may have an idea of what you want your site to look like, but start talking HTML and CSS and we may as well be talking a foreign language. So this section includes some explanations of what languages and methods Web designers use when creating Web sites. If you decide to delve right in to this level, instead of hiring a pro or using WYSIWYG software (refer to Chapter 4), you need to know what's what. Spend a few weeks learning HTML before you jump in and start building your site. People are easily put off by poor design, slow loading sites or areas that are half finished or don't work. So take the time to learn the languages needed and test your site thoroughly before putting it online for all to see.

Choosing a layout

Start by deciding on a layout for your site. Are you going to use a simple two- or three-column layout or something fancier? Where is each element to sit on the page? Find a place for your logo, navigation buttons or links, contact details, introductory text, products and call to action. Are you going to have any feature boxes or promotional items highlighted? Figures 5-12, 5-13 and 5-14 show some standard layout examples.

Start by laying out all the elements of your page in a graphics package like Adobe Photoshop or Paint Shop Pro. Professional Web designers follow this approach, which allows you to move elements around in a pictorial way and helps you decide what your site is going to look like before you get your hands dirty and start coding.

Figure 5-12:
This Web site layout has a header and a three-column layout with the navigation buttons on the left.

Figure 5-13:
This Web site layout has a header with the navigation buttons along the top and a two-column layout. This layout also makes use of feature boxes to highlight the most important things.

Figure 5-14:
This layout has three columns and two sets of navigation. Along the top are the standard site pages such as Home. The side navigation contains the categories of products to navigate its catalogue.

Especially for e-commerce (or online-shopping) sites, the crucial elements are easy-to-use navigation and search features (so shoppers can find their way around), as well as the speed of the checkout or place-an-order process.

Purchasing a design template

Perhaps laying out graphics is not your forte or you want a pretty standard layout and want to save some time. Plenty of Internet sites allow you to download design templates either for a fee or free. The most well known is Template Monster (www.templatemonster.com) where you can browse more than 5,000 Web site templates!

When purchasing a design template, check what file formats you're provided with. At the least it helps to get the Photoshop source file (.PSD). Being provided with the HTML/CSS code for the template can save you a lot of time too. Most template sites allow you to download a free sample so you can see what files they provide and the quality of their designs and code.

Make sure you check the copyright or licence requirements of any templates before you download and use them.

Other template sites worth a look are

- www.boxedart.com
- www.freelayouts.com
- www.interspire.com/templates

All these acronyms — HTML, XML, CSS

After the look and layout of your site is decided, you can roll up your sleeves and start building (or coding) your site. One of the first things you're going to notice is that lots of acronyms are used to describe how Web sites are built, such as HTML, XHTML, XML and CSS. In this section, you find out what these acronyms stand for.

HTML stands for *HyperText Markup Language* and is the markup language or code used to publish Web pages. HTML allows you to specify how information is displayed in a Web browser through a series of tags, surrounded by angle brackets.

TIP

One way to learn how to write HTML is to look at the code behind other existing Web pages. You can find the source code behind a page by choosing 'View' from the top browser tool bar and then clicking 'Source'. This view shows the code in a text editor. You can even save the view to play around with the HTML code and see what each line does.

TECHNICAL STUFF

A quick HTML primer

Thanks to Web page creation tools, you don't have to master HyperText Markup Language (HTML) in order to create your own Web pages, although some knowledge of HTML is helpful when editing pages and understanding how they're put together.

HTML is a markup language, not a computer programming language. You use it in much the same way that editors used to mark up copy before they gave it to typesetters. A markup language allows you to identify major sections of a document, such as body text, headings, title and so on. A software program (in the case of HTML, a Web browser) is programmed to recognise the markup language and to display the formatting elements that you have marked.

Markup tags are the basic building blocks of HTML as well as eXtensible Markup Language (XML). Tags enable you to structure the appearance of your document so that, when the document is transferred from one computer to another, it looks the way you described it. HTML tags appear within angle brackets. Most HTML commands require a *start tag* at the beginning of the section and an *end tag* (which usually begins with a backslash) at the end.

For example, if you place the HTML tags `<b>` and `</b>` around the phrase 'This text will be bold', the words appear in bold type on any browser that displays them, no matter whether the browser is running on a Windows-based PC, a UNIX workstation, a Macintosh, a palm device that's Web enabled, or any other computer.

Many HTML commands are accompanied by *attributes*, which provide a browser with more specific instructions on what action the tag is to perform. In the following line of HTML, `src` is an attribute that works with the `<img>` tag to identify a file to display:

```
<img src="house.jpg">
```

Each attribute is separated from a HTML command by a single blank space. The equal sign (=) is an operator that introduces the value on which the attribute and command functions. Usually, the value is a filename or a directory path leading to a specific file that is to be displayed on a Web page. The straight (as opposed to curly) quotation marks around the value are essential for the HTML command to work.

XML stands for *eXtensible Markup Language*. This markup language allows developers to define their own markup language. For example MathML is a standardised language created in XML to define mathematics. You're probably going to be too busy developing your online business to create your own markup language! However, if you want to learn more, refer to the World Wide Web Consortium (W3C) Web site (www.w3.org).

XHTML stands for *eXtensible HyperText Markup Language*. This stricter and cleaner version of HTML is popular with many Web designers instead of HTML in order to be more compliant with W3C standards (see www.w3.org).

CSS stands for *cascading style sheets*. CSS, as defined by the W3C, is a simple mechanism for adding style such as fonts, colours and spacing, to Web documents.

Cascading style sheets are the tools of choice among designers who want to observe standards that have been established on the Internet and who want to make sure their Web pages appear the same from one browser to another and from one computer to another. If you have a choice as to how you want to lay out a page, and you want to precisely position items while at the same time creating layouts that are easily updatable, we urge you to look into CSS.

CSS is a subject for a book all by itself, so we're not going to get into it in any great detail here. If you want to create full-featured, cutting-edge Web layouts, you need to use CSS. The major Web design programs — Dreamweaver and Expression Web — both support CSS designs. Rather than learning CSS from scratch, choose one of these applications and let it do the work for you.

A *style sheet* is a document that contains the formatting for a Web page. By separating the formatting from the content, you quickly apply the same formatting to multiple Web pages. You can also update the design of an entire Web site easily: Rather than changing a heading from Arial to Verdana 20 separate times on 20 Web pages, for example, you have to change it only once and all the pages that have the style sheet attached to them have their headings updated all at once.

W3C and World standards

W3C stands for the *World Wide Web Consortium*. Created in October 1994, the W3C is working to standardise the Web and creates and maintains WWW standards.

Standards like CSS and XML are important because they enable you to reach the widest set of viewers possible.

The advantages of building a standards-compliant Web site include:

- **Accessibility:** Making it easier for people with special needs to use the Web, as well as people using any size device, from a handheld PDA or phone to a high-end workstation.

- **Stability:** Web standards are designed with forward and backward compatibility in mind — Web pages using old versions of the standards continue to work in new browsers and Web pages using new versions of the standards 'gracefully degrade' to produce an acceptable result in older browsers. Standards-compliant Web sites are easier for any designer to work with; so, if down the track you want to hire a professional designer to add to your site, they're going to be able to understand the code.

- **Visibility:** Search engines can better access and evaluate the information on the pages of your site, and they're indexed more accurately.

When in doubt, hire a pro

Building a Web site, even a small and simple one, is a time-consuming task. While you can build a simple Web site without a lot of technical knowledge, rarely does it look professional, and the potential pitfalls are many.

One of the keys to being a successful business owner is recognising your strengths and weaknesses — 'do what you do best and outsource the rest'!

If you're tempted, due to budget constraints, to use a friend or relative because they have some IT knowledge and are enthusiastic about your business idea, perhaps think about using them to manage the project, and to select and work with the professional Web designer.

In many cases, the initial cost of hiring someone to help you design your online business can be a good investment in the long run. You can save a lot of time and get your Web site online quicker. Keep in mind that after you pay someone to help you develop a look, you can probably implement it in the future more easily yourself. For example:

- ✔ If you need business cards, stationery, brochures, or other printed material in addition to a Web site, hiring someone to develop a consistent look for everything at the beginning is worth the money.
- ✔ You can pay a designer to get you started with a logo, colour selections and page layouts. Then you can save money by adding text yourself.
- ✔ If you're artistically challenged, consider the benefits of having your logo or other artwork drawn by a real artist.

When getting a quote from a Web designer, consider asking the designer to build your site with a content management system (CMS). Having a CMS means your site content is stored in a database and gives you much more control to maintain and add to the Web site after the initial building of the site is complete.

Consider popular CMSs such as:

- ✔ Drupal (`drupal.org`)
- ✔ Joomla (`www.joomla.org`)
- ✔ Plone (`plone.org`)

The ideal Web designer to build your site needs to give a satisfactory answer to the following questions:

- ✔ How long has the Web designer been in business?
- ✔ Is the business a one-man-band or is it an established team?
- ✔ Does the designer have the skills and experience to develop the type of site you have specified?
- ✔ Does the designer seem to be a good listener?
- ✔ Does the designer understand the project?
- ✔ Has the designer built Web sites for your type of organisation before?
- ✔ How much experience does the designer have in developing Web sites similar to the one you're planning to develop?

- ✔ Is what the designer proposes to do for you able to be viewed on a live Web site that you can see and explore?
- ✔ Is the designer's written submission easy to understand?
- ✔ Is the designer's solution value for money?
- ✔ Does the designer's proposal indicate that it is likely to add value to the project beyond merely providing what you asked for?
- ✔ Does the designer appear to be honest and professional?
- ✔ Does the designer's approach allow you to maintain the site easily and cost effectively yourself after it has been launched?
- ✔ Have you spoken to previous clients and heard good things about the designers?

Most professional designers charge $60–$120 an hour for their work. As with anything, you're best to seek more than one quote and not base your final choice on cost alone, but on the merits of each designer. This approach can help to ensure you're happy with the finished result.

The Web site is the main asset of an online business, so investing capital up front to have your site built properly and in a timely manner is money well spent in the long run. Not only does this get you off to a good start, but your site serves you for longer and is easier to maintain and change as your business grows.

Chapter 6

Creating a Secure Shopping Experience

In This Chapter

▶ Understanding the purchasing needs of online consumers

▶ Managing your sales stock: Sourcing, replenishing inventory and fulfilling orders

▶ Protecting your customers' data (and your own) through passwords, firewalls and backups

*A*s the owner of an online business, you need to create the right atmosphere for making purchases. Some simple steps make the customer feel secure so that you're paid promptly and reliably. You also need to protect yourself financially and guard your business data. The whole idea of security can seem intimidating when you consider the viruses and other attacks that are proliferating along with the always-on broadband Internet connections, which are especially vulnerable to these intrusions. In this chapter, we discuss some technologies and strategies that can keep your data secure. Some of these measures are easy to put into practice and especially important for home-based businesspeople. Others are technically challenging to implement on your own. But even if you have your Web host or a consultant do the work, familiarising yourself with Internet security schemes is the prudent way to go.

Fostering a good atmosphere for e-commerce is also a matter of presenting your merchandise clearly and making it easy for customers to find, choose and purchase them. Making changes to your Web site is relatively easy. You can remake your store's *front door* (your home page) in a matter of minutes.

You can revamp your sales catalogue in less than an hour. Making regular improvements and updates to your online store doesn't just mean changing the colours or the layout, which is the part of your operation that customers notice, on your Web site. It also means improving back-office functions that customers don't see, such as inventory management, invoices, labels, packing and shipping. When you test, check and revise your Web site based on its current performance, you can boost your revenue and increase sales as well as make your Web site more usable.

Here's a short list of what you need to do to be a successful e-commerce businessperson: Set up the right atmosphere for making purchases, provide options for payment and keep sensitive information private. Oh, and don't forget that your main goal is to get goods to the customer safely and on time. In this chapter, we describe ways in which you can implement these essential online business strategies to ensure a positive shopping experience for your customers.

Meeting the Needs of Online Shoppers

You've heard it before, but the importance of understanding the needs of online shoppers and doing your best to meet them can't be emphasised enough. That's the best way to have a healthy bank balance.

Showing what you've got

Customers may end up buying an item in a brick-and-mortar store, but chances are that they saw it online first. More and more shoppers are assuming that legitimate stores have a Web site and an online sales catalogue that is likely to include even more items, accompanied by detailed descriptions, than a shopper would find by going to the store in person.

'It's not enough to just say we have this or that product line for sale. Until we actually add an individual item to our online store, with pictures and prices, we won't sell it,' says Ernie Preston, who helped create an 84,000-item online catalogue for a brick-and-mortar tool company that is profiled later in this chapter. 'As soon as you put it in your online catalogue, you'll get a call about it. Shopping on the Web is the convenience factor that people want.'

Making it easy to choose and purchase

Because most customers are comparison shopping, you're wise to put the cost, measurements and other important features next to each item to promote speed and convenience.

Microsoft Office 2007 gives you access to clip-art images that help highlight sales items. Figure 6-1 shows an example of how you can edit an HTML Web page file with Word by inserting an image from the Clip Art task pane. (You can find more clip-art images at the Microsoft Office Clip Art & Media Home, office.microsoft.com/clipart/default.aspx.)

When you make the process of finding products easy (for example, seeing a picture and completing a purchase in minimum clicks), most of your Web site visitors (who are otherwise busy and impatient) are likely to remember and return to your site.

If you have stock you want to clear or particular items on sale, make these clearly visible from the front page to capture impulse buyers who are in a hurry.

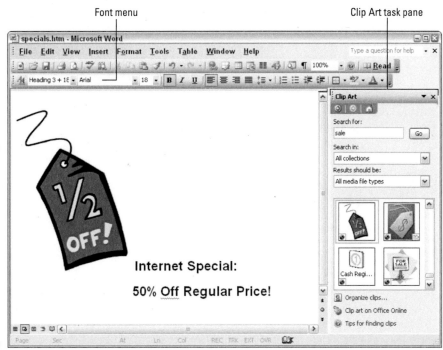

Figure 6-1
Use graphics to call attention to the information your customer wants the most: The price.

Earning trust to gain a sale

Although e-commerce is more and more common, many customers need to have their fears addressed. They want to be sure that providing their names, phone numbers and credit card information aren't going to lead to identity theft or fraudulent charges on their credit card. At the very least, they want to avoid being flooded with unwanted emails. In regard to the sale at hand, many fear that merchandise is going to be paid for but not received.

State your policies clearly and often, providing assurance that you don't give out personal data without consent. If you plan to accept credit card orders, get an account with a Web host that provides a *secure server*, which is software that encrypts data exchanged with a browser. And be sure to include comments from satisfied customers. If you run an eBay store, your feedback rating provides assurance.

You can have your site evaluated and display a recognisable trust seal on your site to build credibility and confidence among your clients. A trust seal is a badge or picture displayed on your Web site to show it has been thoroughly checked and established as a site that can be trusted. Examples of popular trust seals include:

- VeriSign (www.verisign.com.au)
- TRUSTe (www.truste.org)
- Trust Guard (www.trust-guard.com)

Sites like ShopSafe Australia (www.shopsafe.com.au) and New Zealand (www.shopsafe.co.nz) are safe shopping directories. Submitting your Web site is free. ShopSafe examines your site based on a set of criteria and if your application is approved you're listed as a safe shopping Web site. You can also display the ShopSafe logo on your site.

Giving the essentials

Remember that one of the big advantages of operating a business online is space. Not only do you have plenty of room in which to provide full descriptions of your sale items, but you also have no reason to skimp on the details that you provide about your business and services. Here are some suggestions of how to provide information that your customer may want:

- ✔ If you sell clothing, include a page with size and measurement charts.
- ✔ If you sell food, provide weights, ingredients and nutritional information.
- ✔ If you sell programming, Web design or traditional graphic design, provide samples of your work, links to Web pages you've created and testimonials from satisfied clients.
- ✔ If you're a musician, publish a link to a short sound file of your work.

Don't be reluctant to tell people ways that your products and services are better than others. Visit the EziBuy online catalogue (www.ezibuy.co.nz) for good examples of how this well-established marketer describes the quality of its wares.

Managing Goods and Services

Shoppers on the Web are continually in search of The New: The next new product, the latest price reduction or rebate, the latest comment in a blog, or today's headlines. As a provider of content, whether in the form of words, images or products for sale, your job is to manage that content to keep it fresh and available. You also need to handle returns, deal with shipping options and replenish stock when it's purchased as we describe in the sections that follow.

Handling returns

Your returns policy depends on the place where you make your sales. If you sell primarily on eBay, you should accept returns, if only because many of the most experienced and successful sellers do. That doesn't mean you need to accept every single item that is returned. Most businesses place restrictions on when they'll receive a return and send a refund. The items must be returned within 14 days, for instance; the packages must be unopened; the merchandise must not be damaged.

Adding shipping rates

As part of creating a usable e-commerce catalogue, provide customers with shipping costs for your merchandise. Shipping rates can be difficult to calculate. They depend on your own geographic location, the type, size and weight of your merchandise, as well as the location where you're planning to ship. If you're a small-scale operation and you process each transaction manually, you may want to ship everything a standard way (standard post, express post or courier). Then you can keep a copy of your shipper's charges with you and calculate each package's shipping cost individually.

You can also save time by using the shipping calculator provided by Australia Post (www1.auspost.com.au/pac). Just go to the site's home page, choose Calculate postage rates and then select whether you're sending a letter or a parcel within Australia or internationally. In New Zealand, go to the NZ Post home page (www.nzpost.co.nz), select Rate Finder, choose where you're sending the parcel from and to, enter the parcel weight and click Next. You're then asked for the parcel length, width and thickness.

Maintaining inventory

Shoppers on the Web want things to happen instantly. If they discover that you're out of stock of an item they want, they're likely to switch to another online business instead of waiting for you to restock that item. With that in mind, obey the basic principle of planning to be successful: Instead of ordering the bare minimum of this or that item, make sure you have enough to spare. Too much inventory initially is better than running out at some point.

Rely on software or management services to help you keep track of what you have. If you feel at ease working with databases, record your initial inventory in an Access or SQL database. A database forces you to record each sale manually so you know how many items are left. You could connect your sales catalogue to your database by using a program, such as ColdFusion from Adobe. Such a program can update the database on the fly when sales are made. But you may need to hire someone with Web programming experience to set up the system for you and make sure it actually works.

If you use a shopping cart application like osCommerce (www.oscommerce.com) or X-cart (www.x-cart.com), you can choose to have inventory tracked automatically for you. Whether you do the work yourself or use a hosted service, you have to be able to answer basic questions such as:

- ✔ **When should you reorder?** Establish *reorder points* — points at which you automatically reorder supplies (when you get down to two or three items left, for instance).

- ✔ **How many do you have in stock right now?** Make sure that you have enough merchandise on hand not only for everyday demand but also in case a product becomes popular or the holiday season brings about a dramatic increase in orders.

An e-commerce hosting service can also help you with questions that go beyond the basics, such as the past purchasing history of customers. Knowing what customers have purchased in the past gives you the ability to suggest *up-sells* — additional items the person may want. But in the early stages, making sure that you have a cushion of additional inventory for the time when your site becomes a big success is your primary responsibility.

Making Sure Your Business Is Safe

Working at home or even in a small office carries its own set of safety concerns for small-business owners. Chances are you don't have an IT professional at hand to make sure your files and your network are safe from intrusion. Some safe computing practices, such as using password protection, making backups and installing antivirus software, can go a long way towards keeping your data secure, even if you never have to get into more technical subjects such as public-key encryption.

Separating the personal and the professional

Many entrepreneurs who run businesses from their homes face a simple logistical problem: Their work takes over their home. Boxes, computers, phones and other gadgets create disruptions that can drive everyone crazy. Here are some simple steps that can help you set more clearly defined boundaries between work and home life.

When the computer is a group sport

A lot can be said for having at least two separate computers — one for personal use and one for business use. The idea is that you set up your system so that you have to log on to your business computer with a username and password. (For suggestions on how to devise a good password that's difficult to crack, see the section 'Picking passwords that are hard to guess' later in this chapter.)

If you have only one computer, passwords can still provide a measure of protection. Windows gives you the ability to set up different user profiles, each associated with its own password. User profiles and passwords don't necessarily protect your business files, but they convey to your family members that they should use their own software, stick to their own directories and not try to explore your company data.

Folder Guard, a program by WinAbility Software Corporation (www.winability.com/folderguard), enables you to hide or password-protect files or folders on your computer. The software works with Windows 95 or later versions. You can choose from the Standard version (which is intended for home users) or the Professional version (which is designed for business customers). A 14-day trial version is available for download from the WinAbility Web site; if you want to keep the Standard version of Folder Guard, you have to pay US$39.95 (or US$59.95 for the Professional version).

One phone may not be enough

Having a devoted phone line not only makes your business seem more serious, but also separates your business calls from your personal calls. If you need a phone line to connect to the Net, you then have a choice of which line to use for your modem.

The next step is to set up your business phone with its own answering machine or voice mail. You can then install privacy features, such as caller ID, on your business line as needed.

Several useful Web sites provide tips and news on telephone services, not only for small businesses but also for personal use. Check out Consumer NZ (www.consumer.org.nz), PhoneChoice (www.phonechoice.com.au), Small Enterprise Telecommunications Centre Limited (SETEL) (www.setel.com.au) and Australian Telecommunications Users Group Limited (ATUG) (www.atug.com.au).

Heading off disasters

When you're lying awake at night, you can be anxious about all sorts of grim disasters: Flood, fire, theft, computer virus, you name it. Prevention is always better than a cure, so this chapter covers steps you can take to prevent problems. But, should a problem arise, there are also ways to recover more easily.

Insurance ... the least you can do

We can all think of ways to spend money that are a whole lot more fun than paying insurance premiums. Yet, every month or year we pay to protect ourselves in case something goes wrong with our house, car, body and so on. And yes, there's another item to add to the list: Protecting your business investment by obtaining insurance that specifically covers you against hardware damage, theft and loss of data. You can also go a step further and obtain a policy that covers the cost of data entry or equipment rental that would be necessary to recover your business information. Here are some specific strategies:

- ✔ Make a list of all your hardware and software and how much each item cost. Store a copy of the list in a safe place, such as a fireproof safe, filing cabinet or safe-deposit box.

- ✔ Take photos of your computer setup in case you need to make an insurance claim. Put the photos in the same safe place.

- ✔ Save your electronic files on CD or DVD and put the disc in a safe storage location, such as a safe-deposit box.

Investigate the many options available to you for insuring your computer hardware and software. Your current home and/or contents insurance may offer coverage, but make sure the dollar amount is sufficient for replacement. You may need to either increase your coverage or take out an additional home-office policy for computer hardware and software.

If you use a laptop, check whether your insurance covers this precious business asset while in transit or away from your home office.

Think ahead to the unthinkable

The Gartner Group estimates that two out of five businesses that experience a major disaster go out of business within five years. Our guess is that the three that are able to get back up on their feet and running quickly are those that already had recovery plans in place. Even if your company is small, be prepared for trouble such as floods, electrical storms or fires. A recovery effort may include the following strategies:

- **Backup power systems:** What are you going to do if the power goes out and you can't access the Web? Consider a battery backup system, such as APC Back-UPS (www.apc.com/products). This system instantly switches your computers to battery power when the electricity goes out so you can save your data and switch to laptops. A version that runs for five to ten minutes costs US$110. Even more important, make sure that your Web host has a backup power supply so that your store can remain online in case of a power outage.

- **Data storage:** This step is probably the most practical and essential disaster recovery step for small or home-based businesses. Back up your files on to a USB key, portable hard drive or a computer that's not located in the place where you physically work. Also consider storing your files with an online storage service such as CyberSecure (www.cybersecure.com.au), Carbonite (www.carbonite.com.au), Backup247 (www.backup247.com.au) or Back It Up (www.backitup.co.nz).

- **Telecommunications:** Having some alternative method of communication available in case your phone system goes down ensures that you're always in touch. The obvious choice is a mobile phone. Also set up a voice mailbox so that customers and suppliers can leave messages for you even if you can't answer the phone.

Creating a plan is a waste of time if you don't regularly set aside time to keep it up to date. Back up your data on a regular basis, purchase additional equipment if you need it, and make arrangements to use other computers and offices if you need to — in other words, *implement* your plan. You owe it not only to yourself but also to your customers to be prepared in case of disaster.

Antivirus protection without a needle

As an online businessperson, you download files, receive disks from customers and vendors, and exchange email with all sorts of people you've never met before. Surf safely by installing antivirus programs, such as:

- **AVG AntiVirus by GriSoft** (www.avg.com): Many users who find Norton Internet Security too intrusive (it leaves lots of files on your computer and consumes a great deal of memory) turn to this product, which comes in a free version as well as a more full-featured Professional version for US$34.99.

✔ **Norton Internet Security by Symantec Corporation (**www.symantec. com/en/au/product**):** This application, which includes an antivirus program as well as a firewall and lists for $99.95, automates many security functions and is especially good for beginners. A stand-alone version, Norton Anti-Virus, is available for $59.95, but Greg highly recommends the more full-featured package, which includes a firewall that blocks many other dangerous types of intrusions, such as trojan horses.

✔ **VirusScan by McAfee (**www.mcafee.com/au**):** This program is the leading competitor to Norton Anti-Virus. VirusScan is included in McAfee Internet Security, which includes a firewall and costs $99.95, or you can purchase VirusScan on its own for $59.95.

Trend Micro HouseCall (housecall.trendmicro.com/au) is a free online virus scanner for checking if your computer has been infected by viruses or spyware. We don't recommend using this program as your only virus protection because you need something installed locally on your computer to provide full protection. But HouseCall is great if you think you have been infected by a trojan or spyware and your virus software isn't able to clean or remove it. This way, you have another level of checking to be sure your computer is clean.

USB keys or thumbdrives (small storage devices that plug into the USB port on your computer that are often used instead of floppy disks and CDs) are popular little gadgets these days but, due to their miniature size and portability, they're easy to lose or misplace. At the very least, you should password-protect any important files. You can also install protection software designed especially for USB devices, such as VirusScan USB by McAfee (au.mcafee.com/root/package.asp?pkgid=269).

Antivirus protection is another area that demands your attention on a regular basis. Viruses change all the time and new ones appear regularly. The antivirus program you install one day may not be able to handle the viruses that appear just a few weeks or months later. You may want to pick an antivirus program that doesn't charge excessive amounts for regular updates (for instance, those for which you have to pay for a new version every year).

Low- and high-tech locks

If you mention the word 'security' to a Web surfer or Web site owner, she may mention words such as 'security certificate' and 'encryption'. But security doesn't need to start with software. The fact is that all the firewalls and passwords in the world can't help you if someone breaks into your home office and trashes or makes off with the computer that contains all your files.

Besides insuring your computer equipment and taking photos in case you need to get it replaced, you can also invest in locks for your home office and your machines. They may not keep someone from breaking into your house, but they'll at least make it more difficult for intruders to carry off your hardware.

Here are some suggestions for how to protect your hardware and the business data your computers contain:

✔ **Lock your computers:** Kensington (au.kensington.com) and Davko (www.davko.co.nz) offer several varieties of computer locking systems. Ultraviolet pens and data dots (www.datadothb.com.au) are also a great way to mark your equipment in case the police recover it and you are called to identify it.

✔ **Lock your office:** Everyone has locks on the outer doors of their house, but go a step further and install a deadbolt lock on your office door.

✔ **Make backups:** Be sure to regularly back up your information on external hard drives, USB drives, CDs, or similar storage devices. Also consider signing up with a Web-based storage service where files can be transferred from your computer. That way, if your computers and your extra storage disks are lost for whatever reason, you have an online backup in a secure location. Check out CyberSecure (www.cybersecure.com.au) or Back it Up (www.backitup.co.nz).

✔ **Mark your modem:** An innovative theft recovery system called CompuTrace can be installed on your hard drive. If your computer is stolen, the software is activated. When the thief connects an internal modem to a phone line, the authorities are notified. The system works with other types of Internet connections as well, including DSL and cable modems. CompuTrace Plus (www.absolute.com) is offered by Absolute Software Corp. and costs home-office users US$49.95 for one year of monitoring.

Installing firewalls and other safeguards

When you're connected to the Internet, not only can you browse any computers or Web servers connected to the Internet, but you also open your own computer to the world. Anyone clever enough can access your computer — which is why a firewall is needed.

You probably know how important a firewall is in a personal sense. Firewalls filter out unwanted intrusions, such as executable programs that hackers seek to plant on your file system, so they can use your computer for their own purposes. When you're starting an online business, the objectives of a firewall become different: You're protecting not just your own information, but also that of your customers. In other words, you're quite possibly relying on the firewall to protect your source of income as well as the data on your computers.

A *firewall* is an application or hardware device that monitors the data flowing into or out of a computer network and that filters the data based on criteria that the owner sets up. Like a security guard at the entrance to a building, a firewall scans the packets of digital information that traverse the Internet, making sure the data is headed for the right destination and that it doesn't match known characteristics of viruses or attacks. Authorised traffic is allowed into your network. Attack attempts or viruses are either deleted automatically or cause an alert message to appear to which you must respond with a decision to block or allow the incoming or outgoing packets.

Keeping out trojan horses and other unwanted visitors

A *trojan horse* is a program that enters your computer surreptitiously and then attempts to do something without your knowledge. Some people say that such programs enter your system through a back door because you don't immediately know that they've entered your system. Trojan horses may come in the form of an email attachment with the filename extension .exe (which stands for *executable*). For instance, Greg recently received an email that purported to be from Microsoft Corporation and claimed to contain a security update. The attachment looked innocent enough, but had he saved the attachment to his computer, it would have used his computer as a staging area for distributing itself to many other email addresses.

Greg didn't run into trouble, however. His firewall program recognised the attachment and alerted him to the danger. We highly recommend that anyone who has a cable modem, DSL or other direct connection to the Internet install a firewall right away. You can try out the shareware program ZoneAlarm by Check Point, Inc. (www.zonealarm.com) that provides you with basic firewall protection, though more full-featured programs like Norton Internet Security (www.symantec.com/en/au/norton) are probably more effective.

Cleaning out spyware

Watch out for software that 'spies' on your Web surfing and other activities and then reports these activities to advertisers, potentially invading your privacy. Ad-Aware isn't a firewall, exactly, but the software is a useful program that detects and erases any advertising programs you may have downloaded from the Internet without knowing it. Such advertising programs may be running on your computer, consuming your processing resources and slowing operations. Some spyware programs track your activities when you surf the Web; others simply report that they have been installed. Many users regard these spyware programs as invasions of privacy because they install themselves and do their reporting without you asking for it or even knowing they're active.

When Greg ran Ad-Aware the first time, it detected a whopping 57 programs he didn't know about that were running on his computer and that had installed themselves when he'd connected to various Web sites or when he'd downloaded software.

Greg highly recommends Ad-Aware; you can download a version at www. lavasoft.com and try it for free. If you decide to keep it, you pay a US$15 shareware fee. Two other free anti-spyware tools include AVG Anti-Spyware (www.avg.com) and Spybot Search & Destroy (www.spybot.com).

Positioning the firewall

These days, most home networks are configured so that the computers on the network can share information as well as the same Internet connection. Whether you run a home-based business or a business in a discrete location, you almost certainly have a network of multiple computers. A network is far more vulnerable than a single computer connected to the Internet: A network has more entry points than a single computer and more reliance is placed on each of the operators of those computers to observe good safety practices. And if one computer on the network is attacked, others have real potential to be attacked as well.

You probably are acquainted with software firewalls, such as Norton Personal Firewall or ZoneAlarm. Software firewalls protect one computer at a time. In a typical business scenario, however, multiple computers share a single Internet connection through a router that functions as a gateway. Many network administrators prefer a *hardware firewall* — a device that functions as a filter for traffic both entering and leaving it. A hardware firewall may also function as a router, but it can also be separate from the router. The device is positioned at the perimeter of the network where it can protect all the company's computers at once. Examples of hardware are the Cisco (www.cisco.com) ASA line (one example is the ASA 5505, which costs about US$545) and the WatchGuard Firebox X5, which costs about US$655, by WatchGuard (www.watchguard.com).

Companies that want to provide a Web site that the public can visit as well as secure email and other communications services, create a secure sub-network of one or more specially hardened (in other words, secured because all unnecessary services have been removed from them) computers. This kind of network is a *Demilitarised Zone* (DMZ).

Keeping your firewall up to date

Firewalls work by means of *attack signatures* (or *definitions*), which are sets of data that identify a connection attempt as a potential attack. Some attacks are easy to stop: They've been attempted for years and the amateur hackers who attempt intrusions don't give much thought to them. The more dangerous attacks are new ones. These have signatures that emerged after you installed your firewall.

You quickly get a dose of reality and find out just how serious the problem is by visiting one of the Web sites that keeps track of the latest attacks, such as the Distributed Intrusion Detection System or DShield (`www.dshield.org`). On the day Greg visited, DShield reported that the 'survival time' for an *unpatched computer* (a computer that has security software that isn't equipped with the latest updates called *patches*) after connecting it to the Internet was only six minutes. Therefore, such a computer only has six minutes before someone tries to attack it. That scenario should scare you into updating your security software!

Providing security with public keys

The conversations you overhear on a train or bus packed with young teens leave no doubt different segments of society use code words that only their members can understand. Even computers use encoding and decoding to protect information they exchange on the Internet. The schemes used online are far more complex and subtle than the slang used by kids, however. This section describes the security method that is used most widely on the Internet and the one you're likely to use yourself: Secure Sockets Layer (SSL) encryption.

The keys to public-key/private-key encryption

Terms like SSL and encryption may make you want to reach for the remote. But don't be too quick to switch channels. SSL is making it safer to do business online and boosting the trust of potential customers. And anything that makes shoppers more likely to spend money online is something you need to know about.

The term *encryption* is the process of encoding data, especially sensitive data, such as credit card numbers. Information is encrypted by means of complex mathematical formulas — *algorithms*. Such a formula may transform a simple-looking bit of information into a huge block of seemingly incomprehensible numbers, letters and characters. Only someone who has the right formula, called a *key* (which is a complex mass of encoded data), can decode the gobbledygook.

Here's a very simple example. Suppose that your credit card number is 12345, and we encode it by using an encryption formula into something like the following: 1aFgHx203gX4gLu5cy.

The algorithm that generated this encrypted information may say something like: 'Take the first number, multiply it by some numeral and then add some letters to it. Then take the second number, divide it by x and add y characters to the result' and so on. (In reality, the formulas are far more complex than this example, which is why you usually have to pay a licence fee to use them.) Someone who has the same formula can run it in reverse, so to speak, in order to decrypt the encoded number and obtain the original number, 12345.

In practice, the encoded numbers that are generated by encryption routines and transmitted on the Internet are very large. They vary in size depending on the relative strength (or *uncrackability*) of the security method used. Some methods generate keys that consist of 128 bits of data; a *data bit* is a single unit of digital information. These formulas are *128-bit keys*.

Encryption is the cornerstone of security on the Internet. The most widely used security schemes, such as the SSL protocol, the Secure Electronic Transactions (SET) protocol and Pretty Good Privacy (PGP) all use some form of encryption.

With some security methods, the party that sends the data and the party that receives it both use the same key (this method is *symmetrical encryption*). This approach isn't considered as secure as an asymmetrical encryption method, such as public-key encryption, however. In public-key encryption, the originating party obtains a licence to use a security method. (In the following section, we show you how to do this yourself.) As part of the licence, you use the encryption algorithm to generate your own private key. You never share this key with anyone. However, you use the private key to create a separate public key. This public key goes out to visitors who connect to a secure area of your Web site. When they have your public key, users can encode sensitive information and send it back to you. Only you can decode the data — by using your secret, private key.

Dealing with the ATO

Many companies and government agencies make use of public-key cryptography for the security of online transactions. One experience Melissa has had with this type of security is electronically submitting documents to the Australian Taxation Office (ATO) over the Internet. Public-key cryptography uses digital certificates and a pair of unique 'keys' to identify a business or individual involved in a transaction.

When transmitting tax and financial data electronically, security is paramount and digital certificates and keys can provide this safeguard if protected properly. In the case of the ATO, you're issued with a digital certificate. You then receive a PIN number and a password by mail and an access code by email. You need to have all these details handy to install the certificate and identify yourself. You're then asked to set a new password for your digital certificate.

Melissa uses her digital certificate to lodge quarterly business activity statements and annual payment summaries.

Terms to familiarise yourself with include

- **Cryptography:** Converting information into a secret code, using complex mathematical algorithms, so that it can't be read by anyone who doesn't already understand the code.

- **Digital certificates:** An electronic file that contains information which uniquely identifies an individual or business when using online services.

- **Encryption:** The process of applying cryptography to an email message or document so that it can be safely transmitted over networks such as the Internet.

- **Public and private keys:** For maximum security, digital certificates are used in conjunction with public and private keys. When a message is encrypted, the system uses both a public key (which is freely supplied to anyone who needs to receive information from the sender) and a private key (which is known only to the sender, and ensures messages from that sender can't be forged by others).

Getting a certificate without going to school

When you write a cheque at a shop, the checkout operator is likely to make sure you're pre-registered as an approved member and also asks to see your driver's licence. But on the Internet, how do you know that people are who they say they are when all you have to go on is a URL or an email address? The solution in the online world is to obtain a personal certificate that you can send to Web site visitors or append to your email messages.

How certificates work

A *certificate*, which is also sometimes dubbed a Digital ID, is an electronic document issued by a certification authority (CA). The certificate contains the owner's personal information as well as a public key that can be exchanged with others online. The public key is generated by the owner's private key, which the owner obtains during the process of applying for the certificate.

In issuing the certificate, the CA takes responsibility for saying that the owner of the document is the same as the person actually identified on the certificate. Although the public key helps establish the owner's identity, certificates do require you to put a level of trust in the agency that issues it.

A certificate helps both you and your customers. A certificate assures your customers that you're the person you say you are, plus it protects your email communications by enabling you to encrypt them.

Obtaining a certificate from VeriSign

Considering how important certificates are in online security, obtaining one is remarkably easy. You do so by applying and paying a licensing fee to a CA. One of the most popular CAs is VeriSign, Inc., which lets you apply for a certificate called a *Class 1 Digital ID*.

A Class 1 Digital ID is only useful for securing personal communications. As an e-commerce Web site owner, you may want a business-class certificate called a 128-bit SSL Global Server ID. This form of Digital ID works only if your e-commerce site is hosted on a server that runs *secure server software* — software that encrypts transactions — such as Apache Stronghold. Check with your Web host to see if a secure server is available for your Web site.

A VeriSign personal certificate, which you can use to authenticate yourself in email, news and other interactions on the Net, costs US$33.00 per year. Follow these steps to obtain your Digital ID:

1. Go to the VeriSign, Inc. Digital IDs for Secure Email page at

```
www.verisign.com.au/authentication/individual-authentication
/digital-id/
```

2. **Click the Buy Now button.**

   The Personal Digital Certificate Enrolment page appears.

3. **Click Buy Now near the bottom of the page.**

   The site automatically identifies the Web browser you're using. An application form for a Class-1 Certificate appears.

4. **Complete the application form.**

   The application process is pretty simple. The form asks for your personal information and a challenge phrase that you can use in case anyone is trying to impersonate you. You're then asked to enter your credit card information. The form also requires you to accept a licence agreement.

5. **Click the Accept button at the bottom of the screen.**

   A dialogue box appears asking you to confirm your email address. After you confirm by clicking OK, a dialogue box appears asking you to choose a password. When you enter a password and click OK, VeriSign uses your password to generate a private key for you. The private key is an essential ingredient in public-key/private-key technology.

6. **Click OK to have your browser generate your private key.**

   A page appears asking you to check your email for further instructions. In a few minutes, you receive a message that contains a Digital ID PIN.

7. **In your email program, open the new message from VeriSign Customer Support Department.**

8. **Use your mouse to highlight (or select) the PIN and then choose Edit⇨Copy to copy the PIN.**

9. **Go to the URL for Digital ID Services that's included in the email message and paste your PIN in the Enter the Digital ID Personal Identification Number (PIN) box.**

10. **Click Submit.**

    The certificate is generated, and the Digital IDF Installation and Registration Page appears.

11. **Click the Install button.**

    The ID from VeriSign downloads and you can view it with your browser. Figure 6-2 shows Greg's certificate for Netscape Navigator. (Copying this ID, or anyone else's, is pointless because this ID is only your public key; the public key is always submitted with your private key, which is secret.)

Figure 6-2:
A personal certificate assures individuals or Web sites of your identity.

After you have your Digital ID, what do you do with it? For one thing, you can use it to verify your identity to sites that accept certificate submissions. Some sites that require members to log in use secure servers that give you the option of submitting your certificate rather than entering the usual username and password to identify yourself. You can also attach your Digital ID to your email messages to prove that your message is indeed coming from you. See your email program's Help files for more specific instructions.

You can't encrypt or digitally sign messages on any computer other than the one to which your certificates are issued. If you're using a different computer than the one you used when you obtained your certificates, you must contact your certificate issuer and obtain a new certificate for the computer you're now using. Or, if your browser allows transfers, you can export your certificate to the new computer.

Keeping other noses out of your business

Encryption isn't just for big businesses. Individuals who want to maintain their privacy, even while navigating the wilds of the Internet, can install special software or modify their existing email programs in order to encode their online communications.

The NetAlert Web site (www.netalert.gov.au) and the Office of the Privacy Commissioner Web site (www.privacy.gov.au/internet/internet_privacy/) present some good tips and strategies for personal protection on the Internet.

Encryption software for the rest of us

PGP (Pretty Good Privacy), a popular encryption program, has been around about as long as the Web itself. PGP lets you protect the privacy of your email messages and file attachments by encrypting them so that only those with the proper authority can decipher the information. You can also digitally sign the messages and files you exchange, which assures the recipient that the messages come from you and that the information hasn't been tampered with. You can even encrypt files on your own computer.

PGP (www.pgp.com) is a freely available personal encryption program. PGP is a *plug-in*, an application that works with another program to provide added functionality. You can integrate the program with popular email programs such as Eudora and Microsoft Outlook.

In order to use either the free version of PGP or another, commercial version called PGP Desktop, the first step is to obtain and install the program. After you install the program, you can use it to generate your own private-key/public-key pair. After you create a key pair, you can begin exchanging encrypted email messages with other PGP users. To do so, you need to obtain a copy of their public keys and they need a copy of your public key. Because public keys are just blocks of text, trading keys with someone is really quite easy. You can include your public key in an email message, copy it to a file or post it on a public-key server where anyone can get a copy at any time.

After you have a copy of someone's public key, you can add it to your *public keyring*, which is a file on your own computer. Then you can begin to exchange encrypted and signed messages with that individual. If you're using an email application supported by the PGP plug-ins, you can encrypt and sign your messages by selecting the appropriate options from your application's toolbar. If your email program doesn't have a plug-in, you can copy your email message to your computer's Clipboard and encrypt it there by using PGP built-in functions. See the PGP User's Guide files for more specific instructions.

At this writing, the commercial version of PGP's Encryption Platform runs on Windows Vista, Windows XP, Windows 2000, or the Mac OS 10.4 or later.

Encrypting email messages

You can use your existing software to encrypt your mail messages rather than installing a separate program such as PGP. In the following section, we describe the steps involved in setting up Microsoft Outlook 2007 to encrypt your messages.

If you use Outlook, you can use your Digital ID to do the following:

- ✔ **Send a digital signature:** You can digitally shrink-wrap your email message by using your certificate in order to assure the recipient that the message is really from you.

- ✔ **Encrypt your message:** You can digitally encode a message to ensure that only the intended party can read it.

To better understand the technical details of how you can keep your email communications secure, read the Digital ID User Guide, which you can access at

```
www.verisign.com/static/005326.pdf
```

For installation instructions for other email applications including different versions of Outlook, Outlook Express and Thunderbird, see VeriSign's support documentation at

```
https://knowledge.verisign.com/support/digital-id-support/
index?page=content&id=AR654
```

After you have a digital ID, in order to actually make use of it, you need to follow these steps (which apply to Microsoft Outlook 2007):

1. **After you obtain your own Digital ID, the first step is to associate it with your email account. Choose Tools⇨Trust Center⇨E-mail Security.**

2. **Under Encrypted Email, select Settings.**

3. **Under Certificates and Algorithms, you see two Choose buttons.**

   The first button allows you to select a Digital ID to sign your emails and the second allows you to choose a Digital ID to encrypt your email messages.

4. **Click Choose and select your Digital ID for both Signing and Encryption Certificate.**

5. **Click OK.**

   You return to the main Outlook window.

6. **To send a digitally signed email message to someone, click New Mail Message.**

   A new blank email opens.

7. **Under Options, click Digitally Sign Message (envelope with red ribbon).**

   The Sign button enables you to add your Digital ID. The Encrypt button allows you to encrypt your message.

8. **Finish writing your message and then click the Send button.**

   Your encrypted or digitally signed message is sent on its way.

The preceding steps show you how to digitally sign or encrypt an individual message. You have to follow these steps every time you want to sign or encrypt a message. On the other hand, by checking one or more of the options (Encrypt Contents and Attachments for all Outgoing Messages and Add Digital Signature to Outgoing Messages) under Tools➪Trust Center➪ E-mail Security, you activate Outlook's built-in security features for *all* your outgoing messages. (You can still 'turn off' the digital signature or encryption for an individual message by deselecting the Sign or Encrypt buttons in the toolbar of the New Message dialogue box.)

Picking passwords that are hard to guess

You put a lot of effort into picking the names of your kids and pets, and now you get to choose passwords. But, whereas you want others to think the kids' and pets' names are cool, the point of creating a password is to make it difficult for thieves to figure out what it is. That point is true whether you're protecting your own computer, downloading software, subscribing to an online publication or applying for a certificate (as we explain in the section 'Getting a certificate without going to school', earlier in this chapter).

One method for choosing a password is to take a familiar phrase and then use the first letter of each word to form the basis of a password. For example, the phrase 'Every Good Boy Does Fine' would be EGBDF. Then, mix uppercase and lowercase, add punctuation, and you wind up with eGb[d]f. If you *really* want to make a password that's hard to crack, add some numerals as well, such as the last two digits of the year you were born: eGb[d]f48.

Whatever you do, follow these tips for effective password etiquette:

- ✔ **Don't use passwords that are in a dictionary:** It takes time but not much effort for hackers to run a program that tries every word in an online dictionary as your password. So if your password is in the dictionary, eventually, they discover it.

- ✔ **Don't use the same password at more than one site:** Remembering more than one password is a pain, not to mention keeping track of which goes with what. Plus, you tend to accumulate lots of different passwords after you've been online for a while. But if you use the same password for each purpose and your password to one site on the Internet is compromised, all your password-protected accounts are in jeopardy.

- ✔ **Use at least six characters:** The more letters in your password, the more difficult you make the life of the code-crackers.

When choosing and using passwords, duplication is not only boring but also dangerous. Especially important is not re-using the password that you enter to connect to your email, or your account with your Internet service provider as a password to an Internet site — worst of all, your online bank account. If a hacker discovers your password, that person can use it to read your email or wreak havoc with your finances.

Chapter 7

Accepting Payments

*S*tarting a new business and getting it online is exciting, but the real excitement occurs when you get paid for what you do. Nothing boosts your confidence and tells you that your hard work is paying off like receiving the proverbial cheque in the mail, or having funds transferred to your business bank account.

The immediacy and interactivity of selling and promoting yourself online applies to receiving payments, too. You can get paid with just a few mouse clicks and some important data entered on your customer's keyboard. But completing an electronic commerce (*e-commerce* for short) transaction isn't the same as getting paid in a traditional retail store. The challenge with online payments for merchandise is the same as it has always been. Customers can't personally hand you cash or a cheque. They need a reliable way to pay you securely, without worrying that their credit card information may be stolen. You, as a seller, can't verify the user's identity through a signature or photo ID. You need to know the credit card information hasn't been stolen.

In order to get paid promptly and reliably online, you have to go through some extra steps to make the customer feel secure — not to mention protecting yourself, too. Successful e-commerce is about setting up the right atmosphere for making purchases, providing options for payment and keeping sensitive information private. It's also about making sure that the goods get to the customer safely and on time. This chapter describes ways in which you can implement these essential online business strategies.

Sealing the Deal: The Options

As anyone who sells online knows, the point at which payment is transferred is one of the most eagerly awaited stages of the transaction. This moment, though, is also one of the stages that can produce the most anxiety. Customers and merchants who are used to dealing with one another face to face and who are accustomed to personally handing over identification and credit cards suddenly feel lost. On the Web, customers can't see the person they're dealing with.

For customers, paying for something purchased over the Internet is still fraught with uncertainty, even though security is improving. For merchants like you, it can still be nerve wracking; you want to make sure cheques don't bounce and purchases aren't being made with stolen credit cards.

Your goal, in giving your customers the ability to provide payments online, is to accomplish the following:

- **Give the customer options.** Online shoppers like to feel that they have some degree of control. Give them a choice of payment alternatives: Phone, fax, cheque and credit cards are the main ones.

- **Keep payment secure.** Pay an extra fee to your Web host in order to have your customers submit their credit card numbers or other personal information to a secure server — a server that uses Secure Sockets Layer (SSL) encryption to render details unreadable if stolen.

- **Make payment convenient.** Shoppers on the Web are in a hurry. Give them the Web page forms and the phone numbers they need so that they can complete a purchase in a matter of seconds.

Though the goals are the same, the options are different if you sell on eBay or on another Web site that functions as an e-commerce marketplace. If you sell on eBay, either through an auction or an eBay store, you can take advantage of eBay's fraud protection measures: A feedback system that rewards honesty and penalises dishonesty; fraud insurance; investigations staff; and the threat of suspension. These safeguards mean that it's feasible to accept cash and personal cheques or money orders from buyers. If you don't receive the cash, you don't ship. If you receive cheques, you can wait until they clear before you ship.

On the Web, you don't have a feedback system or an investigations squad to reveal dishonest buyers. You can accept cheques or money orders, but credit cards are the safest and quickest option and, accordingly, they're what buyers expect. It's up to you to verify the buyer's identity as best you can in order to minimise fraud.

Enabling Credit Card Purchases

Having the ability to accept and process credit card transactions makes it especially easy for your customers to follow the impulse to buy something from you. You stand to generate a lot more sales than you would otherwise.

But although credit cards are easy for shoppers to use, they make *your* life as an online merchant more complicated. We don't want to discourage you from becoming credit card ready by any means, but you need to be aware of the steps (and the expenses) involved, many of which may not occur to you when you're just starting out. For example, you may not be aware of one or more of the following:

- ✔ **Merchant accounts:** You have to apply and be approved for a special bank account called a *merchant account* in order for a bank to process the credit card orders that you receive. Approval can take days or weeks and often you're required to provide details of your turnover, average transaction amount and an outline of your business plan.

- ✔ **Fees:** Fees can be high, but they vary widely so shopping around pays. Some banks charge a merchant application fee ($50–$600).

- ✔ **Merchant service fees:** All banks and merchant account companies (and even payment companies like PayPal) charge a usage fee, called a *merchant service fee*. Typically, this fee ranges from 1 to 4 per cent of each transaction. You may also have to pay a monthly premium charge in the range of $15–$50 to the bank.

- ✔ **American Express:** If you want to accept payments from American Express cardholders, you can apply online to be an American Express card merchant by going to the American Express Merchant Homepage (home3.americanexpress.com/australia/merchant/) and clicking the Apply to Accept the Card link.

- ✔ **Software and hardware:** Unless you depend on a payment service, such as PayPal, you need software or hardware to process transactions and transmit the data to the banking system. If you plan to accept credit card numbers online only and don't need a physical device to handle actual 'card swipes' you can use a virtual Web terminal. A virtual Web terminal allows you to process transactions with your browser and, ordinarily, is Web-based software provided by your bank or merchant account provider. You pay a monthly fee of around $15 and often a per transaction fee of around $0.50. Other systems require you to get a hardware terminal or phone line, which you lease from the bank as part of your merchant agreement and pay anywhere from $15 to $35 a month to use.

As we move further into the Web's second decade, the payment landscape hasn't changed dramatically. But things have shifted a bit. The changes actually give buyers and sellers more options:

- ✔ **More and more people are paying bills online.** This change has been taking place over several years. This change isn't a great leap to paying for things online with a credit card; consumers are more and more at ease with the process.

- ✔ **PayPal is becoming more widespread.** This payment service is owned by eBay, but it can be used by anyone who wants to send or receive money online. PayPal is used by millions of auction sellers every month, but e-commerce store owners can use it, too.

- ✔ **Overseas consumers are making use of new and innovative payment systems.** At some point, if you accept payments from overseas, you may be asked to accept Western Union money transfers or other payment schemes — a wave of the future as e-commerce becomes globalised.

The steps in the upcoming section, in which we explain how to create your own merchant account, are useful if you run a brick-and-mortar business that is tied to your online store. But if you don't want to go through the trouble, you may consider a payment service like PayPal, Paymate or Flo2Cash.

You also need to watch for credit card fraud, in which criminals use stolen numbers to make purchases. (The hardware store profiled later in this chapter, General Tool & Repair, stopped the problem but only after instituting a policy in which it would no longer accept *any* overseas purchases.) You, the merchant, end up being liable for the fictitious transactions. To combat this crime, before completing any transaction, verify that the shipping address supplied by the purchaser is the same (or at least in the same vicinity) as the billing address. If you're in doubt, you can phone the purchaser for verification — making this check is a courtesy to the customer as well as a means of protection for you. (See the upcoming section 'Verifying credit card data'.) You can do this check yourself or pay a service to check.

Selling legal documents online

Sue Norfolk (Melissa's mum) knows all about the benefits of accepting secure credit card orders online. She started her business Norfolk Corporate Support (NCS) (www.ncs-services. com.au) in 1995. NCS works with lawyers, accountants and public companies and provides corporate registry services, that is, the documentation required to set up new companies, trusts and business structures as well as company, business name, title and bankruptcy searches.

NCS built its first company Web site in 1998, and added secure online ordering in early 2000. In those early days of the Internet, not many accounting or legal businesses had Web sites, and didn't sell their services or legal documents online. Now more than eight years on, Sue is very pleased she added secure online ordering to her site because at least a half of her clients now prefer to order online, and she has also picked up a number of international and interstate clients.

Q. Can you briefly describe your business?

A. Our business is a corporate registry service. We register new companies and business structures and provide all the necessary documentation.

Q. What got you started online?

A. My daughter had her own Web design business and was able to help me create a professional, easy-to-use Web site where our clients could not only order but also pay online. Some of our major competitors were starting to market their business online. The younger generations were using the Internet and were shopping online regularly. We could see that, to stay competitive, we needed to keep up with technology and market our online services to new and existing clients in order to create new opportunities.

Q. What products/services do you sell over the Internet and how long have you been doing this?

A. We sell new company registrations, business name registrations, company, title and bankruptcy searches, as well as provide the documents for the setting up of family trusts and self-managed superannuation funds.

All these services can be ordered and paid for online and we have been doing this since 2000.

Q. How do you process credit card orders?

A. We use a system provided by the National Australia Bank (NAB) called National Secure Internet Payment Service (NSIPS).

The Client/Customer completes the order form for the required service on our Web site. A copy of the order is emailed to our office and the client is directed to a secure payment page on the NAB Web site. The bank processes the payment and sends us a payment receipt via email.

Q. How do you verify the identity of customers who submit credit card numbers to you?

A. The bank NSIPS system verifies the credit card details and accepts or denies the payment in real time.

(continued)

(continued)

Many of our customers who order online are regular clients who are known to us.

If we get an order and payment from an unknown miscellaneous customer, we always try to contact the person to confirm the order and payment.

Q. Do you get many fraudulent credit card orders?

A. In eight years, we have had just two fraudulent credit card orders.

Q. After you receive payment, how do you deliver items?

A. We ask our online customers to advise us via our order form on how and where they would like the documents delivered.

This delivery can be by courier, email, snail mail, Express Post or CD.

Q. Has having ordering available on your Web site been worthwhile?

A. Yes, it has definitely been worth having ordering on our Web site. At least 50 per cent of our existing clients use this facility on a regular basis. We do pick up a relatively small percentage of new miscellaneous customers. A large percentage of these new customers are often interstate or international customers who find us online.

Q. What advice would you give to someone starting a business and who is going to accept online payments?

A. Just four main things:

- Find yourself a good Web designer with experience in setting up online payment facilities.

- Use a reputable secure bank system for processing payments.

- Check out any irregular orders, and always contact any new unknown customers by phone to confirm the validity of the order and or payment.

- Report any suspicious activity to the relevant authorities.

Setting up a merchant account

The good news is that getting merchant status is becoming easier all the time for e-commerce enterprises, as more banks accept the notion that businesses don't have to have an actual, physical storefront in order to be successful. Getting a merchant account approved, however, still takes a long time and some hefty fees are involved as well. Banks look more favourably on companies that have been in business for several years and have a proven track record.

Traditional banks are reliable and experienced, and you can count on them being around for a while. The new Web-based companies that specialise in giving online businesses merchant account status welcome new businesses and give you wider options and cost savings, but they're new; their services may not be as reliable, and their future is less certain.

Visit Google or Yahoo! and do a search for 'credit card merchant services'. If you're overwhelmed with the choices, start with the major banks and compare with a couple of online options such as WorldPay and Authorize.Net.

MyTexasMusic.com, the family-run business we profile in Chapter 1, uses a Web-based merchant account company called GoEmerchant.com (www. goemerchant.com) to set up and process its credit card transactions. This company offers a shopping cart and credit card and debit card processing to businesses that accept payments online. MyTexasMusic.com chose to use GoEmerchant after an extensive search because it found that the company would help provide reliable processing, while protecting the business from customers who purchased items fraudulently.

One advantage of using one of the payment options set up by PayPal Merchant Services (www.paypal.com.au) is that the system (which originated with the well-known companies CyberCash and VeriSign) was well known and well regarded before PayPal acquired it. We describe the widely used electronic payment company in the section 'Choosing an Online Payment System' later in this chapter.

In general, your chances of obtaining merchant status are enhanced if you apply to a bank that welcomes Internet businesses, and if you can provide good business records proving that you're a viable, moneymaking concern.

Be sure to ask about the merchant service fee that the bank charges for Internet-based transactions before you apply. Compare the rate for online transactions to the rate for conventional 'card-swipe' purchases. Some banks and credit card processing companies charge 1 to 2 per cent extra for online sales.

Finding a secure server

A *secure server* is a server that uses some form of encryption, such as SSL, which we describe in Chapter 6, to protect data that you receive over the Internet. Customers know that they've entered a secure area when the security key or lock icon shown in the browser window is locked shut. (Depending on which browser and which version you have, the lock icon appears in a different spot within your browser window. Sometimes this lock is shown at the very bottom of your browser window; other times you see it at the top, next to the address bar.)

If you plan to receive credit card payments, you definitely want to find a Web hosting service that can protect the area of your online business that serves as the online store. In literal terms, you need secure server software protecting the directory on your site that is to receive customer-sent forms. Some hosts charge a higher monthly fee for using a secure server; with others, the secure server is part of a basic business Web site account. Ask your host (or hosts you're considering) whether any extra charges apply.

Verifying credit card data

Unfortunately, the world has some bad people who try to use credit card numbers that don't belong to them. The anonymity of the Web and the ability to shop anywhere in the world, combined with the ability to place orders immediately, can facilitate fraudulent orders, just as it can benefit legitimate orders.

Protecting yourself against credit card fraud is essential. Always check the billing address against the shipping address. If the two addresses are thousands of kilometres apart, contact the purchaser by phone to verify that the transaction is legitimate. Even if it is correct, the purchaser appreciates your taking the time to verify the transaction.

These days, most credit cards have an additional three-digit code printed on the back of the card. These three digits are not embossed like the other 16 digits. This number is called the *CCV number* or *credit card verification number* and is meant to provide an additional check that the person has the physical card in her possession. Most credit card thieves don't have the physical card in front of them and so can't supply these additional three numbers — because either they obtained a fraudulent swipe of the raised digits, or accessed your credit card number via your computer or a Web site you purchased from that doesn't have the correct security in place.

Processing the orders

When someone submits credit card information to you, you need to transfer the information to the banking system. Whether you make this transfer yourself or hire another company to do it for you is up to you.

Do-it-yourself or manual processing

To submit credit card information to your bank, you need POS (point of sale) hardware or software. The hardware, which you either purchase or lease from your bank, is a *terminal* — a grey box of the sort you see at many local retailers. The *software* is a program that contacts the bank through a modem.

The terminal or software is programmed to authorise the sale and transmit the data to the bank. The bank then credits your business bank account, usually within two or three business days. The bank also deducts the merchant service fee from your account monthly.

Automatic processing

You can hire a company to automatically process credit card orders for you. This kind of service is called an *online payment gateway*. An online payment gateway links with your Web site and securely collects credit card details on your behalf, processes the transaction and transfers the funds to your bank account. In most cases, this means that your Web site doesn't need to collect and store credit card details, removing the need for credit card security on your site. It also saves you time manually processing credit card orders and helps you speed up your customer service by reducing the amount of time before goods are sent to customers.

You can look into the different options provided for such services.

In Australia:

- Camtech (www.camtech.com.au)
- eMatters (www.ematters.com.au)
- eSec (www.esecpayments.com.au)
- eWAY (www.eway.com.au)
- SecurePay (www.securepay.com.au)

In New Zealand:

- DPS (www.dps.co.nz)
- PayPro (www.paypro.co.nz)
- Paystation (www.paystation.co.nz)
- Zipzap (www.zipzap.co.nz)

International: WorldPay (www.worldpay.com)

Automatic credit card processing works so fast that your customer's credit card can be charged immediately, whether or not you have an item in stock. If a client receives a bill and is still waiting for an item that is on back order, the person can become very unhappy. For this reason, some business owners, such as Mark Lauer (profiled in the sidebar 'Keeping back-office functions personal'), chose not to use it.

If you have a small-scale Web site — perhaps with only one item for sale — you can use a simple online payment gateway, which enables you to add a Pay Button to a catalogue page that securely processes a customer's payment information. Services such as PayPal (www.paypal.com.au) or Paymate (www.paymate.com.au) are often easier to set up and more cost-effective for Web sites just starting out that have only a low volume of sales. Both you and your customer receive email notifications that the transaction has been completed.

Keeping back-office functions personal

Mark Lauer knows the importance of credit card verification and order processing. Yet, in keeping with the spirit of online business, he tries to make these functions as personal as possible.

Mark is president of General Tool & Repair, Inc., a power tool supplier based in York, Pennsylvania. General Tool & Repair has been in business for 10 years, but seven years ago, General Tool & Repair created a simple Web page on America Online to help promote the company. Within two weeks, an order was received from a customer in Florida.

Since then, Mark has expanded his e-commerce Web site with Microsoft Commerce Server and he set up shop at www.gtr.com.

Mark estimates that General Tool's Web site receives between 10 and 40 orders each day and average online sales amount to US$35,000–US$45,000 per month — an amount that has remained steady in recent years despite economic ups and downs. He believes the site takes the place of 50 salespeople. 'This is all business we never had until two years ago, so it's basically all extra sales for us', he notes happily.

Q. How do you process credit card orders?

A. Our customers send us the credit card information through our Web site and our secure server encrypts the data. But we don't process orders online. We first check to see if we have the item in stock and, if we do, we process the order the next business day. That way, we don't 'slam' the customer's credit card without having the item ready to ship out.

Q. How do you verify the identity of customers who submit credit card numbers to you?

A. We use a program called Authorizer. The program lets you check the shipping address against the address of the credit card owner. If the two addresses are in the same state, you're pretty sure that you can ship the item. Otherwise, you know that you'd better email the card owner and tell the person there's a problem. Sometimes, a customer will want to purchase a gift and have it shipped out of state to a family member and in this case, you should also email the customer just to be sure. We have since upgraded to the multi-merchant version of Authorizer, which lets us accept several different types of credit cards.

Q. Do you get many fraudulent credit card orders?

A. We don't get many bogus orders since we stopped accepting overseas orders altogether. In the past, you could always tell because they didn't have the correct 'ship to' address. Often, the address was in a different country than the credit card holder's residence. If we suspect something, we email or call the customer to confirm. Additionally, Authorizer detects fraudulent credit card orders. Customers don't mind you being extra careful when dealing with their credit card protection, by confirming that it is a legit order. This extra step has gained us many repeat customers.

Q. Whom do you use for shipping?

A. If the customer is affiliated with the military, you're required to use the US Postal Service for shipping. If we're shipping to a business address, such as an office in New York City, we use United Parcel Service (UPS) because they give the option of sending a package 'signature required' which, as it implies, requires someone to sign for an item before they deliver it. We add the UPS charge for 'signature required' to the shipping charge, but we feel that it's worth it because we don't want any items to get lost because they were left without a signature. There have been many instances where a customer's neighbour, employee, or landlord have signed for their package without the customer's knowledge, so it really provides protection for all involved.

Q. How do you tell your customers about shipping options?

A. We offer customers three choices during the purchase process: UPS ground, second-day air and next-day air. We also provide a comment area where shoppers can make shipping requests or provide us with special instructions regarding their orders. That way, they can choose. We don't add on flat-rate shipping or handling charges that might be excessive. There are only five of us here and I can't justify charging someone $25 shipping and handling for a $3 part for a power tool. Our products vary a great deal in price and weight, and we haven't found a way to provide a flat rate for shipping that is fair to everyone, so each order is treated individually. This flexibility in shipping has proven to be a service that sets us apart from the 'Big Box' online power tool providers and customers shop on our Web site because of it.

Choosing an Online Payment System

A number of organisations have devised ways to make e-commerce secure and convenient for shoppers and merchants alike. These alternatives fall into one of three general categories:

- ✔ Organisations that help you complete credit card purchases (for example, VeriSign Payment Services).

- ✔ Escrow services that hold your money for you in an account until shipment is received and then pay you, providing security for both you and your customers.

- ✔ Organisations that provide alternatives to transmitting sensitive information from one computer to another. A number of attempts to create 'virtual money' have failed. However, companies like PayPal let customers make payments by directly debiting their savings or cheque accounts.

In order to use one of these systems, you or your Web host has to set up special software on the computer that actually stores your Web site files. This computer is where the transactions take place. The following sections provide general instructions on how to get started with setting up each of the most popular electronic payment systems.

To work smoothly, some electronic payment systems require you to set up programming languages such as Perl, C/C++, or Visual Basic on your site. You also have to work with techy documents called *configuration files*. This is definitely an area where paying a consultant to get your business set up saves time and headaches and gets your new transaction feature online more efficiently than if you tackle it yourself. PayPal, for instance, provides support in setting up systems for its merchants; you can find an affiliate to help you or call the company directly. Visit the PayPal Merchant Services page (www.paypal.com.au/merchants) for links and phone numbers.

Shopping cart software

When you go to the supermarket or another retail outlet, you pick goodies off the shelves and put them in a shopping cart (or trolley). When you go to the cash register to pay for what you've selected, you empty the cart and present your goods to the cashier.

Shopping cart software performs the same functions on an e-commerce site. Such software sets up a system that allows online shoppers to select items displayed for sale. The selections are held in a virtual shopping cart that 'remembers' what the shopper has selected before checking out.

Shopping cart programs are pretty technical for non-programmers to set up, but if you're ambitious and want to try it, you can download and install a free program — Zen Cart (www.zencart.com). Signing up with a Web host that provides you with shopping cart software as part of its services, however, is far easier than tackling this task yourself.

A shopping cart is often described as an essential part of many e-commerce Web sites, and Web hosts usually boast about including a shopping cart along with their other business services. But the fact is that you don't *have* to use a shopping cart on your site. Many shoppers are put off by them; they're just as likely to abandon a purchase than follow through by submitting payment. Plenty of other e-businesses have users phone or fax in an order or fill out an online form instead. Work out the best solution for your business before jumping in and spending big bucks on a shopping cart solution.

PayPal Merchant Services

A good deal of this chapter is devoted to PayPal and its solutions for online buyers and sellers. The fact is that PayPal is getting bigger and is one of the most recognised payment methods worldwide. This scenario isn't necessarily a bad thing: The more users you have who take advantage of the same services, the more routine payments become and the more customers trust the whole payment process.

PayPal's Merchant Services page (visit www.paypal.com.au and click the Business tab) includes services, such as Payflow, which allows your company to accept payments online, and Web site Payments, which facilitates payment with either credit cards or a PayPal account. Options include

- ✔ **Email payments:** Your customers pay through email communications; you don't even need to have a Web site.
- ✔ **Website payments standard:** Your customers choose an item to buy and are sent to PayPal's site where they can pay either with a credit card, debit card, bank account or with their PayPal account if they have one.

Both Payflow options require that you have a merchant account. The Payflow services do carry some charges and require you to do some work:

- **Payflow Link:** The smallest and simplest of the Payflow payment options, Payflow Link is intended for small businesses that process 200 transactions or fewer each month. You add a payment link to your online business site and you don't have to do programming or other site development to get the payment system to work. You pay a $300 setup fee and a $45.41 monthly fee.

- **Payflow Pro:** With this service, you can process up to 750 transactions per month; additional transactions cost 20 cents each. To use this option, you begin by installing the Payflow software on the server that runs your Web site. The customer then makes a purchase on your site and the Payflow software sends the information to PayPal, which processes the transaction. Payflow Pro carries a $500 setup fee and costs $136.32 per month.

PayPal's personal payment services

PayPal was one of the first online businesses to hit on the clever idea of giving business owners a way to accept credit and debit card payments from customers without having to apply for a merchant account, download software, apply for online payment processing, or some combination of these steps.

PayPal's person-to-person payment services are ideal for transactions on eBay and other sites. In this sense, PayPal functions as a sort of financial middleman, debiting buyers' accounts and crediting the accounts of sellers — and, along the way, exacting a fee for its services, which it charges to the merchant receiving the payment. The accounts involved can be credit card accounts, savings or cheque accounts, or accounts held at PayPal into which members directly deposit funds. In other words, the person making the payment sets up an account with PayPal by identifying which account (credit card or cheque, for example) a payment is to be taken from. The merchant also has a PayPal account and has identified which cheque or credit card account is to receive payments. PayPal handles the virtual card swipe and verification of customer information; the customer can pay with a credit card without the merchant having to set up a merchant account.

PayPal is best known as a way to pay for items purchased on eBay. eBay, in fact, owns PayPal. But the service is regularly used to process payments both on and off the auction site. If you want to sell items (including through your Web site), you can sign up for a PayPal Business or Premier account. You get a PayPal button that you add to your auction listing or sales Web page. (If you sell on eBay, this button is provided automatically.)

The customer clicks the button to transfer the payment from his or her PayPal account to yours and you're charged a transaction fee.

Setting up a PayPal account is free. Here's how you can set up a PayPal Business account (you can visit an online tutorial available at www.paypal-education.com.au/sellersguide):

1. **Go to the PayPal home page (**www.paypal.com.au**) and click the Sign Up button.**

   You go to the PayPal Account Sign Up page.

2. **Click the button next to Business Account, choose your country of residence and click Continue.**

   The Business Account Sign Up page appears.

3. **Follow the instructions on the registration form page and set up your account with PayPal.**

   After you fill out the registration forms, you receive an email message with a link that takes you to the PayPal Web site to confirm your email address.

4. **Click the link contained in the email message.**

   You go to the PayPal — Password page.

5. **Enter your password (the one you created during the registration process) in the Password box and then click the Confirm button.**

   You go to the PayPal — My Account page.

6. **Click the Merchant Services tab at the top of the My Account page.**

7. **Under PayPal Website Payments Standard, Key Features, click Buy Now Buttons.**

   If you want to create a shopping cart, click the Shopping Cart link.

8. **Provide some information about the item you're selling:**

   • Enter a brief description of your sales item in the Item Name/Service box.

   • Enter an item number in the Item ID/Number Box.

   • Enter the price in the Price of Item/Service box.

   • Choose a button that shoppers can click to make the purchase. (You can choose either the PayPal logo button or a button that you've already created.)

9. **When you're done, click the Create Button Now button.**

   You go to the PayPal — Web Accept page, as shown in Figure 7-1.

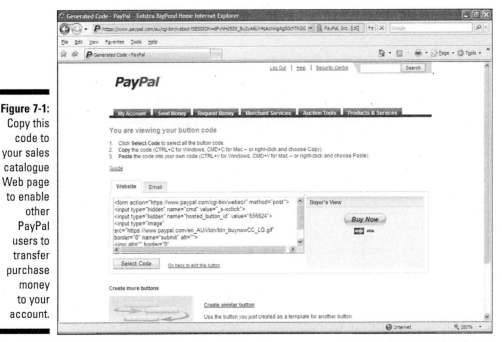

Figure 7-1:
Copy this code to your sales catalogue Web page to enable other PayPal users to transfer purchase money to your account.

10. **Copy the code in the For Websites box and paste it onto the Web page that holds your sales item.**

That's all there is to it. When you receive a payment through eBay, you receive an email notification to that effect. When someone sends you money directly through PayPal, you see that too. You can then verify the payment by logging in to your account on the PayPal Web site.

You should realise that accepting money on PayPal is *not* free. Buyers don't pay to use PayPal, but sellers do. Greg has a Premier account and every time he receives money from an eBay transaction, PayPal takes its fees off the top. For a purchase of about $30, PayPal takes about $1 in fees, for instance.

The nice thing about using PayPal is that the system enables you to accept payments through your Web site without having to obtain a merchant account. Your customers don't have to become PayPal users to pay you via PayPal, but chances are those who buy or sell on eBay already have a PayPal account. The thing to remember is that both you and your customers place a high level of trust in PayPal to handle your money. PayPal does have protection and a claims system in place to investigate both buyer and seller issues. You can investigate the protection options available to make sure you're happy with what PayPal offers in this regard. Go to Google and do a search for **PayPal claims** in order to have the full picture and anticipate problems before they arise.

Micropayments

Micropayments are very small units of currency that are exchanged by merchants and customers. The amounts involved may range from one-tenth of one cent (that's $.001) to a few dollars. Such small payments enable sites to provide content for sale on a per-click basis. In order to read articles, listen to music files or view video clips online, some sites require micropayments in a special form of electronic cash that goes by names such as *scrip* or *eCash*.

Micropayments seemed like a good idea in theory, but they've never caught on with most consumers. On the other hand, they've never totally disappeared, either. The business that proved conclusively that consumers are willing to pay small amounts of money to purchase creative content online is none other than the computer manufacturer Apple, which revolutionised e-commerce with its iPod music player and its iTunes Store. Every day, users pay $1.69 to download a song and add it to their iPod selections. But they make such payments with their credit cards, using real dollars and cents.

In other words, iTunes payments aren't true micropayments. But this system is just about the only really successful system Greg knows that deals in small payments for items purchased or downloaded online. While Greg was preparing this book, he wrote about a system called BitPass that provided a true micropayment system for online merchants. But the company went out of business in 2007. In Australia, bopo by Bill Express allowed consumers to obtain a debit card through newsagents and post offices and deposit money onto the card instead of using a credit card online. However, Bill Express went out of business in 2008. Micropayments simply look like they're unlikely to be a popular option for the majority of online shoppers.

Other payment options

A number of new online payment options have appeared that let people pay for merchandise without having to submit credit card numbers or mail cheques. Here are some additional options to consider:

- **BPAY** (www.bpay.com.au): BPAY allows anyone with an Australian bank account to pay for products and services via their bank's telephone or Internet banking. Billers must be registered for BPAY with their bank and receive a BPAY biller code, which customers quote when paying their bill. The best thing about BPAY is that cleared funds arrive in your bank account within one business day.

- **PayByCash** (www.paybycash.com): Lots of individuals — especially those who live outside the United States — don't have credit cards. Or those who do use a system (for example, the Chinese debit card system) that doesn't link up with the credit card providers in the United States. PayByCash consolidates approximately 25 different payment systems used around the world, ranging from PayPal and Western Union to local systems like eNets in China or Paymate in Australia. There's one big catch, however: PayByCash requires that merchants expect sales of at least $50,000 in US dollars or the equivalent in your native currency.

- **Pago** (www.pago.co.nz): Pago (pronounced 'pay go') is an instant payment tool that allows anyone with a New Zealand bank account to send cleared funds to another person with a New Zealand mobile phone number, a valid email address or a Pago username. When you register, you start with a Pago 'virtual wallet'. You can transfer money from your bank account to your Pago wallet. Pago business members can receive payments of up to NZ$2,500 from other Pago members.

- **Paymate** (www.paymate.com.au): Paymate is an Australian company that provides online payment services to individuals and businesses selling in Australia and New Zealand and clients buying in 52 countries, in either Australian or US currency. Similar to PayPal, you can use Paymate to receive online payments via credit card without the need to have a merchant account with a bank. Sellers can choose to share costs with buyers or absorb all the buyer fees. Paymate assesses the financial risk of buyers and sellers before transactions are approved, which reduces the chance of fraudulent transactions. Integrating Paymate with your Web site, eBay or Trade Me auction listings is easy and approved funds are transferred direct to your bank account.

Which one of these options is right for you? That depends on what you want to sell online. If you're providing articles, reports, music or other content that you want people to pay a nominal fee to access, consider a micropayment system (see the preceding section). If your customers tend to be sophisticated, tech-savvy individuals who are likely to embrace online billing systems, consider PayPal or Paymate. The important things to remember are to provide customers with several options for submitting payment and to make the process as easy as possible for them.

Fulfilling Your Online Orders

Being on the Internet can help when it comes to the final step in the e-commerce dance: Order fulfilment. *Fulfilment* refers to what happens after a sale is made. Typical fulfilment tasks include the following:

- ✔ Packing up the merchandise
- ✔ Shipping the merchandise
- ✔ Solving delivery problems or answering questions about orders that haven't reached their destinations
- ✔ Sending out invoices
- ✔ Following up to see whether the customer is satisfied

Order fulfilment may seem like the least exciting part of running a business, online or otherwise. But from your customer's point of view, it's the most important business activity of all. The following sections suggest how you can use your presence online to help reduce any anxiety your customers may feel about receiving what they ordered.

The back-end (or, to use the Microsoft term, BackOffice) part of your online business is where order fulfilment comes in. If you have a database in which you record customer orders, link it to your Web site so that your customers can track orders. Dreamweaver or ColdFusion can help you set up a database. (Dreamweaver contains built-in commands that let you link to a ColdFusion database.)

Providing links to shipping services

One advantage of being online is that you can help customers track packages after shipment. The TNT Express online order-tracking feature, as shown in Figure 7-2, gets thousands of requests each day and is widely used within Australia. If you use TNT Express, provide a link to its online tracking tool.

Figure 7-2:
Provide links to online tracking services so that your customers can check delivery status.

Other shipping services also provide their own online tracking systems. You can link to these sites, too:

- CourierPost (www.courierpost.co.nz)
- DHL (www.dhl.com.au or www.dhl.co.nz)
- New Zealand Couriers (www.nzcouriers.co.nz)
- PACK & SEND (www.packsend.com.au)
- TNT Express (www.tntexpress.com.au)

Presenting shipping options clearly

In order fulfilment, as in receiving payment, it pays to present your clients with as many options as possible and to explain the options in detail. Because you're online, you can provide your customers with as much shipping information as they can stand. Web surfers are knowledge hounds — they can never get enough data, whether it's related to shipping or other parts of your business.

When it comes to shipping, be sure to describe the options, the cost of each option and how long each option takes. (See the sidebar 'Keeping back-office functions personal' earlier in this chapter, for some good tips on when to require signatures and how to present shipping information by email rather than on the Web.) Here are some more specific suggestions:

- ✔ **Compare shipping costs:** Compare the cost of using standard post to Express Post, a courier or a freight forwarding company. Often the costs depend on the origin, destination, weight and dimensions of a package that you want to ship.

- ✔ **Make sure that you can track:** Pick a service that lets you track your package's shipping status.

- ✔ **Be able to confirm receipt:** If you use Australia or NZ Post for international deliveries, choose a form of post that includes tracking even if the service costs more. For example, with Australia Post, Express Courier or Express Post is available for parcel delivery and includes tracking.

Many online stores present shipping alternatives in the form of a table or bulleted list of options. You don't have to look very far to find an example; just visit the online bookstore Web site The Nile (www.thenile.com.au) and click on Availability & Shipping. On this page you see a two-columned table explaining delivery costs to different locations, as shown in Figure 7-3.

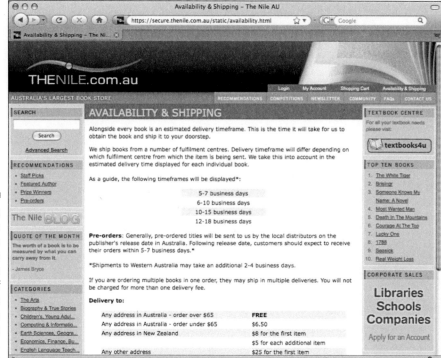

Figure 7-3: Tables help shoppers calculate costs, keep track of purchases and choose shipping options.

Shipping Goods Overseas

Stating the obvious can be useful, so here goes: Don't depend on standard mail (appropriately nicknamed *snail mail*) to communicate with overseas customers. Use email and fax to get your message across — and, if you have to ship information or goods, use airmail express delivery. Surface mail can take weeks or even months to reach some regions of some countries — if it gets there at all.

Your customer may ask you to provide an estimate of your export costs by using a special set of abbreviations called incoterms. *Incoterms* (short for *international commercial trade terms*) are a set of standardised acronyms originally established in 1936 by the International Chamber of Commerce. They establish an international language for describing business transactions to prevent misunderstandings between buyers and sellers from different countries. Incoterms thus provide a universal vocabulary that is recognised by all international financial institutions.

Incoterms are most likely to apply to you if you're shipping a large number of items to an overseas factory rather than, for example, a single painting to an individual's home. But just in case you hit the big time, you should be aware of common incoterms, such as:

- **EXW (Ex Works):** This term means that the seller fulfils his or her obligation by making the goods available to the buyer at the seller's own premises (or *works*). The seller doesn't have to load the goods onto the buyer's vehicle unless otherwise agreed.

- **FOB (Free on Board):** This term refers to the cost of shipping overseas by ship — not something you're likely to do in this high-tech day and age. But if you sell a vintage automobile to a collector in France, who knows?

- **CFR (Cost and Freight):** This term refers to the costs and freight charges necessary to transport items to a specific overseas port. CFR describes only costs related to items that are shipped by sea and inland waterways and that go to an actual port. Another incoterm, CPT (Carriage Paid To) can refer to any type of transport, not just shipping, and refers to the cost for the transport (or *carriage*) of the goods to their destination.

You can find a detailed examination of incoterms at the International Chamber of Commerce Web site (www.iccwbo.org).

If you're planning to deliver goods overseas by mail, you should check whether any paperwork or a permit is required through:

- ✔ The Australian Customs Service Web site (www.customs.gov.au)
- ✔ The New Zealand Customs Service Web site (www.customs.govt.nz)

Some nations require a certificate of origin or a signed statement that attests to the origin of the exported item. Some purchasers or countries may also ask for a certificate of inspection stating that the goods shipped meet the agreed specifications. Inspections are performed by independent testing organisations.

Wherever you ship your items, be sure to insure them for the full amount they're worth — and tell your customers about any additional insurance charges up front. Finally, choose an insurance company that can respond quickly to claims made from your own country *and* from your customer's country.

Getting Paid in International Trade

Having an effective billing policy in place is especially important when your customers live thousands of kilometres away. The safest strategy is to request payment in your own currency (Australian or New Zealand dollars) and to ask for cash in advance. This approach prevents any collection problems and gets you your money right away.

What happens if you want to receive payment in US dollars from someone overseas but the purchaser is reluctant to send cash? You have a couple of options:

- ✔ You can ask the purchaser to send you a personal cheque — or, better yet, a bank cheque — but it's up to the buyer to convert the local currency to US dollars.
- ✔ You can suggest that the buyer obtain an international money order and specify that the money order be payable in US dollars.

Suggest that your customers use an online currency conversion utility, such as the XE Universal Currency Converter (www.xe.com/ucc), to do the calculation.

You can also use an online escrow service — such as Escrow.com (www.escrow.com) or Moneybookers (www.moneybookers.com) — to hold funds in escrow until you and your customer strike a deal. An *escrow service* holds the customer's funds in a trust account so that the seller can ship an item knowing that he or she is going to be paid. The escrow service transfers the funds from buyer to seller after the buyer has inspected the goods and approved them.

Escrow services usually accept credit card payments from overseas purchasers; this service is one way to accept credit card payments even if you don't have a merchant account yourself. The credit card company handles conversion to your local currency.

If you're doing a lot of business overseas, consider getting export insurance to protect yourself against loss due to damage or delay in transit.

Chapter 8

Providing Customer Service with a Virtual Smile

In This Chapter

▶ Building a base of repeat customers through effective communication

▶ Being available 24/7

▶ Finalising sales through chat-based customer service

*W*hen we started selling on eBay, we didn't have to look far to figure out what separated the successful sellers from the struggling ones. Greg had been lucky enough to interview some of the best sellers on the auction site. He discovered that a consistently strong level of customer service prompted buyers to leave glowing feedback, which boosted your reputation. Extras like leaving cards and gifts in packages, making an effort to ship merchandise the same day of purchase, having a clear return policy and sticking to it, and answering questions promptly help to set off a positive feedback cycle: You build your feedback numbers, you build more trust, you inspire more people to buy from you, and on and on. So, when we made an effort to include some 'extras' with our packages and to ship quickly and carefully, we received our own glowing comments of appreciation — which, of course, proved highly satisfying.

Customer service is one area in which small, entrepreneurial businesses can outshine brick-and-mortar stores and even larger online competitors. Whether you're competing in the areas of e-trading, e-music or e-tail sales of any sort doesn't matter. Tools, such as email, RSS feeds and interactive forms, coupled with the fact that an online commerce site can provide information on a 24/7 basis, give you a powerful advantage when it comes to retaining customers and building loyalty. Make no mistake, giving personal attention to customers who call you on the phone or demand instant shipment is hard work. But it pays off in the long run.

What constitutes good online customer service, particularly for a new business that has only one or two employees? Whether your customers are broadband or dial-up, deal with them one at a time and connect one to one. But being responsive and available is only part of the picture. This chapter presents ways to succeed with the other essential components: Providing information, communicating effectively and enabling your clientele to talk back to you online.

Keeping Your Customers in the Loop

In a manner of speaking, satisfaction is all about expectations. If you give your customers what they're expecting or even a little bit more, they're going to be happy. But how do you go about setting their level of expectation in the first place? Communication is the key. The more information you can provide up front, the fewer phone queries or complaints you're likely to receive later. Printed pamphlets and brochures have traditionally described products and services at length. But online is now the way to go.

Say you're talking about a 1,000-word description of your new company and your products and/or services. If that text were formatted to fit on a DL foldout brochure, the contents would cover several panels and take at least a few hundred dollars to print.

On the other hand, if those same 1,000 words were arranged on a few Web pages and put online, they'd probably be no more than 5K–10K in size. The same applies if you distribute your content to a number of subscribers in an email newsletter. In either case, the costs are minimal to publish the information.

And online publishing has the advantage of easier updating. When you add new products or services or even when you want a different approach, it takes only a little time and effort to change the contents or the look.

Providing FAQs

FAQs may not be the most elegant of concepts, but it has worked for an infinite number of online businesspeople and it can work for you. A set of *frequently asked questions* (FAQs) is a familiar feature on many online business sites — so familiar, in fact, that Web surfers expect to find a FAQ page on every business site.

Even the format of FAQ pages is pretty similar from site to site and this predictability is an asset. FAQ pages are generally presented in Q-and-A format, with topics appearing in the form of questions that have literally been asked by other customers or that have been made up to resemble real questions. Each question has a brief answer that provides essential information about the business.

Just because we're continually pushing communication doesn't mean you should bore your potential customers with endless words that don't apply to their interests. To keep your FAQ page from getting too long, we recommend that you list all the questions at the top of the page. This way, by clicking a hyperlinked item in the list, readers jump to the spot on the page where you present the question that relates to them and its answer in detail.

Just having a FAQ page isn't enough. Make sure that yours is easy to use and comprehensive. A good example of a FAQ page is Your Privacy Rights FAQs (www.privacy.gov.au/faqs), on the Web site of the Office of the Privacy Commissioner in Australia. See also QueryElf (www.queryelf.com), which is a searchable database of FAQs from all over the Internet. The site claims to have 1.8 million FAQs!

Sure, you could compose a FAQ page off the top of your head, but sometimes getting a different perspective helps. Invite visitors, customers, friends and family to come up with questions about your business. You may want to include questions on some of the following topics:

- ✔ **Contact information:** If I need to reach you in a hurry by mail, fax or phone, how do I do that? Are you available only at certain hours?
- ✔ **Instructions:** What if I need more detailed instructions on how to use your products or services? Where can I find them?
- ✔ **Service:** What do I do if the merchandise doesn't work for some reason or breaks? Do you have a returns policy?

✔ **Sales tax:** Is GST added to the cost I see on-screen?

✔ **Returns or exchanges:** If I'm not satisfied, can I get my money back or get an exchange? Is there a time limit on this policy?

✔ **Shipping:** What are my shipping options?

You don't have to use the term FAQ, either. Other terms used include how-to, tutorial, fact sheet or knowledge base. The retailer DealsDirect, which does just about everything right in terms of e-commerce, uses the term Help for its list of questions and answers. Go to the DealsDirect home page (www.dealsdirect.com.au) and click the Help link to see how DealsDirect presents the same type of material.

Nothing makes you look worse than an out-of-date FAQ page. Try to keep your page up to date as your business grows. Make sure the questions match sales items and services that you actually provide.

Writing an online newsletter

You may define yourself as an online businessperson, not a newsletter editor. But sharing information with customers and potential customers through an email newsletter is a great way to build credibility for yourself and your business.

For added customer service (not to mention a touch of self-promotion), consider producing a regular publication that you send out to a mailing list. Your mailing list would begin with customers and prospective customers who visit your Web site and indicate that they want to subscribe.

An email newsletter doesn't happen by magic, but it can provide your business with long-term benefits that include:

✔ **Customer tracking:** You can add subscribers' email addresses to a mailing list that you can use for other marketing purposes, such as promoting special sales items for return customers.

✔ **Low-bandwidth:** An email newsletter doesn't require much memory. Such newsletters are great for businesspeople who get their email on the road via laptops, palm devices or appliances that are designed specifically for sending and receiving email.

✔ **Timeliness:** You can get breaking news into your electronic newsletter much faster than you can put it in print.

The fun part is to name your newsletter and assemble content that you want to include. Then follow these steps to get your publication up and running:

1. **Create your newsletter by typing the contents in plain text (ASCII) format.**

   You can also provide a HTML-formatted version. You can then include headings and graphics, which show up in email programs that support HTML email messages.

   If you use a plain-text newsletter, format it by using capital letters; rules that consist of a row of equal signs, hyphens or asterisks; or blank spaces to align elements.

2. **Save your file with the proper filename extension: .txt for the text version and .htm or .html if you send an HTML version.**

3. **Attach the file to an email message by using your email program's method of sending attachments — or paste it into the body of the message in case your recipients don't receive attachments.**

4. **Address your email to the recipients.**

   If you have lots of subscribers (many newsletters have hundreds or thousands), save their addresses in a mailing list.

5. **Send your newsletter.**

Consider using a Web-based email marketing application such as Constant Contact or DIY Email Manager to personalise, track and send a large number of emails at the same time. These software applications are all ways to help your words reach their destination quickly and reliably.

Managing a mailing list can be time consuming. You have to keep track of people who want to subscribe or unsubscribe, as well as those who ask for more information. Web-based email marketing applications, therefore, can save you time and hassles. Useful features include

✔ Managing subscriptions and unsubscriptions

✔ Scheduling emails to go out at a certain time

✔ Tracking to see how many subscribers have opened your email newsletters or clicked on the hyperlinks included in your newsletter

Adobe's Portable Document Format (PDF) enables you to save a publication with the images, special typefaces and other layout features intact. You can save your file as a PDF document and mail it. PDF format often helps to keep the file size small while maintaining the quality of the pictures and layout used. Recipients need the widely available program Adobe Reader to open it. These days, you can download a free add-on for Microsoft Office 2007 to create PDF files from your documents. Alternatively, check out Pdf995 (www.pdf995.com).

Mixing bricks and clicks

If you operate a bricks-and-mortar business as well as a Web-based business, you have additional opportunities to get feedback from your shoppers. Take advantage of the fact that you meet customers personally on a regular basis and ask them for opinions and suggestions that can help you operate a more effective Web site.

When your customers are in the checkout line (the real one with a cash register, not your online shopping cart), ask them to fill out a questionnaire about your Web site. Consider asking questions like the following:

- Have you visited this store's Web site? Are you familiar with it?
- Would you visit the Web site more often if you knew there was merchandise or content there that you couldn't find in our physical location?
- Can you suggest some types of merchandise or special sales you'd like to see on the Web site?

Including your Web site's URL on all the printed literature in your shop is a good idea. The feedback system works both ways, of course: You can ask online customers for suggestions on how to run your bricks-and-mortar shop better and what types of merchandise they'd like to see on your real, as opposed to your 'virtual', shelves.

Adding a human touch to your Web site

Audio is a powerful yet cost-effective marketing tool that can enhance and add value to your Web site.

Adding an audio message to your Web site can assist your site visitors to gain a better understanding of your products or services. Just as a face-to-face meeting increases the opportunity to sell your products or services, audio on your Web site creates a bond/rapport with your Web site visitor.

No longer are you just another Web site among the hundreds or thousands that a prospective client may visit, but your Web site has a human dimension — a voice. This presentation assists in making your Web site visitor feel comfortable and your Web site appear more professional and trustworthy.

Here are some examples of how audio can be used to enhance your Web site:

✔ **Audio testimonials:** Give your Web site visitors the opportunity to hear what your customers think about your business. Testimonials are always a great way to add credibility to your business, but by adding them as audio content, your Web site visitors can hear enthusiastic voices talk about you and your business.

✔ **Instructions:** When giving instructions, a lot of people respond better to the spoken word — making audio a valuable tool. Providing instructions as an audio file can make even the most complex written instructions easier to follow. For example, you may want to simply guide Web site visitors through a task such as ordering products, or offer short tips or tutorials. This method also prevents you from excluding those people who are auditory (not visual) learners. By having instructions in text on your Web site, you're catering for visual learners. When you add audio, you make the process easier for auditory learners, and they understand and relate to your message more easily as well.

✔ **Personal messages:** Adding a personal greeting, introduction or welcome audio message to your Web site is a great way to introduce yourself, your business, products or services. Web site visitors may not read all of your text content or remember what they have read so a personal message increases the chances of them remembering the information about your products or services and your Web site.

✔ **Sales message tool:** Adding audio to your Web site serves as an attention getter. By using audio on your Web site you have the ability to guide your Web site visitor through your site to featured products or services. Audio is a powerful motivator: Your voice can influence and persuade visitors to explore your Web site and therefore stay for longer. Audio improves the 'stickiness' of your Web site.

Creating an RSS feed

Email newsletters and hyperlinks are becoming passé. These days, blogs and RSS feeds are the preferred options for getting the word out about just about anything. The phrase 'send an RSS feed of your Web site or eBay listings' may sound really high-tech and complex. But it's Really Simple — Really Simple Syndication, or RSS, that is.

RSS is a way of converting the contents of a Web page to an eXtensible Markup Language (XML) file so it can be read in a flash by anyone with an *RSS reader* software program. People subscribe to your RSS feed and they receive it each time your site's contents are updated.

RSS is a marketing tool that is widely used in the world of blogs. Like a blog publisher, you can capture an RSS feed of your sales and offer it (you may say, *feed it*) to customers who want to subscribe to it. If you sell through an eBay store (an option we describe in Chapter 9), getting started is easy. Follow these steps:

1. **Subscribe to a feeder program, such as Feedburner (available from** `www.doors2stores.com/resources2.html`**), or one of the readers I describe in Chapter 3.**

2. **Go to My eBay and click the Marketing Tools link.**

3. **Click the button next to Distribute Your Listings via RSS.**

4. **Click Apply.**

5. **Go to your store's home page. Scroll to the bottom of the page, where there is an orange button labelled RSS.**

6. **Click the RSS button on your page, copy the code presented and paste it into your RSS feeder program.**

7. **Post the file and send it through the feeder program. (See eBay seller Doors2Stores's tutorial at** `www.doors2stores.com/resources2.html` **for more information.)**

If you don't sell through eBay, turning your catalogue listings into an RSS feed isn't quite as simple. You need to come up with a standard description for your listings: A listing title, a description and a hyperlink. You then format each item like this:

```
<item>
<title>Model 101 Widget</title>
<description>Check out the 101, the latest and greatest
            widget offering ever!</description>
<link>http://www.mywidgetcatalog.com/widget101.html</link>
</item>
```

You then go to a site such as Feed Validator (feedvalidator.org) to ensure your formatting is correct. Then, subscribe to one of the RSS readers mentioned at searchenginewatch.com2175281 or in Chapter 3 of this book. Copy your feed to the reader and distribute it. More info about creating feeds is at searchenginewatch.com2175271.

Helping Customers Reach You

Greg is the type of person who has an unlisted home phone number. But being anonymous is not the way to go when you're running an online business. (He uses a different number for business calls, by the way.) Of course, you don't have to promise to be available 24/7 to your customers in the flesh. But they need to believe that they can get attention no matter what time of day or night.

When you're online, contact information can take several forms. Be sure to include

- ✔ Your snail mail address
- ✔ Your email address(es)
- ✔ Your phone and fax numbers and a toll-free number (if you have one)

Most Web hosting services (such as the types of hosts that we describe in Chapter 4) give you more than one email inbox as part of your account. So it may be helpful to set up more than one email address. One address can be for people to communicate with you personally and the other can be where people go for general information. You can also set up email addresses that respond to messages by automatically sending a text file in response. (See 'Setting up autoresponders' in the next section.)

Even though you probably won't meet many of your customers in person, you need to provide them with a human connection. Keep your site as personal and friendly as possible. A contact page is a good place to provide photos and some brief biographical information about the people visitors can contact; namely, you and any employees or partners in your company.

Not putting your contact information on a separate Web page has some advantages, of course. Doing so makes your patrons wait a few seconds to access it. If your contact info is simple and your Web site consists only of a few pages, put your contact information on your home page or at the top of each page. This approach saves people going searching — making contacting you quick and easy.

Going upscale with your email

These days everyone under 70 years of age seems to have an email account. But when you're an online businessperson, you need to know more about the features of email than just how to ask about the weather or exchange a recipe. The more you discover about the finer technical points of email, the better you can meet the needs of your clients. The following sections suggest ways to go beyond simply sending and receiving email messages, as well as how to utilise email for business publishing and marketing.

Setting up autoresponders

An *autoresponder* is software that automatically answers emails sent to it. You can set up your autoresponder to send automatic replies to requests for information about a product or service, or to respond to people subscribing to an email publication or service.

You can provide automatic responses either through your own email program or through your Web host's email service. If you use a Web host to provide automatic responses, you can usually set up an extra email address that can be configured to return a text file (such as a form letter) to the sender.

Look for a Web host that provides you with one or more autoresponders along with your account. Typically, your host assigns you an email address that takes the form info@yourcompany.com. In this case, someone at your hosting service configures the account so that when a visitor to your site sends a message to info@yourcompany.com, a file of your choice, such as a simple text document that contains background information about you and your services, automatically goes out to the sender as a reply. Melissa's Web host, WebCentral (www.webcentral.com.au), allows her to create and edit an autoresponse message for each of her email accounts. First, Melissa logs on to her hosting control panel, which is the service provided to customers for changing their email settings. Melissa clicks the Modify or Create a Mailbox link and then selects the Mailbox for which she wants to edit the settings. Melissa then selects Auto-Responder to go to the Responder Settings page, as shown in Figure 8-1. Melissa checks the Auto-Responder On radio button to turn on the feature and then clicks inside the Default Reply text box to set up her autoresponse text.

If the service that hosts your Web site doesn't provide free autoresponders, look into SendFree, an online service that provides you with an autoresponder service for free but that requires you to display ads along with your automatic response. (An ad-free version is available for US$19.97 a month.) Read about it at www.sendfree.com.

Figure 8-1:
Many Web hosts enable users to create their own autoresponse messages.

Noting by quoting

Responding to a series of questions is easy when you use *quoting* — a feature that lets you copy portions of the message to which you're replying. Quoting, which is available in almost all email programs, is particularly useful for responding to a mailing list or newsgroup message because it indicates the specific topic being discussed.

How do you tell the difference between the quoted material and the body of the new email message? The common convention is to put a greater-than (>) character in the left margin, next to each line of the quoted material.

When you tell your email software to quote the original message before you type your reply, it usually quotes the entire message. To save space, you can delete the part that isn't relevant.

For example:

Instead of sending an email that says only:

> yes

Say:

> > Did you order more business cards?
>
> yes

This presentation reminds the recipient exactly what you're referring to, so communication is efficient and has less chance of misunderstandings.

Attaching files

A quick and convenient way to transmit information from place to place is to attach a file to an email message. In fact, attaching files is one of the most useful things you can do with email. *Attaching*, sending a document or file along with an email message, allows you to include material from any file to which you have access. Attached files appear as separate documents that recipients can download to their computers.

Many email clients allow users to attach files with a simple button (usually a paperclip icon) or other command. Compressing a single large file or a lengthy series of attachments by using software, such as StuffIt or WinZip, conserves bandwidth. Using compression is also a necessity if you ever want to send more than one attached file to someone whose email account doesn't accept multiple attachments.

Protocols, such as MIME (Multipurpose Internet Mail Extensions), are sets of standards that allow you to attach graphics and other multimedia files to an email message. Recipients must have an email program that supports MIME (which includes almost all the newer email programs) in order to download and read MIME files in the body of an email message. In case your recipient has an email program that doesn't support MIME attachments or if you're not sure whether it does, you must encode your attachment in a format, such as BinHex (if you're sending files to a Macintosh) or UUCP (if you're sending files to a newsgroup).

Creating a signature file that sells

One of the easiest and most useful tools for marketing on the Internet is a signature file, or sig file. A *signature file* is a text blurb that your system appends automatically to the bottom of your email messages and newsgroup postings. Your signature file should tell the readers of your message something about you and your business. You can include information such as your company name and how to contact you.

Creating a signature file takes only a little more time than putting your John Hancock on the dotted line. First, you create the signature file itself:

1. **Open a text-editing program.**

   This example uses Notepad, which comes built in with Windows. If you're a Macintosh user, you can use SimpleText. With either program, a new blank document opens on-screen.

2. **Press and hold down the hyphen (–) key or the equal sign (=) key to create a dividing line that separates your signature from the body of your message.**

   Depending on which symbol you use, a series of hyphens or equal signs forms a broken line. Don't make this line too long, or it runs onto another line, which doesn't look good; 30 to 40 characters is a safe measure.

3. **Type the information about yourself that you want to appear in the signature, pressing Enter after each line.**

   Include such information as your name, job title, company name, email address and Web site URL, if you have one. A three- or four-line signature is the typical length.

   If you're feeling ambitious at this point, you can press the spacebar to arrange your text in two columns. But the best idea is to keep it fairly plain so that your signature file displays the most important information to everyone you email regardless of what software they use to read their email. Melissa's signature file is shown in Figure 8-2.

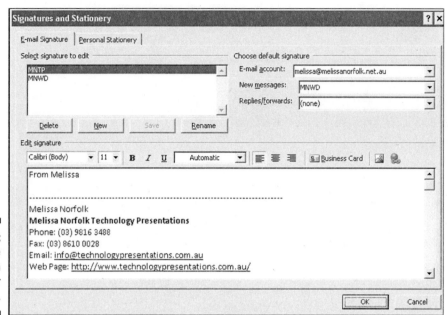

Figure 8-2:
A signature
file often
uses divider
lines.

Always include the URL of your business Web site in your signature file
and be sure to include it on its own line. Why? Most email programs
recognise the URL as a Web page by its prefix (`http://`). When your
reader opens your message, the email program displays the URL as a
clickable hyperlink that, when clicked, opens your Web page in a Web
browser window.

4. **Choose File⇨Save.**

   A dialogue box appears, enabling you to name the file and save it in a
   folder on your hard drive.

5. **Enter a name for your file that ends in the filename extension** `.txt`**.**

   This extension identifies your file as a plain text document.

6. **Click the Save button.**

   Your text file is saved on your computer's hard drive.

If you created a plain-text version of your electronic signature, the next step
is to identify that file to the computer programs that you use to send and
receive email and newsgroup messages. Doing so enables the programs
to make the signature file appear automatically at the bottom of your
messages. The procedure for attaching a signature file varies from program
to program. The following steps show you how to do this using Microsoft
Outlook Express 6:

1. **Start Outlook Express and choose Tools⇨Options.**

   The Options dialogue box opens.

2. **Click the Signatures tab.**

3. **Click New.**

   The options in the Signatures and Edit Signature sections of the Signatures tab are highlighted.

4. **Click the File button at the bottom of the tab and then click Browse.**

   The Open dialogue box appears. This is a standard Windows navigation dialogue box that lets you select folders and files on your computer.

5. **Locate the signature file that you created in the preceding set of steps by selecting a drive or folder from the Look In drop-down list. When you locate the file, click the filename and then click the Open button.**

   The Signature File dialogue box closes and you return to the Options dialogue box. The path leading to the selected file is listed in the box next to File.

6. **Click the Add Signatures to All Outgoing Messages check box and then click OK.**

   The Options dialogue box closes and you return to Outlook Express. Your signature file is added automatically to your messages.

To test your new signature file, choose File⇨New⇨Mail Message from the Outlook Express menu bar. A new message composition window opens. Your signature file appears in the body of the message composition window. You can compose a message by clicking before the signature and typing.

 For instructions on how to set up an email signature in Outlook 2003, see `office.microsoft.com/en-au/outlook/CH010046001033.aspx`. This area on the Microsoft Web site also has instructions for other versions of Outlook, from 2000 to 2007.

Creating forms that aren't formidable

In the old days, people who heard 'here's a form to fill out' usually started to groan. Who likes to stare at a form to apply for a job or for financial aid or, even worse, to figure out how much you owe in tax? But as an online businessperson, forms can be your best friends because they give customers a means to provide you with feedback as well as essential marketing information. With forms, you can find out where customers live, how old they are and so on. Customers can also use forms to sound off and ask questions.

Forms can be really handy from the perspective of the customer as well. The speed of the Internet enables them to shoot off information right away. They can then pretty much immediately receive a response from you that's tailored to their needs and interests.

The two components of Web page forms

Forms consist of two parts, only one of which is visible on a Web page:

- ✔ The *visible* part includes the text-entry fields, buttons and check boxes that an author creates with HTML commands.
- ✔ The *invisible* part of the form is a computer script that resides on the server that receives the page.

The aforementioned script — which is typically written in a language such as Perl, AppleScript or C++ — processes the form data that a reader submits to a server and presents that data in a format that the owner or operator of the Web site can read and use.

How the data gets to you

What exactly happens when customers connect to a page on your site that contains a form? First, they fill out the text-entry fields, radio buttons and other areas you have set up. When they finish, they click a button, often marked Submit, in order to transmit (or *post*) the data from the remote computer to your Web site.

A computer script called a Common Gateway Interface (CGI) program receives the data submitted to your site and processes it so that you can read it. The CGI may cause the data to be emailed to you, or it may present the data in a text file in an easy-to-read format.

You can also create a CGI program that prompts your server to send users to a Web page that acknowledges you received the information and thanks them for their feedback. This is a nice touch that your customers are sure to appreciate.

Writing the scripts that process form data is definitely in the province of Webmasters or computer programmers and is far beyond the scope of this book. But you don't have to hire someone to write the scripts: You can use a Web page program (such as FrontPage or Dreamweaver) that not only helps you create a form but also provides you with scripts that process the data for you. (If you use forms created with FrontPage, your Web host must have a set of software — FrontPage Server Extensions — installed. Call your host or search the host's online Help files to see if the extensions are present.)

Some clever businesspeople have created some really useful Web content by providing a way for non-programmers, such as you and me, to create forms online. Appropriately enough, you connect to the server's Web site and fill out a form provided by the service in order to create your form. The form has a built-in CGI that processes the data and emails it to you. Check out Freedback (`freedback.com`). Another alternative is a free hosted service such as Bravenet (`www.bravenet.com/webtools/emailfwd`).

Making forms easy for your visitors

The aim of a form is to provide a mechanism to collect information you need. This mechanism may be a simple inquiry from your Web site, an order or perhaps a subscription to your email newsletter.

The first step is to decide what information you need to collect, and then you can make the form as short and easy to fill out as possible so people don't get frustrated and leave your Web site without completing the necessary information.

Assume you have an inquiry form on your Web site. Ordinarily, this inquiry is located on the Contact Us page. In order to respond to an inquiry, the minimum information you require is a name, one method of contact and the text that details the sender's inquiry. Any other details are probably a luxury either to help you build a database, measure your marketing or to help you provide a better/more customised response.

The information you want to collect includes

- **First name:** Not necessary but nice to have so that you can personalise your response and address.
- **Surname:** Not necessary for an initial inquiry but handy to have on your database.
- **Email/phone:** Ask for either an email address or phone number, otherwise you have no way to respond to the inquiry! Ask for the customer's preferred method of contact and the best time to call.
- **Address:** Needed if you're going to post a response. Alternatively you could just ask for a city or postcode for marketing purposes so you can track what areas your leads come from.
- **Type of inquiry:** You may provide a drop-down list of choices to save the respondent from typing to fill out this field.
- **Where you heard about us:** Again, provide a drop-down list of choices to save the respondent time.
- **Any other comments:** Allows the respondent to ask more or give you feedback.

Next, decide the type of data to be entered for each field so you can build the form or provide instructions to your Web developer.

The most commonly used field types for Web forms are

- ✔ **Textbox:** Creates a single-line box where someone can type text
- ✔ **Text Area:** Creates a multi-line scrolling text box
- ✔ **File Upload:** Lets the user send you a text file
- ✔ **Checkbox:** Creates a check box
- ✔ **Option Button:** Creates an option button, sometimes called a radio button
- ✔ **Drop-Down Box:** Lets you create a drop-down list
- ✔ **Picture:** Lets you add a graphic image to a form

Figure 8-3 shows the most common form fields as they appear in a Web page form that you're creating.

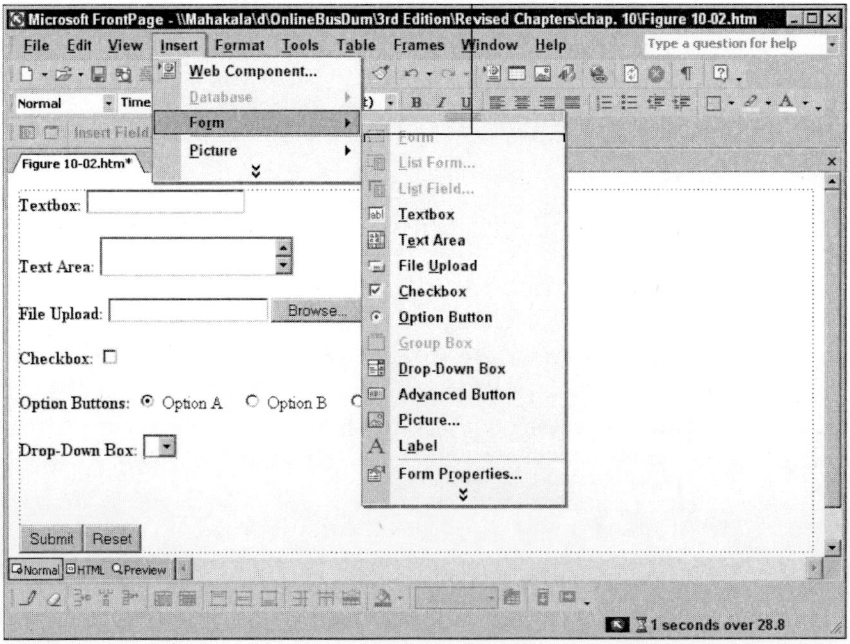

Figure 8-3: FrontPage provides you with menu options for creating form elements.

When you choose Insert⇨Form, FrontPage inserts a dashed, marquee-style box in your document to signify that you're working on Web page form fields rather than normal Web page text.

The Form Page Wizard is a great way to set up a simple form that asks for information from visitors to your Web site. This wizard lets you concentrate on the type of data you want to collect rather than on the buttons and boxes needed to gather it. We show you how to create such a form in the following steps. (These steps are for FrontPage 2002. Version 2003 and the successor program, Expression Web, require similar steps but provide you with more options.)

1. **Choose Start⇨Programs⇨Microsoft FrontPage.**

   FrontPage starts and a blank window appears.

2. **Choose File⇨New⇨Page or Web.**

   The New Page or Web task pane appears.

3. **Click Page Templates.**

   The Page Templates dialogue box appears.

4. **Double-click Form Page Wizard.**

   The first page of the Form Page Wizard appears. (You can click Finish at any time to see your form and begin editing it.)

5. **Click Next.**

6. **Follow the instructions presented in succeeding steps of the wizard to create your form.**

   a. **Click Add and then select from the set of options that the wizard presents you with for the type of information you want the form to present.**

      This may include account information, ordering information and so on.

   b. **Select specific types of information you want to solicit.**

   c. **Choose the way you want the information presented.**

      You have options such as a bulleted list, numbered list and so on.

   d. **Identify how you want the user-submitted information saved.**

      You can choose to save information as a text file, a Web page or with a custom CGI script if you have one.

7. **Click Finish.**

   The wizard window closes and your form appears in the FrontPage window.

When you finish, be sure to add your own description of the form and any special instructions at the top of the Web page. Also add your copyright and contact information at the bottom of the page. Follow the pattern you've set on other pages on your site. You can edit the form by using the Forms submenu options if you want.

Tips for making 'happy' forms!

In general, people hate filling out forms — they're often obstacles that drive away potential customers because they're confusing, obtrusive, lengthy and unresponsive.

Follow these five tips to make your forms — and your visitors — happy. You may want to simply guide Web site visitors through a task such as ordering products, or offer short tips or tutorials:

✔ **Get to the point:** Don't make people scroll down the page to the first input field. If you need to provide instructions, keep them short or include an anchor link (shortcut) straight to the start of the form for those in a hurry.

✔ **Don't ask for too much information:** Visitors are reluctant to volunteer information, especially if what you're asking for seems irrelevant. For example, if you have an email newsletter subscription form, visitors need to provide their email address, but they're probably not likely to be comfortable providing their street address, age and gender. If you do ask for extra information, clearly indicate why you're asking for it and what you intend to do with it.

✔ **Make navigation easy:** You can use JavaScript to place the cursor at the start of the first field automatically when the form loads.

Other handy features include being able to use the tab key to move through the fields; and for a drop-down list, to type in the first letter of a chosen answer which enables you to jump down to the first option in the list starting with that letter (which is especially quick and handy for a long list).

✔ **Add help information:** Don't state the obvious. Fields such as first name and surname are probably self explanatory, but for date or email you may explain or show an example of desired format, such as DD/MM/YYYY.

Some field types allow you to pre-fill fields with a default value. For example, if you have a country field you may make the default value Australia or New Zealand if most of your customers come from these countries.

✔ **Keep it neat:** Make the form easy to read by lining up form elements in columns with the field names in the first column and the input boxes, selections and check boxes in the second column. If your form is easy to read and your customer can distinguish one line or field from another, the form is easier to fill out.

✔ **Provide a clear confirmation message:** What can your visitors see after the form is submitted? At a minimum, you need to clearly confirm that the form has been received — send them to a page on your Web site that confirms the form has been sent. You should also tell them what happens next: For example, Your feedback is answered within two business days, or Your order is processed within 72 hours.

Making Customers Feel They Belong

In the old days, people went to the market often, sometimes on a daily basis. The shopkeeper was likely to have set aside items for their consideration based on individual tastes and needs. More likely than not, the business transaction followed a discussion of families, politics and neighbourhood gossip.

Good customer service can make your customers feel like members of a community that frequent a small family-owned store on the corner of their block — the community of satisfied individuals who regularly use your goods and services. In the following sections, we describe some ways to make your customers feel like members of a group, club or other organisation. Then they're going to return to your site on a regular basis and interact with a community of individuals with similar interests.

Putting the 'person' into personal service

How often does an employee personally greet you when you walk through the door of a store? On the Web as well as in real life, people like a prompt and personal response. Your challenge is to provide live customer support on your Web site.

Some Web sites do provide live support so that people can post a question to someone in real-time (or close to real-time) using Internet technologies, such as chat and message boards. The online auction giant eBay has a New Users Board, for example, where beginners can post questions for eBay support staff, who post answers in response.

An even more immediate type of customer support is provided by *chat* in which individuals type messages to one another over the Internet in real-time. You can see an example of this in action at DealsDirect (www.dealsdirect.com.au) by clicking Contact Us and then Live Chat, or at eBay Australia (www.ebay.com.au) by clicking Live Help. One way to add chat to your site is to start a Yahoo! Group, which is described in the 'Starting a Yahoo! Group' section later in this chapter.

LivePerson (www.liveperson.com) provides a simpler alternative that allows small businesses to provide chat-based support. LivePerson is software that enables you to see who is connected to your site at any one time and instantly lets you chat with them, just as if you're greeting them at the front door of a brick-and-mortar store.

LivePerson works like this: You install the LivePerson Pro software on your own computer (not the server that runs your site). With LivePerson, you or your assistants can lead the customer through the process of making a purchase. For instance, you may help show customers what individual sale items look like by sending them an image file to view with their Web browsers. You can try out LivePerson Pro for free for 30 days and then pay US$99.99 a month thereafter.

CASE STUDY

Adding the personal touch that means so much

Sarah-Lou Morris started her business out of an apartment in London, England, in 1997. She developed a herbal insect repellent — Alfresco — while working in a botanical and herbal research centre. Since then, sales have grown quickly — often doubling each year. One key to Morris's quick success is that no products are in direct competition with her lotion. Another key component is her personal approach to serving her customers, who include movie stars on location and other prominent entertainers like Sir Paul McCartney.

Morris describes her Web site and operation (www.alfresco.uk.com), as shown in the accompanying figure, as 'an extremely lively business ... an ever-growing, 24/7-demanding teenager that could easily drain my resources if I didn't keep a *very* tight shop'. Over the years, she stuck to basic business practices and focused on cultivating the customer base she had already developed through selling her product by word of mouth. (The trendy term for this type of publicity is *viral marketing;* see Chapter 10 for more on this topic.) She started a fan club for Alfresco and she has personally visited some of her best customers.

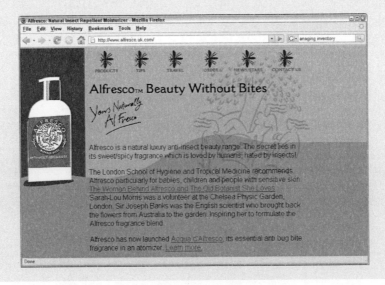

Q. How have you been able to keep a steady flow of business amid the ups and downs of the world economy?

A. We have built a bigger and bigger customer base by constantly giving good service to customers. We send out special editions for frequent buyers, have a fan club and encourage customers to make recommendations. We listen to our customers — why wouldn't we? Our site could be more automated, making it easier for us to run, but we'd lose the personal touch. It's still rewarding, and I think profitable in the long term, to take a phone call or email from some VIP in Rome or a badly bitten Chinese customer wanting quickly to buy what a friend just bought. The effort is still geared towards turning the products into a worldwide addiction-by-Internet.

Q. What are the one or two most important things people should keep in mind if they're starting an online business these days?

A. It isn't necessary to spend fortunes setting it up. Find a host that has been in business a number of years. (There *are* experts now.) A clean database that really works for you is vital because your customers are the most precious things a business can have. Keep in touch with them. Treat them with care and respect.

Q. What's the single best improvement you've made to your site to attract more customers or retain the ones you've had?

A. Putting on a special code that only special customers or fan club members can access for discounts and so on. For example, Royal Bank of Scotland employees have a special code dedicated to them.

Q. Is this a good time to start an online business?

A. It's a great time to start an e-commerce biz for a number of reasons, not the least being that the technical support is now well and truly in place. Let's just say more people know what they're doing than in earlier years. Secondly, most new customers aren't as concerned about credit card security, as there really has been hardly any fraud.

Q. What advice would you give to someone thinking of starting a new business on the Web?

A. Your customer is King, Queen, Prince and Princess. Whatever you would like yourself is what you should aim to offer. 'Do as you would like to be done by' should be your motto. Expose yourself any which way and as often as is acceptable to as many well-targeted customers as possible. Most of all, keep a positive attitude. Sir Paul McCartney once said to me when I felt depressed and almost ready to give up, 'Always have faith'. I'm glad I listened to him!

Not letting an ocean be a business barrier

You're probably familiar with terms such as 'global village' and 'international marketplace'. But how do you extend your reach into the huge overseas markets where e-commerce is just beginning to come into its own? Increasingly important is making sure products are easily and objectively described with words as well as clear images and diagrams, where necessary. You can effectively overcome language and cultural barriers in other ways, some of which are commonsense while others are less obvious.

Keep in mind the fact that shoppers in many developing nations still prefer to shop with their five senses. So that foreign customers never have a question on how to proceed, providing them with implicit descriptions of the shopping process is essential. Make information on ordering, payment, execution and support available at every step.

Customer support in Asia is, in many ways, a different creature than in the West. Although personalisation still remains critical, language and translation gives an e-commerce site a different feel. A Western site that may work well by looking clean and well organised may have to be replaced with the more chaotic blitz of characters and options often found more compelling by Eastern markets. In Asia, Web sites tend to place more emphasis on colour and interactivity. Many e-commerce destinations choose to dump all possible options on the front page instead of presenting them in an orderly, sequential flow.

Enhancing your site with a discussion area

Can we talk? Even pet birds like to communicate by squawks and sometimes by words as well. A small business can turn its individual customers into a cohesive group by starting its own discussion group on the Internet. Discussion groups work especially well if you're promoting a particular type of product or if you and your customers are involved in a provocative or even controversial area of interest.

The three kinds of discussion groups are

✔ **A local group:** Some universities create discussion areas exclusively for their students. Other large companies set aside groups that are restricted to their employees. Outsiders can't gain access because the groups aren't on the Internet but rather are on a local server within the organisation.

✔ **A Usenet newsgroup:** Individuals are allowed to create an Internet-wide discussion group in the alt or biz categories of Usenet without having to go through the time-consuming application and approval process needed to create other newsgroups.

✔ **A Web-based discussion group:** Microsoft FrontPage includes easy-to-use wizards that enable you to create a discussion area on your business Web site. Users can access the area from their Web browsers without using special discussion-group software. The problem with this approach is that Microsoft no longer supports FrontPage and in order to get the discussion area to actually work, you need a server that supports the FrontPage Server Extensions. As an alternative, you can start a Yahoo! Group, which we describe in the upcoming section named (surprise!) 'Starting a Yahoo! Group'.

Of these three alternatives, the first isn't appropriate for your business purposes. So what follows focuses on the latter two types of groups.

In addition to newsgroups, many large corporations host interactive chats moderated by experts on subjects related to their areas of business. But small businesses can also hold chats, most easily by setting up a chat room on a site that hosts chat-based discussions. But the hot new way to build goodwill and establish new connections with customers and interested parties is an interactive Web-based diary — a *blog* (short for Web log). Find out more about blogs in Chapter 3.

Starting an alt discussion group

Usenet is a system of communication on the Internet that enables individual computer users to participate in group discussions about topics of mutual interest. Internet newsgroups have what's referred to as a hierarchical structure. Most groups belong to one of seven main categories: comp, misc, news, rec, sci, soc and talk. The category name appears at the beginning of the group's name, such as rec.food.drink.coffee. In this section, we discuss the alt category, which is just about as popular as the seven other categories and enables individuals — like you — to establish their own newsgroups.

In our opinion, the biz discussion groups aren't taken seriously because they're widely populated by unscrupulous people promoting get-rich-quick schemes and egomaniacs who love the sound of their own voices. The alt groups, although they can certainly address some wild and crazy topics, are at least as well known and often address serious topics. Plus, the process of setting up an alt group is well documented.

The prefix `alt` didn't originally stand for *alternative*, although it has come to mean that. The term was an abbreviation for Anarchists, Lunatics and Terrorists, which wasn't so politically incorrect back in those days. Now, `alt` is a catchall category in which anyone can start a group, if others show interest in the creator's proposal.

The first step to creating your own `alt` discussion group is to point your Web browser to Google Groups (`groups.google.com`) or launch your browser's newsgroup software. To start the Outlook Express newsgroup software, click the plus sign next to the name of the newsgroup software in the program's Folders pane (this assumes you have already configured Outlook Express to connect to your ISP's newsgroup server) and access the `alt.config.newgroups` group. This area contains general instructions on starting your own Usenet newsgroup. Also look in `news.answers` for the How to Start a New Usenet Newsgroup message.

To find out how to start a group in the `alt` category, go to Google (`www.google.com`), click Groups, and search for the How to Start an Alt Newsgroup message. Follow the instructions contained in this message to set up your own discussion group. Basically, the process involves the following steps:

1. **Write a brief proposal describing the purpose of the group you want to create and include an email message where people can respond with comments.**

   The proposal also contains the name of your group in the correct form (`alt.groupname.moreinfo.moreinfo`). Try to keep the group name short and official looking if the form is for business purposes.

2. **Submit the proposal to the newsgroup** `alt.config`.

3. **Gather feedback to your proposal with email.**

4. **Send a special message, or a *control message*, to the news server that gives you access to Usenet.**

   The exact form of the message varies from server to server, so you need to consult with your ISP on how to compose the message correctly.

5. **Wait a while (a few days or weeks) as *news administrators* (the people who operate news servers at ISPs around the world) decide whether to adopt your request and add your group to their list of newsgroups.**

Before you try to start your own group, look through the Big 7 categories (comp, misc, news, rec, sci, soc and talk) to make sure that someone else isn't already covering your topic.

Starting a Yahoo! Group

When the Internet was still fresh and new, Usenet was almost the only game in town. These days, the Web is pretty much (along with email) the most popular way to communicate and share information, which is why starting a discussion group on the Web makes perfect sense! A Web-based discussion group is somewhat less intimidating than others because it doesn't require a participant to use newsgroup software.

Yahoo! Groups are absolutely free to set up. (To find out how, just go to the FAQ page, help.yahoo.com/l/au/yahoo7/groups/original/, and click the Starting and Managing a Group link.) They not only enable users to exchange messages, but they can also communicate in real time by using chat. And as the list operator, you can send email newsletters and other messages to your participants, too.

Simply operating an online store isn't enough. You need to present yourself as an authority in a particular area that is of interest. The discussion group needs to concern itself primarily with that topic and give participants a chance to exchange views and tips on the topic. If people have questions about your store, they can always email you directly — they don't need a discussion group to do that.

Part III
Running and Promoting Your Online Business

Glenn Lumsden

'I've optimised my search engine hit-rate by including every word in the English language on my Web site.'

In this part . . .

*I*f you've never run an online business before and you're starting out from scratch, consider starting out on one of the online auction marketplaces. eBay and Trade Me in particular are remarkable because they give you an opportunity to develop a regular source of income in a matter of a few months, or even a few weeks without having to set up your own Web site.

Chapter 9 shows you how to turn your online sales activities into a part- or full-time business. Chapter 10 discusses how to embrace advertising and publicity in ways that attract and keep your customers. Chapter 11 explains how search engines find your site and how to make sure you're reaching the most people possible with the best message you can convey. You no doubt already use Google several times a day, but Chapter 12 explains the basics of making Google work for you.

Chapter 9

Running a Business through Online Auctions

*T*he popularity of online auctions is growing at a rapid rate due to being one of the easiest ways to make money online — so it may just be the perfect place for you to test the waters for your new business idea.

Sales through online auctions are already in the tens of billions of dollars and this amount is predicted to grow steadily over the next few years. You would have heard of eBay which is the biggest player in the market worldwide. So what about in Australia and New Zealand? Well in Australia eBay.com.au is definitely the most used online auction site with more than 5 million Australian members, followed by the home-grown OZtion, which hit 300,000 members in mid-2008. In New Zealand, home-grown Trade Me is not only the largest online auction site but is also the most visited Web site in New Zealand. As of June 2008, Trade Me had more than 2 million members and 1.2 million live auctions, as opposed to eBay New Zealand which had just 7,600 live auctions.

Online auctions are convenient and easy to use for both buyers and sellers, even for newbies — hence their appeal. More and more often, when consumers are looking to purchase rare or unusual items or simply to save money, they automatically turn to a popular online auction site. For sellers of all sorts, an online auction is a viable place to find customers and boost revenue.

Chances are you've already bought or sold some things yourself through an online auction site. Where else can you start from zero and have a business up and running in a matter of weeks or perhaps even days?

Selling occasionally to make a few extra dollars and doing what thousands have already done — selling through online auctions as a means of self-employment — are quite different approaches though. eBay itself has estimated that as many as 450,000 individuals run a business on the auction site full time. Countless others do it on a permanent part-time basis to help boost the family income. Whatever the reason, you can't overlook online auctions as a way to get a first business off the ground. With online auctions, you don't necessarily have to create a Web site, develop your own shopping cart, or become a credit card merchant: The auction site handles each of those essential tasks for you. But that doesn't mean developing your own online auction business is easy. You need a dose of hard work and commitment, combined with the important business strategies we discuss in this chapter.

Running a business through an online auction site doesn't necessarily mean you depend on this as the sole source of your income. It might mean you sell via online auctions part time for some supplementary income each month. This chapter assumes that you want to sell regularly on auctions and build a system for successful sales that can provide you with extra money, bill-paying money or 'fun money.'

Understanding eBay Auctions

In any contest, you have to know the ground rules. Anyone who has held a garage sale knows the ground rules for making a person-to-person sale. But eBay is different, and not just because auctions are the primary format. eBay gives its members many different ways to sell, and each sales format has its own set of rules and procedures. It pays to know something about the different sales so that you can choose the right format for the item you have.

This section assumes that you have some basic knowledge of eBay and that you have at least shopped for a few items and possibly won some auctions. When it comes to putting items up for sale, eBay gets more complicated. You have the following sales options:

- ✔ **Standard auctions:** This is the most basic eBay auction: You put an item up for sale, and you specify a starting bid (usually, a low amount from $1–$9.99). You don't have a reserve price; the highest bidder at the end of the sale wins (if there is a highest bidder). Standard auctions and other auctions on eBay can last one, three, five, seven or ten days. The ending time is precise: If you list something at 10.09 am on a Sunday and you choose a seven-day format, the sale then ends at 10.09 am the following Sunday.

- ✔ **Reserve auctions:** A *reserve price* is a minimum price you specify in order for a successful purchase. Any bids placed on the item being offered must be met or exceeded; otherwise, the sale ends without the seller being obligated to sell the item. You know if a reserve price is present by the message `Reserve Not Yet Met` next to the current high bid. When a bid is received that exceeds the reserve, this message changes to `Reserve Met`. The reserve price is concealed until the reserve is met.

  Reserve prices aren't used as often on eBay as in the past; instead, set a starting bid that represents the minimum you want to receive.

- ✔ **Multiple-item auctions:** This type of sale, also known as a Dutch auction, is used by sellers who want to sell more than one identical item at the same time. The seller specifies a starting bid and the number of items available; bidders can bid on one or more items. But the question of who wins can be confusing. The bidders who win are the ones who placed the lowest *successful* bid. In a Dutch auction, a *successful* bid doesn't necessarily mean the *lowest* bid though. It is a bid that is still above the minimum price, based on the number of items being offered. For instance, suppose six items are offered, and ten bidders place bids. The six lowest bids are successful. One bidder bids $20 each for two items. Another bids $24 for one. Three others bid $18, two others bid $14 and three bid $10. The winners are the ones who bid $24, $20 and $18, respectively. The others lose out because only six items are available.

- ✔ **Fixed-price Buy It Now (BIN) sales:** A *BIN price* is a fixed price that the seller specifies. Fixed prices are used in all eBay Stores: The seller specifies that you can purchase the item for, say $10.99; you click the Buy It Now button, agree to pay $10.99 plus shipping, and you instantly win the item.

✔ **Mixed auction/fixed price sales:** BIN prices can be offered in conjunction with standard or reserve auctions. In other words, even though bidders are placing bids on the item, if someone agrees to pay the fixed price, the item is immediately sold and the sale ends. If a BIN price is offered in conjunction with a standard auction, the BIN price is available until the first bid is placed; then the BIN price disappears. If a BIN price is offered in conjunction with a reserve auction, the BIN price is available until the reserve price is met. After the BIN price disappears, the item is available to the highest bidder.

Those are the basic types of sales. You can also sell automobiles on eBay Motors (cars2.ebay.com.au). By knowing how eBay sales work and following the rules competently, you gradually develop a good reputation on the auction site.

How you sell is important, but the question of exactly *what* you should sell is one you should resolve well before you start your eBay business. Most people begin by cleaning out their closets and other storage areas, but that inventory doesn't last more than a few weeks. Start by selling something you love, something you don't mind spending hours shopping for, photographing, describing and, eventually, packing up and shipping. Sell something that has a niche market of enthusiastic collectors or other customers. Do some research on eBay to make sure a thousand people aren't already peddling the same things you hope to make available.

Building a good reputation

To run a business on eBay, you need a steady flow of repeat customers. Customer loyalty comes primarily from the trust that is produced by developing a good reputation. eBay's feedback system is the best indicator of how trustworthy and responsive a seller is because past performance is a good indication of the kind of service a customer can expect in the future. Along with deciding what you want to sell and whether you want to sell on eBay on a part- or full-time basis, you need to have the development of a good reputation as one of your primary goals as well.

Learning from the pros: Greg's story

I was assigned, as part of the research for a book I was writing, to attend a convention in Atlanta of the Professional eBay Sellers Alliance (PeSA). PeSA members are among the elite of the eBay merchant association. Just to get into the group, you have to meet two of three criteria: gross eBay sales income of US$25,000 per month, eBay fees of US$1,500 per month or 500 positive feedbacks in the past 30 days.

These are hard-working, enterprising and successful individuals. But when I spoke to them and got to know them, I realised that they weren't very different from me: Other than a strong business sense and drive, most of them were normal folks with families who hadn't been selling professionally until they discovered eBay.

I left the meeting inspired not only to write my book but to start selling on my own. I have always collected antiques and other items and I like 'scrounging' for used items that are valuable. I am lucky enough to have a network of good second-hand shops in my area. I had already found some shoes at my local store that I knew cost US$350 new. They weren't new but were in good condition and only cost a few dollars. I bought some shoes for myself and gave others to friends or relatives.

Now, I've started buying shoes to resell on eBay. At first, it felt strange to be shopping for 'business' purposes at the store where I had previously shopped only for enjoyment and for my own benefit. It took me a few weeks to get over this, but it was easy to do so when I had made a few sales — of my own merchandise and some antiques sold on behalf of my mother — and realised I was a legitimate businessperson.

Before too long, I easily achieved my initial goal of making US$300 to US$400 a month in sales. I decided to put into practice the most important lesson I have gained from the PowerSellers I'd met: In order to make more money on eBay, you need to increase your volume. This sounds deceptively simple. But the tendency is to start slow — perhaps putting ten items up for sale in a week. Putting up ten items for sale three, five or even seven days a week is much more work. But the extra time and labour does pay off: The more you can put up for sale, the more you actually sell.

To make a long story short, I became a PowerSeller in only about three months. I got a special icon next to my User ID. As a PowerSeller, I attracted more bids and more sales. After a year, I had raised my feedback rating to nearly 400. I found out a great deal about eBay and had some extra spending money besides. I got a debit card through eBay's payment service PayPal (www.paypal.com) and used the money I collected from my eBay sales to pay daily expenses as well as some bills.

Feedback, feedback, feedback!

eBay's success is due in large measure to the network of trust it has established among its millions of members. The *feedback system*, in which members leave positive, negative or neutral comments for the people with whom they conducted (or tried to conduct) transactions is the foundation for that trust. The system rewards users who accumulate significant numbers of positive feedback comments and penalises those who have low or negative feedback numbers. By taking advantage of the feedback system, you can realise the highest possible profit on your online sales and help get your online business off the ground.

Scientific studies probably can't show how feedback numbers affect sales, but we've heard anecdotally from sellers that their sales figures increase when their feedback levels hit a certain number. The number varies, but it appears to be in the hundreds — perhaps 300 or so. The inference is that prospective buyers place more trust in sellers who have higher feedback numbers because they have more experience and are presumably more trustworthy. Those who have a PowerSeller icon are even more trustworthy (see the section 'Striving for PowerSeller status' later in this chapter).

eBay members take feedback seriously. You're going to see this after you start selling. If you don't leave feedback for your buyers after the transaction has ended, they start reminding you to do so. You're in control of the feedback you leave; don't feel coerced to leave comments unless you want to. Otherwise, the feedback system isn't going to be of value. To read someone's feedback, click the number in parentheses next to his or her User ID.

Developing a schedule

One thing that can boost your reputation above all else on eBay is timeliness. If you respond to email inquiries within a few hours or at most a day or two, and if you can ship merchandise quickly, you're virtually guaranteed to have satisfied customers who leave you positive feedback. The way to achieve timely response is to observe a work schedule.

The tedious and time-consuming bit is taking and retaking photos, editing those photos, getting sales descriptions online, and doing the packing and shipping required at the end of a sale. The only way to come up with a sufficient number of sales every week is to come up with a system. And a big part of coming up with a system is developing a weekly schedule that spells out when you need to do all of your eBay activities. Table 9-1 shows a possible schedule.

Table 9-1	eBay Business Schedule	
Day of Week	*First Activity*	*Second Activity (optional)*
Sunday	Get 7-day sales online	Send end-of-sale notices
Monday	Packing	Emails
Tuesday	Shipping	Emails
Wednesday	Plan garage sales	Take photos
Thursday	Go to garage sales	Prepare descriptions
Friday	More sales	Prepare descriptions
Saturday	Respond to buyer inquiries	Get some sales online

Is something conspicuously missing from the proposed schedule in Table 9-1? A day of rest maybe? You can certainly work in such a day on Sunday (or whatever day you prefer). If you sell on eBay part time, you can probably take much of the weekend off. But most full-time sellers (and full-time self-employed people in general) are likely to tell you that finding a day to take off is difficult, especially when responding to customer emails within a day or two of their receipt is so important. You don't have to do everything all by yourself, however. You can hire full- or part-time help, which can free up time for family responsibilities.

Sunday nights are generally considered the best times to end eBay sales because that's when most potential buyers are available. But if you have an item for sale that someone really wants, any night of the week attracts buyers. And you can try starting a five-day sale on a Tuesday night so it ends on the following Sunday night; that way, you don't have to work on Sunday.

Creating an About Me page

One of the best ways to build your reputation on eBay is to create a Web page that eBay makes available to each member free of charge called About Me. Your About Me page should talk about who you are, why you collect or sell what you do, and why you're a reputable seller. You can also talk about an eBay Store, if you have one, and provide links to your current auction sales. Creating an About Me page takes only a few minutes (not much longer than filling out the Sell Your Item form to get a sale online, in fact). If you want to include a photo, take a digital image and edit it in an image-editing program, such as Paint Shop Pro or Photoshop, just as you would any other image. But a photo isn't absolutely necessary. Glenda from Million Dollar Baby (the eBay seller profiled in the sidebar 'Making money doing what you love') has a simple About Me page, as shown in Figure 9-1.

Figure 9-1: An About Me page can be simple; it can contain links to your eBay Store and your eBay auction sales.

When you've decided what you want to say on your About Me page, you need to save a digital photo if you want to include one. You then need to upload your photo to the Web server where you usually store your photos. Make note of the URL that identifies the location of the photo (for example, `www.myphotohost.com/mydirectory/photoname.jpg`).

Then follow these steps to create your About Me page:

1. **Click My eBay on the navigation bar near the top-right corner of virtually any eBay page.**

   A login page appears.

2. **Type your User ID and password and then click Sign In Securely.**

   The My eBay page appears.

3. **Click Personal Information under the My Account heading in the links on the left-hand side of the page.**

   The My eBay Account: Personal Information page appears.

4. **Scroll down to the About Me link and click Edit.**

   The About Me page appears.

5. **Scroll to the bottom of the page and click Create My Page.**

   The Choose Page Creation Option page appears.

6. **Leave the Use Our Easy Step-By-Step Process option selected and click Continue.**

   The About Me: Enter Page Content page appears.

7. **As indicated on the page, type a heading and text for your page. Label your photo and enter the URL for the photo in the Link to Your Picture text box. You can also type links to favourite pages and your own Web page if you have one. When you're done, click Continue.**

   The Preview and Submit page appears, as shown in Figure 9-2.

8. **Choose one of three possible layouts for your page, and preview your page content in the bottom half of the page. When you're done, click Submit.**

   Your page goes online.

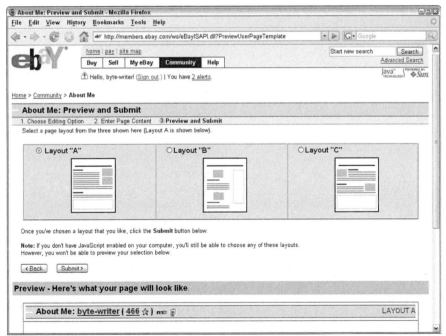

Figure 9-2:
Take a few
minutes to
proofread
your About
Me page
before
you post it
online.

Like any Web page, you can change your About Me page at any time by following the preceding steps.

Another way to ensure a good reputation as a seller is to participate actively in eBay's discussion boards. Pay special attention to boards that pertain to the type of merchandise you buy and sell. Responding to questions from new users and offering advice based on your experience boosts your standing within the user community.

Preparing sales descriptions that sell

How do you actually go about selling on eBay? The aim is similar to other forms of e-commerce: You select some merchandise, take photos, type descriptions and put the descriptions online in a catalogue. But some critical differences are apparent as well. You don't have to specify a fixed price on eBay; you can set a starting bid and see how much the market can bear. All sales descriptions aren't created equal, however. Many sellers would argue that clear, sharp photos are the most important part of a description and that, if you show the item in its best light photographically, it practically sells itself. We're of the opinion that a good heading and descriptions that include critical keywords are just as important as good photos. The art of creating descriptions is best discovered by inspecting other people's sales listings; the essentials are described in the sections that follow.

Details, details

The primary way of getting your sales online is eBay's Sell Your Item form. You can access this form at any time by clicking Sell on the eBay navigation bar, which appears at the top of just about any page on the eBay Web site. The Sell Your Item form is easy to use, so we don't step you through every nuance and option. In this section, however, we do point out a few features you may overlook that can help you get more attention for your sales.

The Sell Your Item form is by no means the only way to get eBay sales online. Many full- or part-time businesspeople use special software that allows them to upload multiple images at once or schedule multiple sales so they all start and end at the same time. The auction services Vendio (www.vendio.com), Auctiva (www.auctiva.com) and inkFrog (www1.inkfrog.com) offer eBay auction-listing tools. In addition, eBay offers two programs you might find helpful:

✔ **Turbo Lister** (pages.ebay.com.au/education/learn-to-sell-turbolister.html): Turbo Lister is a free program that provides sellers with design templates they can use to add graphic interest to their sales descriptions. This is the program Greg uses. It takes a lot of memory and is sometimes slow to run but, as shown in Figure 9-3, Turbo Lister enables you to format auctions quickly and re-use standard elements such as your shipping or returns policies.

✔ **Selling Manager** (pages.ebay.com.au/education/learn-to-sell-sellingmanager.html): Selling Manager is sales and management software — also a free program. It provides you with convenient lists that allow you to track what you have up for sale, which sales have ended, which items have been purchased, and what tasks you have yet to do — for instance, sending emails to winning bidders or relisting items that don't sell the first time.

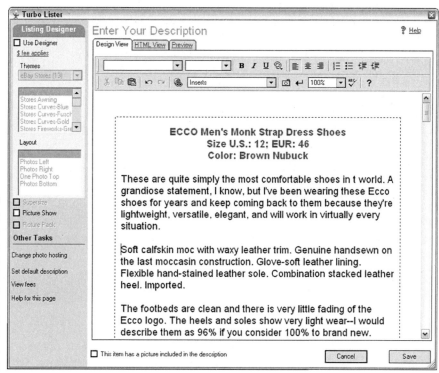

Figure 9-3: You prepare sales descriptions with the Sell Your Item form or with software like Turbo Lister.

Choosing a second category

One of the first things you do in the Sell Your Item form is to choose a sales category in which to list your item. We highly recommend using the search box at the top of the Select Category page. Enter a keyword and click Find. You're presented with a detailed list of sales categories. The list is ranked in order of the ones that are most likely to sell items matching your desired keywords. The categories near the top of the list are the ones to choose.

We also recommend paying an extra dollar or so (when you choose a second category, your listing fee is doubled) and listing the item in a second category — especially if the second category has a percentage ranking almost as high as the first.

Focusing on your auction heading

The *heading* of an eBay sales description is the six or seven words that appear in a set of search results or in a set of listings in a category. In other words, this is the set of words that a potential customer initially sees when he or she is deciding whether to investigate a sale and possibly bid on it. Keep your heading short and specific. Include dates, colours or model numbers if applicable. Try to pick one word that may attract a buyer, such as Rare, Hard-to-Find, Mint, New or something similar.

Be sure to work keywords into your auction title — brand names or phrases that shoppers may search for on eBay. Your sale is more likely to turn up in search results with desirable brand names like Gucci, Versace and so on. Be as specific as you can; include sizes, colours and original retail prices in your headings, too.

Choosing a good ending time for your sale

With eBay, the starting time isn't what counts, but the ending time that makes a difference. The more attention you can get at the end of a sale, the more likely you are to make a profit. Most sales get attention on weekends, when the majority of shoppers aren't working. In our experience, the optimal time is to have the sale end at a time on a Saturday afternoon or Sunday evening (though Wednesday evenings are also good — we're not sure why).

Of course, bidders can come from all over the world, and what's Sunday afternoon in California is Monday morning in Australia. But don't worry too much about such distinctions: Pick an ending time that's convenient for eBay shoppers in your own country to be present — not in the middle of a workday but on the weekend.

In eBay's early days, if you wanted a sale to end at a particular time (say, 7 pm on a Sunday evening, when lots of bidders are available), you had to physically be present to create the description at a certain time. For instance, if you wanted such a sale to last seven days, you had to list it at precisely 7 pm the preceding Sunday. Now, you don't have to be physically present exactly a week, five days, three days or one day before you want your sale to end: You can specify an ending time when you fill out the Sell Your Item form or with Turbo Lister, though you have to pay an extra listing fee of $.20 for each sale you schedule.

Adding keywords

You don't have to make your auction description overly lengthy. The length isn't what counts; it's the number of keywords you include. A *keyword* is a word or phrase that describes the item you have for sale and that prospective buyers are likely to enter in their eBay searches. If your description contains a keyword that someone enters, your sale shows up in search results. And just appearing in the search results is half the battle: If a buyer can find your item, he or she can then follow through with the purchase.

The more keywords you can add to your description, the more frequently the sale is found by searchers. So, thinking of all the terms that someone would use when looking for your item and adding as many of those keywords as you can to the heading as well as to the body of the description is to your advantage. If you're selling an electric drill, for example, use keywords such as *cordless, electric, 3/8-inch, Black & Decker,* or anything else a potential buyer is likely to enter.

Upgrading your listings

Near the end of the Sell Your Item form, a series of items gives you the option to specify whether you want to upgrade your listings. *Upgrade,* in this case, is adding graphic highlights that are intended to help your listing stand out from those around it, either in search results or on category pages. You can choose from the options shown in Table 9-2.

Table 9-2	Listing Upgrades	
Upgrade	**Description**	**Cost**
Highlight	A coloured strip is drawn across auction title.	$3.00
Bold	The auction title is formatted in bold type.	$2.00
Gallery	A thumbnail image appears next to auction title.	$0.59
Gallery Featured	A Gallery image appears in a 'feature' area at the top of Gallery pages.	$14.95
Home Page Featured	Your auction title is listed randomly along with other sales on eBay's home page.	$49.95

Of these, the single most cost-effective upgrade, in our opinion, is the Gallery thumbnail image, which costs only $.59 cents and calls more attention to your sales listing — especially when you consider that most other listings around yours also have Gallery images.

Note: Although you don't pay to register for an account on eBay or to fill out the Sell Your Item form, eBay charges you an Insertion Fee when you actually put an item up for sale. The Insertion Fee is based on the starting price of the auction. The fee is only $.30 for a starting bid of $0.99 or less, which explains why most starting bids are less than $1. A Final Value Fee is also charged at the end of the auction, and it depends on the sale price. On a sale of $75, the Final Value Fee is $3.94; at $1,000, it is $29.38. For a detailed explanation of the formula used to calculate fees, see `pages.ebay.com.au/help/sell/fees.html`.

Including clear images

No matter how well written your auction's headings and description, all your work can quickly be undone by digital images that are dark, blurry, or that load too slowly because they're too large in either physical or file size. The same principles that you use when capturing digital images for your e-commerce Web site apply to eBay images: Make sure you have clear, even lighting (consider taking your photos outdoors); use your camera's auto-focus setting; crop your images so they focus on the merchandise being sold; and keep the file size small by adjusting the resolution with your digital camera or your image editing software.

Some aspects to posting images along with auction descriptions are unique to eBay:

- ✔ **Close-ups:** If what you're selling has important details, such as brand names, dates and maker's marks, you need to have a camera that has *macro capability* — that is, the ability to get clear close-ups. Virtually all digital cameras have a macro setting, but it can be tricky to hold the camera still enough to get a clear image (you may need to mount the camera on a tripod). If you use a conventional film camera, invest in a macro lens.

- ✔ **Image hosting:** If you run a business on eBay and have dozens or even hundreds of sales items online at any one time, you can potentially have hundreds of image files to upload and store on a server. If you use eBay Picture Services as your photo host, the first image for each sale is free. Each subsequent image costs $.25. Finding an economical photo hosting service, such as Auctiva (www.auctiva.com), PixHost (www.pixhost.com) or Auction-Images (auction-images.com) is worth your while.

- ✔ **Multiple images:** You never hear an eBay shopper complaining that you included too many images with your auction listings. As long as you have the time and patience as well as an affordable image host, you can include five, six or more views of your item (for big objects like automobiles and other vehicles, multiple images are especially important).

Be sure to crop and adjust the brightness and contrast of your images after you take them, using a program such as Paint Shop Pro by Corel (www.corel.com) or Adobe Photoshop Elements (www.adobe.com).

If you want to find out more about creating sales descriptions (and practically every aspect of buying or selling on eBay, for that matter) take a look at *eBay PowerSeller Business Practices For Dummies* by Marsha Collier (Wiley Publishing, Inc.).

Being flexible with payment options

Payments may seem like the most nerve-racking part of a transaction on eBay. They have been, in the past; but as time goes on, eBay provides more safeguards for its customers. That doesn't mean you're not going to run into the occasional bidder who doesn't respond after winning your auction, or whose cheque bounces. But as a seller, you have plenty of protections: If someone doesn't respond, you can relist your item; if someone's cheque bounces, you don't lose your sales item because you hold on to it while the cheque clears.

You should accept the most popular forms of payment: direct bank deposit, credit card, either by using your merchant credit card account if you have one (refer to Chapter 7), or by using PayPal (www.paypal.com). PayPal is by far the most popular option. In the case of PayPal, you're charged a nominal fee (2.4 per cent of the amount plus a 30-cent fee) when a buyer transfers money electronically to your account. You can also enable buyers to use the basic forms of payment such as personal cheques and money orders although transactions can take more time due to waiting for the post and for funds to clear.

Don't accept other forms of payment from buyers. Occasionally, a buyer insists on sending you cash in an envelope; you should insist, in turn, that the buyer sends a money order instead. COD (Collect on Delivery) is expensive and cumbersome; it makes the delivery service responsible for collecting your money, and if the buyer isn't home when the delivery people arrive, you may have to wait a long time to get paid. For example, Western Union wire transfers are notorious for being used by scam artists — though Greg has used Western Union money order payments with no problem.

Providing good customer service

When you sell on eBay on a regular basis, you need to develop a good reputation. One way to achieve that goal is to provide a high level of customer service to your buyers. The single best way to do *that* is to be responsive to email inquiries of all sorts. This means checking your email at least once a day and spending lots of time typing messages. If you take days to get back to someone who asks you about the colour or the condition of an item you have for sale, it may just be too late for that person to bid. And a slow response to a high bidder or buyer after the sale can make the buyer nervous and result in neutral feedback — not a complaint about fraud or dishonesty, but a note about poor service. Such feedback is considered as bad as a negative comment on eBay.

Setting terms of sale

One aspect of good customer service is getting back to people quickly and communicating clearly and with courtesy. When you receive inquiries, always thank prospective customers for approaching you and considering the sale; even if they don't end up placing bids, your goodwill is bankable, so to speak.

Another way to be good to your customers is to be clear about how you plan to ship your merchandise and how much it is going to cost. When you fill out the Sell Your Item form (which we discuss further in the earlier section 'Details, details'), you can specify either an actual *shipping cost* (a cost based on weight and the buyer's residence) or a *flat shipping fee* (a shipping fee you charge for all of your items).

The moment you specify a shipping charge in the Sell Your Item form, you set eBay's automated Checkout system in motion. The Checkout system enables buyers to calculate their own shipping charges. The advantage to you, as the seller, is that you don't need to send your buyers a message stating how much they need to pay you.

Packing and shipping safely

One of the aspects of selling on eBay often overlooked (not by *buyers*) is the practice of packing and shipping. After sending out payment for something, buyers often wait on pins and needles, eagerly hoping to receive their items while dreading an unresponsive seller who refuses to ship their purchases. Besides the danger of fraud, the buyer sweats on the danger that the item you send is going to be damaged in transit.

Be sure to use sturdy boxes when you ship and that you take care to adequately cushion your merchandise within those boxes. Your buyer prefers to receive a box from a seller who stuffed the insides with bubble wrap and newspaper. If you're shipping something particularly fragile, consider double-boxing it: Put it in a box, place the box in a larger one, and put cushioning material between the two. Your customers are going to be pleased to receive the merchandise undamaged, and you get good feedback as a result.

Place a thank-you note, business card or even a small gift inside the box with your shipment. It spreads good feelings and reminds buyers how to get in touch with you in the future.

Moving from auctioneer to eBay businessperson

eBay sellers don't start out saying, 'I'm going to be a PowerSeller, and I'm going to sell full time on eBay for a living!' Rather, they typically start out on a whim. They find an object lying in a box, in the cellar or on a shelf, and they wonder: Will anyone pay money for this?

That's what happened to Glenda (profiled in the sidebar 'Making money doing what you love') who was nearing retirement and had worked in retail baby shops for 19 years. Four years ago she took a basic computer course not wanting to be left behind in her job. She started out on eBay selling a couple of pieces of furniture she needed to get rid of from around the house. She then sewed a couple of things and placed them on eBay and they were snapped up! This got her thinking about earning a bit of an income from home in her retirement.

Opening an eBay store

An *eBay Store* is a Web site within eBay's own voluminous Web empire. It's a place where sellers can post items for sale at fixed prices. The great advantage of having a store is that it enables a seller to keep merchandise available for purchase for 30, 60, 90 or even an unlimited number of days at a time. It gives customers another way to buy from you, and it can significantly increase your sales, too. eBay itself, at a recent eBay Live event, made the claim that eBay Stores brought about a 25 per cent increase in overall sales.

Starting an eBay Store is a big undertaking, and something you should only do when you already have a proven system for selling items on eBay at auction. You should also have a ready source of inventory with which you can stock your store. The problem with stores is that they cost $14.95 and up per month, depending on the package you choose, and you have to sell that much just to break even every month. For sellers who have a small profit margin, it can sometimes be a struggle to make back that monthly payment, especially in the slow months.

As soon as you know what you want to sell and you have good-quality inventory to offer (not just castoffs that went unsold at auction), go to the eBay Stores home page (`stores.ebay.com.au`) and click the Open a Store link to get the ball rolling. You need to decide on a name for your store and you need to organise your merchandise into sales categories. You also need to tend and update your store to make it a success. But having a store can be a key step towards making an eBay business work, and if you're serious about making eBay a regular source of income, we encourage you to give the store option a try.

An article in *E-Commerce Times* describes different strategies for getting your eBay Store listed in many of the major search engines. You can read the article at www.ecommerce-guide.com/news/news/article. php/3375851.

Striving for PowerSeller status

PowerSellers are among the elite on eBay. Those members who have the coveted icon next to their names feel justifiably proud of their accomplishments. They have met the stringent requirements for PowerSellers, which emphasise consistent sales, a high and regular number of completed sales, and excellent customer service. Moving from occasional seller to PowerSeller is a substantial change — and can be quite a thrill. Requirements include

- ✔ At least 100 unique feedback results — 98 per cent of which are positive
- ✔ A minimum of $2,000 of average gross monthly sales for three consecutive months
- ✔ A good standing record — achieved by complying with eBay Listing Policies
- ✔ An average of four monthly listings or more for three consecutive months

In return for the hard work required to meet these standards, PowerSellers do get a number of benefits. These include invitations to eBay events, business templates with a special logo on it, a special discussion board just for PowerSellers, and more. The big benefit is that the number of bids and purchases go up because buyers have more confidence in you.

The PowerSeller program isn't something you apply for. eBay reviews your sales statistics and invites you to join the program when you meet the requirements. You can find out more about the requirements and benefits of the PowerSeller program at pages.ebay.com.au/services/buyandsell/ powersellers.html.

CASE STUDY

Making money doing what you love

PowerSeller and eBay Store owner Glenda, hadn't touched a computer until four years ago. Now in her late 50s, and with three grown-up sons, she is retired and earns a decent living on eBay doing what she loves — sewing! Her business, Million Dollar Baby (www.milliondollarbaby.com.au), started out on a whim — she had sewn cot sheets for a few friends who'd had trouble finding certain sizes and colours in retail stores. Having worked in the retail baby-supplies industry for 19 years, she also had a pet hate for the amount mums were charged for often substandard products that had loose threads when opened or didn't hold up after the first time through the washing machine. In 2005, she started out sewing a couple of individual items and selling them on eBay and they were whipped up in a flash. The business grew from there and she was able to quit her job in June 2007 to concentrate full time on her business.

Million Dollar Baby now averages between 120 and 150 orders a month and Glenda works seven days a week from her home in Beaudesert in Queensland. She specialises in cot and cradle sheets for babies, including hard-to-get sizes and styles, and offers 17 different colours. After her initial setup costs, the business has very low ongoing overheads and sales have doubled for each of the last three years in a row.

In the early days of business, Glenda used the Internet a lot for market research to investigate sizes, colours and prices of other baby-linen manufacturers but found the offerings very limited, especially in Australia — hence her niche! Now she supplies a couple of baby-supplies stores, and childcare and medical centres, but prefers to concentrate on retail sales direct to the public and gets great satisfaction out of the hundreds of thank-you emails she receives from happy customers. As the business grows, she sets herself annual goals to keep her focused but has avoided hiring staff at this stage, preferring to do all the sewing herself to keep control of the quality of her product.

Q. What do you think has led to your success on eBay?

A. Having a quality product at a reasonable price and offering good old-fashioned service.

Q. Has it been of benefit to your business having an eBay Store?

A. Yes, definitely, although sometimes I get mad at the amount I pay out in fees ($400–$500 a month) it allows me more features with my listings. I usually have about 70 items listed at a time and it is easier and cheaper to link to other items in my store so eBay browsers can see my other products.

Q. What one piece of advice would you give to new eBay members hoping to generate an income through online auctions?

A. Find a niche. Don't pick a product line already saturated on eBay with lots of competition. Perfect your offer by offering good prices, be honest and provide great customer service. Listen to your customers.

Q. I see you have a Web site, too. Tell me about how you came to set up your Web site. Was it a hard task? Has the Web site been helpful for your business?

A. First off I tried to create my Web site myself and this was a disaster due to my limited computer skills and not knowing what I was doing. I later found someone on eBay who helped me re-do my Web site for under $400. He was fabulous — he helped me link my Web site up to my eBay store and I can email him anytime I need help. My Web site only costs me Web hosting of $70 a year, which is a lot cheaper than my eBay Store fees. It has been a big learning curve, but I now know more about getting listed in the search engines and using Google Adwords — and my Web site generates a decent number of orders.

Source: These materials have been reproduced with the permission of eBay Inc.
© 2008 EBAY INC. ALL RIGHTS RESERVED.

trademe.co.nz: Where Kiwis Buy and Sell

Trade Me is a household name in New Zealand. If you live in New Zealand and use the Internet, you're almost guaranteed to be a Trade Me member — out of a population of 4.1 million, around 2 million are active Trade Me members. Started in 1999 by Kiwi Sam White, the Web site sold to Fairfax for NZ$700 million in 2006. Trade Me is still by the far the number one Web site in New Zealand and beats eBay New Zealand by a mile! So if you're going to start an online auction business in New Zealand, you may want to strongly consider Trade Me instead of eBay.

Trade Me allows you to list general items for sale as well as vehicles and property. You can also advertise a job or look for a flatmate.

When starting out, your first task must be to familiarise yourself with how Trade Me works, so list a couple of second-hand items from around the house that you want to get rid of and see how you go. Next, you need to decide what you want to sell on a regular basis and how to source these items. Depending on the volumes you plan to sell, you can either list items as a private seller or alternatively set up your own Trade Me Store. This section describes your options and all things required to develop your own online business on Trade Me.

Only members located in New Zealand and Australia can buy and sell items on Trade Me.

Reputation and feedback matters

Selling on Trade Me is as simple as listing your item, setting a sale price and a reserve price, members then bid and the highest bidder when the auction closes wins the item. The simplicity of the process heralds its success — along with the critical feedback system.

If you're going to purchase over the Internet from a complete stranger, you need to be able to trust that the item is going to arrive as described, is going to be of a certain quality and is going to be good value for your money. To build a successful online business on Trade Me, you need to work hard to develop a good and trustworthy reputation. Trade Me provides authentication, user feedback and trust ratings to help you do this.

Getting authenticated

If you're serious about selling on Trade Me, you must become an *authenticated member*. You can only sell items if you're an authenticated member — this classification is identified by a single red star beside your name.

Buyers look to see if a trader is authenticated and then check the feedback rating before making a decision to bid for items. To gain authentication you need to credit your Trade Me account with a minimum of NZ$10. This amount is added to your account balance and used towards your listing fees when you start trading.

Authenticated members have a few additional features available to them including the ability to list items for sale, place bids over NZ$5,000, bid on an unlimited number of auctions and purchase items using 'buy now'.

Authentication earns you your first star, and the number of stars you have represents your feedback rating.

Collecting feedback equals greater trust

Each time you sell an item, both you and the buyer have the opportunity to post feedback about each other. This feedback represents how smoothly the transaction goes and how easy the person is to deal with. This impression is usually based on how well each person communicates, how fast the buyer pays for the goods, how quickly the seller delivers the goods and whether the goods arrive in the condition advertised.

You can then review a member's feedback to see what other traders say, which helps you assess whether the trader is reliable to deal with or not. Similarly your potential customers can review your feedback before deciding to bid on your auctions, so you should work hard to build and maintain your rating. This work is hard work and becomes more time consuming the more items you list for sale because you need to be available to respond to any questions prior to the auction closing, and to finalise the transaction and ship the goods quickly when each auction ends. Your feedback rating is displayed in brackets next to your trader username.

Placing and managing listings

To place a listing, follow these steps:

1. **Click the Sell tab on the menu at the top of any page.**

   You must be based in New Zealand or Australia and be an authenticated member.

2. **Choose the type of item you're listing from the selection that appears.**

   Your choices are: General item; Car, motorbike or boat; Property; Job or Flatmate wanted. Each attracts a different listing fee, so check the cost before proceeding.

   In many cases, you can likely select General Item. Listing a General Item is free, which means you don't incur any fees unless the item sells.

3. **Choose General Item and Click Next.**

   The Member Login page appears.

4. **Enter your email address and password to login.**

5. **Select the category to list your item under.**

6. **Start entering the details.**

   Depending on the category you choose, you may need to fill out different fields. The most common ones are the Listing Title (or headline), the price, the listing duration and the payment methods you wish to accept.

7. **Enter the item description.**

   A text field appears to allow you to enter the description of your item. Include keywords and phrases (such as brand names and model numbers) because these help your customer to find the item.

8. **Upload a picture.**

   Trade Me site software allows you to upload pictures under 5MB from your computer's hard drive. Photos must be in either `.gif` or `.jpg` format and you can upload one photo for free. Additional photos attract a fee.

9. **Choose any Premium Extras.**

   You have the option to choose add-ons such as Bold, Gallery and Featured. Bold and Featured options both help to make your listing more prominent, and Gallery allows you to add extra images to your listing. Choose the options appropriate for your item.

10. **Check your details.**

    You then have the option to check all details of your listing and you can choose either Start My Auction or Edit to change any details. Your auction then becomes live on the site.

A couple of useful Web pages to visit are

✔ **Seller Acceleration Centre** `www.trademe.co.nz/Help/Seller AccelerationCentre.aspx`: Provides useful tips for sellers running a business and wanting to automate and speed up their activities.

✔ **Site Statistics** `www.trademe.co.nz/Community/SiteStats.aspx`: Provides up-to-date and useful stats such as how many items are for sale on Trade Me, how many visitors the site is getting and what day of the week and time of the day is most popular. This information can help you decide what time of day to end your listings.

CASE STUDY

Finding a niche through your passion or hobby

Sandra loves to decorate cakes but when she tried to source cake-decorating supplies in New Zealand she found her options were very limited. This discovery led her to online auction site Trade Me, first as a buyer and, very soon after, as a seller. She realised that others like her were looking for novelty cake pans, cupcake papers, display stands and the like, but no-one was supplying these kinds of things.

Finding her niche, she started Kiwi Cakes when she knew she would not be returning to work after the birth of her second child. She now sells cake-decorating supplies to both amateur and professional cake-decorating enthusiasts. She began trading purely on Trade Me (User ID bejewelled), then later, as demand grew, she opened her own online store as well (kiwicakes.co.nz). She now makes a reasonable living from these combined. She sells items on Trade Me daily and is one of the top 25 Trade Me traders (www.stuff.co.nz/4305436a13. html).

Q. What do you think has led to your success on Trade Me?

A. I offer great service. If I say I'm going to do something, I do it. I have a fantastic range of products not readily available in New Zealand.

Q. Do you have a Trade Me Store?

A. No, I do not. While I'm aware of the benefits of one, I'm happier with my Trade Me listings because not many people look at store listings compared to auctions. My own Web site has features a Trade Me store can't offer, such as product reviews and top sellers, and I believe I get more trade from there than I would from a Trade Me Store.

Q. What one piece of advice would you give to new Trade Me members hoping to generate an income through online auctions?

A. If you have a passion for something and it is not readily available in New Zealand — there is an opening for you. Research is a *must*. And do your homework on what being in business means. Don't forget that when importing into New Zealand as a business, taxes beyond GST are payable on parcels. The profit margins on goods brought into the country aren't what they seem at first glance. Don't underestimate the time involved and expense of customs clearances.

If you're going to start an online business, make sure you're passionate about the products, because some days it can be all hard slog. Loving your product is what gets you through.

After the auction closes

As with any retail sales business, one of the keys to success is good customer service. When building a successful Trade Me business, developing this core value means being conscientious about how quickly you respond to buyer questions prior to an auction closing, and how quickly you communicate and deliver the item after the auction closes.

When an auction closes, the successful bidder sees your email address appear next to the listing. Both the buyer and the seller receive an automated email that details the item and the successful bidder. You should then communicate with the buyer by email to confirm payment details and deliver the item as quickly as you can.

If you respond quickly, offer reasonable postage rates and deliver quality items as described, your customers are more likely to leave positive feedback, buy from you again and tell their friends, which is exactly what you need to build your business.

Build your own Trade Me Store

As soon as you get serious and you're selling regular and large volumes on Trade Me, you can look at starting a Trade Me Store. A Trade Me Store may be an alternative to starting your own e-commerce Web site. You pay a monthly fee of NZ$79 to keep your store online, which is less than you would spend to build your own site, plus you get access to a large number of potential buyers who visit Trade Me daily. Other benefits include a link to your Web site (if you have one), your own Trade Me Web address and promotion on the Store's section of the Trade Me site.

To qualify for your own Trade Me Store you must

- Have at least 50 unique feedback results — 98 per cent of which are positive
- Pay at least NZ$300 in success fees, which equates to monthly sales of between NZ$3,000 and $5,000
- Be a registered company and be registered for GST
- Provide a minimum 30-day warranty on sale items

Chapter 10

Advertising and Publicity

. . . .

In This Chapter

▶ Getting your business name into the market price

▶ Finding free advertising for businesses on a budget

▶ Placing banner ads

▶ Broadening your customer base by shipping overseas

. . . .

*E*ver heard of the Mentos and Diet Coke guys? Fritz Grobe and Stephen Voltz put a video called 'Diet Coke and Mentos Experiments' on YouTube in May 2006 showing what happens when you combine (well, yeah) Mentos breath mints with Diet Coke. That video has been viewed more than 7 million times. Its makers appeared in Las Vegas and on *The US Ellen DeGeneres Show*, and earned $28,000 from ad spots posted at the end of the video.

It doesn't stop there. A musical group called OK Go achieved notoriety on YouTube; the Apple Pink Nano iPod gained a following on the free Web host (and social networking site) MySpace — and so did Pugster, an online retailer of Italian charms. And perhaps you remember a low-budget movie that came out in 1999 called *The Blair Witch Project*. The cost to create this horror film was less than $100,000, and yet the movie made more than $120 million at the box office.

In all these cases, word of mouth generated the attention — with a little help from the Web. As time goes on, such stories are only growing more common, as more innovative online advertising venues become available, and more imaginative people find ways to get their work before the public. The Web can be a cost-effective way for a small-business owner such as you to get a potential customer's attention. In fact, the most successful advertising strategies often involve one individual connecting with another. Targeted, personalised public-relations efforts work online because cyberspace is a personal place where intimate communication is possible. Blanketed advertising strategies of the sort you see in other media (most notably, display ads, commercials or billboards) are expensive and don't always work for online businesses. Why? They lack the personal edge you get with e-commerce; the Web is a one-to-one communications medium. Successful e-commerce sites, such as eBay, thrive not just because you can find bargains there but also because they promote community through features such as newsletters and message boards.

Internet advertising is becoming big business, but entrepreneurs like you can benefit from it as well. Usually, the more effort you put into attracting attention to your business, the more visits you receive. So, as far as Web promotion is concerned, if you don't blow your own horn, there's a danger that it may not get blown at all.

In this chapter, we describe cost-effective, do-it-yourself advertising techniques for the online entrepreneur who has a fledgling business on a tight budget.

Coming Up with a Marketing Strategy

Half the battle with running a successful online business is developing a plan for what you want to do. The next step is to get noticed. The following sections describe two strategies for making your company name more visible to online customers.

A brand that speaks for you

In business-speak, *branding* has nothing to do with rounding up cattle and everything to do with ramping up your profits. Branding is the process of raising awareness of a company's name and logo through advertising, public relations or other means.

Despite recent economic slowdowns, the Web is still a great place for developing a business brand. Forecasts indicate that global online advertising revenue (the amount that businesses spend to advertise online) is set to reach $81 billion annually by 2011. In Australia, online advertising is the third largest medium approaching $1.5 billion annually behind only metropolitan TV ($3 billion) and metropolitan newspapers ($2.8 billion).

Online advertising works because you don't have to get potential shoppers to dress up, drive across the city and find a parking spot. Web users sit only centimetres from their screen or handheld device, which means your Web page can easily get a user's undivided attention — if your content is compelling enough, that is. Don't be shy about providing links to click, thumbnail images to view and the like. Previous studies have found that Web advertising that doesn't seem like advertising — that is, interactive and entertaining — is supported and liked by consumers, and that brands advertised on the Web were seen as forward-thinking.

But don't rely on your Web page alone to spread your name. Make use of the whole Internet — including email, online communities, competitions and promotions. These days you have plenty of options to get the word out about your online business, such as the following:

- **Banner ads:** This type of ad is similar to the traditional print ads that you can place in a newspaper. See the 'Waving a banner ad' section, later in this chapter, for more information.

  Pop-ups are fairly common on the Web, but many users dislike them, and they slow down the browsing/shopping process as well. This delay dampens the enthusiasm of impulse buyers. Before you use them, consider both the upside and downside, as described in the 'Pop-up (and under, and over) ads' section, later in this chapter.

- **Blogs:** These are online diaries that you can create to engage connections with your customers and other interested individuals; you can use them to build visibility and generate advertising revenue.

- **Classifieds:** You can advertise your goods on a classified ad site such as Craigslist (www.craigslist.org), Trading Post (www.tradingpost.com.au) or Gumtree (www.gumtree.com.au or www.gumtree.co.nz).

- **Interstitials:** These pop-up ads appear in a separate window while a Web page is loading.

- **Keyword searches:** You can pay search services to make your site appear more prominently in search results.

- **MySpace and Facebook:** A growing number of businesses are using these popular sites to promote themselves and their products. In fact, LinkedIn (www.linkedin.com) is a social-networking site created especially for business owners and professionals.

- **Newsletters:** You can generate goodwill and drive business to your Web site by distributing an email newsletter.

- **Partnerships:** Find businesses whose goods and services complement yours and create links on each other's Web sites.

A Web site can also promote a brand that has already become well known through traditional sales and marketing strategies. The click-and-mortar version of the Gap (www.gap.com) works in conjunction with the clothing retailer's brick-and-mortar stores. The Web site provides a selection of styles and sizes that's generally wider than what customers can find in stores. The Gap continues to rank in the US National Retail Federation's Stores magazine's (www.stores.org) Top 100 retailers, with $15.7 million in revenue in 2007.

You may not have thousands of dollars to spend on banner ads, but they aren't the most effective forms of online advertising any more, anyway. Just as effective, is to start with some simple, cost-effective techniques like this one: Make sure that your signature files, your domain name and your email address all refer to your company name as closely as possible. Developing name awareness may take longer, but this approach is a perfect place to start.

Being selective about your audience

Traditional broadcast advertising, such as commercials or radio spots, works kind of like standing on top of a tall building and screaming: 'Hey everyone, come to my store.' Such ads deliver short bits of information to huge numbers of people — everyone in the coverage areas who happens to be tuned in at a particular time. The Internet has its own form of broadcasting — getting your company mentioned or advertised on one of the sites that draws millions of visitors each day.

But where the Internet really excels is in one-to-one communication of the kind that TV and radio can't touch. I suggest that you try your own personalised forms of online advertising before you attempt to blanket cyberspace with banner ads. Often you can reach small, *targeted* groups of people — or even one prospect at a time — through free, do-it-yourself marketing strategies. These strategies include using the right keywords, sending newsletters, and taking part in mailing lists and newsgroups, all of which we discuss in the next section.

Painting a new business scenario

Marques Vickers has appeared in this book through several editions when he was primarily an artist based in California. His life has changed dramatically, and though he says he doesn't spend as much time online as he used to, he's an example of someone who has been able to change his life and circumstances dramatically, in part through the Web. 'I can clearly say that Internet access enabled me to pursue my present course even if it meant shifting directions,' he declares.

Through his self-named Web site (www.marquesv.com), he still markets his own painting, sculpture and photography, as well as his books on marketing and buying fine art online. He first went online in November 1999, and his art-related sites have received anywhere from 25,000 to 40,000 visits per month.

Q. What are the costs of running all your Web sites and doing the associated marketing?

A. Out-of-pocket expense is approximately US$29 monthly for a Web site hosting and Internet access package. New domain name registrations and renewals probably add another US$250 because I own more than 20 domain names.

Q. What would you describe as the primary goals of your online business?

A. My initial objective was to develop a personalised round-the-clock global presence in order to recruit sales outlets, sell directly to the public, and create a reference point for people to access and view my work. I also have an intuitive sense that an online Web site presence is going to be a marketing necessity for any future visual artist and a lifelong exposure outlet. Having an online presence builds my credibility as a fine artist and positions me to take advantage of the evolution of the fine arts industry, too.

Q. Has your online business been profitable financially?

A. Absolutely — but make no mistake, achieving sales volume and revenue is a trial-and-error process and involves a significant time commitment. I'm still perfecting the business model, and it may require years to achieve the optimum marketing plan.

Q. How do you promote your site?

A. With the Internet, you're layering a collective web of multiple promotional sources. Experimentation is essential because recognition isn't always immediate but may ultimately be forthcoming as postings in cyberspace are often stumbled across from unforeseen sources. I try multiple marketing outlets including paid ad positioning services, such as Overture and Google, bartered advertising space and reciprocally traded links. Some have had moderate success, some unforeseen and remarkable exposure. Unlike traditional advertising media that have immediate response times, the Internet may lag in its response. It is a long-term commitment and one that can't be developed by short-term tactics or media blitzes.

(continued)

(continued)

Q. Do you create your Web pages yourself or do you work with someone to do that?

A. I'm too particular about the quality of content to subcontract the work out. Besides, I know what I want to say, how I want to say it, and am capable of fashioning the design concepts I want to integrate. The rectangular limitations of HTML design make colour a very important component, and the very minimal attention span of most Web viewers means that you'd better get to the point quickly and concisely. The more personalised, timely and focused your content, the more reason an individual has to return to your Web site and ultimately understand your unique vision of what you're trying to create. A Web site is an unedited forum for telling your version of a story and a means for cultivating a direct support base.

Q. How are you using the Web these days?

A. A year and a half ago, I uprooted from northern California with my wife, and we moved to the Languedoc region of southern France. I decided to focus my activities on areas more interesting to me and pursue a completely different direction. Much of the process is detailed in a column I write called 'An American in the French Languedoc' (`www.the-languedoc-page.com/articles/`). I'm still doing my artwork, but my primary 'work' is buying and renovating houses (`www.UniqueSeek.com`). I've taken a decided step back from the pace of northern California. I still use the Internet for promoting the houses I renovate, however.

Q. What advice would you give to someone starting an online business?

A. Don't hesitate one minute longer than necessary. Read substantially and from a diverse selection of sources on the subject. Subscribe to ezines on related subject matter and query the Webmasters of sites that impress you with their content. Go to informational seminars; ask questions. Experiment with marketing ideas and by all means, consider it a lifelong project. The Internet is continuing to evolve, and the opportunities have never been more prevalent.

Adopting Publicity Strategies That Are Free

In the following sections, we describe some ways that you can publicise your online business yourself — for free. Prepare, however, to devote several hours a week to corresponding by email and applying to have your business listed in search services, Internet indexes or Web sites that have a customer base similar to yours.

The best way to generate first-time and return visits to your business site is to make yourself useful as well as ornamental. The longer people are inclined to stay on your Web site, the more likely they are to acquire your goods or services. (Refer to Chapter 5 for some specific suggestions on generating compelling, useful content.)

A newsletter for next to nothing

It used to be said that the pen is mightier than the sword, but these days nothing beats a well-used mouse. No longer do you have to spend time and money to print a newsletter on actual paper and distribute it around the neighbourhood. Now that you're online, you can say what you want — as often as you want — with your own publication. Online newsletters also help meet your clients' customer service needs, as we discuss in Chapter 8.

Many of the suggestions in this section apply to an even easier way of getting the word out: creating a blog. With a blog, you don't have to worry about design, distribution and organisation issues, either; you just have to focus on putting out comment that your readers can actually find useful and that can encourage them to return on a regular basis.

Publish or perish

The work of producing an online newsletter is offset by the benefits you get in return. You may obtain hundreds — even thousands — of subscribers who find out about you and your online business.

The MailChimp Resource Center (`www.mailchimp.com/resources`) has an Email Marketing Beginners Guide — free to download and well worth a read.

In order for your publishing venture to run smoothly, however, you have some areas to consider:

- ✔ **Audience:** Identify your readers and make sure your content is useful to them. (This last item certainly applies to business blogs: Keep the personal news about your trip to Europe or your new puppy for a personal blog; focus on your area of expertise and present news and tips for readers who are going to be interested in them.)

- ✔ **Design:** You have two choices: You can send a plain-text version that doesn't look pretty but that everyone can read easily, or you can send a formatted HTML version that looks like a Web page but is only readable by people who can receive formatted email.

    HTML email, because of its additional text-formatting capabilities and graphics, puts more creative options at the marketer's disposal. HTML also has more potential problems and an increased chance that your email may not be viewed properly.

    If you're running your first campaign, you may want to stick to doing a plain-text-based email. Because this version is easy to put together yourself, you can concentrate your efforts on getting the copy and call to action perfect.

- ✔ **Staff:** You don't have to do it all. Delegate the editing function to someone else, or line up colleagues to function as contributors.

✔ **Topics:** If you run out of your own topics to write about, look to others for inspiration. Identify magazines in your field of business so you can quote articles. Get on the mailing list for any press releases you can use.

The power of opt-in email newsletters

Publishing a simple opt-in email newsletter (or *ezine*), as little as once a month, can help you increase sales — guaranteed.

✔ **Capturing the email addresses of your Web site visitors:** This is one of the most important benefits: If Melissa visits your site today but isn't ready to buy from you today, you're likely to have lost her forever when she clicks away. But, if you invite Melissa to sign up for your free newsletter that features helpful information on the topic at hand, she's going to be happy to sign up.

Now you've got Melissa to market to — over and over — as long as you continue to give her the practical content you promised. She gets to learn all about your services and products while you gain her trust. This method is especially powerful because statistics show that consumers don't usually purchase a product or service until after they've seen multiple messages about it!

✔ **Maintaining contact:** An email newsletter is a cost-effective way to maintain contact with your clients and/or prospects.

Unless you continually follow up with clients and prospects, they soon forget about you. But phoning or writing to each and every one of them every week is near impossible!

So, a properly implemented email newsletter achieves the same goal — keeping you in the back of their minds in an unobtrusive way. This constant contact makes these recipients more likely to think of you when they need a product or service like yours and helps to turn prospects into customers and customers into repeat sales.

✔ **Promoting your products or services — credibly and subtly:** Instead of 'blowing your own trumpet' and simply 'saying' how great your business is, an ezine allows you to 'show' how great you are by sharing your expertise through tips, case studies or client testimonials. You're avoiding simple bragging, and are instead offering useful information that demonstrates your knowledge.

✔ **Positioning yourself as an expert in your field:** By showcasing your knowledge and skills, you're likely to attract more and better clients. And by sharing what you know well, you're saying: 'Hey, I really know my stuff! I'm an expert.'

✔ **Spreading the word:** If your email newsletter contains useful, quality articles and tips, your readers are very likely to pass it on to friends and colleagues — this form of marketing is called *viral marketing*.

Most ezine publishers begin with just a few dozen subscribers who are their clients and associates. But after several months, you can have thousands of readers on your list — thanks to viral marketing mixed with some promotional legwork.

With the proliferation of *SPAM* (junk email), however, you need to be aware of not misusing email marketing or purchasing illegitimate bulk email lists — because bad news about your business email marketing practices is going to spread much faster than good news.

Newsletters work only if they appear on a regular basis *and* they consistently maintain a high level of quality. Whether yours comes out every week, every month or just once a year, your subscribers expect you to re-create your publication with every new issue. Keep your newsletter simple and make sure you have the resources to follow through.

Extra! Extra! Read all about it!

After you do your planning, the actual steps involved in creating your newsletter are pretty straightforward. Because you're just starting out, we suggest you concentrate on producing only a plain-text version of your newsletter. Later on, you can think about doing a HTML version as well.

People like receiving inside tips and suggestions in plain text; they're happy that they don't have to wait for graphics files to download. Figure 10-1 shows an example newsletter that uses a typical plain-text arrangement.

Before you do anything about preparing your email newsletter, check with your ISP to make sure you're permitted to have a mailing list or send bulk email. Even if your newsletter is a simple announcement that you send out only once in a while (in contrast to a discussion list, which operates pretty much constantly), you're going to be sending a *lot* more email messages through your ISP's machines than you otherwise would.

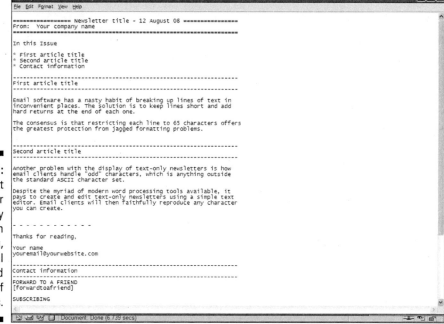

Figure 10-1: A plain-text newsletter typically begins with a heading, a horizontal divider, and a table of contents.

Keep the size of your newsletters small; about 40K is the biggest email file you can comfortably send. Reducing the file size of your newsletter keeps your readers from getting irritated about how long your message takes to download or open. And keeping your customers happy should be one of your highest business priorities.

When you're all set with the prep work, follow these general steps for an overview of how to create and distribute your publication:

1. **Open a plain-text editor, such as Notepad (Windows) or SimpleText (Mac).**

2. **Start typing.**

   Just because your newsletter is in plain text doesn't mean that you can't spice it up. Consider the following low-tech suggestions for emphasising text or separating one section from another:

   - **Lines/Dividers:** You can create your own homemade horizontal rules by typing a row of equal signs, hyphens or asterisks to define headings and separate sections.

   - **Blank spaces:** Don't underestimate white space. Use blank space throughout to separate sections and keep your newsletter neat and tidy.

   - **Lists:** Use a single dash or asterisk for bullet points. Using short paragraphs and bulleted lists keeps the newsletter concise and easy to read.

   DON'T USE ALL CAPITAL LETTERS! On the Web, excessive use of all capital letters is seen as shouting. It is also a common method spammers use to get attention. So avoid using excessive capital letters or having all your headings in capital letters; instead, use dividing lines to highlight the headings from the other text.

3. **Save your file.**

   Be sure to proofread the whole newsletter before sending it. Better yet, enlist the help of an objective viewer to read over the text for you. Ask him or her to make suggestions on content, organisation and format, as well as to look for typos.

4. **Open your email program's address book, select the mailing list of recipients and compose a new message to them.**

5. **Attach your newsletter to the message, or paste it into the body of the message, and send it away.**

Don't flood your Internet service provider's mail server with hundreds or thousands of messages at one time; you may crash the server. Break the list into smaller batches and send them at different times.

Be sure to mention your newsletter on your Web page and to provide an email address where people can subscribe to it. In the beginning, you can ask people to send subscription requests to you. If your list swells to hundreds of members, consider automated mailing-list software or a mailing-list service to manage your list (see the sidebar 'Managing your campaigns and mailing list').

Managing your campaigns and mailing list

When you make the decision to run your own email campaigns and look after your own mailing list you can run into problems. The first is being able to send large amounts of email and have them arrive at their intended location. The second is that you assume the responsibility of processing requests to subscribe and unsubscribe from the list. This updating can be very time consuming and can start eating into the time that you need to spend on your other business activities. You have a couple of options to make life easier:

✔ **Purchase desktop mailing-list software:** This type of program makes sending large amounts of email easier and also automatically adds or subtracts individuals from a mailing list in response to special email messages that they send to you. You can usually manage your email campaigns and mailing list from your home computer. Check out Gammadyne Mailer (gammadyne.com/mmail.htm) or Mailloop (www.mailloop.com).

✔ **Choose to use Web-based email marketing software:** The benefits of Web-based software are that you don't have to download and install anything on your local computer, you don't need to purchase multiple licences if you have more than one computer, you can access your campaigns from anywhere you have Internet access and you don't need to leave your computer on while your newsletter is sending.

Two other major advantages are that managing subscriptions and unsubscriptions is automated for you (saving you time), and you have access to detailed statistics about the success of your campaign. This information ordinarily includes how many subscribers open the email, who they are and when they open your message, as well as whether they click on any links inside the email or forward the message on to a friend. Check out Constant Contact (www.constantcontact.com) or DIY Email Manager (www.diy-email-manager.com).

Timing is everything

When is the best time to send your email? Great question. In fact, the audience you select, the subject line, the mailing list you're using and the timing all have an impact on the overall results of your email campaign. Of course the answer is likely to be different if you're selling executive diaries to business people as opposed to disposable cameras for weddings — so you need to consider when members of your target audience are likely to be in front of a computer.

In general, the best days to send your email are Tuesdays, Wednesdays and Thursdays.

What's wrong with the rest of the days?

- ✔ Well, on Monday your recipients are recovering from the weekend and are less likely to be in business mode yet. They may have a number of things to do over the course of the day and they often arrive in the morning to a flooded inbox after the weekend. So your Monday message gets lost in the crowd or sent straight to the trash can!

- ✔ On Friday, they're too busy wrapping things up and planning the weekend.

- ✔ If you're targeting a business audience, they're generally out of the office on Saturdays, Sundays and public holidays.

Avoid sending at a time of day when people's inboxes are likely to be overcrowded (that is, over the weekend, at the beginning of a business day or over lunch time) — this way your message has more chance of being read.

Increasing Web site traffic by writing articles

Most new, small-business Web sites take months to average just a few hundred visitors a week. Many of these sites stall indefinitely at this level. Unfortunately, income generation is very limited with these relatively low numbers.

Why so little traffic? Most small-business owners simply don't have a marketing budget big enough to properly 'kick off' a new Web site. What's more, Web promotion and getting noticed on the Internet is getting harder as more new sites are launched daily.

One of the best ways to promote your Web site is by writing articles that you can post on your Web site, in your email newsletter, on your blog, in other e-newsletters and submit to sites that provide free content to e-newsletter publishers. This approach can help you to develop credibility and build both your traffic and email database.

So, exactly what do you need to do? The answer is simple. Write about what you do. That's it. Nothing more. Plan to write a new article every week. Then do two things:

- ✔ **Email your best articles to other publishers and Webmasters:** (Check out `ezinesearch.com`.) Here are a few tips to maximise the effectiveness of your articles:

  - Keep articles short and to the point. They must act as a free sample that entices your reader to go to your Web site for more.

  - Present articles as a tip or a solution to a problem.

  - Write in easy to understand 'layman's' terms.

  - Whenever possible, write from personal experience. People love to hear other people's experiences and stories. This approach also tends to hold their attention longer.

  - Be extra-careful to avoid spelling and grammatical errors. A sloppy presentation makes you lose credibility.

  - Don't make articles sound like a sales pitch; offer honest, value-adding advice.

  - Don't forget the most important part: Always include a 'resource box' or 'by-line' at the end of your article. This element is a small paragraph (no longer than six lines) with your name, the name of your business, a short tagline and that all-important link to your Web site.

- ✔ **Post each article as a stand-alone Web page on your site (with reprint rights):** This approach allows more Webmasters easy access to your articles. It also attracts more traffic through the search engines (see Chapter 11 for more tips on maximising your search engine position).

Write articles on topics, keywords and phrases you wish to be found under in the search engines. Every article posted should be *keyword rich* (include the words you want to be found by several times throughout). This method helps with search engine ranking and targeted traffic. Next, carefully choose the 'title' of article Web pages. Examples of clever article titles include:

- ✔ Advertising in ezines — Ezine advertising that works!
- ✔ Direct Email Marketing. Using direct email to sell.

Notice the important components of the titles:

- ✔ Catchy, interesting titles
- ✔ Alphabetically strategic first word
- ✔ Most important words are repeated
- ✔ Popular keywords

If you're careful to employ ALL of these features, collectively they add up to better search engine placement.

The last thing when building your 'article' Web pages is to place a link to your home page on every article. Readers who find your articles and want more information about the topic they're researching, can always simply click to your main site! Starting to get the picture?

Every week, build another page. The result is different keyword-rich pages, different subjects, and all linked to your Web site home page.

Participating in mailing lists, discussion forums and newsgroups

Many areas of the Internet can provide you with direct access to potential customers as well as a chance to interact with them. Two of the best places to market yourself directly to individuals are mailing lists and newsgroups. Mailing lists and newsgroups are highly targeted and offer unprecedented opportunities for niche marketing. Using them takes a little creativity and time on your part, but the returns can be significant.

Get started by developing a profile of your potential customer. Then join and participate in lists and newsgroups that may provide customers for your online business. For example, if you sell memorabilia of movie stars to fans online, you may want to join some newsgroups started by the fans themselves.

Email newsletters versus blogs

In marketing terms, email newsletters are a *push strategy* and blogs are a *pull strategy*. This means that with newsletters you push out content to subscribers at a time that suits you, but with blogs people go to your blog when they're seeking information on your topic. In general, newsletters are often for longer communications sent less often (monthly or weekly); whereas, blogs are for short tips or bursts of information on a daily basis.

The great news is that you can use them to cross-promote one another. Promote your blog in your newsletter and vice versa. So, should you publish a blog, a newsletter or both? Melissa suggests both. They both serve different purposes and have different communication styles that appeal to different audiences.

According to Technorati (technorati.com) some 112 million blogs exist worldwide (more than 250,000 in Australia); and 175,000 new blogs are being launched daily. Here's why:

✔ For individuals, blogs can be a way to express your views, build a social community with a similar hobby or interest, keep a travel diary or keep family and friends, who may not be physically close, updated with all your news and photos.

✔ For business, blogs can help you build stronger relationships with important target groups such as clients, the media, the general public and/or shareholders.

✔ Blogs are simple, low-cost PR — a simple and fast way to put information online.

✔ Blogs establish expertise. A blog can position you and your company as the expert and can raise your visibility with your target market.

✔ Blogs extend communications and customer relationships. Blogs enable companies to present a human face and voice to the public. Blogs allow you to join customer discussions, respond to concerns, provide tips and insights or receive feedback.

✔ Blogs build community. You can use blogs to grow group support around a cause, political issue, technology or hobby related to your product.

✔ Blogs can test ideas or products. Because blogs are informal and conversational in nature, you can publish an idea and see whether it generates any interest or buzz.

✔ Blogs promote higher search engine rankings. Google and other search engines reward sites with a lot of content that is updated often and have many inbound links.

For example: Telstra's blog nowwearetalking aims to communicate with shareholders about new technologies (www.nowwearetalking. com.au).

Other corporates using blogs include Dell (www.direct2dell.com); McDonald's (csr.blogs.mcdonalds.com); Boeing (www.boeingblogs.com/randy).

And from the norm to the novel: *The Age* (www.blogs.theage.com.au); Pigs Will Fly (www.pigswillfly.com.au); Freaked-Out Fathers (www.freakedoutfathers.com); Grab Your Fork (www.grabyourfork.blog spot.com).

So, if you're prepared to add something at least every week or two, then adding a blog to your site is probably a good idea because a good blog can help you build traffic, communicate and more importantly build trust. Many businesses choose to host their blog separately from their main business Web site. This approach can be useful because it separates the formal from the conversational and casual, and prevents these two styles from conflicting. But don't be surprised if your blog starts getting more traffic than your main site!

Where can you find these discussion forums? Topica (`lists.topica.com`) maintains a mailing-list directory that you can search by name or topic; it includes thousands of mailing lists. (Topica also helps you create your own email newsletter, by the way.) Refdesk.com (`www.refdesk.com`) maintains links to Web sites, organised by category, that help you locate and participate in newsgroups, mailing lists and Web forums.

A few newsgroups (in particular, the ones with `biz` at the beginning of their names) are especially intended to discuss small-business issues and sales:

- ✔ `alt.business.consulting`
- ✔ `alt.business.home`
- ✔ `aol.commerce.general`
- ✔ `biz.marketplace.discussion`
- ✔ `biz.marketplace.international.discussion`
- ✔ `biz.marketplace.services.discussion`
- ✔ `misc.entrepreneurs`

The easiest way to access newsgroups is to use Google's Web-based directory (`groups.google.com`). You can also use the newsgroup software that comes built into your Web browser. Each browser or newsgroup program has its own set of steps for enabling you to access Usenet. Use your browser's online help system to find out how you can access newsgroups.

Mailing lists

A *mailing list* is a group of individuals who receive communications by email. Two kinds of mailing lists are common online:

- ✔ **Discussion lists:** These are lists of people interested in a particular topic. People subscribe to the list and have messages on the topic delivered by email. Each message sent to the list goes to everyone in the group. Each person can reply either to the original sender or to everyone in the group, too. The resulting series of messages on a topic is called a *thread*.

- ✔ **Announcement lists:** These lists provide only one-way communication. Recipients get a single message from the list administrator, such as an attached email newsletter.

Discussion lists are often more specific in topic than newsgroups. These lists vary from very small lists to lists that include thousands of people. An example of a discussion list is ROOTS-L, which is a mailing list for individuals who are researching family history. People on this list exchange inquiries about ancestors that they're seeking and announce family-tree information they've posted online.

By making contributions to a mailing list, you establish a presence; so, when members are looking to purchase the kind of goods or services you offer, they're likely to come to you rather than to a stranger. By participating in the lists right for you, you also find out invaluable information about your customers' needs and desires. Use this information to fine-tune your business so that it better meets those needs and desires.

Marketing through lists and newsgroups requires a low-key approach. Participating by answering questions or contributing your opinion to ongoing discussion topics is far more effective than blatant self-promotion (which can often get you banned).

Always read the welcome message and list guidelines that you receive upon joining a mailing list. Figure out the rules before you post. Lurk in the background for a few weeks to get a feel for the topics and participants before you contribute. Allow your four-to-six-line signature file to establish your identity without selling your wares directly. Also, remember to spell-check and proofread your messages before you send them.

Discussion groups

Discussion groups provide a different form of online group participation. On the Internet, you can find discussion groups in an extensive network called Usenet. America Online and CompuServe also have their own systems of discussion groups that are separate from Usenet. One of the easiest ways to access newsgroups, however, is with your Web browser. Just point it to Google Groups (`groups.google.com`). Many large corporations and other organisations maintain their own internal discussion groups as well. In any case, you can also access discussion groups with your Web browser's newsgroup or email software. Microsoft Outlook Express can connect to newsgroup postings, for instance.

You can promote yourself and your business in discussion groups in the same way that you can make use of mailing lists — by participating in the group, providing helpful advice and comments, and answering questions. Don't forget that newsgroups are great for fun and recreation, too; they're a good way to solve problems, get support and make new friends. For more information on newsgroups, refer to Chapter 8.

Holding a contest — everyone's a winner

In Chapter 1, we describe how cartographer John Moen uses competitions and other promotions to attract attention to his online business. Remember that everyone loves to receive something for free. Holding a competition can attract visitors to your Web site, where they can find out about the rest of your offerings — the ones you offer for sale, that is.

You don't have to give away cars or trips around the world to get attention. SoftBear Shareware LLC — a company that offers Web hosting and manages several Web sites — gave away teddy bears and other simple items on its Web site (www.799bear.com). SoftBear's owner, John Raddatz, discontinued the competition, but he still provides free online games and a scholarship competition on other sites. When we asked John whether such competitions had helped gain attention for his business, he responded as follows:

> 'YES, YES, YES. Contests have increased traffic to my site. The response averages about 350 entries per month. I offer contests, free screensavers and software, which still attract quite a few people from all over the world. My number-one contest draw is at Ice Puck University (www.ipucku.com), where I offer a free hockey diploma every month. My Johnny Puck Web site (www.johnnypuck.com) has spawned a local UHF TV show here in Muskegon, Michigan. You must offer something for free to draw people in to your site. Then you can draw their attention to your main offerings.'

Cybersurfers regularly take advantage of freebies online, for example, by downloading shareware or freeware programs. They get free advice from newsgroups, and they find free companionship from chat rooms and online forums. Having already paid for network access and computer equipment, they actually *expect* to get something for free.

Your customers keep coming back if you devise as many promotions, giveaways or sales as possible. You can also get people to interact through online forums or other tools, as we describe in Chapter 5.

Waving a banner ad

We're not as big a fan of traditional banner ads as we are of the other strategies that we discuss in this chapter — especially where small entrepreneurial businesses are concerned. But banner ads have hardly gone away. You see them on the Microsoft Office Live hosting site, and on popular sites like Friendster (www.friendster.com) and MySpace (www.myspace.com). The latter venue reportedly attracts a billion page views per month, so that site is a nearly irresistible place for advertisers. In general, though banner ads are being used online less frequently than *targeted ads* — that is, ads that appear when specified keyword searches are conducted on sites such as Google (www.google.com) and Yahoo (www.yahoo.com).

Banner ads are like the traditional print ads you might take out in local newspapers. In some limited cases, banner ads are free, as long as you or a designer can create one. Otherwise, you have to pay to place them on someone else's Web page, the same way you pay to take out an ad in a newspaper or magazine.

Even these days, however, many commercial operations *do* use banner ads successfully on the Web. Banner ads can be effective promotional tools under certain circumstances:

- ✔ If you pay enough money to keep them visible in cyberspace for a long period of time
- ✔ If you pay the high rates charged by the most successful Web sites, which can steer you the most traffic

Banner ads differ from other Web-specific publicity tactics in one important respect: They publicise in a one-to-many rather than a one-to-one fashion. Banner ads broadcast the name of an organisation indiscriminately, without requiring the viewer to click a link or in some respect choose to find out about the site.

Staking your claim

You have to pay the piper in order to play the banner-ad game. In general, Web sites have two methods of charging for banner ads:

- ✔ **CPM, or Cost Per Thousand:** This is a way of charging for advertising based on the number of people who visit the Web page on which your ad appears. The more visits the Web site gets, the higher the ad rates that site can charge. In this type of advertising, you have to pay depending on the number of times your ad is *viewed*, regardless of whether anyone clicks on it or not to actually visit your site.
- ✔ **CTR, or Click-Through Rate:** A *clickthrough* occurs when someone clicks a banner ad that links to your (the advertiser's) Web site. (Virtually all banner ads are linked this way.) In this case, you're billed after the ad has run for a while and the clicks have been tallied.

Say 100,000 people visit the site on which your banner runs. If the site charges a flat $20 CPM rate, your banner ad costs $2,000 (100 × $20). If the same site charges a $1 per clickthrough rate, and 2 per cent of the 100,000 visitors click through to your site (the approximate average for the industry), you pay the same: $2,000 (2,000 × $1).

Obviously, the more popular the site on which you advertise, the more your ad costs. For example, ninemsn has a minimum booking of $10,000 for a month (as at March 2008). Not all advertising sites are so expensive, of course.

These days, many advertisers are following Google's lead and charging for ads with a Cost Per Click (CPC) model, or some form of CPC. CPC is similar to CTR in that you, the advertiser, pay when someone clicks a link or graphic image that takes that person to your Web site. But the big difference is that in Google's CPC model, *you* determine how much you pay for each click; in traditional CTR, the advertisers set the rates. In this system, the advertiser only pays when someone actually clicks on an ad. In the case of Google's AdWords program (adwords.google.com), the amount paid per click is one that the advertiser decides by placing bids on keywords used to display the ad. See Chapter 11 for more information.

CPM rates are difficult to calculate because of the number of repeat visitors a site typically receives. For example, a Web page designer may visit the same site a hundred times in a day when testing scripts and creating content. If the site that hosts your ad charges a rate based on CPM, make sure that they weed out such repeat visits. You're better off advertising on sites that charge not only on a CPM basis, but on a click-through basis as well — or, better yet, *only* on a click-through basis. The combination of CPM and CTR is harder for the hosting site to calculate but ultimately fairer for you, the advertiser.

Positioning banner ads can be a substantial investment, so be sure that your ad appears on a page whose visitors are likely to be interested in your company. If your company sells automotive parts, for example, get on one of the Yahoo! automotive index pages.

Designing your ad

The standard 'medium rectangle' and 'large rectangle' banner ads are the most popular ones. Some standard square configurations or small button-like shapes are common, too. The measurements for ads usually appear in pixels, the most common size being a 468-×-60-pixel ad. The rectangular ads appear most often at the top of a Web page, so they load first while other page contents have yet to appear; smaller ads may appear anywhere on a page. (Ensuring that your ad appears at the top of a Web page is always a good idea.)

Many banner ads combine photographic images, type and colour in a graphically sophisticated way. However, simple ads can be effective as well. You can create your ad yourself if you have some experience with a graphics program such as Paint Shop Pro. (You can download a trial copy of Paint Shop Pro at www.corel.com.)

Need some help in creating your own banner ad? If you have only a simple, text-only ad in mind and you don't have a lot of money to spend on design, try a create-your-own-banner-ad service or software program. Greg has had mixed results with the online banner-ad services such as The Banner Generator, provided for free by Prescient Code Solutions (www.coder.com/creations/banner). See Figure 10-2 for an ad that he created in just a couple of minutes by using a shareware program called Banner Maker Pro (www.bannermakerpro.com).

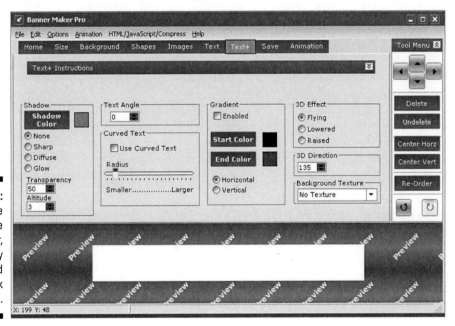

Figure 10-2: With the right choice of colour, a text-only banner ad can look good.

Profiting from someone else's banner ads

Banner ads may be out of favour, but they're not dead by any means. When used economically and targeted to the right audience, banner ads can help you achieve one of your goals: attracting visitors to your Web site. Attract enough visitors, and banner ads can help you achieve another, even more important goal: making money.

If you attract thousands or (if you're lucky) even millions of visitors to your site each month, you become an attractive commodity to advertisers looking to gain eyespace for their own banner advertisements. By having another business pay you to display their ads, you can generate extra revenue with very little effort.

Of course, the effort involved in soliciting advertisers, placing ads, keeping track of how many visitors to your site actually click ads and getting paid *is* considerable — but you don't have to manage ads yourself.

For John Moen, owner of a pair of map-related Web sites (including Graphic Maps, which is profiled in Chapter 1), the move from marketing his own Web site to becoming an advertiser came when his WorldAtlas.com (www.worldatlas.com) site began to attract 3 million hits a month. He turned to advertising giant DoubleClick (www.doubleclick.com) to serve the ads and handle the maintenance.

'We place their [DoubleClick's] banner code on our pages, and they pay us monthly for page impressions, direct clicks, page hits and the like,' says John. 'They [DoubleClick] also provide a daily report on site traffic. With their reports, I can tell which page gets the most hits and at what time of day. Banner advertising now pays very well.'

Understanding Guerrilla Marketing and Advertising Strategies

We didn't make up the term *guerrilla marketing*. As you may already know, the term appears in the titles of a series of popular books by Jay Conrad Levinson and Michael McLaughlin. It appears to be a buzzword that encompasses many (actually sensible) marketing techniques — from providing good customer service to knowing what your competition is doing. It also means going beyond the passive placement of ads on Web pages or other venues, and taking a proactive, aggressive approach to getting your business name and brand in the marketplace. With competition growing all the time among online businesses, it pays to know all the options when dealing with online advertising — including the ones we describe in this section.

Pop-up (and under, and over) ads

When you visit some Web sites a window pops up asking you to make a choice about what you want to see next or to confirm you're over 18 years of age (if the site is about alcohol, for example). Other sites typically urge you to sign up for news alerts or subscribe to a newsletter. Anything you can do to induce your visitors to identify themselves and provide contact information, from an email address to a street address, is to your advantage. But I would urge you to tread carefully when using pop-up windows.

If your Web site becomes popular enough, you may be approached by a company that wants to place its ad on your page, either as a banner ad that is part of the page or as a window that does one of several things:

- **Pops up:** This type of ad window is probably the most common one. It appears when a page is viewed and pops up in a smaller window on top of the page you want to view. These ads work best when their content is related to the page you're opening: Subscribe to our newsletter, buy our book, attend our seminar, or other supplementary information.

- **Pops under:** When you open Web pages on many sites that display ads, a new window opens. But this window, which contains an ad unrelated to the Web page, opens underneath the primary window. Its content is only visible when the user specifically tries to close it, or closes or minimises the other window(s) sitting on top of it.

- **Pops on top:** These ads, also called *interstitials*, totally replace the content you want to view. You're forced to look at them for a period of time and close them before you can view the page you wanted to see. I see these ads used on online magazines from time to time. When you click an article, a totally new window appears, with animated content, and it is big enough that it completely covers the article you want to read. You have to close the ad window in order to keep reading.

According to an article by usability expert Jakob Nielsen titled 'The Most Hated Advertising Techniques' (www.useit.com/alertbox/20041206.html) 95 per cent of Internet users hate pop-ups and 69 per cent use pop-up blockers.

Many Web surfers consider pop-up ads annoying and think worse of advertisers who use them. Since 2004, almost all Web browsers have built-in pop-up blocking features and many people also use other pop-up blocking utilities like the add-on Google Toolbar and firewalls like Norton Internet Security. A pop-up blocking utility can stop pop-up ads from appearing in the first place, and as a result many sites have stopped using pop-ups for advertising.

Some examples of legitimate uses for pop-up windows, however, are

- Showing a *thumbnail* (a small version of a picture) to speed up your Web site and including a link underneath it to view a larger version of this image.
- Providing instructions throughout a form on your Web site, in which case you can place help links next to some of the fields that need further explanation and these instructions may open up in a small pop-up window.

Perhaps try *pagepeel* instead (www.webresourcesdepot.com/pagepeel-type-banner-application-pageear). Remember the roll-down corners at the top of some Web sites that encourage you to click on them? These type of ads take up less real estate on your home page and are more unobtrusive because they give visitors the option to click on them or not (as opposed to pop-up windows that pop up uninvited!).

Adding life to your ads

Ads on billboards, the sides of buildings, the sides of buses, the lights on top of cabs, and the pages of a newspaper and magazine have one thing in common: They basically sit there and don't do anything. They can have lights pointed at them, and magazine ads for perfumes can be given their own scent — but that's about it.

On the Web, ads can get interactive in several different ways. The aim is to gain more attention from the jittery, hurried Web surfer who is, after all, looking for something else on the current Web page. You see several examples of interactive ads on news sites such as *The Age* (www.theage.com.au) and Stuff (www.stuff.co.nz). One ad for Honda shows the new Legend taking corners, and another health insurance ad presents a slide show of a straight face turning into a smile to advertise dental cover.

Creating ads that appear to move around is easy. You need software that's used to create animated GIF images, such as GIF Construction Set Professional, a Windows-only program available for US$24.99 (`www.mindworkshop.com/alchemy/gifcon.html`), or the Macintosh application Gif.glf.giF, available for US$28 (`www.peda.com/ggg`). When you create the initial ad image and save it in GIF format, you create a series of variations and string them together to create the animation. The animation software leads you through the process.

Minding Your Ps and Qs (Puns and Quips)

What is it that attracts shoppers to your business and encourages them to place orders from thousands of kilometres away? The answer lies with what you have to sell and how you present it. But how can customers understand what you're selling if they speak a different language? You must make your site accessible to *all* your potential customers.

Speaking their language

Put yourself in your customer's shoes. Suppose that you're from Spain. You speak a little English, but Spanish is your native tongue, and other Romance languages, such as French or Italian, are definitely easier for you to understand than English. You're surfing around an Internet shopping directory and you come across sentences such as

> Hey mate, get your missus to bail up the ankle biters and get ready for some you-beaut stuff.

> Our site has some fair dinkum bargains. Like this real ace cable modem. Bring ya moolah!

Get the picture? Your use of slang and local dialect may have customers from your own hometown or region in stitches, but it can leave many more people scratching their heads and clicking to the next site. The first rule in making your site accessible to a worldwide audience is to keep your language simple so people from all walks of life — and various places on the planet — can understand you.

Using the right salutations

First impressions mean a lot. The way you address someone can mean the difference between getting off on the right foot and stumbling over your shoelaces. The following useful titbits are from the International Addresses and Salutations Web page (www.bspage.com/address.html), which, in turn, borrowed them from Merriam Webster's *Guide to International Business Communication*:

- ✔ In Austria, address a man as *Herr* and a woman as *Frau*; don't use *Fräulein* for business correspondence.

- ✔ In southern Belgium, use *Monsieur* or *Madame* to address someone, but the language spoken in northern Belgium is Flemish, so be sure to use *De heer* (Mr) when addressing a man, or *Mevrouw*, abbreviated to *Mevr.* (Mrs), when addressing a woman.

- ✔ In India, use *Shri* (Mr) or *Shrimati* (Mrs). Don't use a given name unless you're a relative or close friend.

- ✔ In Japan, given names aren't used in business. Use the family name followed by the job title. Or, add *-san* to the family name (for example, Fujita-san), or the even more respectful *-sama* (Fujita-sama).

Making your site multilingual

Adding multilingual content to your Web site is a nice touch, particularly if you deal on a regular basis with customers or clients from a particular area. You can either hire someone to prepare the text in one or more selected languages or use a computer program to do the work for you. Regional differences abound, so be prudent and find a person familiar with the area you're trying to target, and ask that person to read your text before you put it up on the Web or in your newsletter. Have a friend — not the absence of orders for your goods — tell you you're committing a cultural *faux pas*. That way you can fix it before you put it out there. Then provide links to the Web pages that contain the translated text right on your site's home page, like this:

```
Read this page in:
French
Spanish
German
```

One translation utility that's particularly easy to use — and, by the way, free — is available from Yahoo!. Just follow these steps to get your own instant translation:

1. **Connect to the Internet, launch your Web browser, and go to** `au.babelfish.yahoo.com`**.**

   The Yahoo!7 Babel Fish Translation page appears.

2. **If you have a specific bit of text that you want to translate, click in the text box on this page and either type the text or paste it from a word-processing program. If you want the service to translate an entire Web page, enter the URL in the text box.**

   Be sure to include the first part of the URL (for example, `www.mysite.com` rather than just `mysite.com`).

   Obviously, the shorter and simpler the text, the better your results.

3. **Choose the translation path (that is, *from* what language you want to translate) by clicking the Select From and To Languages drop-down list.**

   At this writing, the service offers translation to or from Chinese, Dutch, English, French, Greek, Korean, Spanish, German, Italian, Japanese, Portuguese and Russian.

4. **Click the Translate button.**

   Almost as fast as you can say, 'Welcome to the new Tower of Babel,' a new Web page appears on-screen with the foreign-language version of your text. (If you selected a Web page to translate, the Web page appears in the new language. The title of the page, however, remains in the original language.)

Instead of creating a foreign-language version of your Web page, you can provide a link to the Yahoo! translation page on your own page. That way, your visitors can translate your text for themselves.

You don't have to translate your entire Web site. Just providing an alternate version of your home page may be sufficient. The important thing is to give visitors an overview of your business and a brief description of your products and services in a language they can understand easily. Always include a mailto link (refer to Chapter 5) so that people can send mail to you. However, if you're not prepared to receive a response in Kanji or Swahili, request that your guests send their message in a language you can read.

Although you probably don't have sufficient resources to pay for a heap of translation services, having someone translate your home page so you can provide an alternate version may be worthwhile — especially if you sell products that are likely to be desirable to a particular market where a different language is the order of the day. Consider hiring a competent graduate student to do some translation for you. Plenty of translation services are available online — search Google or Yahoo! for 'translation services'.

Using the right terms

Sometimes communicating effectively with someone from another country is a matter of knowing the terms used to describe important items in that language. The names of the documents you use to draw up an agreement or pay a bill are often very different in other countries than they are in your own. For example, if you're an Australian merchant and someone from Europe asks you to provide a *proforma invoice*, you may not know what the person wants. You're used to hearing the document in question called a *quote*.

When you and your European buyer have agreed on terms, a *Commercial Invoice* is an official form you may need to use for billing purposes. Many of these forms have to do with large-scale export/import trade, and you may never have to use them. But if you do undertake trade with people overseas, be aware that they may require you to use their own forms, not yours, in order to seal the deal. To avoid confusion later on, ask your overseas clients about any special requirements that pertain to business documents before you proceed too far with the transaction.

Marketing through global networking

Jeffrey Edelheit knows the potential for making connections around the world by taking advantage of the networking value of the World Wide Web. Edelheit, a business planning and development consultant based in Sebastopol, California, supports fledgling entrepreneurs' dreams of getting their businesses off the ground. You can find some of his advice for small-business owners on the Bplans.com Web site www.bplans.com. He also helps established business people extend their reach by looking at ways of gaining greater market exposure — including going online. In addition, Jeffrey works closely with management and staff to develop the internal systems necessary to build a strong operational base for the company.

Edelheit provides the following guidance:

- **Be deliberate in the creation of your Web site:** 'I've worked with clients who are able to attract overseas customers and express themselves through creating their own Web sites,' he says. A well-thought-out Web site can create a relationship between you and your customers; in other words, the stronger the relationship, the greater the opportunity for sales.

- **Know your market:** Jeffrey goes on to say, 'The most important suggestion I can make is to know the overseas market that you want to reach and be aware of the issues associated with doing business there. I recommend getting contact information for an international trade group from the country's consulate.'

- **Research shipping costs and regulations:** Shipping costs and restrictions are among the most common problems new businesspeople encounter when dealing with foreign customers, he says. 'Check with the customs service in your country and find out what the duty charges are before you ship overseas. Once, in the 1980s, a company I was working with shipped an IBM computer to Sweden, but because there were still restrictions on exporting high-tech equipment, I nearly got arrested by the US Customs for not having received the required special clearance.'

- **Avoid being ethnocentric:** Also be aware of how consumers in other cultures regard your products, he suggests. Make sure that nothing about your products would be considered offensive or bad luck to someone from another part of the world.

- **Be visible:** Edelheit emphasises that after you figure out the inside tricks to the search engines and cooperative links, you have an unlimited potential to reach people. He believes that one of the keys to a successful Web site is providing information that your targeted market would find useful — and then providing product offerings as an attractive supplement.

'Consumers, whether in this country or overseas, want to know who they're doing business with, and want to develop a relationship with that person. A commercial Web site not only enables you to express yourself, but lets you create a "value-added" experience for your customers,' he concludes.

Chapter 11

Search Engine Optimisation

*1*f you can get your business mentioned in just the right place, customers can find you more easily. For example, start-up business Watersaversigns.com came up with an idea for a simple sign people could place in their gardens to tell passers-by they use recycled water to water their gardens. Sales started slowly but as soon as the sign was featured on the front page of the local newspaper and mentioned on radio, sales soared. The signs are now stocked by a national supermarket chain as well as a national hardware chain and most orders are big bulk orders rather than ones and twos!

On the Web, search engines are the most important places to get your business listed, with 49 per cent of Internet users using search engines on a daily basis, second only to email, which is used daily by 60 per cent of Internet users (Pew Internet report, August '08).

The key requirements for any business are to match your products or services with potential customers, to ensure that your company shows up in lots of search results, and to have your site near the top of the first page. *Search engine marketing* is the range of marketing techniques required to make a Web site visible on search engines and directories so that it attracts visits from its target audience. You have two kinds of search results:

- ✔ **Organic (or natural) search results:** *Organic results* are ranked according to relevance to the search terms. You don't pay a fee for sites ranked in the organic search results. These free listings are usually shown on the left-hand side of the browser window.

- ✔ **Paid search results:** *Paid results* are those listings that require a fee. These paid results are usually shown on the right hand side of the browser window. The most widely used form of paid listing is Pay Per Click (PPC) advertising; for example, Google AdWords (refer to the section 'Getting Started with Google AdWords', later in this chapter).

Search engine optimisation (SEO) is a set of practices designed to improve your site's placement in the organic search results and is a cost-effective form of advertising that any Web site owner can tackle. SEO gives you a measure of control over the quality of your placement in search results. This chapter describes strategies for improving both SEO and PPC advertising.

Understanding How Search Engines Find You

Have you ever wondered why some companies manage to find their way to the top page of search engine results — and occasionally pop up several times on the same page — while others get buried deep within pages and pages of Web site listings? In an ideal world, search engines would rank e-commerce sites by how well designed they are and how responsive their owners are. But with so many millions of Web sites crowding the Internet, the job of processing searches and indexing Web site URLs and contents has to be automated. Because the process is computerised, you can perform some magic with the way your Web pages are written that can help you improve your placement in a set of search results.

Your site doesn't necessarily need to appear right at the top of the first search results page. But you have to keep in mind that consumers on the Web are in a rush, and if you can get your site on the first page of search results — if not at the top of that page — you get more attention. The important thing is to ensure that your site appears before that of your competition. To begin, you need to think like a searcher, which is probably easy because you do plenty of Web-based searches yourself. How do you find the Web sites you want? Two things are of paramount importance: keywords and links.

Keywords are key

A *keyword* describes a subject that you enter in a search box in order to find information on a Web site or on the wider Internet. Suppose you're trying to find something for your son to wear at his christening or you want to source a copy of a great book your friend recommended. You'd naturally enter the term **boys christening outfit** or **Starting an Online Business For Dummies** respectively, into the search box on your favourite search engine, click a button — Search, Search Now, Go, or something similar — and then wait a few seconds for search results to gather.

When you send a keyword to a search service, you set a number of possible actions in motion. First the keyword is processed by a script on a Web server operated by the search service. The script makes a request (which in computerspeak is a *query*) to a database file. The database contains contents culled from millions (even billions, depending on the service) of Web pages.

The database contents are gathered from two sources. In some cases, search services employ human editors who record selected contents of Web pages and write descriptions for those pages. But Web pages are so changeable that most of the work is actually done by computer programs that automatically scour the Web (*spiders*). These programs don't record every word on every Web page. Some take words from the headings; others index the first 50 or 100 words on a Web site. Accordingly, when searching for boys christening outfit on Google, the sites listed at the top of the first page of search results have two attributes:

- ✔ Some sites have the phrase 'christening outfit' in the URL, such as `www.googoogear.com.au/christening_outfits.html`.
- ✔ Other sites have the phrases boys christening or christening outfit mentioned several times at the top of the home page.

Observers agree that including the most relevant keywords in the titles and headings of the Web page is essential. In addition, pages that are updated with fresh content on a regular basis and are thus re-indexed frequently get good search placement as well.

Wordtracker (`www.wordtracker.com`) does daily surveys of the keyword queries made to various search engines. This program creates lists of the most popular search terms it finds. In turn, you can feed in the keywords you want to rank under and Wordtracker provides results on how popular these search terms are at the moment. You can then use this information to write your Web site text accordingly. This can help you maximise the number of visits to your site or just to make your site more prominent in a list of search results.

Adding your site's most important keyword to the URL is one solution to better search placement. But you can't always do this. When choosing keywords, your job is to load your Web site with as many words as you can find that are relevant to what you sell. You can do this by:

- Burying keywords in the <meta> tags in the HTML for your home page so they're not visible to your visitors but do appear to the spider programs that index Web pages (see the section, 'Adding keywords to your HTML', later in this chapter).
- Adding keywords to the headings and initial body text on your pages. Check out the section, 'Adding keywords to key pages', later in this chapter.

A keyword doesn't have to be a single word. You can use a phrase containing two or more words. In fact, most people (58.93 per cent) use two- or three-word phrases in search engines to find what they're looking for compared to 15.22 per cent of people who use a single word (OneStat, Oct '07). So think beyond single words to consider phrases people might enter when they're trying to find products or services you're offering.

Links help searchers connect to you

Keywords aren't the only things that point search services to Web sites. Services, like Google, keep track of the number of links that point to a site. The greater the number of links, the higher that site's ranking in a set of Google search listings. And, if the URLs that form the links make use of your keywords, you get a particularly good result. Suppose your ideal keywords are 'New Zealand wine'. The ideal URL would be www.newzealandwine.com, www.newzealandwine.co.nz and so on. You could create the following HTML link to your e-commerce Web site on a personal Web page or an eBay About Me page (refer to Chapter 9):

```
<a href="http://www.newzealandwine.com"> Visit our New
Zealand Wine Store </a>
```

Such a link is doubly useful: A search service, such as Google, would find your desired keywords ('New Zealand wine') in the visible, clickable link on your Web page as well as in the HTML for the link.

Three tips for better search engine ranking

Did you know 87 per cent of Internet users find Web sites through search engines? Can they find you?

The most popular search engines in Australia are Google, Yahoo! and ninemsn. How well do you rank in these engines?

Web sites can be a powerful marketing tool because you can reach a large audience on a small budget. But so can your competitors.

One way to gain a competitive advantage is through search engine optimisation or SEO.

What is SEO?

Search engine optimisation is the process of improving a Web site for higher search engine rankings.

Every search engine uses its own unique formula, or algorithm, to index and score Web sites.

Here are three tips for improving your search engine ranking:

✔ **Choose your keywords:** Think in terms of what keywords and phrases your target market is likely to type into a search engine. By using these keywords frequently you tell the search engines what you do. Then place these keywords in your copy and in the HTML code behind each page.

Tip: 81 per cent of search engine queries contain more than one word. What does this mean? Single words are often too generic so use 'key phrases' instead of just one word.

✔ **Repeat key phrases throughout your Web site content:** People visit Web sites for content — they want information. Search engines rank Web sites based on how much content they have and how relevant it is to the search term query.

A good rule to follow is to include a minimum of 100–250 words of informative text on every page. Focus on one or two key phrases per page and use the selected phrases several times throughout the text, as some search engines reward for repetition. The higher up on the page the phrase appears the better.

Tip: The trick is to use the most important keywords as much as possible without compromising readability. You tread a fine line between writing for the search engines and writing for your site visitors.

✔ **Create effective Page Titles:** A HTML Page Title describes the contents of your Web page in one sentence. The title is likely to appear in search engine results and in bookmarks, and is also the first thing a search engine's spider sees on your page. Since your title is seen by both readers and search engines, your word choice is particularly important.

Tip: To find the 'title' of any Web page, load the page in your browser, right click on the page with your mouse and choose View Source. The title is contained between the HTML tags <title> </title> and should be within the top 4–6 lines of the HTML code.

Don't repeat the same keyword in your title more than twice and don't use all CAPS (capital letters) because some search engines penalise your site for this practice.

Don't forget the human touch

Search engines don't work solely by means of spiders (computer programs that automatically scour Web pages) and by paid advertisements. Computer programs are perceived as the primary source, but the human factor still plays a role. Yahoo!, one of the oldest search engines around, originally compiled its directory of Web sites by means of real live employees. These days, its Web directory (`dir.yahoo.com`) isn't as easy to find on Yahoo! as it once was. But editors still index sites and assign them to a New Additions category, which includes sites that are especially cool in someone's opinion.

There's almost no way to make sure that a human editor indexes your Web site. The only thing you can do is to make your site as unique and content rich as possible. That helps your business not only show up in directories and search results but also drum up more paying customers for you, too.

Having your site added to the Yahoo! Directory greatly increases your e-commerce site's visibility. But Yahoo! charges a US$299 fee for businesses that want to be included. Focus on free directories, like MSN and Google, and try to improve your visibility that way before you spend the big bucks.

Taking the initiative: Paying for ads

You can't get much better placement than right at the top of the first page of a set of search results, either at the top of the page or in a column on the right side. An even better idea is to highlight your site's name and URL in a colour. The only way to get such preferred treatment is to pay for it. And that's just what a growing number of online businesses are doing — paying search engines to list their sites in a prominent location. See the sidebar 'Paying for search listings can pay off' for more information.

Knowing who supplies the search results

Another important thing to remember about search engines is that they often gather results from *other* search services. You may be surprised to find that if you do a search of the Web on America Online (AOL), your search results are primarily gathered from Google — because AOL has a contract with Google to supply such results. Not only that, but many search services are owned by parent search services. Just what are the most popular search services, and where do they get their results? A rundown appears in

Table 11-1. The services are presented in rank order, beginning in the first row with Google, which is number 1.

Table 11-1	Internet Search Services			
Parent Company	*Its Search Services*	*URLs*	*Source (Search Results)*	*Source (Paid Listings)*
Google	Google	`www.google.com`	Google	Google
Yahoo!	AltaVista, AllTheWeb	`www.yahoo.com, www.altavista.com`	Yahoo!	Yahoo!
Microsoft	Live Search	`www.live.com`	Yahoo!	Yahoo!
Ask Network	Ask	`www.ask.com`	Ask	Google
AOL	AOL Search, Netscape Search	`search.aol.com`	Google	Google
Excite (owned by Ask Jeeves)	Excite, IWON, MyWay.com	`www.excite.com, home.iwon.com, www.myway.com`	Google	Google
InfoSpace	Dogpile, WebCrawler	`www.dogpile.com, www.webcrawler.com`	Lycos	Enhance Interactive
Lycos	Lycos, HotBot	`www.lycos.com, www.hotbot.com`	LookSmart, Yahoo!	Google

The important thing to note is that many of the most popular search engines receive their listings not from their own database of Web sites but from other search services. If you pay for a listing with Google, in other words, your ad is likely to appear not only on Google but also on HotBot, Lycos, Ask, AOL Search, and other places. By getting your site in the Yahoo! database, you appear in Yahoo! search results as well as MSN Search.

These are by no means the only search services around. Other search engines focus on Web sites and Internet resources in specific countries. You can find more of them by going to Search Engine Watch (`searchenginewatch.com`).

Going Gaga over Google

When talking about search engines, Google is at the top of the heap. In fact, Nielsen/NetRatings and comScore Networks both consistently reported that more than 40 per cent of all search referrals are done by Google. The next highest competitor, Yahoo!, typically has between 25 and 29 per cent of the search market business.

Google is a runaway success thanks to its effectiveness. You're simply more likely to find something on Google, more quickly, than you are on its competitors. Any search engine placement strategy has to address Google first and foremost. But that doesn't mean you should ignore Google's competitors, such as Yahoo! and Windows Live Search.

Googling yourself

To evaluate the quality of your search results placement on Google, start by taking stock of where you currently stand. Go to Google's home page (www.google.com) and do a search for your own name or your business's name (a pastime now called *egosurfing*). See where your Web site turns up in the results and also make note of which other sites mention yours.

Next, click Advanced Search or go directly to www.google.com/advanced_search?hl=en. Under the heading Page-specific Tools, enter the URL for your e-commerce site in the Links text box and then click Search. The results that appear in a few seconds consist of Web sites that link to yours. The list suggests the kinds of sites you should approach to solicit links. It also suggests the kinds of informational Web sites you might create for the purpose of steering business to your Web site. (See the section 'Maximising links' later in this chapter, for a specific example.)

Playing Google's game to reach #1

Not long ago, some bloggers got together and decided to play a game called *Google bombing*. The game is simple: It consists of making links to a particular Web site in an attempt to get that site listed on Google. The more links the site has pointing to it, the higher that site appears in a set of search results. Of course, the links that are made all have to be connected with a particular keyword or phrase.

The Google game applies to your e-commerce Web site, too. Suppose you sell yo-yos, and your Web site URL is `www.yoyoplay.com`. (This site is actually one of the sites run by Lars Hundley, the entrepreneur we profile in the sidebar 'Paying for search listings can pay off' later in this chapter.) The game is to get as many other Web sites as possible to link to this URL. The terms that a visitor clicks to get to this URL can be anything: *Yo-Yos, Play Yo-Yos* and so on. The more links you can make, the better your search results are.

Getting started with Google AdWords

When most people think about search engine marketing, they immediately think about a single program: Google AdWords. AdWords revolutionised advertising on the Web and, not incidentally, has made a fortune for Google as a company. What makes AdWords special is its do-it-yourself aspect, which puts a huge amount of control in the hands of individual businesspeople. You decide what to advertise; you specify how much you want to pay every time someone clicks one of your ads; you write the ads; you fine-tune your advertising programs to bid higher on those that are getting results and end the ones that aren't getting much attention.

This section presents you with a brief introduction on how to get started with AdWords. It isn't meant to be the last word on the subject. Entire books could be written about AdWords, and they have. Consult *Search Engine Optimization For Dummies,* 3rd Edition, by Peter Kent, or *Building Your Business with Google For Dummies* by Brad Hill (both published by Wiley Publishing, Inc.).

Getting the big picture

What is AdWords? This service is provided by Google and allows individuals and companies to take out ads that appear at the top or along the right-hand side of a page of Google search results. Do a search on Google right now, and you can see what I mean: They're the ads enclosed in small boxes and that contain links to Web sites. Perhaps you have clicked those ads yourself, perhaps not. The fact is that hundreds of thousands — perhaps millions — of clicks are placed on those ads every single day. Every time someone clicks an ad, the person who placed the ad is charged a small fee by Google (which is why they're called pay-per-click or PPC ads).

If the 'clicker' goes on to make a purchase on the Web site that is being advertised, or if he or she fills out a form or takes out a new membership, however, the person who took out the AdWords ad (for the purposes of this discussion, we'll call this person the affiliate) earns money in two possible ways. If your own Web site is being advertised, you make money from the purchase. If you advertise someone else's site and that site pays affiliates, you earn a referral fee. The exact fee varies from site to site. On eBay, a purchase can earn the affiliate a sizeable fee of 40 per cent or more. In Australia or New Zealand, a new registration can earn the affiliate as much as $22. If that click cost 10 cents, that's a huge profit — even if it takes a hundred clicks before someone takes one of the actions that earn the affiliate a referral fee.

One thing that makes AdWords effective is that the ads are targeted. The ads only appear on search results that are similar to the product or service being advertised. The connection between the advertiser and search results is made by keywords that the affiliate associates with the ad. If the affiliate is advertising a site that sells dog and cat supplies and specifies keywords like dog food, cat collar, flea spray, and the like, the ad appears when a Web surfer searches for those terms. Another advantage is that you write the ad, and you specify how much you're willing to pay for each click: You're in control.

You might think that specifying common keywords is a good thing because it causes your advertised site to appear in its AdWords ad more often: More people likely search for 'dog' or 'cat' than 'dog food' or 'dog hip dysplasia', for instance. But your goal is to target your search and find just the shoppers who are hunting for what the advertiser wants. If 100,000 people view your ad with the keyword 'dog' and only 2 clicks are made, the ad is ineffective. If 100 people view the ad for 'dog flea collars' but 30 clicks are made and they lead to 10 purchases, you have a far more effective ad.

Signing up for the service

Taking out an account with AdWords is the easy part. Before you start, you need to decide what you want to advertise. For this example, I assume you're advertising your own Web site. You can also advertise for someone else, as long as you're willing to pay for the 'clicks'.

You also need to obtain a Google account, with a username and password. You do this by going to Google's home page, clicking the Sign In link, and clicking the Create an Account Now link.

After you sign in, follow these steps:

1. **Go to the Google Advertising Programs page.**

   Click Advertising Programs at the bottom of the home page, or go directly to www.google.com.au/intl/en/ads/.

2. **Click Google AdWords to go to your page on the AdWords site.**

3. **Click the My Account tab, fill out the first online form and click Continue. Follow the steps shown on the screens that follow to finish creating your account.**

After you have an account set up on AdWords, you can move to the next step: advertising your products.

Writing AdWords ads

When you have the URL of the Web page you want to link to, return to your AdWords window and click the Campaign Management tab. Under the Campaign Summary heading, click the New online campaign link and from the drop-down menu choices that appear choose Start with keywords. When the page shown in Figure 11-1 appears, follow these steps:

1. **In the Name Your Campaign box, enter the name of the business you're advertising.**

2. **In the Name Your Ad Group box, enter a name that describes your ad.**

   This name is only for your convenience and can be as simple as Web site Ad.

3. **Select a language and location, if you wish to target your ad to a particular group of Web surfers.**

Figure 11-1:
Name your ad campaign and ad group, even if you're only creating one ad.

4. **Click Continue.**

   The Create Ad page appears; see Figure 11-2.

5. **Write an attention-grabbing, click-inducing, action-producing ad for this product.**

   And you only have 35 characters per line to do so — you see in a moment just how short a space that is.

6. **Write a heading (25 characters or less) in the Headline box.**

7. **Write lines 1 and 2 (each 35 characters or less).**

8. **In the box next to Display URL, type the URL that appears in the body of the ad.**

9. **In the Destination URL box, type the same URL as the Display URL.**

   If you're advertising as an affiliate for a Web site like Amazon.com, this box contains a complex link you need to obtain from Amazon.com. Here's an example of an ad I wrote:

   ```
   Martial Arts Supplies
   Equipment Uniforms Belts Protective
   Wear for Karate, Boxing and more
   www.samuraimartialarts.com.au
   ```

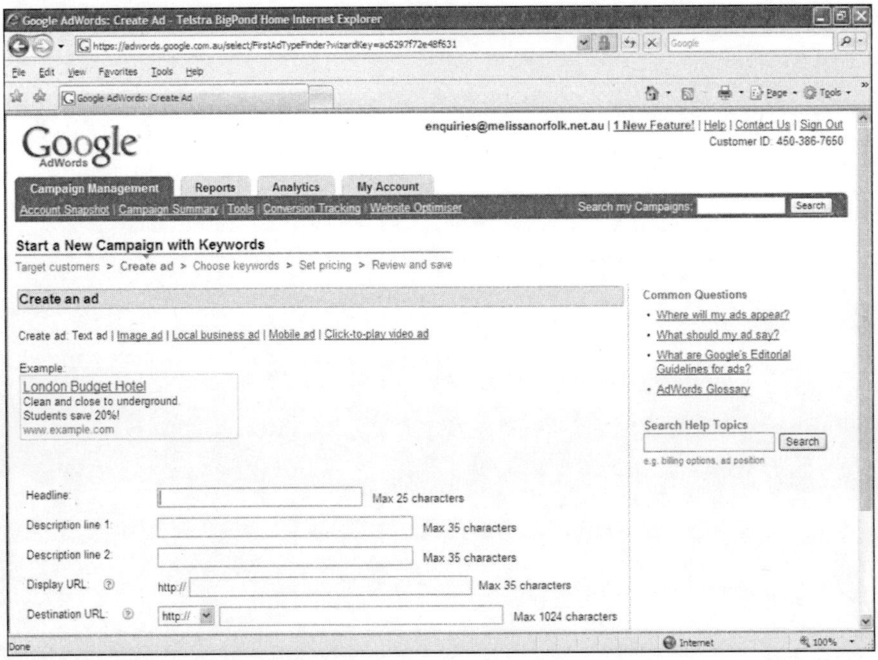

Figure 11-2: Create a short ad that induces clicks and purchases.

10. **When you're done, click Continue.**

Don't be surprised if the page refreshes with some instructions in pink informing you that you need to do some rewriting. Google monitors copyright and trademark issues carefully, and if you violate its rules, it keeps telling you until you get your ad right.

When you have everything right, the Choose Keywords page appears, as shown in Figure 11-3.

11. **Choose keywords to accompany your ad.**

You can use Google's suggestions, which are presented on this page. Or you can consult an online service such as Wordtracker (www.wordtracker.com), which suggests keywords for you.

Eventually, you launch your campaign, which goes online in a matter of minutes, if it meets Google's review standards. Once your ad is online, you can create variations and see which ones get the best results. It can be quite an entertaining game to see which of your ads gets lots of page views, and which attracts clicks.

Monitor your ads closely so you don't spend too much on 'clicks' that don't lead to purchases.

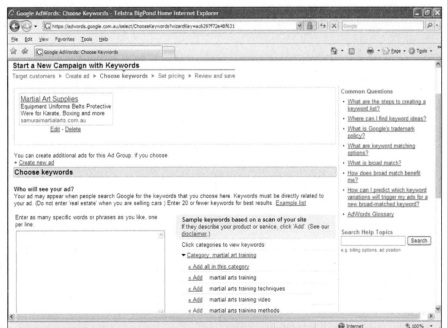

Figure 11-3:
Choose your keywords.

Leaving a Trail of Crumbs

In order to improve your site's search placement, make it easy for searchers to find you. Leave a trail of digital crumbs, add keywords to the HTML for your Web pages, and make sure your site is included in the most popular services databases.

Keep in mind that most Web surfers don't enter single words in search boxes. They tend to enter phrases. Combinations of keywords are extra effective. If you sell tools, don't just enter *tools* as a keyword. Enter keywords, such as *tool box*, *power tool*, *tool caddy*, *pneumatic tool*, *electric tool* and so on.

Adding keywords to your HTML

What keywords should you add to your site? Take an old-fashioned pencil and paper and write all the words you can think of that are related to your site, your products, your services or you — whatever you want to promote, in other words. You may also enlist the help of a printed thesaurus or the one supplied online at Dictionary.com (www.dictionary.com). Look up one term associated with your goods or services, and you're likely to find a number of similar terms. Tools such as Wordtracker.com can also be used to find similar terms.

Where to put the <meta> tag

Every Web page is enclosed by two specific tags: <html> and </html>. These tags define the page as being an HTML document. The <html> tag goes at the beginning of the document and </html> goes at the end.

Between the <html> and </html> tags reside two main subdivisions of a Web page:

- ✔ **The header section:** This section, enclosed by the <head> and </head> tags, is where the <meta> tags go.
- ✔ **The body section:** This section, enclosed by the <body> and </body> tags, is where the contents of the Web page — the part you actually see on-screen — go.

You can list each individual page on your Web site separately in the search engines — your business interests are best served by listing in as many places as possible to build traffic to your site. Hence, you're best to include <meta> tags on every page on your site.

How to create a <meta> tag

The following steps show how to add your own ⟨meta⟩ tags from scratch to the source code of a Web page by using Microsoft FrontPage. (Microsoft has stopped supporting this program in favour of a new package called Expression Web. But FrontPage is still widely used, and I include it as an example because the steps shown here are similar for other Web page editors, including Expression Web itself, where you access the Code tab rather than the HTML tab.) These steps presume that you've already installed Internet Explorer and FrontPage 2002, created your Web site's home page, and saved it on your computer with a name like index.htm or index.html. To add ⟨meta⟩ tags to your site's home page, start FrontPage and follow these steps:

1. **Choose File⇨Open.**

   If you already have your Web site open, you can double-click the page in the FrontPage Folder List.

   Either way, the Open File dialogue box appears.

2. **Find your Web page document.**

   - If the file resides on your computer's hard drive, locate the Web-page file in the standard Windows navigation dialogue box, and then click the Open button.

   - If the file resides on the Web, enter the URL in the Location box of the Open File dialogue box and then click OK.

   The Web page opens in the Normal pane of the FrontPage window. To add the ⟨meta⟩ tags, you must type them directly into the HTML source code for the page.

3. **Click the HTML tab near the bottom of the FrontPage window.**

   FrontPage displays the HTML source code for your Web page.

4. **Scroll to the top of your page's HTML source code, between the ⟨head⟩ and ⟨/head⟩ tags, and enter your keywords and description.**

   Use the following format:

   ```
   <meta name="description" content="Your short Web site
   description goes here.">
   <meta name="keywords" content="keyword1, keyword2,
   keyword3 and so on">
   ```

   The output appears in the View HTML window, as shown in Figure 11-4.

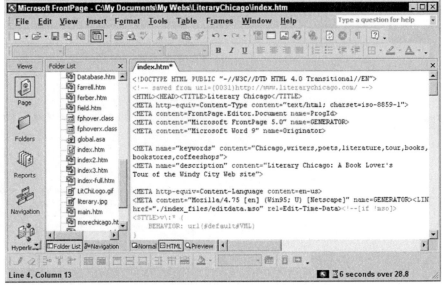

Figure 11-4:
Insert your
<meta> tags
in the HEAD
section of
your HTML
document.

5. **Click the Normal tab to close the View HTML window.**

   The View HTML window closes, and you return to the FrontPage window. Your additions aren't visible on the Web page because they're intended for search engines, not visitors to your site.

   Note: If you use FrontPage 2003, you view HTML code in the Code or Code and Design pane instead of clicking the HTML tab.

6. **You can now make more changes to your page, or you can save your Web page and then close FrontPage.**

Most Web page editors make this user friendly for you: You can type your information in specially designated boxes. Figure 11-5 shows Expression Web's commands; open the page you want to edit by choosing File⇔Properties, and type the words in the Keywords box. You can also write your official description in the Description box.

Page Properties `[?][X]`

General | Formatting | Advanced | Custom | Language | Workgroup

Location: `unsaved:///Untitled_1.htm`

Title: `NewCor Home Page`

Page description: `A group of design and marketing professionals who provide corporate visibility and branding services.`

Keywords: `Web design, marketing, writing, editing, advertising, graphic image, brand, visibility, public relations`

Base location:

Default target frame: `...`

Background sound

Location: `Browse...`

Loop: `0` `☑ Forever`

`OK`   `Cancel`

Figure 11-5: Some Web page editors make it easy to add keywords and descriptions for search services to find.

You can also spy on your competitors' Web sites to see if they added any keywords to their Web pages by following these steps:

1. **Go to your competitor's home page and choose View⇨Source if you use Internet Explorer or choose View⇨Page Source if you use Mozilla Firefox.**

   A new window opens with the page source supplied.

2. **Scroll through the code, looking for the `<meta>` tags if they're present. (Press Ctrl+F, enter META, and click the Find button if you can't find them on your own.)**

   If the page's author used `<meta>` tags to enter keywords, you see them on-screen. They should appear towards the top of the code.

3. **Make note of the keywords supplied and see if you can apply any to your own Web site.**

Keywords, like Web page addresses, are frequently misspelled. Make sure you type several variations on keywords that might be subject to typos: for instance, **Parramatta**, **Paramatta**, **Paramata** or **Papatoetoe**, **Pappatoetoe**, **Papatoitoi** and so on. Don't worry about getting capitalisation just right, however; most searchers simply enter all lowercase characters and don't bother with capital letters at all.

Besides keywords, the `<meta>` tag is also important for the `description` command, which enables you to create a description of your Web site that search engines can index and use in search results. Some search services also scan the description for keywords; so make sure that you create a description at the same time you type your keywords in the `<meta>` tags.

Don't place too much importance on picking the ultimate, perfect keywords for use with your `<meta>` tags. They're not all that effective any more — not with search placement on Google, for instance. Keeping your content updated and promoting links to other Web sites are just as effective.

Registering your site with Google

Google has a program — Googlebot — that automatically indexes Web pages all over the Internet. However, you don't have to wait for Googlebot to find your site: You can fill out a simple form that adds your URL to the sites indexed by this program. Go to `www.google.com/addurl.html`, enter your URL and a few comments about your site, and click the Add URL button. That's all there is to it. Expect to wait a few weeks for your site to appear among Google's search results if it doesn't already appear there.

Getting listed on Yahoo!

If you want to get the most bang for your advertising buck, get your site listed on the most popular locations in cyberspace. For several years now, the many sites owned by Yahoo! have ranked in the top two or three most popular sites on the Internet in the Media Metrix Top 50 list of Web Properties published by comScore Media Metrix. Although many people think of Yahoo! primarily as a search engine, the site is also a categorical index to Web sites. Getting listed on Yahoo! means being included on one of its index pages. An *index page* is a list of Web sites grouped together by category, much like a traditional *Yellow Pages* phone book.

Aside from its steadily increasing size and popularity, one thing that sets Yahoo! apart is the way in which it evaluates sites for inclusion on its index pages. For the most part, real human beings do the Yahoo! indexing; they read your site description and your own suggested location and then determine what category to list your site under. Usually, Yahoo! lists sites in only one or two categories, but if Yahoo! editors feel that a site deserves its own special category, they create one for it.

The Yahoo! editors don't even attempt to process all the thousands of site applications they receive each week. Reports continue to circulate on the Web as to how long it takes to get listed on Yahoo! and how difficult it is to get listed at all. The process can take weeks, months or even years. Danny Sullivan, the editor of *Search Engine Watch*, estimates that only about a quarter of all sites that apply get listed. That's why Yahoo! has now instituted an Express listing system — your business site gets reviewed in exchange for a US$299, non-refundable annual fee, though you *still* aren't given a guarantee of a listing. Find out more at `help.yahoo.com/help/us/bizex/index.html`.

Search Engine Watch (`searchenginewatch.com`) is a great place to go for tips on how search engines and indexes work and how to get listed on them.

Paying for Yahoo! Search Marketing

What *can* you do to get listed on Yahoo!? You can always sign up for Yahoo!'s paid search option (also called sponsored search), Yahoo! Search Marketing (`searchmarketing.yahoo.com/en_AU/`). Paid search won't get you listed in the Yahoo! Directory, but it does ensure with some measure of certainty that you at least appear in search results on the site.

What sets Yahoo! Search Marketing apart is that an editorial teams reviews your keywords and ads, much like the Web site listings at Yahoo!. Google AdWords listings are also reviewed thoroughly, but the results come back in a matter of seconds and appear to be automated. Yahoo! Search Marketing originally used Google's search technology, but developed its search marketing system based on companies, like Inktomi and Overture, which it began purchasing after 2002. Yahoo! is a notable search engine because its search results mix together organic results and paid listings, and the paid ads appear at the top, along the right, and the bottom of a results page.

Listing in the Yahoo! index

If you want to show up in the Yahoo! Directory, here is a three-step suggestion:

1. **Make your site interesting, quirky or somehow attention grabbing.**

   You never know; you may just stand out from the sea of new Web sites and gain the attention of one of the Yahoo! editors.

2. **Go ahead and try applying to the main Yahoo! index.**

   You can at least say you tried!

   a. **Go to** www.yahoo.com, **find the category page that you think should list your site, and click the Submit Your Site link at the very bottom of the page.**

      The Yahoo! Submit Your Site page appears.

   b. **Click the Yahoo! Standard link.**

   c. **Verify that the Yahoo! category shown is the one in which you want to be included and then click Continue.**

   d. **On the form that appears, provide your URL and a description for your site.**

      Make your description as interesting as possible while remaining within the content limit. (If you submit a too-lengthy description, Yahoo! asks you to revise it.)

3. **Try a local Yahoo! index.**

   Major areas around the country as well as in other parts of the world, have their own Yahoo! indexes. Go to Yahoo! Local Australia & NZ au.local.yahoo.com/ and apply it, as we describe in the preceding step. Your chances are much better of getting listed locally than on the main Yahoo! site.

Getting listed with other search services

Search services can steer lots of business to a commercial Web site, based on how often the site appears in the list of Web pages that the user sees and how high the site appears in the list. Your goal is to maximise your site's chances of being found by the search service. But Google is hard to crack, and Yahoo! charges for commercial sites that want to be listed. What about other search services?

Not so long ago, search services allowed you to list your site for free. After that, services adopted policies that guaranteed listings in their index only if you paid a subscription fee. These days, the pre-eminence of Google and Yahoo! has changed the playing field even further. Some services have consolidated; others 'borrow' the search technology used by the competition. And only a few search services provide you with a Submit Your Site or an Add a URL link that enables you to include your site in their index.

One of the few sites that allows individuals to submit personal or commercial Web sites for addition in its index is the Open Directory Project (dmoz.org/add.html). The advantage is that other well-known search services (AOL Search, Google, Netscape Search and Yahoo! Search) use Open Directory data to update and augment their own databases. After you get your site in the Open Directory, anywhere from a few days to a few weeks later, you're likely to see it appear in other directories as well.

Follow these steps to submit your site to the Open Directory:

1. **Connect to the Internet, start your Web browser, and go to the Open Directory home page at** dmoz.org.

   The ODP — Open Directory Project home page appears.

2. **Enter the name of the site you want to add in the box at the top of the page and click Search.**

   A set of search results appears.

3. **Check to see whether your site is included already in the directory.**

   If it isn't, scan the search results for the category 'tree' that appears at the end of each listing, and find the category that fits your own site. A category tree looks like this:

   ```
   Regional: Oceania: New Zealand: Business and Economy:
   Shopping
   ```

4. **Click the category tree.**

   The Category page on the Open Directory appears.

5. **Click the Suggest URL link near the top of the Category page.**

   The Submission form appears.

   Not all categories in the Open Directory include Suggest URL links. If you don't see one, that particular category doesn't allow submissions. But others do: Click a more specific subcategory to suggest your site.

6. **Type the URL as well as a brief but specific description for your site and then click Submit.**

   Your page is submitted to one of the Open Directory staff members who reviews it to decide whether the site is suitable for inclusion in the directory. The process of adding your site may take several weeks.

Businesses on the Web can get obsessed with how high their sites appear on the list of search results pages. If a Web surfer enters the exact name of a site in the HotBot or WebCrawler search text box, for example, some people just can't understand why that site doesn't come back at the top — or even on the first page — of the list of returned sites. Of the millions of sites listed in a search service's database, the chances are good that at least one has the same name as yours (or something close to it) or that a page contains a combination of the same words that make up your organisation's name. Don't be overly concerned with hitting the top of the search-hit charts. Concentrate on creating a top-notch Web site and making sales.

Paying for search listings can pay off

Listing with search sites is growing more complex all the time. Many sites are owned by other sites. On top of that, you can list your products on shopping aggregation sites as well. You can make the consolidation of search sites work to your advantage by choosing a few services carefully: You can then find your business listed with many other sites.

Lars Hundley, who in 1998 started his first online store, Clean Air Gardening, has received lots of publicity thanks to energetic marketing and good use of search engine resources. 'I use Yahoo! Search Marketing (formerly known as Overture) and Google AdWords. I also sometimes use shopping aggregation sites, like Yahoo! Shopping, Shopzilla and Shopping. com.' He hosts Clean Air Gardening and other e-commerce sites with Yahoo! Small Business. Other informational sites are hosted on his own Web server.

Hundley uses many of the search engine placement tools that this chapter covers. He says, 'I also use tools, like Wordtracker and the Overture search term suggestion tool (acquired by Yahoo!), to make sure that I use important keywords in all my product descriptions. I always try to name and describe things in the words that people are searching for, and I think that really pays off over time.'

Not only that, but he uses his previous journalism experience to write and distribute his own press releases and pitch articles to magazines, such as *U.S. News & World Report*, *The Wall Street Journal*, *This Old House* and others. Then he has an email marketing campaign: 'With Clean Air Gardening, I use Constant Contact to manage an email newsletter that I send out every two weeks. I have approximately 10,000 subscribers. I use the newsletter to give gardening tips and promote my products at the same time — they are informational, but they also show how you can use Clean Air Gardening products for more successful gardening.' It's hard to argue with success: Hundley reports that Clean Air Gardening brought in gross revenues of more than $1.5 million in 2006.

Adding keywords to key pages

Earlier in this chapter, we show you how to add keywords to the HTML for your Web pages. Those keywords aren't ones that visitors normally see, unless they view the source code for your Web page. Other keywords can be added to parts of your Web page that are visible — parts of the page that programs called *crawlers* or *spiders* scan and index:

- **The title:** Be sure to create a title for your page. The title appears in the title bar at the very top of the browser window. Many search engines index the contents of the title because it appears not only at the top of the browser window but at the top of the HTML, too.

- **The headings:** Your Web page's headings should be specific about what you sell and what you do.

- **The first line of text:** Some search services index every word on every page, but others limit the amount of text they index. So the first lines might be indexed, but others aren't. Get your message across quickly; pack your first sentences with nouns that list what you have for sale.

The best way to ensure that your site gets indexed is to pack it with useful content. I'm talking about textual content: Search programs can't view photos, animations or sounds. Make sure your pages contain a significant amount of text as well as these other types of content.

Web sites that specialise in SEO talk about *keyword density*: The number of keywords on your page, multiplied by the number of times each one is used. Keyword density is a way to gain a good search engine ranking. In other words, if you sell shoes and you use ten different terms once, you don't get as good of a ranking compared to the use of six or seven words that appear twice or a handful of well-chosen keywords used several times each.

Don't make your pages hard to index

Sometimes, the key to making things work is simply being certain that you're not putting roadblocks in the way of success. The way you format Web pages can prevent search services from recording your text and the keywords you want your customers to enter. Avoid these obvious hindrances:

- ✔ **Your text begins too far down the page.** If you load the top of your page with images that can't be indexed, your text is indexed that much slower, and your rankings suffer.

- ✔ **Your pages are loaded with Java applets, animations and other objects that can't be indexed.** Content that slows down the automatic indexing programs reduces your rankings, too.

- ✔ **Your pages don't actually include the ideal keyword phrase you want your searchers to use.** If you have a business converting LP records to CDs, you want the phrase 'LP to CD' or 'convert LPs to CDs' somewhere on your home page and on other pages as well.

Every image on your Web page can and should be assigned a textual label (also known as *ALT text* because the `alt` element in HTML enables it to be used). The immediate purpose of the label is to tell visitors what the image depicts in case it can't be displayed in the browser window. (ALT text is actually required by the W3 Consortium to make sites more accessible — see www.w3.org/TR/WAI-WEBCONTENT for more information.) Another technique to produce more keyword density is to assign keywords or keyword phrases to describe your images.

Maximising links

Along with keywords, hyperlinks are what search engines use to index a site and include it in a database. By controlling two types of links, you can provide search services with that much more information about the contents of your site:

- ✔ The hyperlinks contained in the bodies of your Web pages
- ✔ The links that point to your site from other locations around the Web

The section 'Links help searchers connect to you', earlier in this chapter, mentions the links in the bodies of your own Web pages. One of the most effective tricks for increasing the number of links that point to your online store is to create several different Web sites, each of which points to that store. That's just what Lars Hundley did with his main e-commerce site, Clean Air Gardening (www.cleanairgardening.com). 'Creating my own network of gardening sites that provide quality information helps me rise to the top of the search engines in many categories,' says Lars. 'People find the content sites sometimes and click through to Clean Air Gardening to buy related products.'

It's true: Do an Advanced Search on Google for sites that link to www.cleanairgardening.com. First, some sites are just a sampling that link to Clean Air Gardening and that aren't run by Lars:

✔ Garden Tool Buyer's Resource (www.gardentoolguide.com)

✔ Master Composter (www.mastercomposter.com)

✔ National Gardening Association (garden.garden.org)

✔ Organic Gardening (www.organicgardening.com)

You might also find these sites farther down in the search results that are run by Lars:

✔ Compost Guide (www.compostguide.com)

✔ Gardening Guide Home (www.gardenplantcare.com)

✔ Guide to Using a Reel Mower (www.reelmowerguide.com)

✔ Organic Garden Tips (www.organicgardentips.com)

✔ Organic Pest Control (www.organicgardenpests.com)

✔ Rain Barrel Guide (www.rainbarrelguide.com)

For the sites that Lars doesn't run himself, he solicits links. 'I also exchange links with other high-ranking related sites, both to improve my rankings and to provide quality links for my visitors. If you stick with quality links, you can never go wrong.' For more about Lars and how he uses the Yahoo! Search Marketing (formerly Overture) to help users find him on the Web, refer to the sidebar 'Paying for search listings can pay off'.

The SEO Suite Standard Edition (www.dynamicwebrank.com/seo_suite) evaluates the contents of your Web pages for mistakes that can keep your site from appearing high in a list of search results. You can download and try the software for 30 days; if you decide to keep it, you pay US$149.

Monitoring Traffic: The Science of Web Analytics

How do you monitor how many visitors are coming to your Web site and how they find you? One way is to analyse your Web site statistics (also known as *log file analysis*). Your Web host should provide access to your Web site statistics as part of your hosting package, so if you don't know how to access these details contact your Web host.

Web site statistics are commonly a summary or graphical representation of the raw log files on the server that hosts your Web site. These statistics report on things like:

✔ How many people look at your site

✔ Which pages they look at

✔ Which referring sites are sending traffic to your Web site

Web hosts commonly use software such as AWStats or WebTrends to provide these reports to you.

Another term commonly used is *Web analytics*. This practice is simply an in-depth way to look at the activity on your Web site. For example, instead of just looking at how many people visit your home page, you can also analyse how they move around the page and what they click on next to take a chosen path through your site.

Analysing the activity on your Web site can help you identify how to improve your site for both visitors and search engine placement.

Understanding your Web site statistics

Wow, the graph that you just printed out with your Web site statistics for the previous month looks nice, and some of the numbers are very impressive, but do you really understand what the terminology means and which figures are the most important on your statistics report. Or perhaps you're asking: 'What are Web site statistics?' or have never actually printed them out!

First of all, the terminology used in Web statistic reports isn't too confusing:

- **Bandwidth:** The amount of data (measured in megabytes) transferred from your host's server to an Internet user's computer. For example, someone views your home page which contains text and images that add up to say 1Mb. If 50 people view this page, then the amount of data transfer would be 50Mb. Your Web host specifies the amount of *bandwidth* (data transfer) that your hosting plan includes each month. If you exceed this you're charged for additional bandwidth. If you have a large site with lots of traffic, keep an eye on this statistic.

- **Hits:** A request made to the server where your Web site is hosted. Each file requested is counted as a *hit*. For example, your home page may be a single .html page with five images on it. The number of hits recorded is six, as your .html page is one file and each image is also counted as a file. Therefore, looking at how many hits your Web site receives isn't a very good statistical indicator.

- **Number of visits:** The number of times that your site has been visited. When you compare it with the number of unique visitors, this stat gives you an idea of the number of people who are returning to your site.

- **Page:** A single page of your Web site, it may be your home (index) page, contact us page, about us or another page within your Web site.

- **Pages viewed or Pages URL:** A statistic that shows how many people are visiting each page. You may find you have an even amount of traffic visiting each page on your site or maybe that the majority of people are only visiting your home page and not going any further.

- **Referrers or referring URLs:** The Web site address where a visitor was before they came to your site. This stat gives you some idea of the Web sites or search engines that are referring traffic to your site, and is also useful when considering your marketing plan. For example, you may get some good traffic via Yellow Pages Online, so it may be worthwhile considering including extra in your marketing budget for a slightly higher profile advert.

- **Search key phrases and keywords:** The words and phrases that people are using to find businesses like yours. Taking notice of this stat is important because it may be good to weave more of the popular words into your content.

- **Unique visitors:** A single individual person who views your Web site within a specified time period such as a day or a month. Each person visiting your site is counted only once, no matter how many times they visit your Web site.

- **Visits duration:** This statistic shows how long people are spending at your site. If they're not staying long you may need to review your content or add an attractor to have them stay longer and view more of your site.

The statistics you need to take the most notice of are the following:

✔ Key phrases and keywords

✔ Pages visited

✔ Referring URLs

✔ Unique visitors

Understanding your Web site statistics is important and you do need to keep an eye on them. They can help you direct your marketing plan, alert you to which pages on your Web site are more popular and which ones need attention, where your traffic is coming from, which keywords people are using from your content and whether you need to consider rewriting your content to include more keywords and key phrases.

If you're not sure how to access your Web site statistics, contact your Web host or Web designer and find out how.

Digging deeper with Web analytics

Web analytics allow you to dig deeper and look at statistics that can give you greater insight into how visitors are using your Web site. After all, being able to measure how people are using your site can highlight what is working, what is not and ultimately help you to improve your site for a greater return on investment.

Path Analysis or Click Path

Path Analysis allows you to see how visitors are moving through your Web site, which pages they enter and exit by and which are the most common pathways through your site. Do a lot of your visitors arrive on your home page and then not go any further? Or perhaps most don't enter your site via the home page but instead arrive on a specific product or service page.

Being able to monitor whether visitors are finding the pages you want them to or taking the actions you want them to take, such as subscribing to a newsletter or purchasing a product is very useful. For example, perhaps you're launching a new product and have placed ads on other Web sites or on Google AdWords. Hopefully, you're directing people straight to the page about this new product and not to your home page. Then, to judge the effectiveness of your copy and online advertising, measuring how many people are entering your Web site via this new page is important.

Time spent

Measuring the amount of time visitors are spending on your site is also a very handy statistic. This helps you determine whether visitors are taking a quick look, then leaving, or whether they're hanging around a bit longer and actually reading your material with the view to possibly taking action. If the majority of your visitors aren't staying long, this stat is a red flag for you to review your site content and look at ways to attract and hold visitors' attention.

Search engines, such as Google, also measure the amount of time visitors spend on your site and this information contributes to where your site is placed in their rankings. For search engines, this measure is called *stickiness* and is calculated according to the time that elapses between a user clicking on your link on the search engine's results page and returning to click on the next link in the search listing.

Conversions

Converting browsers to clients or customers is the name of the game. A *conversion* is when a visitor to your site takes a desired action. So, how do you track whether people are taking action?

If you have a fill-in inquiry form you're able to measure how many people visit this page compared to how many people fill it out. If lots of people are arriving on this page but not going any further, perhaps the form is too difficult to understand or requires too many details. Review your form and then test the results.

If you have a shopping cart, or online ordering system, check how many people are visiting a product page, viewing details and even adding the product to the shopping cart but then not checking out. This stat can give you some clues into where you may need to simplify the ordering process.

Discovering trends

Monthly History graphs allow you to review visitor data over time. This can help you identify your ability to attract visitors and grow your Web site traffic based on your promotional activities or seasonal factors in your industry. For example, nurseries and garden shops can generally see increased traffic during the spring and summer months.

Your overall aim should be to see a gain in visitors over time. These graphs allow you to compare this month to last month as well as June this year with June last year, to measure whether growth is being achieved.

Reviewing Days of the Month graphs may show patterns of usage. For example, a business-related Web site ordinarily has higher traffic during the week with less traffic over weekends and holidays. But leisure and entertainment sites may find the opposite.

Measuring the impact of changes

Lastly, think about monitoring these statistics before and after you make changes to your Web site to measure the impact of these changes. Ultimately, you're aiming to increase traffic and sales over time, so tweak away and monitor results for continued improvement.

Software to assist with SEO

Some software options are specifically designed to help improve SEO, such as:

- Apex Pacific's SEO Suite (www.apexpacific.com/seo_suite)
- Trellian's SEO Toolkit (www.trellian.com)
- WebTrend's WebPosition (www.webposition.com)

These kinds of tools allow you to find the right keywords, optimise each page on your site for the search engines, submit your pages, analyse the number of other sites that are linking to your site and find out whether your site pages have been indexed by the search engines.

Chapter 12

Taking Advantage of Google's Tools

In This Chapter

▶ Making your e-commerce site easier to find in Google's Web directory

▶ Using Google tools

▶ Doing business research with Google

*L*ong ago, Main Street was the place to see and be seen as well as make money as a merchant in many small towns in Australia and New Zealand. Later, the shopping centre attracted sellers of all sorts along with curious shoppers. Those marketplaces haven't gone away altogether, but these days, Google is the newest and best-known, single online resource for businesses around.

Google started as a *search engine* — a Web site that organised the contents of the entire Internet and made information easy to find. It turns out that the same approaches that apply to organising content and presenting search results apply to merchants as well as their goods and services. Google now makes millions by giving online businesspeople the ability to pay for ads that steer consumers to their Web sites. The site has branched out to supply a host of new services, including free email, Web hosting and business applications. You owe it to yourself to pay attention to what Google has to offer and take advantage of the services that can help you. This chapter examines the many ways the current 'big guy' among online companies can help your business get organised and connect with customers — to get yourself *Googled*, in other words.

Spreading the Word with Google

The fact that Google has become a verb as well as a noun shows how the search engine name has become a part of mainstream culture. When consumers want to find anything online, most of them turn to Google. Conversely, when new businesspeople create their first e-commerce Web sites, they also turn to Google to help them get found by those same consumers. After you get your site online, you do *search engine optimisation* (SEO), the practice of optimising your content to get the best placement in Google's search results. The sections that follow briefly summarise the basics of using Google for marketing and publicity, two of the most important ways in which Google can help small businesses.

The practice of SEO is so important that Chapter 11 examines it in depth.

Getting yourself listed in the Google Directory

The Holy Grail for many online businesspeople is a ranking right at the top of Google's search results — or at least on the first page of search results.

When you do a search for the term 'nanny' on Google Australia (at least, at the time we wrote this chapter) and scan the first page of search results, you find Dial-An-Angel's Web site (www.dialanangel.com) listed at number three in the first page of ten search results. Dial-An-Angel provides a range of services such as childcare, housekeeping, in-home nursing and gardening. The business launched a new Web site last year and has done a lot of work to get ranked under key terms related to the services it offers. The business has submitted the site to Google and other search engines, updated the site frequently, spent a lot of time wording its content and naming its pages to have search engine friendly URLs, and more.

Following any or all of these steps is a good idea. But you can improve your search engine ranking with two simple and practical ways:

- Submitting your site for inclusion in Google's directory
- Exchanging links with other Web sites

Submitting your site for inclusion

Perhaps the simplest and most practical approach all businesses can take is to add your URL to the Google Directory. I mention how to do this — by accessing Google's form for submitting a Web page URL to the directory (www.google.com/addurl) — in Chapter 11. But I didn't mention one thing you should do when you fill out this form: Create your own description of your Web site. The description you type appears in Google's search results. For instance, with the dialanangel.com site, the Google search result description looks like this:

```
Find a nanny or housekeeper at Dial-An-Angel. We have
qualified ...
Dial-An-Angel will solve your childcare problem with our
professional nannies and nanny housekeeper services ...
```

The ellipses (...) are shown because the descriptions are too long to fit in the search results. Nevertheless, what does appear gets the message across. By taking the time to submit your own description rather than waiting for Google's spiders to index your site, you can control exactly what appears in the search results and in the directory as well. (A longer description you type appears in Google's directory to the Web.)

The *Google Directory* is a Yahoo!-style index to the contents of the Internet, arranged by category. Most people access the Google database of Web sites by using its well-known search page, which is also the site's home page. To find the Directory, you have to burrow into the site: Go to the home page, click 'more', 'click even more', and when the More Google Products page appears, click Directory under the Search heading.

Exchanging links with other Web sites

Google's engine is smart enough that it doesn't necessarily give a good ranking to Web sites that have added keywords and descriptions to their Web pages. The search engine favours sites that are frequently updated and that are popular. A sign of popularity, from the search index program's point of view, is the number of links made to a page. The higher the number of links, the more valuable the page must be, and the higher the ranking that is given. For example, a lot of Australian accounting and finance companies include links on their site to the ATO (Australian Taxation Office): This link is one of the reasons why when you type 'tax' into Google Australia the ATO comes up on top.

One of the best ways to get better visibility in search results, then, is to get other sites to link to you. How do you do it? You might automatically start thinking of programs or technological shortcuts that can create links for you on other people's Web sites. Such tools are available, but the best way is to roll up your sleeves and create links the old-fashioned, time-consuming, human way: Look for sites that have products and services that complement yours, approach the owners of those sites, and ask to exchange links ('I'll publicise your site if you publicise mine.'). You find some examples of such links in Chapter 11.

Avoid so-called *free link* or *banner exchanges* because these options are often set up purely to collect and sell large email lists. As a result, Google doesn't look favourably on these services and the practice may affect your ranking negatively. You may also notice a huge increase in the amount of spam you receive.

Find quality links. What I mean by this suggestion is don't exchange links with just anybody. If a site is reputable and ranks well itself, it is likely to be much better for your own ranking than exchanging links with a small site that is ranking poorly or currently not ranking in Google at all itself.

Optimising your site for better search results

For just about all online businesses, getting a good ranking in Google search results is very important. Google's exact formula for determining search result rankings is a well-kept secret. But again, you can take some simple and practical approaches to better your chances of getting placed near the top of the first page. Chapter 11 describes such strategies in more detail; we cover two other tips in the following sections.

Keeping it fresh

When you submit your site for inclusion in the Google Directory, you read the following instructional note: 'Google updates its index on a regular basis, so updated or outdated link submissions are not necessary. Dead links will "fade out" of our index on our next crawl when we update our entire index.'

In other words, Google continually re-indexes the Web and ignores sites that are considered dead. A *dead site* is one that hasn't been updated for a long time and that doesn't receive many (or any) visits. To avoid becoming one of these cobWeb sites, update some of your content on a regular basis.

You don't have to update your whole site. If you have a blog online, you only have to make an entry every week (or better yet, every day) to keep your site fresh. Otherwise, make a commitment to change something — anything — on your site every week or so. This change can be something as insignificant as a price change or as significant as the page title. Just add a bit of information as often as you can; you not only improve your search results but, by this practice, you also keep your visitors coming back to you on a regular basis.

Some sites (for example, Google Guide, www.googleguide.com) claim that popular Web pages are re-indexed as often as they're updated. However, Greg doubts whether this is true. Matt Cutts, a Google employee, states in his blog (www.mattcutts.com/blog) that from 2000 to 2003, the index was updated about once a month. But, in the summer of 2003 he comments that Google 'switched to an index that was incrementally updated every day (or faster)'. This scenario seems impossible, but just in case it has a ring of truth, you have another incentive to update your site as often as you can.

Building in keywords

When Google's automated indexing programs scour Web pages, they ignore common words such as *the*, *at*, *is*, *a*, *how* and so on. What do they pay attention to? *Keywords* — nouns and verbs that individuals may enter into Google's search box when they're looking for your site.

To determine what keywords your customers are likely to enter into the Google search box when they're looking for you or your services, use a service like Wordtracker (www.wordtracker.com), which suggests likely terms for you based on the name and content of your Web site.

Keywords do make a difference — especially if you place them in strategic locations like the title of your page, the headings, and the first 50 or so words of text on a page. Sprinkle your Web page text with key terms and don't worry about repeating them from page to page. The more frequently they appear, the better your chances of ending up number one.

Having Google's spider programs crawling through your Web pages isn't always a good idea. Some Webmasters don't like to give all their content (such as newspaper or magazine articles) away for free. However, you can block indexing programs like Google's from including your pages in their index. Include a simple text file named robots.txt and identify the automated program you want to block, or the pages on your site that you don't want indexed. You then post this text file on your Web site. Google itself provides instructions for people who want to block indexing programs at www.google.com/support/Webmasters/bin/answer.py?answer=40360.

How does your site rank? A peek behind the scenes

Google keeps its algorithm for ranking pages secret. But generally known is that Google assigns a Web page a score called a *PageRank*. The PageRank is based on lots of different and complex factors. In December 2003, a patent application was filed by a group of Google employees with the US Patent and Trademark Office. You can view this application, which is number 0050071741, by doing a search for that number on the office's Web site (www.uspto.gov).

The patent application is lengthy, but it includes the following clues to how Google ranks pages:

✔ The history of the Web page is important. This factor includes the date the page was first discovered by a search engine.

✔ The frequency with which the content of the Web page changes is also important. This factor includes an average time between the changes, a number of changes in a time period, and a comparison of a rate of change in a current time period with a rate of change in a previous time period.

✔ The number of new pages associated with the document matters as well.

✔ The amount of content that changes as a proportion of the amount of content in the entire document matters, too.

✔ How frequently the document is associated with search queries is taken into account.

These points are just a few of the 63 separate claims listed in the patent request. You can read a detailed interpretation of the patent request at www.seomoz.org/articles/google-historical-data-patent.php. The claims all boil down to making your page worthwhile, keeping it up to date, and exchanging as many links as you can to other quality Web sites.

Highlighting your location with Google Maps

Google Maps allows you to search for a location or address and find a map of it. This tool is very useful for giving people directions to your shop, office or home, for instance. It is possible to add your business to Google Maps and link to your Google Map from your Web site.

1. **Visit the Google Maps home page.**

   In Australia, go to maps.google.com.au and in New Zealand go to maps.google.co.nz.

2. **Do a search for your address and check that your business is not already listed.**

3. **Next, click on the link Put your business on Google Maps.**

4. **Sign in to your Google Account.**

   If you already have a Google Account, sign in with your email and password. If you don't have a Google Account, click Sign up for an account now.

5. **Follow the instructions to create a listing.**

   After you submit your business information, you need to be able to verify your information by phone or by mail to your business address. After verification, your information should be added within six weeks.

Google Maps is currently available in these countries: Andorra, Australia, Austria, Belgium, Brazil, Canada, China, Czech Republic, Denmark, Finland, France, Germany, Gibraltar, Greece, Hungary, Ireland, Italy, Japan, Liechtenstein, Luxembourg, Monaco, Netherlands, New Zealand, Norway, Poland, Portugal, Russia (Moscow only), San Marino, Singapore, Slovakia, South Africa, Spain, Sweden, Switzerland, Turkey (Istanbul only), United Kingdom and United States.

A street with a (Google) view

At the time of writing this chapter, Google had just released Google Street View in Australia (maps.google.com.au/help/maps/streetview/) and plans to release it in New Zealand before the end of 2008. So, if you do a search for your home or office address, you may even see a photo of your house!

Street View is an additional feature of Google Maps and allows you to search for an address, see photos, zoom in and pan around. You can also get directions if you put in the address you're leaving from and the address you're heading to.

The response to Google Street View is mixed:

- One man proposed to his girlfriend via Street View (www.news.com.au/technology/story/0,25642,24147587-5014115,00.html).

- Others (for example, privacy activists) are concerned about this amount of detail being available for all the world to see (www.smh.com.au/news/biztech/google-backlash-over-street-view/2008/08/05/1217701932020.html).

Useful Google Tools

Other than Google's core services, search and advertising, the company has now built and acquired a whole range of additional tools available via the top left set of links when you visit Google.com. True to the company mission 'to organise the world's information and make it universally accessible and useful' all these tools are simple and easy to use and many of them are free.

In this section, we explore just some of these tools that may be useful to you in running your online business.

Delivering the goods with Gmail

Aside from its search service, Google's Gmail email service must be one of its most popular applications. Many of our friends have Gmail accounts; a group Greg belongs to distributes a mailing list with a Gmail account, too.

Anyone can sign up for a Gmail account by visiting `mail.google.com/mail/signup`.

Many of the business services offered by Google require you to have a Google Account. This option is free to obtain, and it opens the door to a variety of services, so we encourage you to obtain one. Go to the Google home page, click Sign In, and click Create an Account Now under the Don't have a Google Account? heading.

One of the best aspects of using Gmail, in fact, is the ability to create email lists. Another is the fact that you get a whopping 7GB of storage space for your email messages. (That's the space available at this writing; Google increases it periodically.) But wait, there's more: You can also redirect your email from other accounts into your Gmail account so it becomes a single point of contact for your correspondence.

Configuring email for you and your co-workers is the same as activating a start page: From the Dashboard page, click the Activate Email link. You have to change your mail exchange records to direct your email through Google's servers, if you're using *Google Apps* with a domain you own already (see the warning in the next paragraph). Google Apps is a hosted service allowing businesses to use a suite of Google products, such as email and Google Calendar, on their own domain name for example, `www.yourbusiness.com`. After you configure your email, you're presented with a robust interface, as shown in Figure 12-1.

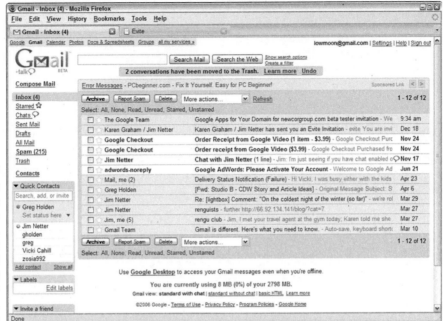

Figure 12-1:
Gmail is
a full-
featured,
Web-based
email
client that
is widely
popular.

You're encouraged to follow an optional set of steps before you start using Gmail for your domain. Google requires you to have it host your domain email. Chances are if you already own a domain, you have existing email service with it. If you activate your email through Google, Google is your email host. You may not want to do this; if you're happy with the email service you already get from your existing domain host, you can skip the email activation. Click Inbox to start using your email without having Google function as your host.

Staying in touch with Google Talk

Google Talk is Google's chat interface. (Don't ask me why they didn't simply call it Google Chat.) Google Talk (www.google.com/talk) has two interfaces. One is a stand-alone chat (I mean, Google Talk) window; the other is a window that appears within the Gmail interface (see Figure 12-2). You need to download and install the chat application so you can start using it. Though the file is small and installs quickly, you may prefer to simply 'reply by chat' from within your Gmail application. You don't have to activate the chat function within Gmail; it's available automatically.

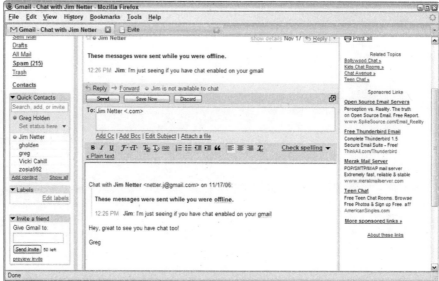

Figure 12-2:
You can use Google Talk as a stand alone application or through Gmail.

To send a message, your recipient needs to be saved as a Gmail Contact (click Contacts on the left side of the Gmail window to add the individual). Then click the person's name under Contacts, click Chat, type your message in the text field, and press Enter. Your recipient has to be online at the same time in order to respond; the chat window indicates whether the person is currently online.

Keeping track with Google Calendar

Google's Calendar application gives members of a workgroup the ability to do some advance planning and get on the same schedule with regard to upcoming meetings, deadlines and events. The Calendar is one of the simplest Google applications to use. Just go to the Calendar page (www.google.com/calendar), sign in with your Google account details, and you access the colourful calendar, as shown in Figure 12-3. Here's how to move around in Calendar:

- ✔ **Move forward or back a month:** Click the left or right blue arrows.
- ✔ **Add an event:** Click the rectangle located at the intersection of the date and time you want. A window pops up; type the event details in the What field. Click Create Event to add it to the calendar.

All the members of the same workgroup access the same shared calendar, so it can be used as a planning tool to keep everyone abreast of the same milestones that need to be met and meetings that can't be missed.

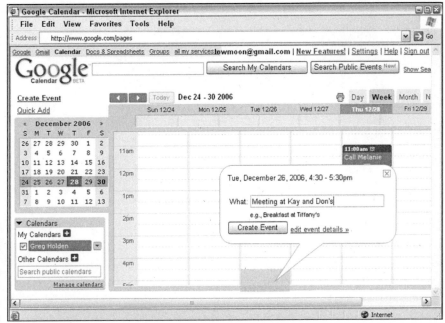

Figure 12-3:
Google
Calendar is
simple and
easy to use.

Creating and sharing documents with Google Docs

Google Docs allows you to create and share documents, spreadsheets and presentations. You can start a new document from scratch or via a template, or upload an existing document from your computer and edit it. Then you have access to your documents from anywhere you have Internet access, and you can also choose who to share them with if you're collaborating either with an individual or a team of people. For example, if you're preparing a business plan, a budget or a marketing brochure you may have other staff members adding content, your accountant looking over the figures and your copywriter writing and proofreading your marketing copy.

Other Google gadgets

Google is constantly adding to its suite of products, so your time is well spent keeping an eye on what Google is offering. You can do this by visiting Google's front page and clicking on the About Google link underneath the search box. Next, click on Google Services & Tools (which is underneath the Our Products heading). You arrive on a Web page that lists all the available tools and gadgets.

In this section, we introduce a few of Google's other handy gadgets.

Google Alerts

Google Alerts allows you to sign up for email updates of recent search results. This tool allows you to keep an eye on your business name, your own name or your competitor's name(!) on Google. Melissa has an alert set up in her own name that allows her to keep up to date with which Web sites have published her name. Often this result is due to one of her articles being published on another Website or another site linking to her site. Google Alerts makes monitoring this scenario on a regular basis very handy.

Google Notebook

Google Notebook allows you to browse or conduct research and save relevant clippings, information and Web page addresses all in one place as you go. You may wish to research your product offering, your competitors or marketing ideas, for example. You can use this handy tool instead of relying on browser bookmarks or history to remember and re-access the key information that you find while conducting research.

Google Book Search

Google Book Search allows you to conduct searches on the full text of books, view and read sample pages, and find out where to buy titles you're interested in. For example, when conducting research, you can read a small amount of a book on a chosen topic without having to buy it. If the book is really helpful and worth buying, reading a sample is enough to help you make a buying decision.

Googling Business News and Trends

In order to be a smart businessperson, you need to be aware of trends and news that can affect the field in which you do business. Google can help you keep on top of the latest trends in a more targeted way than by simply scanning Google News headlines. The following sections examine options for making your site more valuable by addressing current tendencies among the customers you want to reach.

Looking up newspaper and magazine articles

Often, you have to prepare reports for your company. You need to find news articles on topics related to your company's business activities. One of the most convenient clearinghouses for such information is Google News (news.google.com). You can search this part of the Google empire by entering a word or phrase in the box at the top of the Google News page and clicking Search News.

You can choose to see the top stories by country from the drop-down menu at the top of the page or jump straight to your country by visiting

- ✔ news.google.com.au in Australia
- ✔ news.google.co.nz in New Zealand

Click News Alerts in the column on the left side of the Google News home page. Your browser goes to the Your Google Alerts page, where you can enter search terms that trigger an email alert to be sent to your Gmail address.

Searching through blogs

When you click the More link on the Google home page and choose Blogs from the pop-up menu that appears, your browser displays the Google Blog Search page (blogsearch.google.com). The Blog Search interface is quite intuitive; it resembles the main Google Web search engine. If you simply enter **Business Trends** in the search box and click Search Blogs, you turn up plenty of blogs that have Business Trends as part of their titles, for instance. You also find posts about business trends in the current year.

If you click Advanced Blog Search, you access a form that allows you to filter results so that you get posts published within a certain date range or with a specific URL, for instance.

Working smarter with Google Analytics

This business service helps you analyse who visits your Web site so you can determine which one of your advertising campaigns is most effective at driving your business. To get started, follow these steps:

1. **Go to the Google Analytics home page (**`www.google.com/analytics`**) and sign in with your Google account password.**

2. **When the Getting Started page appears, click Sign Up.**

   The New Account Sign Up page appears.

3. **Enter your Web site's URL and time zone and then click Continue.**

4. **Enter your contact information, including your phone number, and click Continue.**

   The Terms of Service appear.

5. **Read the Terms of Service, click Yes, and click Create New Account.**

   The Analytics: Tracking Instructions page appears, with a block of code you need to copy to any pages you want to track.

6. **Copy the code that begins with** `<script>` **and ends with** `</script>`.

7. **Open your Web site's home page in a Web editor or in a program such as Notepad. View the code for your home page and paste the block of Google Analytics code just before the** `</body>` **tag.**

   By doing so, you allow Google to run a script that tracks who comes to your Web page and run reports on where they come from.

   You find this near the bottom of the Web page (see Figure 12-4). Greg has isolated the bottom of his own home page's code so you can see where the block should go.

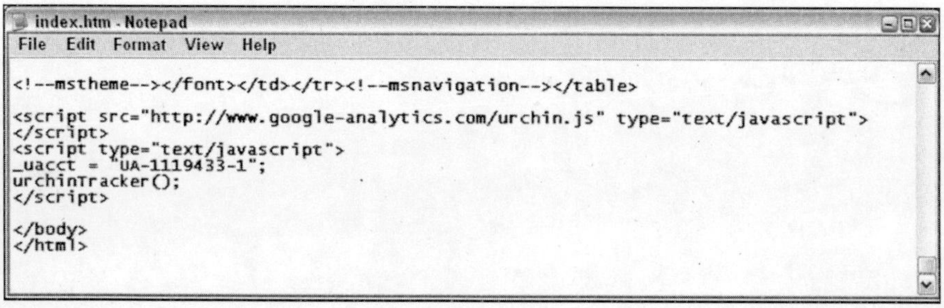

Figure 12-4:
You allow Google to track your visitors and analyse where they come from.

```
index.htm - Notepad
File   Edit   Format   View   Help

<!--mstheme--></font></td></tr><!--msnavigation--></table>

<script src="http://www.google-analytics.com/urchin.js" type="text/javascript">
</script>
<script type="text/javascript">
_uacct = "UA-1119433-1";
urchinTracker();
</script>

</body>
</html>
```

8. **Save your Web page file and upload it to your server.**

9. **Return to the Google Analytics page and click Continue.**

10. **When the Analytics Settings page appears, click Check Status to see if your page has the tracking code added correctly.**

11. **Review your page and then click Done.**

    The Analytics Settings page re-appears.

12. **Click View Reports to view the analysis of your page.**

    You can view settings for the past several days; over the coming weeks, you can view more data pertaining to your site.

We discuss Web site statistics (or log file analysis) in Chapter 11. Google Analytics can also provide similar statistics such as the number of unique visitors to your site and which Web sites referred them; but, more interesting, are the reports that tell you more about *visitor behaviour*, or what visitors do when they arrive on your site. The Site Overlay feature allows you to track where users are clicking after they arrive on a page. Other useful features include benchmarking your site against others in your industry and analysing where users are leaving your site. For example: 100 people may add a product to their shopping cart but only 21 actually check out, pay and complete their purchase online. Being able to track where people are abandoning their purchase helps you improve your site to overcome these problems.

You can also integrate Google Analytics with your advertising campaigns on Google AdWords to track your keyword effectiveness and measure your return on investment. AdWords, one of Google's most popular resources, gives you a cost-effective way to take out paid search ads that steer people to your Web site. You find out more about AdWords in Chapter 11.

Part IV
The Necessary Evils: Law and Accounting

Glenn Lumsden

'No Mr Brown, you may not change your name to Mr Amazon-eBay-In-The-Nude.'

In this part ...

Before you can start raking in the big (or at least
moderate) bickies on the Web, you have to dot all
your *i*'s and cross your *t*'s. Along with the flashy parts
of an online business — the ads, the Web pages and the
catalogue listings — you have to add up the numbers and
complete any necessary paperwork.

This part addresses the aspects of doing business online
that have to be covered in order to pay taxes, take
deductions and observe the law. You may think of them
as necessary evils that help you avoid trouble. Chapter 13
gives you information on trading names, trademarks and
copyright as well as the various legal forms of business
set up that are available. Chapter 14 goes on to describe
useful accounting tools as well as how to make sure you
hang on to as many of your hard-earned profit dollars as
possible.

Chapter 13

Keeping It All Legal

* *

In This Chapter

▶ Using trademarks to protect your company's identity

▶ Avoiding copyright infringement

▶ Deciding on your business structure

▶ Keeping on the right side of the law

* *

*A*s the field of e-commerce becomes more competitive and enterprising businesspeople find new ways to produce content online, e-litigation, e-patents, e-trademarks, and other means of legal protection multiply correspondingly. The courts are increasingly called upon to resolve smaller e-squabbles and, literally, lay down the e-law.

Many of the recent legal cases in the news concern the proliferation of content on popular file-sharing sites and other Web resources. For instance, in 2006 in the United States, the Chicago Lawyers' Committee for Civil Rights Under Law sued the popular classified service Craigslist for violating the Federal Fair Housing Act because of real estate postings that contained discriminating messages, such as 'No Minorities'. The suit was eventually dismissed because under the Communications Decency Act, Craigslist is regarded as an 'interactive computer service' rather than a publisher of information.

The effect on sites that publish copyrighted content, such as YouTube, is unclear. But others who publish information online can be liable if they break the law. In the United States, a Florida woman was awarded US$11.3 million in a defamation lawsuit filed against a Louisiana woman who posted messages on the Internet calling her a 'crook', a 'con artist' and a 'fraud'. The case was seen as a warning to bloggers and other Web site owners. The point: Be sure what you publish doesn't break the law.

In previous years, big e-commerce players, such as Microsoft and Google, were involved in patent and trademark disputes. In summer 2004, for instance, Microsoft settled a lawsuit it filed in the U.S. District Court by paying US$20 million to stop a company — Lindows.com — from infringing on its trademarked name Windows. As a new business owner, remember that ignorance isn't an excuse. This area may well make you nervous because you lack experience in business law and you don't have lots of money with which to hire lawyers and accountants. You don't want to be discovering for the first time about copyright law or the concept of intellectual property when you're in the midst of a dispute. In this chapter, we give you a snapshot of legal issues that you can't afford to ignore. Hopefully, this information can help you head off trouble before it occurs.

The Department of Innovation, Industry and Tourism publishes the 'Legal Issues Guide for Small Business', which is freely available online and well worth a look. Visit sblegal.industry.gov.au.

Trading Names and Trademarks

A *trading name* is the name by which a business is known in the marketplace. A trading name can also be *trademarked*, which means that a business has taken the extra step of registering its trading name so that others can't use it. At the same time, as a business owner you're at an advantage to realise that a trading name can be a trademark even though it hasn't been registered as such. The IP Australia defines a trademark as 'a word, phrase, letter, number, sound, smell, shape, logo, picture, aspect of packaging or a combination of these, used to distinguish the goods and services of one trader from those of another'. Big corporations protect their trading names and trademarks jealously, and sometimes court battles erupt over who can legally use a name.

Although you may never get in a trademark battle and you may never trademark a name, be careful which trading name you pick and how you use it. Choose a trading name that's easy to remember so that people can associate it with your company and return to you often when they're looking for the products or services that you provide. Also, as part of taking your new business seriously and planning for success, you may want to protect your right to use your name by registering the trademark.

You can trademark any visual element that accompanies a particular tangible product or line of goods, which serves to identify and distinguish it from products sold by other sources. In other words, a trademark isn't necessarily just for your business's trading name. In fact, you can trademark letters, words, names, phrases, slogans, numbers, colours, symbols, designs or shapes. Take a look at the cover of this book. Look closely and see how many TM or ® symbols you see. The same trademarked items are shown on the Dummies Web site, which is shown in Figure 13-1.

You can use the ® (Registered symbol) next to your trademark as soon as your trademark is registered. Anyone can use the TM mark because the mark doesn't indicate that the trademark is registered.

For most small businesses, the problem with trademarks isn't so much protecting your own as it is stepping on someone else's. Research the name you want to use to make sure you don't run into trouble.

Figure 13-1:
You don't have to use special symbols to designate logos or phrases on your Web site, but you may want to.

Determining whether a trademark is up for grabs

To avoid getting sued for trademark infringement and having to change your trading name or even pay damages if you lose, conduct a trademark search before you settle on a trading name. The goal of a trademark search is to discover any potential conflicts between your trading name and someone else's. Ideally, you conduct the search before you actually use your trading name or register for an official trademark.

The following list details two ways that you can do a trademark search:

- **Conduct a search online:** You can use the Web to help you conduct a trademark search at the Intellectual Property Office of New Zealand (www.iponz.govt.nz) or IP Australia (www.ipaustralia.gov.au). Both these government-run Web sites allow you to conduct a trademark search — and both are convenient and free.

- **Pay a professional search firm to do the research for you:** Look for professional search firms in the *Yellow Pages* under Trade Marks Attorneys. You can expect to pay between $90 and $390 per trademark searched. More complete searches that cover registered and unregistered marks that are similar to the one you want to use can cost several hundred dollars.

Cyberspace goes beyond national boundaries. A trademark search in your own country may not be enough. Most industrialised countries, including Australia, have signed international treaties that enable trademark owners in one country to enforce their rights against infringement by individuals in another country. Conducting an international trademark search is difficult to do yourself, so you may want to pay someone to do the searching for you.

The consequences of failing to conduct a reasonably thorough trademark search can be severe. In part, the consequences depend on how widely you distribute the protected item — and on the Internet, you can distribute it worldwide. If you attempt to use a trademark that's been federally registered by someone else, you could go to court and be prevented from using the trademark again. You may even be liable for damages and attorney's fees. So you're best to be careful.

Protecting your trading name

The legal standard is that you get the rights to your trading name when you begin using it. You get the right to exclude others from using it when you register. But when you apply to register a trademark, you record the date of its first use. Effectively, then, the day you start using a name is when you actually obtain the rights to use it for trade.

After researching your trading name against existing trademarks, you can file an application with the Intellectual Property Office of New Zealand (www.iponz.govt.nz) or IP Australia (www.ipaustralia.gov.au). In New Zealand it costs NZ$112.50 (per class) to file a trademark application and, as soon as your application is accepted, another 3–6 months go by before you find out whether your trademark has been successfully registered. In Australia it can cost up to $500 (per class) to file a trademark application and, again, turnaround times are slow. Your application isn't looked at for up to 3 months and then, if accepted, it can be a further 6 months before your trademark is registered.

Trademark registration can take 6–24 months. That lead time is why it is critical to take all the necessary steps before submitting your application. Both the Aussie and Kiwi Web sites spell out what checks you need to conduct prior to submitting an application. Having an application returned isn't uncommon. Often, an applicant receives correspondence that either rejects part of the application or raises a question about it. If you receive such a letter, don't panic. You need to go to a lawyer who specialises in or is familiar with trademark law and who can help you respond to the correspondence. In the meantime, you can still operate your business with your trading name.

Trademarks listed in the trademarks register last for 10 years and are renewable. You don't have to use the TM or ® symbol when you publish your trademark, but doing so impresses upon people how seriously you take your business and its identity.

Protecting and building a brand — Roses Only

Online flower retailer, Roses Only, began in 1995 and, as business rapidly expanded, it realised the need to protect its trademark and build a distinctive brand.

Roses Only uses the Internet as a sales tool and provides boxed flowers, and now fruit, to a growing market in Australia, New Zealand and the United Kingdom. Its main target market is men shopping for flowers who want something luxurious without too high a price. The three things that influence its buying decision are speed, convenience and roses.

In 1998, when founder James Stevens sought to protect his brand he was concerned because 'roses' and 'only' are generic words so he decided to hire intellectual property lawyers (Spruson & Ferguson). He went on to trademark both the words 'roses only' and the distinctive two branches with thorns image (check out the image/logo at rosesonly. com.au).

In 2005, when the business expanded into fresh fruit delivery, the words 'fruit only', again with the stylised branches, were trademarked.

Roses Only has registered trademarks in New Zealand and the United Kingdom. The business has also protected the trademark under the Madrid Protocol international trademark system (www.wipo.int/madrid/en) to cover the markets earmarked for possible expansion including the United States and Japan.

On occasion, Roses Only has had to take action to protect its brand. Such as when another large online flower retailer registered the name Flowers Only. Stevens put forward a case to auDA, the Australian Domain Name Administrator, that the only reason the other business would register flowersonly.com.au was so customers would get confused and think it was a division of Roses Only. Roses Only were successful in this case, auDA determined that the other retailer had acted in bad faith, and had to return the address to Roses Only.

Making sure your domain name stays yours

The practice of choosing a domain name for an online business is related to the concept of trading names and trademarks. With cybersquatters and other businesspeople snapping up domain names since 1994 or so, your ideal name is unlikely to be available in the popular .com domain. Here are two common problems:

✔ Someone else has already taken the domain name related to the name of your existing business.

✔ The domain name you choose is close to one that already exists or to another company with a similar name. (Remember the Microsoft Windows – Lindows.com dispute that we mention at the beginning of this chapter?)

If the domain name that you think is perfect for your online business is already taken, you have some options. You can contact the owner of the domain name and offer to buy it. Alternatively, you can choose a domain name with another suffix. If a dot-com name isn't available, try the old standby alternatives, .org (which, in theory at least, is for not-for-profit organisations) and .net (which is for network providers).

You can also choose one of the newer *Top-Level Domains* (TLDs), a second set of domain name suffixes that were made available a few years ago, which include the following: .biz for businesses, .info for general use and .name for personal names. You can find out more about the more recent TLDs at the InterNIC Web site, www.internic.net/faqs/new-tlds.html.

You can always get around the fact that your perfect domain name isn't available by changing the name slightly. Rather than treesurgeon.com, you can choose tree-surgeon.com or treesurgery.com. But be careful, lest you violate someone else's trademark and get into a dispute with the holder of the other domain name. A court may order you to stop using the name and pay damages to the other domain name's owner.

On the other hand, if you've been doing business for a while and have a trademarked name, you may find someone else owns the domain name. You can assert your rights and raise a dispute yourself. To resolve the dispute, you could go to a group like the WIPO Arbitration and Mediation Center (www.wipo.int/amc/en/center/index.html) or ICANN, the Internet Corporation for Assigned Names and Numbers (www.icann.org). But first, find out more about what constitutes trademark infringement and how to enforce a trademark.

Practising Safe Copyright

What's the difference between a trademark and a copyright? *Trademarks* are covered by trademark law and are distinctive words, symbols, slogans or other things that serve to identify products or services in the marketplace. *Copyright*, on the other hand, refers to the creator's ownership of creative works, such as writing, art, software, video or cinema (but not names, titles or short phrases). Copyright also provides the owner with redress in case someone copies the works without the owner's permission. Copyright is a legal device that enables the creator of a work the right to control how the work is to be used.

Even if nobody ever called you a nerd, as a businessperson who produces goods and services of economic value, you may be the owner of intellectual property. *Intellectual property* refers to works of authorship as well as certain inventions. Because intellectual property may be owned, bought and sold just like other types of property, you're best to know something about the copyright laws governing it. Having this information maximises the value of your products and keeps you from throwing away potentially valuable assets or finding yourself at the wrong end of an expensive lawsuit.

Copyright you can count on

A little bit about copyright law … For copyright protection to be put in place your work needs to be original (yours!) and in a material form such as written down, recorded or on disk — it can't be just floating around in your head.

Copyright protects many different items. These include

- ✔ **Artistic works:** For example, paintings, drawings, photos and logos
- ✔ **Dramatic works:** For example, scripts, screenplays and choreography
- ✔ **Film, sound recordings and broadcast:** For example, TV and radio
- ✔ **Literary works:** For example, books, reports and Web site content
- ✔ **Published editions:** For example, layout and typography, and cover design
- ✔ **Music:** For example, online distribution of digital music and music videos

Items not protected by copyright include

- ✔ Ideas
- ✔ Information
- ✔ Names, titles and slogans

Everything you see on the Net is copyrighted, whether or not a copyright notice actually appears. Copyright exists from the moment a work is fixed in a tangible medium, including a Web page. For example, plenty of art is available for the taking on the Web, but look before you grab. Unless an image on the Web is specified as being copyright free, you violate copyright law if you take it. HTML tags themselves aren't copyrighted, but the content of the HTML-formatted page is. General techniques for designing Web pages aren't copyrighted, but certain elements (such as logos) are.

Who owns copyright?

The creator of the material is the first owner of copyright. Copyright lasts for the life of the creator +70 years. The creator of the work may choose to assign or license copyright to someone else. You can also leave your copyright to someone else — via your will.

Ownership of copyright can take many forms, including

- ✔ If you hire a freelance copywriter to write material for you, by default the person owns copyright as the creator of the material — unless you have a written agreement with the copywriter that copyright is transferred to you upon payment at the completion of the project.
- ✔ If the copywriter is employed on a permanent basis (as an employee), the employer owns copyright.
- ✔ If you hire a casual or contract employee, a copyright clause should be included in the employment agreement.

If you hire someone else to write copy for you, always have a written agreement as to who owns copyright of the finished work. If this agreement is then infringed, you can take legal action.

When do you need permission of the copyright owner?

You need permission of the copyright owner if you wish to use all or any *substantial part* of work which is copyright — with or without a copyright notice. A substantial part is an important, essential or distinctive part of the work. Remember everybody's view on what is important, essential or distinctive varies.

You need permission of the copyright owner to

- ✔ Adapt; publish; rent or re-broadcast
- ✔ Communicate that work to the public (including by fax, email or use on the Internet)
- ✔ Perform the work in public
- ✔ Reproduce or copy the work (some exceptions apply to research or personal use)

If you find you need to use a piece of material and you can't find the copyright owner, you can make use of a number of collecting societies to help you. The most common society is Copyright Agency Limited (www.copyright.com.au).

You can purchase individual or blanket licences. These collecting societies are not-for-profit and have copyright owners as their members.

For more information about copyright law, contact the following organisations:

- **In Australia:** Copyright law is governed by the Copyright Act of 1968. For more information on copyright law in Australia visit the Web site of the Australian Copyright Council (www.copyright.org.au).

- **In New Zealand:** The Copyright (New Technologies) Amendment Bill was passed in April 2008. This is an amendment to the Copyright Act of 1994 and seeks to better allow for Internet content such as text, images and audio. For more information on copyright law in New Zealand, visit the Web site of the Copyright Council of New Zealand (www.copyright.org.nz).

Making copyright work for you

A copyright — which protects original works of authorship — costs nothing, applies automatically and lasts more than 50 years. When you affix a copyright notice to your newsletter or Web site, you make your readers think twice about unauthorised copying and put them on notice that you take copyright seriously.

Creating a good copyright notice

While actually placing a copyright notice on your work isn't necessary, doing so is a good idea because the practice serves as a reminder to others that you have put in time, effort, skill and creativity to produce that piece of work.

Copyright notices identify the author of a given work (such as writing or software) and then spell out the terms by which that author grants others the right (or the *licence*) to copy that work to their computer and read it (or use it). The usual copyright notice is pretty simple and takes this form:

```
Copyright © 2009 [Your Name] All rights reserved
```

You don't have to use the © symbol, but the practice does make your notice look more official. In order to create a copyright symbol that appears on a Web page, you have to enter a special series of characters in the HTML source code for your page. For example, Web browsers translate the characters © as the copyright symbol, which is displayed as © in the Web browser window. Most Web page creation tools provide menu options for inserting special symbols such as this one.

Copyright notices can also be more informal, and a personal message can have extra impact. The graphic design company Echoed Sentiments Publishing (www.espconcepts.com) includes both the usual copyright notice plus a very detailed message about how others can use its design elements (www.espconcepts.com/gratis_design_elements.html).

Stop, thief ...

Have you ever been in the situation, where you've walked in the front door of your home and you know you've been burgled? Your personal items have been disturbed and items are missing. You felt violated and angry. How dare someone come in and take your stuff.

Obvious signs show you when you've been burgled in your home; but it's not so obvious when your Web site copy and images are stolen. Physically, nothing looks amiss. Unless you're browsing the Web and you're lucky enough to stumble across your words or image, you don't know. The thieves — they've stolen your work ... but what can you do about it?

If you think someone has infringed on your copyright:

1. **Check whether your suspicion really is an infringement.**

   Consider whether the infringement is a substantial part of your work or just using the underlying ideas. Ideas aren't copyright.

2. **Check whether any outstanding contractual issues exist between you and the other party.**

3. **Contact the person and ask whether he knows he has infringed on your copyright.**

   Try to commence informal negotiations where you may ask for a fee or retraction.

If you're the creator and first owner of copyright of the work, you may be able to receive some assistance in this area from the Australian Copyright Council.

4. **Send a letter of demand.**

   See a solicitor to have a letter of demand drafted. ***Note:*** From here on in, is where you begin to spend larger sums of money to fight your case.

5. **Consider court action — via the Federal Magistrates Court.**

   This approach is your last avenue.

If the roles are reversed and you're contacted by a copyright owner, you need to check whether you've infringed on her copyright and find out whether she really is the copyright owner. If you receive a letter of demand, contact a solicitor immediately.

Basically, to protect yourself from infringing on someone else's copyright, use your own material or get permission to use material, for example, purchase royalty-free images from a reputable image library. Don't steal someone else's stuff ... yes, it's a big wide world out there, but at times you get to see how remarkably small it really is.

More information, fact sheets and books are available from the Australian Copyright Council (www.copyright.org.au).

Protection with digital watermarks

In traditional offset printing, a *watermark* is a faint image embedded in stationery or other paper. The watermark usually bears the name of the paper manufacturer, but it can also identify an organisation for which the stationery was made.

Watermarking has its equivalent in the online world. Graphic artists sometimes use *digital watermarking* to protect images they create. This process involves adding copyright or other information about the image's owner to the digital image file. The information added may or may not be visible. (Some images have copyright information added, not visible in the body of the Web page but in the image file itself.) Other images, such as the one shown in Figure 13-2, have a watermark pasted right into the visible area, which makes it difficult for others to copy and re-use them.

Digimarc (www.digimarc.com), which functions as a plug-in application with the popular graphics tools Adobe Photoshop (www.adobe.com) and Paint Shop Pro (www.corel.com), is one of the most widely used watermarking tools.

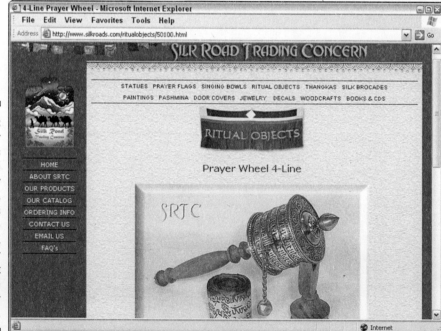

Figure 13-2:
If your products are particularly precious, such as unique works of art, assert your copyright over them on your Web site.

Deciding on a Legal Form for Your Business

When starting a business, your best approach is to investigate your options and decide on what *business structure* is best for you before you start trading. A business structure is the form or type of business you register yourself as, with the relevant governing body, and it allows you to define your business for taxation and licensing purposes. You have a number of options from which to choose, and the choice can affect the amount of taxes you pay and your liability in case of loss. The following sections describe your alternatives.

If you're looking for more information, Veechi Curtis explores the legal and financial aspects of starting and operating a small business in *Small Business For Dummies,* 2nd Edition (Wiley Publishing Australia Pty Ltd).

Deciding on the right business structure for you can be a difficult process, and a number of factors need to be considered such as the number of business owners, tax liabilities, personal exposure and establishment costs. Make discussing your own situation with your accountant or business adviser a critical step before making your decision.

Sole trader

As a *sole trader*, you're the only boss. You make all the decisions and you get all the benefits. On the other hand, you take all the risk, too. This business structure is the simplest and least expensive type of business because you can run it yourself. You don't need an accountant or lawyer to help you form the business, and you don't have to answer to partners, or shareholders, either.

A sole trader has the choice to trade under her own name or under a registered business name. A registered business name has no legal implications other than allowing you to use and trade under that name instead of your own. So you're still personally liable for any losses and you're liable to pay tax as an individual.

Partnership

A *partnership* enables a group of people to contribute their time, talents and money towards the business. In a partnership, you share the risk and profit with at least one other person. Ideally, your partners bring skills to the endeavour that complement your own contributions. One obvious advantage to a partnership is that you can discuss decisions and problems with your partners. All partners are held personally liable for losses. The rate of taxes that each partner pays is based on his or her percentage of income from the partnership.

If you decide to strike up a partnership with someone, drawing up a *Partnership Agreement* is a good idea. Although you're not legally required to do so, such an agreement clearly spells out the duration of the partnership and the responsibilities of each person involved. Without such an agreement, the division of liabilities and assets is considered to be equal, regardless of how much more effort one person has put into the business than the other.

Company

A *limited liability (or private) company* is a separate legal entity established for the sole purpose of carrying out business.

The advantages of setting up as a company are

- ✔ **Limited liability:** One of the biggest advantages of the company structure is that the legal liability of your company's shareholders is limited to their share capital (that is, how much money they pay for their shares in the company). This means that, in most cases, the personal assets of shareholders cannot be seized to pay company debts. However, company directors may still be liable for any debts, liabilities and legal actions held against their company, in certain circumstances, such as when the directors have allowed the company to continue trading when insolvent.

- ✔ **Less tax to pay:** Companies may also pay less tax than other business structures such as sole traders and partnerships. Companies are taxed on their profits at the company tax rate which may be lower than the marginal tax rates of its individual shareholders.

- ✔ **Control:** You can also use a company structure to effectively separate the management and ownership aspects of the business. For example, the managers of the business can be appointed directors of the business and the owners of the business can be shareholders of the company.

The disadvantages of a company business structure are

- ✔ **High set-up and operating costs:** The cost of establishing a company is higher than many other structures such as a sole trader. There are ongoing costs of compliance, such as the costs of preparing and submitting annual statements and any fees for accounting and legal services.

- ✔ **Responsibilities of directors:** The directors of the company have certain legal obligations. If directors fail to meet these requirements they may be held personally liable for the debts of the company.

 The legal and other requirements for setting up a business structure in Australia and New Zealand, while similar, are slightly different in each country. The best place to check and source information about starting a business, registration requirements and business structures is

- ✔ **In Australia:** business.gov.au (`business.gov.au`). In Australia, you need to register for a business name with the relevant office in each state, taxation is managed by the ATO (`www.ato.gov.au`) and company registrations are managed by ASIC (`www.asic.gov.au`).

- ✔ **In New Zealand:** business.govt.nz (`business.govt.nz`). In New Zealand, you're not required to register your business or trading name, taxation is managed by IRD (`www.ird.govt.nz`) and company registrations are managed by the New Zealand Companies Office (`www.companies.govt.nz`).

Keeping Out of Legal Trouble

There are many legal issues to be aware of when it comes to Web sites and e-commerce and how you manage your risks. You need to ensure that the content of your Web site is accurate and complies with current law. And you need to regularly review the Web site after it is up and running to ensure it continues to comply. This section gives you some general guidance on possible ways to manage your risk. (And, of course, obtaining your own specific legal advice is essential.)

Publishing your policy statements

Publishing your policies on your Web site often helps to establish customer loyalty, trust and confidence at the same time as providing a level of protection against the legal risks associated with having a Web site. The important thing is that your policies are clear and easy to understand and not hidden away (in the small print) on your Web site.

You may have your policies all laid out in one document or, alternatively, you can separate them out and provide them on the relevant areas of your site.

Your policy statements may include

- Copyright and intellectual property
- Delivery
- Jurisdiction
- Privacy
- Purchasing
- Returns and refunds
- Security
- Terms and conditions

Understanding the importance of a privacy policy

A privacy policy explains to your Web site visitors what personal information you collect about them from your Web site and how you're going to use and store it.

In the most basic terms, most potential customers just want to know that you're going to securely store their personal details and you're not going to hassle them for life, or pass (or sell) their details on to a third party. With the rise in junk email, direct mail and telemarketing (especially those annoying uninvited dinner-time calls), people are more wary about sharing their personal details and concerned about how these details are to be used.

Having a policy that clearly explains what information you collect on your Web site and how it is used can help to put your site's visitors' minds at ease. Collecting information includes both the obvious information collection methods such as filling in an inquiry form or placing an order, as well as the not-so-obvious methods such as what Web site statistics you collect from each visitor who comes to your site.

Figure 13-3 illustrates a basic sample to get you started:

Privacy Policy

Your privacy is important to us.

Who we are

This Web site is operated by Privacy Palms [Business Name]. Our postal address is PO Box 123, Privacy Palms, NSW 0000. You can also reach us by email at info@privacypalms.com or by phone at + 02 1234 5678.

Information collected

We only ask for your personal information when it is required to respond to an inquiry you have submitted on our Web site or to subscribe you to our email newsletter. This information is only used to fulfil your request and is not passed on to any third party. You may contact us at any time to find out what personal information we have recorded and to request the information be changed, updated or deleted.

We only record your email address if you have given it to us to subscribe to our monthly newsletter. If you have given us your email address in the past but no longer want to receive our newsletter, please email us at the address mentioned above.

When you visit our Web site, our Web host automatically records general information about your visit, but does not record any personal information about you. This information is recorded and used for statistical purposes only and includes: Your server address; the date and time; pages you have accessed and documents you have downloaded while on our site; the previous site you visited; and the type of browser used.

Figure 13-3: A privacy policy explains how you use a visitor's personal information.

Depending on the size of your business or the industry you belong to you may also be required to be compliant with the privacy legislation in your country.

- **In Australia:** The *Privacy Act 1988* establishes National Privacy Principles (NPPs). For more details, visit the Privacy Commissioner's Web site (www.privacy.gov.au).
- **In New Zealand:** The *Privacy Act 1993* sets out 12 privacy principles for how personal information can be collected, used, stored and disclosed. For more details, visit the Privacy Commissioner's Web site (www.privacy.org.nz).

Talking terms and conditions

On a Web site, terms and conditions outline the manner in which the Web site is to be used and the specific obligations that each user must accept prior to using the Web site. These general usage terms and conditions should be separate from any policies or terms you have for making a purchase on the Web site.

Here are the types of things to include in your online business terms and conditions:

- Terms of use — what the user is allowed to do
- Warning — states that if the user doesn't agree with any of the terms and conditions, she should immediately exit the Web site
- Terms for linking to other sites
- Privacy statement — asserts ownership of copyright and all intellectual property rights
- Disclaimer for all liability (in accordance with the law)

Chapter 14

Online Business Accounting Tools

In This Chapter

▶ Discovering simple accounting methods

▶ Choosing user-friendly accounting software or online services

▶ Keeping tax records and taking business deductions

*S*ome people have a gift for keeping track of figures, recording financial information, and completing regular compliance tasks for their business accounts. And others have the shoe box under the bed and what can only be described as a 'dog's breakfast' — relying on their accountant to make sense of the mess annually. Melissa is pretty good with figures and likes to stay on top of things. She checks her business bank account daily and performs regular weekly, monthly, quarterly and annual tasks so that she always has a good picture of her business's financial status. After 10 years in business, she knows the value of having good accounting procedures, especially those that relate to an online business.

Without having at least some minimal records of your day-to-day operations, you don't have any way — other than the proverbial 'gut feeling' — of knowing whether your business is truly successful. Besides that, banks and the Australian Taxation Office (ATO) or New Zealand's Inland Revenue Department (IRD) don't hold gut feelings in high regard! When the time comes to ask for a loan or to pay taxes, you're set to regret not having records close at hand. Even if you sell on eBay, you can't rely on the auction site to keep records for you; your records are only kept on My eBay for 60 days, and PayPal doesn't record payments by cheque or money order.

In this chapter, we introduce you to some simple, straightforward ways to handle your online business's financial information — and all businesspeople know that accurate record keeping is essential when revenues dwindle and expenses must be reduced. This chapter shows you the most important accounting practices and software that can help you tackle the essential financial tasks you need to undertake to keep your new business viable.

ABCs: Accounting Basics for Commerce

The most important accounting practices for your online business are the following:

- **Deciding on your business structure:** Are you going to be a sole trader, partnership or company? (See more about determining a legal structure for your business in Chapter 13.)
- **Establishing good record-keeping practices:** Record expenses and income in ways that can help you at tax time.
- **Obtaining financing when you need it:** Although getting started in an online business doesn't cost a lot, you may want to expand someday, and good accounting can help you do it.

Accounting may not be the sexiest of topics (unless, of course, you're married to an accountant; in that case, you have a financial expert at hand and can skip this chapter!). Then again, unexpected cash shortages or other problems that can result from bad record keeping can unravel the best of businesses.

Good accounting is the key to order and good management for your business. How else can you know how you're doing? Yet many new businesspeople are intimidated by the numbers game. Use the tool at hand — your computer — to help you overcome your fear: Start keeping those books!

Choosing an accounting method

Accepting that you have to keep track of your business's accounting is only half the battle; next, you need to decide how to do it. The point at which you make note of each transaction in your books and the period of time over which you record the data make a difference not only to your accountant but also to agencies such as the ATO or IRD. Even if you hire someone to keep the books for you, knowing what options are open to you is most beneficial to running your business.

The relevant authorities make reference guides available on their Web sites:

- In Australia: Consult the ATO Tax Basics for Small Business (www.ato.gov.au/content/downloads/BUS25193n1908_06_08.pdf).
- In New Zealand: Consult Smart Business IR320 (http://www.ird.govt.nz/forms-guides/title/forms-s/ir320-guide-smart-business.html).

You have two possible methods of totalling income and expenses — cash-basis versus accrual-basis accounting. Don't be intimidated by these terms. Exactly where and how you do the recording is up to you. You can take a piece of paper, divide it into two columns labelled *Income* and *Expenses*, and do it that way. (We describe some more high-tech tools later in this chapter.) These methods are just two standard ways of deciding when to report your income and expenses:

- ✔ **Cash-basis accounting:** You report income when you actually receive it and expenses when you pay them. This method is the easy way to report income and expenses, and probably the way most new small businesses do it.

- ✔ **Accrual-basis accounting:** This method is more complicated than the cash-basis method, but if your online business maintains an inventory, you must use the accrual method. You report income when you actually receive the payment; you write down expenses *when services are rendered* (even though you may not have made the cash payment yet). For example, if a payment is due on 1 December, but you send the cheque on 8 December, you record the bill as being paid on 1 December, when the payment was originally due.

Accrual-basis accounting creates a more accurate picture of a business's financial situation. If a business is experiencing cash flow problems and is extending payments on some of its bills, cash-basis accounting provides an unduly rosy financial picture, whereas the accrual-basis method would be more accurate.

Knowing what records to keep

When you run your own business, being meticulous about recording everything that pertains to your commercial activities pays dividends (so to speak). The more you understand what you have to record, the more accurate your records are going to be — and the more deductions you can take, too. Go to the office supply store and get a financial record book — a *journal* — which is set up with columns for income and expenses. Or, if you prefer doing it all on your computer, install one of the accounting software packages discussed in the section 'Accounting Software for Your Business', later in this chapter.

Tracking income

Receiving cheques for your goods or services is the fun part of doing business, and so income is probably the kind of data that you're going to look forward to recording.

You need to keep track of your company's income (or, as it is sometimes called, your *gross receipts*) carefully. Not all the income your business receives is taxable. What you receive as a result of sales (your *revenue*) is taxable, but loans that you receive aren't. Be sure to separate the two and pay tax only on the sales income. But keep good records: If you can't accurately report the source of income that you didn't pay taxes on, the tax office labels it *unreported income*, and you have to pay taxes and possibly fines and penalties on it.

Just how should you record your revenue? For each item, write down a brief, informal statement. This is a personal record that you may make on a slip of paper or even on the back of a payment cheque. Be sure to include the following information:

- ✔ Amount received

- ✔ Type of payment (credit card, direct bank deposit, cash or cheque)

- ✔ Date of the transaction

- ✔ Name, model number and description of the item purchased

- ✔ Name of client or customer

- ✔ Goods or services you provided in exchange for the payment

Collect all your cheque stubs and revenue statements, in date order, in a folder labelled *Income* so that you can find them easily at tax time.

Assessing your assets

Assets are resources that your business owns, such as your office and computer equipment. *Equity* is your remaining assets after you pay your creditors.

Any equipment you have that contributes to your business activities constitutes your assets. Equipment that has a life span of more than a year is expected to help you generate income over its useful life; therefore, you must spread out (or, in other words, *expense*) the original cost of the equipment over its life span. Expensing the cost of an asset over the period of its useful life is *depreciation*. To depreciate an item, estimate how many years you're going to use it and then divide the original cost by the number of years. The result is the amount that you report in any given year. For example, if you purchase a computer that costs $3,000 and you expect to use it in your business for five years, you expense $600 of the cost each year.

Depending on the type of asset, the total cost and the size of your business, slightly different rules for calculating depreciation apply — so be sure to check with the relevant tax office or your accountant before calculating your depreciation deductions.

Keep records of your assets that include the following information:

✔ Name, model number and description

✔ Purchase date

✔ Purchase price, including fees

✔ Date the item went into service

✔ Amount of time the item is put to personal (as opposed to business) use

File these records in a safe location along with your other tax-related information.

Recording payments

Even a lone entrepreneur doesn't work in a vacuum. An online business owner needs to pay a Web host, an ISP and, possibly, Web page designers as well as other consultants. If you take on partners or employees, things get more complicated. But in general, you need to record all payments such as these in detail as well.

Your accountant is likely to bring up the question of how you pay the people who work for you. You have two options: You can treat them either as full- or part-time employees or as independent contractors. The relevant tax office uses a stringent series of guidelines to determine who is a contractor and who is a full-time employee. Refer to the Web sites for the ATO (www.ato.gov.au) or IRD (www.ird.govt.nz), which discuss the employee/independent contractor subject in detail.

Hiring independent contractors rather than salaried workers is far simpler for you: You don't have to pay benefits, such as superannuation, to independent contractors, and you don't have to withhold payroll taxes. Just be sure to get tax invoices from any independent contractor who works for you. If you have full-time employees whom you pay an hourly wage, things get more complicated, and you had best consult an accountant to help you set up the salary payments.

Listing expenses

When keeping track of your expenses, the practice of breaking expenses into two categories is often useful:

- **Cost of goods sold**, or 'cost of sales', include any costs that can be directly attributed to the goods or services you sell. The most obvious examples of this are that if you make furniture or clothes, the materials you purchase to produce your product are a 'cost of sales' or if you buy goods wholesale and then on sell them, the cost of your inventory is also a 'cost of sales'.

- **Other or indirect expenses** include all other expenses incurred in running your business such as the telephone bill, postage and bank fees.

Get a big folder and use it to hold any receipts, contracts, cheque butts, credit card statements or invoices that represent expenses. Maintain a record of expenses that includes the following information:

- Date the expense occurred

- Name of the person or company that received payment from you

- Type of expense incurred (equipment, utilities, supplies and so on)

Recalling exactly what some receipts were for is often difficult a year or even just a month after the fact. Be sure to jot down a quick note in your cheque book for cheques written and on copies of receipts to remind you what the expense involved.

Understanding the Ps and Qs of P&Ls

You're likely to hear the term *profit-and-loss statement* (also called a P&L) thrown around when discussing your online business with financial people. The P&L is a report that measures the operation of a business over a given period of time, such as a week, a month or a year. The person who prepares the P&L (either you or your accountant) adds up your business revenues and subtracts the operating expenses. And, presto, the remaining amounts are either the profits or the losses.

Most of the accounting programs listed in the next section include some ways of presenting profit-and-loss statements and enable you to customise the statements to fit your needs.

Accounting Software for Your Business

The well-known, commercial accounting packages, such as Quicken and MYOB, let you enter your sales and expenses and then prepare statements and reports. Stick with these programs if you are relatively handy on a computer because they're the most commonly used, can save you time, give you a quick and accurate picture of your business at any time, and your accountant can easily work with electronic records. Otherwise, go for a simpler method such as keeping a journal (refer to the section 'Knowing what records to keep' earlier in this chapter) and hire an accountant to help you.

- ✔ **MYOB:** The two products most suitable for a small or home-based business are MYOB BusinessBasics or MYOB Accounting. The cost of the most basic solution starts at $149.

- ✔ **Quicken:** The two products most suitable for a small or home-based business are QuickBooks EasyStart or Quicken Home & Business (or QuickBooks Small Business in New Zealand). The cost of the most basic solution starts at $139.

Check that the software and version you choose suits your business setup. To help you decide, ask the following questions:

- ✔ Are you operating on a cash or accrual basis?

- ✔ Do you have inventory to account for?

- ✔ Do you employ staff?

- ✔ Is your software compatible with your accountant's software?

You can seek help from your accountant or financial adviser if you're not sure which accounting software to choose.

Whatever program you choose, make sure that you keep accurate books and set up privacy as well as backup systems that prevent your kids from wiping your business records.

If your business is a relatively simple sole proprietorship, you can record expenses and income by hand and add them up at tax time. Then complete your tax return yourself. Alternatively, you can record your entries and turn them over to a tax adviser who prepares a profit-and-loss statement and tells you the balance due on your annual tax.

Other software alternatives include

- ✔ **Accomplish CashManager:** A 100 per cent New Zealand owned and operated company. Its product is available in Australia, New Zealand and the United Kingdom, and allows all the basic bookkeeping functionality you would expect to record your income and expenses, prepare activity statements and reports such as a profit and loss statement. Lite, Standard and Plus versions are available, depending on your requirements, starting at around NZ$475.

- ✔ **eRecord:** A free tool provided by the ATO. This accounting software is aimed at small businesses that operate on a cash basis, have just one bank account and are currently keeping their records on paper.

- ✔ **Xero:** An online product available in Australia, New Zealand and the United Kingdom that claims to be 'the world's easiest accounting system'. Because it is an online application you and your accountant can access your business finances from anywhere in the world and enter data or produce reports. Fees are NZ$49 excluding GST per month to access your online account.

The Taxman Cometh: Concerns for Small Business

After you make it through the start-up phase of your business, surprise, surprise, you can now concern yourself with taxes. Here, too, a little preparation up front can save you lots of headaches down the road. But as a hard-working entrepreneur, time is your biggest obstacle.

In an Institute of Chartered Accountants in Australia survey, 78 per cent reported that they found it 'very or quite difficult' to meet deadlines. Yet advance planning is really important for taxes. In fact a legal requirement means that businesses must keep records appropriate to their trade or business and then store the prepared records for a period of 7 years. The ATO or IRD has the right to view these records if they want to audit your business's (or your personal) tax return. If your records aren't up to scratch the penalties can be severe.

The taxation and reporting requirements for Australia and New Zealand include the following:

- ✔ If your business is based in Australia, you need to be concerned about an Australian business number (ABN), business activity statements (BAS), goods and services tax (GST), pay as you go (PAYG) instalments, PAYG withholding, payment summaries and tax returns.

- ✔ If your business is based in New Zealand, you need to be concerned about income tax, GST and pay as you earn tax (PAYE).

In the next section, we look into these taxation and reporting requirements in more detail.

To charge or not to charge GST

If you're registered for GST and selling goods or services that are subject to GST, you're required to include GST when you make a sale and, also, to provide the customer with a tax invoice that shows the amount of GST charged.

In Australia:

- ✔ You're required to register for GST as soon as your turnover reaches $75,000 or more a year.

- ✔ The standard Australian tax year is 1 July to 30 June each year.

- ✔ GST is charged on most goods and services sold at a rate of 10 per cent. Quite a few goods and services are on the GST-free list — some of these include most basic foods, precious metals, some medicines and international mail, to name a few. Check the ATO Web site (www.ato.gov.au) for other GST-exempt goods and services.

- ✔ If you're registered for GST, you're required to report to the ATO on a regular basis.

- ✔ Depending on your turnover and other eligibility requirements, you may be able to calculate, report and/or pay GST monthly, quarterly or annually.

In New Zealand:

- ✔ You're required to register your business for GST as soon as your turnover reaches NZ$40,000 or more a year.
- ✔ The standard NZ tax year is 1 April to 31 March each year.
- ✔ GST (or goods and services tax) is charged on most goods and services sold, at a rate of 12.5 per cent. Goods and services exempt from GST include rent on a private residential property and some financial services such as bank fees.
- ✔ If you're registered for GST, you're required to report to the IRD on a regular basis.
- ✔ Depending on turnover, you can elect to file tax returns, every six months, two months or monthly.

Remembering other business taxes

Unfortunately, more than one tax is payable out of your hard-earned income, and those taxes that you need to pay depend on your business structure and whether your business is based in Australia or New Zealand.

Income tax (personal)

If you operate your business as a sole trader or partnership, you include your business income in your personal tax return and you're taxed at individual tax rates. In New Zealand, individual tax rates range from 19.5 per cent to 39 per cent depending on your annual earnings. In Australia, tax rates range from 0 per cent to 45 per cent depending on annual earnings. If you're an employee of your company, you have to lodge a personal income tax return, also. Tax returns are required to be lodged annually, so check with ATO or IRD Web sites for the relevant lodgement deadlines.

Income tax (business)

If you operate your business as a company, you're required to lodge an annual tax return for the company. The rate of tax that companies have to pay is 30 per cent both in Australia and New Zealand.

Paying tax on income throughout the year

Australia and New Zealand have systems for collecting income tax from companies throughout the year instead of waiting until the end of financial year.

In New Zealand, if your 'tax to pay' figure on your last return was more than $2,500 you're liable for *provisional tax* (a way of paying your tax through the year as the income is received). The provisional tax you pay during the year is offset against your end-of-year tax payable figure.

In Australia, you're required to make instalment payments during the income year towards your *expected* tax liability on your business income. These instalments are called pay as you go (PAYG) instalments — you pay these instalments quarterly or six monthly depending on your circumstances. Your actual tax liability is worked out at the end of the income year when your annual income tax return is assessed. Your instalments for the year are credited against your assessment to determine whether you owe tax or are owed a refund by the ATO.

Capital gains tax

New Zealand does not have capital gains tax but Australia does. Capital gains tax is payable on the capital gains you make — such as the sale of an asset. Visit the ATO Web site (www.ato.gov.au) for a step-by-step guide to capital gains tax.

Withholding tax from salaries and wages

If you have employees, you're required to withhold PAYG tax in Australia and PAYE tax in New Zealand. The tax office provides up-to-date tables on personal tax rates and how much you're required to withhold depending on the staff members' total earnings or salary.

Fringe benefits tax (FBT)

A *fringe benefit* is a 'payment' to an employee, but in a different form to salary or wages. Examples include using a work car for private use, cheap loans, gym membership or free concert tickets. Fringe benefits tax (FBT) is payable by employers and is assessed on the value of the fringe benefits provided to employees or their associates. Depending on whether your business is based in Australia or New Zealand requirements differ for registering for FBT and lodging returns either quarterly or annual. So check with the ATO or IRD.

Deducing your business deductions

One of the benefits of starting a new business, even if the business isn't profitable in the beginning, is the opportunity to take business deductions and reduce your tax payments. Always keep receipts from any purchases or expenses associated with your business activities. Make sure you're taking all the deductions for which you're eligible. We mention some of these deductions in the following sections.

Your home office

If you work at home (and we're assuming that, as an entrepreneur, you probably do), set aside some space for a home office. This area isn't just a territorial thing. It can result in some handy business deductions, too.

What you deduct depends on the amount of space in your home you use for your business and whether or not your home is your principal place of business. You can claim deductions for expenses such as utilities, business phone and depreciation of office furniture.

Your computer equipment

Computer equipment is probably the biggest expense related to your online business. But taking tax deductions can help offset the cost substantially. The key is showing the ATO or IRD (by reporting your income from your online business on your tax return) that you used your PC and related items, such as modems or printers, for business purposes. You track what you spend on computer equipment and include it in your annual tax return. Depending on the value of the equipment, this amount may affect whether you can claim the expense in one tax year or need to spread it out or depreciate it for the useful life of the equipment.

In case you're ever audited, be sure to keep some sort of record detailing all the ways in which you put your computer equipment to use for business purposes.

Other common business deductions

Many of the business-related expenses that you can deduct are listed on ATO or IRD Web sites. The following is a brief list of some of the deductions you can look for:

- Advertising fees
- Computer supplies
- Internet access charges
- Office supplies
- Shipping and delivery
- Utilities fees that pertain to your home office

Part V
The Part of Tens

Glenn Lumsden

'No wonder your business is on the slide ...
look at the state of your Web site!'

In this part ...

If you're like most people, you have one drawer in the kitchen filled with utensils and other assorted objects that don't belong anywhere else. Strangely enough, that very place is where you can almost always find something to perform the task at hand with.

Part V of this book is a collection of miscellaneous secrets arranged in sets of ten; hence, The Part of Tens. Filled with tips, cautions, suggestions and examples of new ways to make money online, this part presents many kinds of information that can help you plan and create your business presence on the Internet.

Chapter 15

Ten Must-Have Features for Your Web Site

· ·

*Y*ou can put any number of snazzy features on your Web site. If you ever meet with a Web design firm, you're sure to hear about all the cool scripts, animations and other interactive add-ons that can go on your pages. Some pizzazz isn't a bad thing, especially if you're just starting out and need to set yourself apart from the competition. Interactive features and a well-designed Web site give you an air of competence and experience, even if your online business is brand new.

But the Web site features that count towards your bottom line are the ones that attract and retain customers and induce them to return to you regularly. Along with the bells and whistles, your business home on the Web needs to have some basic must-haves that shoppers expect. Make sure your site meets the minimum daily requirements: It needs to be easy to find, loaded with content, include content and background information about you, and include features that make shopping easy and secure. This Part of Tens chapter describes ten specific features that help you achieve these objectives.

Secure Some Easy-to-Remember URLs

Names are critical to the success of any business. A name becomes identified with a business, and people associate the name with its products and its level of customer service. When a small company developed a software product called Lindows, software giant Microsoft sued and eventually paid $20 million to stop the infringement on its well-known, trademarked product Windows.

Write down five or six names that are short and easy to remember and that would represent your business if included in a URL. Do a domain name search and try to find the one you want. (A good place to search is MelbourneIT, `whois.melbourneit.com`.) Try to keep your site's potential name as short and as free of elements such as hyphens as possible. A single four- to ten-character name in between the `www.` and the `.com` sections of the URL is easy to remember.

Domain names are cheap, especially if you can lock them up for several years at a time. A name in the `.com` domain is still the most desirable type of URL suffix because it's the one that most consumers expect to see when they're trying to find your Web site's URL. Even if you can get a `.com` name, purchase domain names in other popular domains, such as `.net` and `.org`. That way, you protect your URL from being poached by competitors who are trying to copy you. If your URL is easily misspelled, consider purchasing a domain name that represents a common misspelling. That way, if shoppers make a typing error, they're still directed to your site.

Provide a Convenient Payment Method

Shoppers go online for many reasons, but those reasons don't include a desire for things to be complex and time consuming. No matter how technically complex getting your business on the Internet may be, shoppers still want things to be quick and seamless. At the top of the list of seamless processes is the ability to pay for merchandise purchased online.

You don't have to get a merchant account from a bank to process your own credit card payments. You don't need to get point-of-sale hardware, either. Since Greg has been selling on eBay, he's become quite used to the convenience and reliability of eBay's electronic payment service PayPal. You don't have to offer items for sale on eBay to use PayPal; if you have an account with PayPal, you can add PayPal 'Buy' buttons to your Web pages and send your customers to PayPal to send you the money using their credit cards. Chances are that many of your prospective customers already have accounts with PayPal if they use eBay. Greg did, so his purchase process was completed in less than a minute. Set yourself up as a seller with PayPal and Paymate and then accept money orders, personal cheques and direct bank deposit. If you can take the additional step of getting a shopping cart and a credit card payment system, so much the better.

Promote Security, Privacy and Trust

Even shoppers who have been making purchases online for years still feel uncertainty when they type their credit card number and click a button labelled Pay Now, Purchase or Submit to a commercial Web site. We're speaking from personal experience.

What promotes trust? Information and communication. Shoppers online love getting information that goes beyond what they can find in a printed catalogue. Be sure to include one or more of the following details that can make shoppers feel good about pressing your Buy Now button:

- ✔ An endorsement from an organisation that is supposed to promote good business practices, such as TRUSTe (www.truste.org)
- ✔ A privacy statement that explains how you handle customers' personal information
- ✔ Detailed product descriptions that show you're knowledgeable about a product

Another thing that promotes trust is information about who you are and why you love what you do, as described in the section 'Help Your Customers Get to Know You' later in this chapter.

Choose Goods and Services That Buyers Want

Every merchant would love to be able to read the minds of his or her prospective customers. On the Internet, you have as much chance of reading someone's mind as you have of meeting that person face to face. Nevertheless, the Internet does give potential buyers several ways to tell you what they want:

- ✔ Come right out and ask them. On your Web site, invite requests for merchandise of one sort or another.
- ✔ After a purchase, do some *upselling*: Suggest some other items you would like your customers to buy from you.
- ✔ Visit message boards, newsgroups and Web sites related to the item you want to sell.

- ✔ Make a weekly (remember that Saturdays and Sundays are the best days for auctions to end) search of eBay's completed auctions to see what has sold, and which types of items have fetched the highest prices.

- ✔ Track the way customers use your site; evaluate what works and what doesn't; and adjust your sales effort accordingly.

An article titled 'The New E-Marketing Must-Haves: Video and Rich Media' (www.ecommercetimes.com/story/62961.html) suggests that attracting shoppers through better product views, features and information through audio, video, 360-degree views, zooming and flash will help increase conversions.

Have a Regular Influx of New Products

With a printed catalogue, changes to sales items can be major. The biggest problem is the need to physically reprint the catalogue when inventory changes. One of the biggest advantages associated with having an online sales catalogue is the ability to alter your product line in a matter of minutes, without having to send artwork to a printer. You can easily post new sales items online each day, as soon as you get new sales figures.

One reason to keep changing your products on a regular basis is that your larger competitors are doing so. DealsDirect, which has a well-designed and popular online sales catalogue (www.dealsdirect.com.au), puts out new products on a regular basis and announces them in an email newsletter to which loyal customers can subscribe.

Optimise Your Site for Search Engines

There's a reason why search engine optimisation (SEO) is the subject of its own chapter (Chapter 11) and why so many Web site owners are immediately concerned with it. SEO is a low-cost and effective way to help your site be found by exactly the people who are looking for the content you're offering.

In order to carry out SEO, you need to leave a 'trail of crumbs' for your prospective customers. Any Web site must have them. They include

- **Headings that contain keywords:** Along with indexing page titles, the consensus is that search engines like Google also index the main headings on Web pages.
- **Page titles that get indexed:** The more keywords you add, the better the chances that your site turns up in Google and other search results.
- **Text that contains specific keywords about your site:** The first paragraph or two of text is the most important because this bit of text is most likely indexed.

After you do these things, you can take a few more steps to make your site easy to find. When most people think about advertising on the Internet, they automatically think about banner advertisements placed on someone else's Web page. A banner is only one kind of online ad, and possibly the least effective. Make use of all the advertising options going online brings you, including the following:

- **Link exchanges:** 'You link to my Web site, and I'll link to yours,' in other words. This is especially effective if you're linking to a business whose Web site ranks well and whose products and services complement your own.
- **Multipe Web sites:** If you have three Web sites, you immediately have two sites linking to each one of yours. Your ability to exchange links with other Web sites triples, too.
- **Word-of-mouth:** Bloggers do this all the time: One person mentions something in another blog, that blogger mentions someone else and so on.

In addition, you need to register your site to make sure it appears in the directories to the Web that the search engines provide (refer to Chapters 11 and 12 for more information).

Be Current with Upkeep and Improvements

Do you have a favourite blog, comic strip or newspaper columnist that you like to visit each day? We certainly do. If these content providers don't come up with new material on a regular basis, you get discouraged. Your loyal customers hopefully feel the same way about your Web site, eBay store or other sales venue.

Melissa knows what you're thinking: You have so many things to do that you can't possibly revisit your Web site every day and change headings or put new sales online. You have to get the kids off to school, pack up some merchandise, run to the post office, clean up the house — the list goes on and on. You can't be two places at once. But two people can. Hire a student or friend to run your site and suggest new content for you. In a five-minute phone conversation, you can tell your assistant what to do that day, and you can get on with the rest of your many responsibilities.

Personally Interact with Your Customers

The fact that personal touch counts for so much in Internet communication is a paradox. With rare exceptions, you never meet face to face with the people with whom you exchange messages. Maybe the lack of body language and visual clues make shoppers and other Web surfers hungry for attention. But the fact is that impersonal, mass email marketing messages (in other words, *spam*) are detested; but quick responses with courteous thank-yous are eagerly welcomed.

You can't send too many personal email messages to your customers, even when they're making only an inquiry and not a purchase. Not long ago, Greg asked some questions about a heater he was thinking of buying online. He filled out the form on the company's Web site and submitted his questions. The representative of the company got right back to him.

'First of all, let me thank you for your interest in our product,' the letter began. She proceeded to answer Greg's questions and then finished with another thank-you, adding 'If you have any further questions, please don't hesitate to ask'. Greg didn't hesitate: He asked some more, she answered, and again said, 'Don't hesitate to ask' at the end. This approach may possibly be all 'form letter' material, added to the beginning and end of every inquiry, but it makes a difference. Greg eventually purchased the item.

Don't be afraid to pour on the extra courtesy and provide complete answers to every question: Just tell yourself each answer is worth an extra dollar or two in sales. It probably is.

Help Your Customers Get to Know You

The personal touch counts for a lot, even when your Web site isn't promoting your own professional services. Your Web site should find a way to make a personal connection with your visitors. Many site owners achieve this goal by creating a blog. Blogs, though, are more appropriate for personal Web sites. E-commerce sites can still achieve a personal touch by including some content:

- ✔ An About Me or About Us page
- ✔ A newsletter
- ✔ A mission statement or a history of the company

Look at the Shiana Web site (www.shiana.com). This site contains all these links, even though its main purpose is to sell jewellery. The Shiana site talks about itself and its mission to appeal to people who are going to be induced to purchase in order to help the tribe that makes the jewellery. Even if you don't have a charitable mission to talk about, some essential background about you, why you started your business and what your goals are builds trust in your shoppers. Be sure to tout your experience, your background, your family or your hobbies — anything to reassure online shoppers that you're a reputable person who is looking out for their interests.

Provide Lots of Navigation Options

Links, menus and other navigation options aren't quite as essential as they used to be because you can establish a regular income on eBay without having any Web site at all. But even if you become a well-established eBay seller, you're going to want a Web site at some point or other. How do you make your site well organised? Make sure your site incorporates these essential features:

- **Navigation buttons:** Consumers who are in a hurry (in other words, almost all consumers) expect to see a row of navigation buttons along the top or one of the sides of your home page. Don't make them hunt; put them in the same place on every page on your site — if your site is quite large, provide additional options such as a search facility.

- **A site map:** A page that leads visitors to all areas of your site can prevent them from going elsewhere if they get lost.

- **Links that actually work:** Nothing is more frustrating than clicking a link that's supposed to lead to a photo and/or a bit of information that you really want and to come up with the generic Page Not Found error message.

- **Links that indicate where a customer is on the site:** Such links are helpful because, like a trail of breadcrumbs, they show how the customer got to a particular page. Here's an example:

```
Clothing > Men's > Sportswear > Shoes > Running
```

When your site grows to contain dozens of pages and several main categories, links that look like this can help people move up to a main category and find more subcategories.

Be the first to visit your Web site and test it to make sure that the forms, email addresses and other features function correctly. If someone sends you an email message only to have it bounce back, you're more likely to lose that customer — a customer who may well conclude that you aren't monitoring your Web site or your business. At the very least, open your site in Microsoft Internet Explorer, Netscape Navigator and Firefox to make sure that your text and images load correctly.

Chapter 16

Ten Hot New Ways to Make Money Online

· ·

*N*ot so long ago, starting an online business primarily meant creating a Web site and organising it in a businesslike manner. You would create a catalogue, add a shopping cart and payment system, and hope customers would find you. You may be in an online shopping directory with other online businesses.

These days, you don't have to create a full-fledged Web site to sell online. The hottest way to make money is to create a store on eBay and become a PowerSeller. Using an online service such as eBay (or Trade Me) helps individuals get their product online and market themselves to the public. You may have to pay a small monthly hosting fee and sales commission. But the benefits are huge: You don't have to do all the work of creating a catalogue and payment system, and you can put your products in the marketplace and streamline your processes without a huge upfront cost of setting up an e-commerce Web site.

This chapter presents ten innovative approaches to making money online. By following one or more of these relatively simple options, you can start generating income quickly and painlessly. You may not make a fortune, but you focus attention on yourself and your business that can brighten your life even while it puts some extra cash in your pocket.

Start a Blog

Adding the personal touch separates the Mum and Dad businesses from the soulless warehouses. Nowadays, however, you're likely to be greeted with a cheery hello even when you wander into a discount warehouse. So the precedent has definitely been set for mixing the family into business. With a blog of the sort we describe in Chapter 3, growing numbers of enterprising individuals are combining the personal and business areas of their lives into a single Web page. Everyone's creating a blog these days, it seems: Lars Hundley, the entrepreneur we mention in Chapters 3 and 11, finds time to maintain three separate blogs; Kathie Thomas, who we profile in Chapter 5, has several as well.

The advantage of a blog is that you can give customers a window into your soul — or at least into your business sense. That approach can build trust, which in turn, can build business. You may not want to define yourself with your strong religious preferences or passionate view on the results of the latest election, but posting a few photos of your children or pets can be a definite asset. You may also wish to include a narrative of your latest family vacation. On a slightly more businesslike side, having a link to the text of a paper you presented at the latest professional conference you attended is really great. Of even more relevance may be a series of photos showing the happy day that the new press was delivered to your printing plant, accompanied by examples of new brochures that feature the results of its bells and whistles. Whatever the subject, the goal is to keep the tone of the text upbeat and breezy, friend to friend.

Julie Powell decided to methodically work her way through all the recipes in Julia Child's classic Mastering the Art of French Cooking. She started a blog, *The Julie/Julia Project* (blogs.salon.com/0001399/), in which she described her attempts to create each dish in the book, chronicling her successes and failures. Because of the popularity of her Web site, she landed a deal for a real book that, she reports, enabled her to leave her day job as a secretary.

Turn Your Hobby into a Business

Greg is a perfect example of a person who started a new career thanks to the Internet. He started when the World Wide Web was new, and lots of people who were previously not all that comfortable with the computer were trying to go online. Nowadays, beginner's books compete with instructional Web sites, especially now that modern babies seem born with computer mice in their hands. So he's not recommending that you follow in his exact footsteps. But the point is that you should take anything you love and are good at and then turn it into a Web site.

Similarly, Melissa started experimenting with building Web pages while studying computer science at uni in the early days of the Internet (1992 to 1995). She started building Web sites for friends and family members on her weekends and after hours, and her first small paid jobs were purely through word-of-mouth recommendation. Today, her Web design business is ten years old, operates from a commercial office and employs several full-time staff. Her two biggest lead generators are still word-of-mouth referrals and her Web site, which ranks very well in Google.

In Chapter 9, we profiled Glenda of Million Dollar Baby who loves to sew. She combined her passion for sewing and her experience in the retail baby industry to retire (give up her day job) and generate a decent income selling handmade cot sheets through eBay and her Web site.

One of Greg's favourite online people, a Wisconsin woman known as The Butter Cow Lady and who has gained local fame through her butter sculptures, sells her autobiography on her site (www.thebuttercowlady. com). On the Web, you're limited only by your imagination as to what you can sell. Take what you know and love and run with it.

Let Craigslist Help You Sell

Lots of people know about *Craigslist*, the popular and widespread classified ad service that exists in 450 cities around the world. But we continually meet people who have heard of eBay and Amazon.com and are still unfamiliar with the site created by Craig Newmark in San Francisco back in 1995.

Craigslist (www.craigslist.org) isn't primarily a commercial marketplace. Users can post ads for a wide variety of services: notices of events, rides, politics and holiday rentals. But people who use Craigslist enjoy it as a place to sell things they have a hard time offering anywhere else. You can sell heavy furniture and appliances to local buyers who can pick them up from you in person. You can sell pets as well. Craigslist allows sellers to post photos of their merchandise for sale; it employs extensive controls to cut down on spam. If you're looking for local buyers for what you have to sell, you're likely to find this one of the best marketplaces around.

Inspire Others with Your Thoughts

Sometimes, you end up making a huge change in your life without really trying. You put something online that's sincere, heartfelt, and that you think may help some other people. You find out that tons of people are out there who feel the same way.

We're reminded of the story of Reata Strickland, a Webmaster and Sunday school teacher in Tuscaloosa, Alabama. She was touched by a short story called 'Interview with God'. She spent a couple of days turning the story into a Web page presentation. She put the pages online, felt good that she had done so, and moved on to other things. In the meantime, the site took on a life of its own. Reata was soon notified by her church's Internet service provider (ISP) that her site had attracted 500,000 visitors. Before long, the site was getting two million visitors a month. Reata has since made herself into a marketable personality, giving talks, creating new presentations, and selling merchandise related to the short story 'Interview with God' and similar products. She also wrote a 64-page book — *Interview with God*. It was all unplanned, but she embraces her success and makes the most of it: You can, too.

You can find the original 'Interview with God' presentation and more about Reata Strickland at momentswithgod.com (www.reata.org).

Create a 'Lens' with Squidoo

The innovative Web site Squidoo gives you the ability to attract affiliate revenue by recommending services and Web sites you know about. You attract and keep visitors by providing compelling content. You use your knowledge and experience to create a 'lens' through which others can view a particular subject. Some of the revenue you generate from your referrals can go to charity; some of it can go to you.

If you're passionate or knowledgeable about a particular topic and willing to share what you know, you're going to find Squidoo an easy and possibly profitable way to get attention and perhaps a few bucks as well. Find out more at www.squidoo.com.

Open the Tip Jar

PayPal has a donations (or tip jar) feature that you can use to add a button to your blog or Web site in an effort to solicit donations from faithful visitors who find value in what you do.

First, you need to apply for a PayPal account if you don't already have one by going to the PayPal home page (www.paypal.com.au) and clicking Sign Up Now. Obtaining an account and setting up the Donation service is free. Go to the PayPal Directory of Features page (www.paypal.com/au/cgi-bin/webscr?cmd=p/xcl/rec/donate-intro-outside) and click Learn More in the Donations row. Follow the steps on subsequent screens to set up a Donation button. This button, labelled Make a Donation or something similar, enables individuals to send payments to your PayPal account.

Give Out Not-So-Free Advice

The Internet has always been a great place to get questions answered. Over the years, the newsgroups that populate Usenet have been the primary resources for answers and support. You can also start a Web site on which you offer your consulting services. If you know something about a given topic such as computers or the repair and maintenance of other objects, you can answer questions and earn a few bucks either by becoming a professional blogger and writing for a popular blog, through your own blog or through a site similar to the former Google Answers site. (At the time of writing, Google Answers has been retired and is no longer accepting new questions.) You can also gather tips, tricks and instructions pertaining to your field of interest: Rod Stephens does just that on his VB Helper site (www.vb-helper.com) where he gathers information on the Visual Basic programming language. He also solicits donations via the Amazon.com Tip Jar (similar to the PayPal Donation feature mentioned in the previous section).

Become a Wealth of Information

What's that you say? You don't have a pet, you can't draw, you don't have any products to sell and you're not a professional contractor. Never fear. On the Web, information sells. Chances are you have a wealth of information about one topic in particular. You know a lot about your family history, you know everything there is to know about collecting coins, you're a genius with identifying rocks or you're an avid birdwatcher. Create a Web site in which you put every bit of information you have online. Make your site the one and only, the greatest resource ever devoted to this topic. Follow the example of the Urban Legends Reference Pages (www.snopes.com), a Web site started in 1995 by a husband-and-wife team living in California. The site collects urban legends of all sorts and reports on whether they're actually true; it makes enough money from ads to keep it going. Mad about cars since his sixth birthday, Alborz Fallah created CarAdvice.com.au (www.caradvice.com.au) to provide unbiased information to car enthusiasts online. He studied IT in Queensland but decided to pursue his true passion with an online business all about cars! The main thing about both of these sites is that they're a labour of love for their creators.

Need Income? Just Ask!

It sounds odd, but if you present yourself in the right way on the Web and you simply ask for money, you just may get it. The most famous case is that of Karyn Bosnak. When she found herself buried in $20,000 of credit card debt, she created a Web site called SaveKaryn.com (www.savekaryn.com). She asked for donations to help her out of debt. In just 20 weeks, her site received nearly two million visits, and she wasn't in debt any more — especially because her book *Save Karyn* was published in several languages, too.

When blogger Andrew Sullivan (www.andrewsullivan.com) was in need of funds to keep his blog online, faithful readers donated more than $70,000. Sullivan was well established by that time, and people knew he would use the money to keep providing them with the opinions and insights they were used to. Present yourself in an open, positive manner and readers are likely to respond to you, too.

Be advised that the field of virtual begging is already very crowded. Just check the Google Directory at directory.google.com/Top/Society/People/Requesting_Help/Debt_Reduction. These people have created Web sites seeking donations so they can get out of debt. You have to find a way to distinguish yourself from the crowd if you want attention for your financial needs.

Expand Your Existing Business to the Web

Expanding your business to the Web isn't new, of course. But a surprising number of established businesspeople haven't done it yet. Many of the lawyers Greg knows have no idea what to do with the Web. The same goes for other service providers — from dentists to plumbers to auto mechanics. It can be as simple as listing a fee schedule, your hours and where to park when customers come to your facility. Or you can expand a bit to include references from satisfied customers.

The point is that these days a large percentage of the population is sitting at the computer already hooked up to the Internet. When they suddenly realise that they need their suit drycleaned for a meeting the next day or that their kids need school supplies, they're more likely to call up information on service providers by using a search engine than they are to flip through the phone book and make a call to find out locations and hours.

The following example didn't fit under any of the previous categories, but the story's inspiring, and it shows how anyone with imagination and 'chutzpah' can make money online. A young (he was aged 21 in 2005, when he got this idea) British man named Alex Tew was broke and having a hard time meeting school expenses when he got the idea of selling individual pixels on a single Web page to advertisers for $1 per pixel. A *pixel* is a tiny bit of digital information; every image on a computer screen is made up of them. Alex's Web page has exactly 1 million of them, which is called the Million Dollar Homepage. By late 2006, the space on the page was sold out, and Alex had made his goal: He earned a million dollars for creating a single Web page. You can read more about this amazing success story at www.milliondollarhomepage.com.

Another site pinpoints the accidental success of Matt Harding who, while travelling, decided to film himself dancing in front of some of the best-known sites around the world. He placed that film on his Web page for his friends to see and three years and more than 20 million viewers later he is an Internet celebrity. US Company, StrideGum (www.stridegum.com) funded two further trips for Matt to make more videos. Read more about Matt's travels at wherethehellismatt.com.

Chapter 17

Ten Must-See Online Business Success Stories

. . . .

A bit of inspiration goes a long way when starting a new online business. At first, you may struggle to come up with an idea for your business and, after you think it through, getting started may seem overwhelming or all too hard. This chapter presents ten success stories to motivate you as well as to demonstrate how others start with an idea and not much money, and yet build a successful online business. Many of these examples are considered the 'big guys' nowadays, but the important thing to remember is they all started somewhere!

realestate.com.au

realestate.com.au started back in 1995 with capital of $24,000 that included some computer equipment. Founders Karl Sabljak and Martin Howell worked in the lounge room (and later expanded to the garage) of Karl's home in a north-east suburb of Melbourne. They used a pair of baby monitors to communicate between the two parts of the house, worked to a very tight budget and kept costs to a minimum. At first, Karl and Martin kept their day jobs and worked long hours after work building their online business. After 18 months they moved to their first office location in Surrey Hills.

Now part of the REA Group, the publicly listed company has operations in ten countries, 22 Web sites and reached $156 million in revenue in 2008.

As at June 2008, REA Group's Web sites attract more than 8.2 million unique visitors each month.

The shame in this story is that the original founders gave up a large percentage of their equity in the business quite early on. So, while they live comfortably and made quite a bit of money out of it — they could have made significantly more!

You can visit realestate.com.au

- ✔ **In Australia:** www.realestate.com.au
- ✔ **In New Zealand:** www.allrealestate.co.nz

RedBalloon Days

Online gift retailer RedBalloon Days started in 2001, and now operates in Australia and New Zealand selling experiences as gifts on the Internet. The experience can be horse riding, a winery tour, a spa treatment or a dance lesson.

The business was started by Naomi Simson who was driven by the need to spend more time with her family after her first child turned one — she realised she was tired of trying to balance a corporate job and family life. Her idea was modelled on a similar idea in the United Kingdom. She has set an ambitious company goal of supplying a RedBalloon Days experience to 10 per cent of Australians by 2015.

The business was started with a budget of $100,000, and from the date the first marketing plan was written in April of 2001 until the Web site was launched in October of the same year, seven months had gone by. In 2008, RedBalloon Days' turnover is estimated to be in the vicinity of $20 million. Naomi is still having fun running a business that brings people pleasure, has written her own book, is an active blogger and is regularly invited to speak about her online business success.

Visit the RedBalloon Days Web sites:

- ✔ **Australian Website:** www.redballoondays.com.au
- ✔ **New Zealand Website:** www.redballoondays.co.nz
- ✔ **Blog:** www.naomisimson.com

Stayz

If you've ever tried to book holiday accommodation for a short break in Australia you may have heard of Stayz.com.au. Started by a husband-and-wife team in their garage in an outer Sydney suburb, Rob and Audrey Hunt estimate they spent $30,000 during their first 12 months to start up their online business. The business started in 2001 and originally operated under the name OzStays.com.au. In 2005, Stayz was sold to Fairfax Media for $12.7 million.

Rob came up with the idea originally because he wanted an easy way for Audrey to manage bookings for their beach house via an Internet-based calendar. The first Web site for their holiday property cost $1,000 and, slowly, over time they added more properties to their site. Property owners gave them feedback about what they would like to see on the Web site.

Stayz.com.au generates income from the properties that list or advertise on the Web site. Now a part of the Fairfax group of Web sites it is linked in and advertised heavily on its network of sites that include news sites `theage.com.au` and `smh.com.au`; car site `drive.com.au`; and real estate site `domain.com.au`.

Visit Stayz at `www.stayz.com.au`.

YouTube

The online video-sharing Web site YouTube was founded in February 2005 by three former employees of PayPal. It very quickly grew in popularity and was bought out by Google for US$1.65 billion in October 2006. If only your online business could be such an instant success, hey!

YouTube started without much of a business plan or structure. The aim was to allow people to easily post, share and watch videos on the Internet. But the instant success of the site has been attributed to the fact that the site had no formal structure and users of the site had the freedom to choose how they wanted to use it. In much the same way as MySpace and Facebook grew in popularity the year before (2004), people started using the site as part of their social networking — in ways such as uploading videos and linking to them from their MySpace or Facebook profiles. The word spread virally about this new site and YouTube now handles hundreds of millions of requests to view videos daily, and receives more than 13 hours of video every minute.

Now owned by Google, YouTube has had its fair share of trouble with huge bandwidth costs due to the amount of video being hosted on the site as well as a range of copyright issues with users uploading copyrighted material. But all three founders are now independently wealthy and living comfortably thanks to this online business idea.

Visit YouTube at `www.youtube.com`.

SEEK

SEEK was formed in November 1997 by three ambitious guys all with very different skills and experience. None, however, had any skills in recruitment or Web development.

Now Australia's largest and most popular online employment Web site, SEEK Limited is a publicly listed company estimated to be worth more than $2 billion and has expanded operations to both New Zealand and the United Kingdom.

At the time SEEK was launched, newspapers were still the most popular way to advertise job vacancies, but not anymore! SEEK beat Australia's media executives to the punch recognising the potential of the Internet. Now SEEK clearly dominates the online employment market hosting more job ads and jobseekers than any other employment Web site.

In Australia, SEEK currently hosts around two-thirds of all online job ads (over 200,000 at any one time) and attracts nearly 2.8 million unique browsers a month, which is more than double that of its nearest competitor (Nielsen NetRatings, February 2008). In New Zealand, SEEK hosts over 20,000 job ads at any given time and attracts over 400,000 unique browsers, which is equivalent to approximately 20 per cent of the New Zealand working population.

Visit SEEK

- ✔ **In Australia:** `www.seek.com.au`
- ✔ **In New Zealand:** `www.seek.co.nz`

The Bub Hub

Today, The Bub Hub is one of Australia's leading parenting Web sites. It was launched in 2002 by husband-and-wife team Brad and Hilary Lauder shortly after the birth of their first child — being inspired to create an online resource for new and expecting parents. Initially, The Bub Hub was launched in Queensland only but, due to the great feedback they received from the general public, they soon launched Australia-wide.

The Bub Hub is a comprehensive directory listing products, services and local activities available to parents. You can list free on the site but each listing is human-moderated to check the content's suitability for the site. The Bub Hub also features support forums, which have proved popular with mothers and now have more than 28,000 members. The site earns its income through advertisers: With more than 200,000 unique site visitors per month (Nielsen NetRatings, March 2008) the Web site has attracted big name advertisers, including Coles, Bonds, Heinz and Huggies.

You can visit The Bub Hub at www.bubhub.com.au.

Trade Me

New Zealand's largest online auction Web site, Trade Me, is a true success story. Started in 1999 by Kiwi Sam White with NZ$12,000, the site sold to Fairfax for NZ$700 million in 2006. Trade Me is the most-visited Web site in New Zealand — an estimated 60 per cent of all New Zealand Web site visits are to this NZ site.

As the story goes, Sam had the idea for Trade Me in 1998 when he was shopping for a second-hand heater. He visited an online classified site and contacted a few sellers only to find the listings were out of date and the heaters already sold. Trade Me was born. At this online auction site, sellers can list items for sale by auction with a reserve price, and buyers make bids. The winning bidder at the closing time is the successful buyer of the item. Buyers and sellers can then post feedback about each other and whether they're happy with the transaction. The feedback system is one of the reasons the site is so successful because the feedback option allows buyers to check out the reputation of sellers before deciding to deal with them.

eBay tried to enter the New Zealand market in 2001, but had little success. As at June 2008, Trade Mc had more than 2 million members and 1.2 million live auctions, as opposed to eBay New Zealand, which had only 7,600 live auctions.

Check out Trade Me at www.trademe.co.nz.

Wotif

Founder of Wotif, Graeme Wood, was consulting to an hotelier who was having trouble advertising and filling vacant rooms at the last minute. Often, lead times didn't allow sufficient time to advertise last-minute rooms via traditional methods such as newspapers, and those options weren't cost effective given the discounted rates that rooms had to be offered at.

Graeme thought the Internet was the perfect medium to deliver this last-minute listing need and managed to get three other associates to invest. Wotif had start-up costs of $200,000 and launched in March 2000 in the middle of the dotcom crash. The company now has offices in Australia, Canada, New Zealand, Singapore and the United Kingdom.

Wotif has a simple business model: Any form of accommodation can list on the Web site for nothing but Wotif gets 10 per cent of the cost of any booked accommodation. Now more than 2 million bookings are made through the Web site each year.

Visit Wotif at www.wotif.com.

Qbik's Wingate

New Zealander Adrien de Croy started software development company Qbik in 1995. His big break was quite accidental. Adrien had just turned 27 and was an Internet consultant with a masters degree in electronic engineering. He was sharing a flat with a few mates addicted to surfing the Web and got frustrated having to wait hours to check his email. So, in a matter of hours, he wrote a program that allows multiple computers to share a single Internet connection. His friends convinced him to put it up on the Internet and charge for it and after the first week Adrien was receiving 200 to 300 emails a day.

Wingate had another lucky break in 1998 when Compaq signed a deal to bundle Wingate with Compaq home PCs. Adrien is now a multi-millionaire and, while still being involved at Qbik, he also has time to indulge in his passions for cars (driving a Ferrari!) and music.

You can visit Wingate at: www.wingate.com.

RSVP

Launched in Australia on Valentine's Day 1997, RSVP was the brain child of Stephen Mulcahy. At first it was an on-the-side project of software company Access Systems. RSVP is a dating site where members are invited to upload their profile and start looking for their perfect match. The original site was modelled on a US dating Web site. Because the Internet allows a certain amount of anonymity the medium has become an alternative way to meet people away from bars and singles clubs.

RSVP has a strict code of conduct: The site monitors all photos and profiles uploaded to maintain a certain standard thus helping its patrons, especially women, to feel safe using the Web site. Initially, RSVP started with just a few hundred members but, today, boasts over 1 million members and many happily-ever-after stories of RSVP weddings and babies! With initial start-up costs of approximately $250,000, RSVP's growth was slow to start but, as it caught on, the site captured the attention of Fairfax who purchased it in mid-2005 for $38.9 million.

Visit RSVP at www.rsvp.com.au.

Index

• *D* •

• *Y* •

• *Z* •

Notes

Notes

FOR DUMMIES®

Business & Investment

1-74031-109-4
$39.95

1-74031-124-8
$39.95

0-7314-0838-1
$54.95

0-7314-0715-6
$39.95

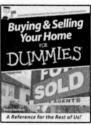

1-74031-166-3
$39.95

0-7314-0724-5
$39.95

1-74031-146-9
$39.95

0-7314-0710-5
$39.95

0-7314-0787-3
$39.95

0-7314-0762-8
$39.95

1-74031-091-8
$39.95

0-7314-0746-6
$29.95

FOR DUMMIES

Reference

0-7314-0723-7
$34.95

0-7314-0699-0
$34.95

1-74031-157-4
$39.95

0-7314-0721-0
$34.95

1-74031-007-1
$39.95

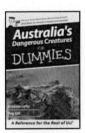

0-7314-0722-9
$29.95

0-7314-0594-3
$24.95

0-7314-0752-0
$34.95

Technology

0-7314-0759-8
$39.95

0-7314-0761-X
$39.95

0-7314-0941-8
$39.95

1-74031-159-0
$39.95

FOR DUMMIES®

Health & Fitness

Australian Editions

Breast Cancer
1-74031-143-4
$39.95

Menopause
1-74031-140-X
$39.95

Food & Nutrition
0-7314-0596-X
$34.95

Diabetes
1-74031-094-2
$39.95

Fitness
1-74031-009-8
$39.95

Weight Training
1-74031-044-6
$39.95

Yoga
1-74031-059-4
$39.95

Pilates
1-74031-074-8
$39.95

Golf
1-74031-011-X
$39.95

Cricket
1-74031-173-6
$39.95

Aussie Rules
0-7314-0595-1
$34.95

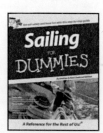

Sailing
0-7314-0644-3
$39.95

For Dummies, the Dummies Man logo, A Reference for the Rest of Us! and related trade dress are trademarks or registered trademarks of Wiley. All prices are GST-inclusive and subject to change without notice.